OHIO ADMINISTRATIVE LAW

Baldwin's OHIO HANDBOOK SERIES

Administrative Law Committee
Ohio State Bar Association

WITHDRAWN

Editor-in-Chief

David Wm. T. Carroll
Smith & Schnacke
Columbus

Banks–Baldwin Law Publishing Company

This book is sold with the understanding that the publisher is not engaged in furnishing any legal or other professional advice. Although prepared by professionals, this book should not be used as a substitute for professional services in specific situations. If legal advice or other expert assistance is required, the services of a specialist should be sought. Non-attorneys are cautioned against using these materials on behalf of others or engaging in conduct which might be considered the unauthorized practice of law.

Copyright 1985
Banks-Baldwin Law Publishing Company
ISBN 0-8322-0069-7

No part of this book may be reproduced or transmitted in any form or by any means, electronic or mechanical, including photocopying, recording, or by any information storage and retrieval system, without prior permission in writing from the publisher.

Foreword

The rise of state administrative agencies is generally regarded as the most significant legal trend affecting the daily life of Ohio citizens in this decade. As the agencies' powers and duties have increased, their output of new rules and opinions has grown tremendously, and the number of people affected continually expands. Administrative law is no longer the exclusive domain of a few experts in Columbus. Every attorney in general practice can expect to encounter administrative law cases in the normal course of his clients' businesses.

The purpose of this handbook is to explicate the state administrative law process and to facilitate practice before Ohio's major agencies. Under the direction of David Wm. T. Carroll, Chairman of the Editorial Subcommittee, ten members of the Ohio State Bar Association's Administrative Law Committee (see inside back cover) contributed text on the two primary functions of administrative agencies—rulemaking and adjudication—as well as judicial review of agency action. (The latter is discussed in terms of the Administrative Appellate Procedure Act as well as appeals from decisions of agencies of political subdivisions.) In addition, eleven practitioners (see About the Authors) share their expertise in regard to eight major agencies.

Chapters 7 through 21 deal with practice before the Bureau of Employment Services, Division of Securities, Environmental Protection Agency, Department of Human Services, Liquor Control Commission, Public Utilities Commission, Department of Natural Resources, and Bureau of Workers' Compensation. The authors offer succinct, readable discussions of the petitions and claims, hearing procedures, permissible evidence, and other matters unique to each agency. An organization chart and a flow chart illustrating the agency's adjudicatory process are included for each.

For convenient reference, the Ohio Administrative Procedure Act (RC Chapter 119), Administrative Appellate Procedure Act (RC Chapter 2506), and other statutes affecting general rulemaking powers are reprinted from *Baldwin's Ohio Revised Code Annotated*. For space reasons, however, neither the statutes governing operation, powers, and duties of specific agencies nor the full text of their administrative rules are included. Instead, cross references to applicable sections of the Revised Code and Ohio Administrative Code are provided throughout the authors' text. In addition to a Table of Cases and a Table of Laws and Rules Construed, a detailed index provides access by subject, agency name, and popular phrases used in practice.

We thank David Wm. T. Carroll who, as Chairman of the Editorial Subcommittee and Editor-in-Chief, devoted many hours to researching, reviewing, and coordinating the project; and Dean Frederick Davis of the University of Dayton School of Law who kindly evaluated the manuscript.

The Publisher

Cleveland, Ohio
November 1985

Preface

With each tax increase, our state government grows, creating more opportunities and problems for lawyers and their clients. Increasingly the forum in which client interests are threatened—and thus need to be protected—is the administrative agency. To the uninitiated, an agency's practices may appear foreign and arcane. The uninitiated are correct—until they first appear before the agency.

The Administrative Law Committee of the Ohio State Bar Association originally conceived the *Ohio Administrative Law Handbook* as a general introduction to administrative law in Ohio. The "first edition," distributed to participants in a 1981 conference on the subject, addressed only the Ohio Administrative Procedure Act (RC Chapter 119). When P. J. Lucier, President of Banks-Baldwin Law Publishing Company, approached the Committee about publishing its then partially completed revision, he suggested that the "second edition" should also focus on practice before specific agencies. Unfortunately, all agencies cannot be covered in a single volume; we thus selected the agencies in this book based on: (1) the likelihood of a nonspecialist receiving a client call involving the agency; and (2) the availability of qualified authors willing to share the fruits of their experience.

With selfless generosity, our contributing authors agreed to reveal the secrets of their practices before their respective agencies. We asked each to approach his subject by telling a first-timer what he or she should know about the agency's procedure before walking in the door. We hoped to provide the nonspecialist with as much practical information as possible.

How many times have we lawyers received a late Friday afternoon call from a client who had planned to attend a Monday morning license-revocation hearing alone, but began to wonder if maybe he should have an attorney with him? No book can supply all the answers for such a situation, and this is no exception. It does not address questions of substantive law governing the agencies. It *does* seek to tell a first-timer what to expect when he enters one of the major agencies. Additional helpful information can often be obtained by calling the assistant attorney general handling the case for the agency.

For agencies not specifically discussed, the first three chapters provide an overview of the Administrative Procedure Act as it applies to all Ohio agencies. Procedures governing adjudications of political subdivisions, under RC Chapter 2506, are covered briefly in Chapter 5. They may raise issues different from those involving state agencies (e.g., home rule for municipalities).

In addition to the authors, members of the Editorial Subcommittee, and the Banks-Baldwin editorial staff, this work is the product of many people. My secretary, Janice Irvine, my paralegal assistant, Mary Jane Dickenson, and others in the Columbus office of Smith & Schnacke helped me tremendously in coordinating the project when client matters took precedence. I am certain that my fellow authors are similarly indebted to their staffs. I would like especially to thank Banks-Baldwin Law Publishing Company for its willingness to undertake the project, with its attendant financial risks, in order to provide Ohio lawyers with a useful guidebook in a relatively enigmatic area of law.

I hope that *Ohio Administrative Law* will live through future editions and revisions. If such are warranted, particularly by sales, the book may be expanded to include articles on other agencies. Thus, if you find the book helpful or have suggestions for improvement (e.g., expansion, focus, or specific practice tips), please contact either Banks-Baldwin Law Publishing Company or the Chairman of the Administrative Law Committee of the Ohio State Bar Association.

> David Wm. T. Carroll
> Chairman, Editorial Subcommittee
> Administrative Law Committee
> Ohio State Bar Association

Columbus, Ohio
November 1985

About the Authors

David Wm. T. Carroll (Editor-in-Chief) is a partner in the law firm of Smith & Schnacke, working in the firm's Columbus office. He received his undergraduate degree from Ohio State University and his law degree from Capital University Law School. Mr. Carroll joined the Ohio State Bar Association's Administrative Law Committee in 1979 and served as Chairman from 1982 to 1984. He has also served as a referee for the Ohio Department of Education. He is a member of the Columbus Bar Association and the Litigation Section of the American Bar Association.

Gary W. Auman (co-author, Chapter 21, "Guide to the Ohio Workers' Compensation System") is also a partner of Smith & Schnacke where he has headed the firm's workers' compensation team since 1981. A graduate of the University of Louisville and the Ohio State University College of Law, Mr. Auman has lectured to the Southwest Ohio Self Insured's Association and the Ohio and Miami Valley Safety Conferences. He is a member of the Ohio State Bar Association's Workers' Compensation Committee and the Labor Law Section of the American Bar Association.

William A. Carroll (author, Chapter 9, "Division of Securities, Ohio Department of Commerce" and Chapter 23, "Afterword") was graduated from Fordham University School of Law in 1943. He was admitted to the New York Bar in 1943, the New Jersey Bar in 1947, and the Ohio Bar in 1953, when he began practicing administrative law. From 1953 to 1956, he was an Assistant Attorney General, representing the Divisions of Securities and Building & Loans, the Departments of Agriculture and Education, the Ohio Racing Commission, and all licensing boards and commissions authorized under RC Title 47. From 1956 to 1958, he served as Ohio Director of Commerce and Commissioner of Securities. Since 1959, he has engaged in the general practice of law and has served as a referee for the Ohio Department of Education. He was the single commissioner appointed by the Ohio Supreme Court (1977-83) to determine victims of crime compensation cases in the Ohio Court of Claims.

Russell S. Frye (co-author, Chapter 11, "Ohio Environmental Protection Agency, the Environmental Board of Review, and the Hazardous Waste Facility Board") is a partner in the law firm of Smith & Schnacke. He earned his undergraduate degree from Princeton University and his law degree from the University of Denver College of Law. His articles have appeared in *Environmental Analyst* and the journals of the Air Pollution Control Association and the Water Pollution Control Federation; and he co-authored the *Clean Water Act Permit Guidance Manual* (Executive Enterprises, Inc. 1984). Mr. Frye has lectured on environmental law at the University of Virginia, the Institute of Paper Chemistry, and the Ohio Water Pollution Conference. He is a member of the Ohio Bar Association's Environmental Law Committee and the Natural Resources Law and Administrative Law Sections of the American Bar Association.

Gary L. Jones (author, Chapter 15, "Ohio Department of Liquor Control and the Liquor Control Commission") practices law in Columbus. He received his undergraduate degree from Ohio State University and his law degree from the Franklin University Law School (later merged with Capital University Law School). From 1971 to 1974, Mr. Jones was Chief of the Permit Division of the Ohio Department of Liquor Control. He is the editor of Title 43, "Liquor," in *Baldwin's Ohio Revised Code Annotated*.

Michael F. Krall (co-author, Chapter 21, "Guide to the Ohio Workers' Compensation System"), currently in private practice in Dayton, was formerly associated with the law firm of Smith & Schnacke, where he was a member of the workers' compensation team from 1983 to 1985. He previously served for two years as Counsel for the Administrator of the Ohio Bureau of Workers' Compensation. He received both his undergraduate and law degrees from the University of Dayton. Mr. Krall is a frequent speaker before business groups concerned with the Ohio workers' compensation system.

Martin H. Lewis (co-author, Chapter 11, "Ohio Environmental Protection Agency, the Environmental Board of Review, and the Hazardous Waste Facility Board") is associated with the law firm of Smith & Schnacke, working in the firm's Columbus office. He received his undergraduate degree from Yale University and his law degree from the National Law Center at George Washington University. Before entering private practice in 1983, Mr. Lewis served for four years as an Assistant Attorney General in the Environmental Enforcement Section. He is currently a member of the Columbus and American Bar Associations.

Jay McKirahan (author, Chapter 19, "Ohio Department of Natural Resources") is a partner in the Columbus law firm of Zingarelli & McKirahan. A graduate of Muskingum College and the University of Michigan Law School, he served from 1972 to 1975 as an Assistant Attorney General in the Environmental Enforcement Section. In 1975, he co-authored an article entitled "Strip Mining: The Ohio Experience" for the *Capital University Law Review*.

John W. Maurer (author, Chapter 7, "Board of Review of the Ohio Bureau of Employment Services") has served as a refereee on the Board of Review since 1979. From 1970 to 1977, while studying for his undergraduate and law degrees at the University of Akron, he worked as an auditor in the Bureau's Compliance Section. He taught business law at the University of Akron during 1978-79. Mr. Maurer currently chairs the Committee on State Central Panel Systems of the National Conference of Administrative Law Judges (Judicial Administration Division, American Bar Association). He is also a member of the National Association of Administrative Law Judges and the Administrative Law Section of the American Bar Association.

Robert L. Mullinax (author, Chapter 13, "Ohio Department of Human Services") is Chief Legal Counsel for the Ohio Department of Human Services. After obtaining both his undergraduate and law degrees from the University of North Carolina, he served as a Senior Staff Attorney with the Ohio State Legal Services Association from 1973 to 1983. During that time, he authored the "Ohio Advocates Guide to Public Assistance Programs." In 1980, Mr. Mullinax was named the Outstanding Attorney in Legal Services by the National Clients Council.

William S. Newcomb, Jr. (co-author, Chapter 17, "Public Utilities Commission of Ohio") is a partner in the Columbus law firm of Vorys, Sater, Seymour and Pease. He received both his undergraduate and law degrees from Ohio State University. Mr. Newcomb was affiliated with PUCO from 1976 to 1981, serving as Director of the Legal Department (1976-77), as a Commissioner (1977-80), and as Chairman (1980-81). He has also chaired the National Association of Regulatory Utility Commissioners' Committee on Administration (1979-81) and the Columbus Bar Association's Energy Committee (1983-85).

Sheldon A. Taft (co-author, Chapter 17, "Public Utilities Commission of Ohio") is also a partner in the firm of Vorys, Sater, Seymour and Pease. He received his undergraduate degree from Amherst College and his law degree from Harvard Law School. From 1969 to 1971, he served as Assistant Attorney General and Chief Legal Counsel to PUCO. Mr. Taft currently chairs the Public Utilities Committee of the Ohio State Bar Association and is a member of the American Bar Association's Public Utilities Section.

Table of Contents

TEXT

Chapter		Page
1	Rulemaking	3
3	Adjudication	25
5	Miscellaneous Judicial Review of Agency Action	47
7	Board of Review of the Ohio Bureau of Employment Services	51
9	Division of Securities, Ohio Department of Commerce	61
11	Ohio Environmental Protection Agency, the Environmental Board of Review, and the Hazardous Waste Facility Board	77
13	Ohio Department of Human Services	95
15	Ohio Department of Liquor Control and the Liquor Control Commission	107
17	Public Utilities Commission of Ohio	119
19	Ohio Department of Natural Resources	139
21	Guide to the Ohio Workers' Compensation System	149
23	Afterword	169

OHIO REVISED CODE—Selected Provisions

Chapter		
101	General Assembly	173
111	Secretary of State	174
119	Administrative Procedure	179
2506	Appeals from Orders of Administrative Officers and Agencies	259

APPENDICES

A.	Table of Cases	287
B.	Table of Laws and Rules Construed	295
C.	Bibliography	297

INDEX

Index 301

Abbreviations

Abs	Ohio Law Abstract
Am Jur 2d	American Jurisprudence, Second Series
APA	Administrative Procedure Act
App	Ohio Appellate Reports
App(2d)	Ohio Appellate Reports, Second Series
App(3d)	Ohio Appellate Reports, Third Series
App R	Rules of Appellate Procedure
Art	Article
Assn	Association
Bd	Board
BTA	Board of Tax Appeals (Ohio)
Cal(2d)	California Reports, Second Series
Cal Rptr	California Reporter
Capital L Rev	Capital University Law Review
CDHS	County Department of Human Services
Cf	compare
CFR	Code of Federal Regulations
Ch	Chapter
Cir	Circuit Court
Co	Company
Comm	Commission
Commrs	Commissioners
Corp	Corporation
CP	Common Pleas Court
DC	District Court
Dept	Department
DHO	District Hearing Officer
Dist	District
DRG	Diagnosis Related Groups
EBR	Environmental Board of Review
ed	edition
EFC	Electric Fuel Component
e.g.	*exempli gratia*, for example
EPA	Environmental Protection Agency (Ohio)
F(2d)	Federal Reporter, Second Series
FCC	Federal Communications Commission
GCR	Gas Cost Recovery
H	House Bill
HWFB	Hazardous Waste Facility Board
Inc	Incorporated
JCARR	Joint Committee on Agency Rule Review
LEd(2d)	Lawyers' Edition, United States Supreme Court Reports, Second Series
LSC	Legislative Service Commission
Minn Stat	Minnesota Statutes
Misc	Ohio Miscellaneous Reports
Mo Rev Stats	Missouri Revised Statutes
NE	Northeastern Reporter
NE(2d)	Northeastern Reporter, Second Series
NLRB	National Labor Relations Board
Nos.	Numbers
NPDES	National Pollutant Discharge Elimination System
NY	New York Court of Appeals

NY	New York Reports
NYS(2d)	New York Supplement, Second Series
OAC	Ohio Administrative Code
OAG	Opinions of the Attorney General (Ohio)
OBR	Ohio Bar Reports
O Const	Ohio Constitution
ODHS	Ohio Department of Human Services
ODNR	Ohio Department of Natural Resources
OGBR	Oil and Gas Board of Review
Ohio St LJ	Ohio State Law Journal
OO(3d)	Ohio Opinions, Third Series
OS	Ohio State Reports
OS(2d)	Ohio State Reports, Second Series
OS(3d)	Ohio State Reports, Third Series
P	Pacific Reporter
PUCO	Public Utilities Commission of Ohio
RBR	Reclamation Board of Review
RC	Ohio Revised Code
RR	Railroad
S	Senate Bill
SCt	United States Supreme Court Reporter
SE(2d)	Southeastern Reporter, Second Series
SEC	Securities Exchange Commission
Supp	Supplement
UAW	United Auto Workers
US	United States Reports
USC	United States Code
US Const	United States Constitution
v	versus
W Va	West Virginia Reports

TEXT

Chapter
- 1 Rulemaking
- 3 Adjudication
- 5 Miscellaneous Judicial Review of Agency Action
- 7 Board of Review of the Ohio Bureau of Employment Services
- 9 Division of Securities, Ohio Department of Commerce
- 11 Ohio Environmental Protection Agency, the Environmental Board of Review, and the Hazardous Waste Facility Board
- 13 Ohio Department of Human Services
- 15 Ohio Department of Liquor Control and the Liquor Control Commission
- 17 Public Utilities Commission of Ohio
- 19 Ohio Department of Natural Resources
- 21 Guide to the Ohio Workers' Compensation System
- 23 Afterword

Chapter 1

Rulemaking

By Editorial Subcommittee of the
Administrative Law Committee of the
Ohio State Bar Association

1.01 Introduction
1.02 Types of rules
1.03 Constitutional issues applicable to rulemaking
1.04 Adoption of rules under RC 111.15
1.05 The formal and informal aspects of the Ohio rulemaking process
1.06 Judicial review
1.07 Emerging issues

1.01 Introduction

Administrative rulemaking can be the most efficient and powerful method of government regulation. The procedural rights of affected individuals are typically reduced to a minimum in the rulemaking process, and Ohio courts have shown a great reluctance to critically review administrative rulemaking actions.

Rulemaking can generally be defined as an administrative action that resembles legislation. This is in contrast to the quasi-judicial function of administrative adjudication, which is the case-by-case application of predetermined legal obligations (established either by statute or by rule) to the facts and circumstances peculiar to a specific party.

The definition of a rule is given in the Ohio Administrative Procedure Act as follows:

> "Rule" means any rule, regulation, or standard, having a general and uniform operation, adopted, promulgated, and enforced by any agency under the authority of the laws governing such agency, but it does not include regulations concerning internal management of the agency which do not affect private rights.[1]

Administrative rules, to the extent that they are consistent with the statutes enabling their adoption, constitute law that is judicially enforceable in the same manner as statutes.[2] Once adopted, an administrative rule is as binding on the agency that created it as it is on anyone else.[3]

In theory, rules apply generally and adjudications determine the rights of specific persons or entities. In practice, however, this distinction becomes blurred. Agencies often adopt rules which in effect render decisions affecting only specific persons or entities.

---

[1] RC 119.01(C).

[2] E.g., Kroger Grocery & Baking Co v Glander, 149 OS 120, 77 NE(2d) 921 (BTA 1948).

[3] See Cleveland Electric Illuminating Co v Williams, 55 App(2d) 272, 380 NE(2d) 1342 (Franklin 1977), cert denied 439 US 865, 99 SCt 189, 58 LEd(2d) 175 (1978).

The number of agencies that have been created and authorized by statute to promulgate rules, and the number of rules that each agency promulgates, have been dramatically increasing. In 1977, RC 103.05 was amended to establish an Ohio Administrative Code, consisting of all currently effective administrative rules adopted pursuant to RC Chapter 119, 111.15, 4141.14, and 5703.14. The codification of those rules by the Legislative Service Commission was intended to facilitate publication of such rules by private publishing companies.[4]

CROSS REFERENCES

See Whiteside, Ohio Appellate Practice, Text 21.01, 23.01

1.02 Types of rules

It is important to distinguish the various types of administrative rules that agencies promulgate. Procedural rules are those that establish procedures to be followed in agency proceedings. In the case of adjudicatory proceedings, such procedural rules would be comparable to the Ohio and Federal Rules of Civil Procedure. In the case of rulemaking proceedings, procedural rules might address such topics as the form and substance of notices and the rules of order and procedure to be followed at public hearings. Procedural rules would not necessarily (or likely) fall into the category of "regulations concerning internal management of the agency which do not affect private rights." The "internal management" regulations that are exempt from the definition of a "rule" in RC 119.01 relate to such things as organizational structure, personnel promotion policies, budgeting, and management policies.

Substantive rules have the force and effect of law and prescribe some right, duty, liability, or standard for decision-making. Examples of substantive rules include the Ohio Building Code, hazardous waste regulations, and air and water pollution regulations. Once promulgated, substantive rules are binding and determinative of the legal obligations involved unless vacated, modified, or rescinded.

Some substantive rules are self-executing, while others require further administrative application or interpretation in order to be given final effect. A self-executing rule is one that embodies the agency's final definition of the legal obligations of regulated parties and is directly enforceable without further agency action. A rule that is not self-executing requires a further exercise of agency discretion to implement.

1.03 Constitutional issues applicable to rulemaking

A leading commentator in the field of administrative law has pointed out that "[t]he administrative process has developed in spite of the dominant

---

[4]RC 103.05. The Official Edition of the Ohio Administrative Code is published by Banks-Baldwin Law Publishing Co.

theoretical thinking, not in response to it."[5] Thus, major building blocks of our system of government such as separation of powers, the nondelegation doctrine, due process, and equal protection of the law have been, in some cases, reshaped to accommodate the perceived need for practical answers to immediate problems. The influence of the development of the administrative rulemaking process on several basic theories of government is discussed below.

(A) Separation of powers and nondelegation doctrines

The separation of power among the executive, legislative, and judicial branches of government is a cornerstone of the structure of federal and state government in the United States. For example, section 1 of Article II of the Ohio Constitution provides that "[t]he legislative power of the state shall be vested in a General Assembly," and the Ohio Supreme Court has held that "that body may not abdicate or transfer to others the essential legislative functions with which it is vested."[6] Furthermore, section 26 of Article II of the Ohio Constitution inhibits the General Assembly from delegating its power to make laws. Simply put, administrative agencies have no lawmaking power under the Ohio Constitution, and no such powers may be delegated.

How then can agencies, which are independent of the General Assembly, promulgate rules which have the full force of law within a regulated community? The answer, as developed by the Ohio Supreme Court, is that the General Assembly is prohibited from delegating *essential* legislative functions but may permit administrative bodies to administer laws already in existence. In other words, "The true distinction . . . is between the delegation of power to make the law, which necessarily involves a discretion as to what it shall be, and conferring an authority or discretion as to its execution, to be exercised under and in pursuance of the law."[7]

The line between lawmaking and the exercise of discretion in executing the law is often unclear, thereby endangering the basic theories of separation and nondelegation of powers. But the administrative rulemaking process has developed because administrative rulemaking is essential for dealing with matters which cannot be managed by the General Assembly. The distinction between lawmaking and discretion in the execution of the law can in practice be characterized as unformed clay which may be shaped to fit the needs of the moment.

While the courts have understood that the requirements of modern government compel delegation of legislative authority to administrative agencies, they have insisted that the delegation of rulemaking power by the General Assembly must be complete in all its terms and cannot be implied. In addition, the courts require that rulemaking authority be linked with meaningful standards to guide the administrative agency as it develops sub-

---

[5] 1 Davis, *Administrative Law Treatise* 59 (2d ed 1978).
[6] Belden v Union Central Life Insurance Co, 143 OS 329, 329, 55 NE(2d) 629 (1944), appeal dismissed by 328 US 674, 65 SCt 129, 89 LE 548 (1944).
[7] Cincinnati, Wilmington & Zanesville RR Co v Clinton County Commrs, 1 OS 77, 88-9 (1852).

stantive rules of general applicability.⁸ So long as the legislative enactment provides proper standards to guide an administrative agency vested with rulemaking authority, it is no violation of the constitutional prohibition against delegation of legislative power for the General Assembly to permit an agency to flesh out the structure it has established.

When called upon to determine the sufficiency of a standard to guide an administrative agency, Ohio courts have generally presumed that administrative action was not arbitrary or unwarranted. The courts recognize that the legislature cannot provide all the details and that discretion must be vested in administrative agencies. If the legislature provides an intelligible principle and the administrative agency uses the principle as its guide, the delegation of legislative power is permissible. Despite this generally liberal position, various standards have been held to be insufficient to serve as rulemaking guides for administrative agencies.

For example, a statute that granted an examiner of steam engineers the power to issue a license if "upon examination, the applicant is found trustworthy and competent," was held to be an unlawful delegation of legislative power because no standard was provided as to qualifications of steam engineers; the decision was left to the opinion of the examiner, who had unlimited discretion.⁹ Similarly, a statute authorizing the establishment of "fair and reasonable minimum prices" for dry cleaning was held to be an insufficient standard in the absence of an intelligible principle by which the price was to be determined.¹⁰

Another problem in the area of delegation of authority arises when an agency adopts a rule that incorporates by reference future amendments to federal regulations. Although the authors are aware of no Ohio case deciding the propriety of such an incorporation by reference, the Ohio Supreme Court in *Cleveland v Piskura*¹¹ held that a municipal ordinance could not constitutionally incorporate by reference later administrative determinations of a federal administrative body.

(B) Due process

The United States Supreme Court has described the procedural requirements respecting rulemaking as follows:

> Interpreting [the rulemaking] provision of the [federal Administrative Procedure] Act in *United States v. Allegheny-Ludlum Steel Corp.,* ... and *United States v. Florida East Coast R. Co.,* ... we held that generally speaking this section of the Act established the maximum procedural requirements which Congress was willing to have the courts impose upon agencies in conducting rulemaking procedures. Agencies are free to grant additional procedural rights in the exercise of their

---

[8] See Yee Bow v Cleveland, 99 OS 269, 124 NE 132 (1919), appeal dismissed by 255 US 578, 41 SCt 320, 65 LE 794 (1921); Raabe v State, 7 App 119, 28 CC(NS) 169 (Lucas 1917).

[9] Harmon v State, 66 OS 249, 64 NE 117 (1902).

[10] State ex rel Schneider v Gullatt Cleaning & Laundry Co, 32 NP(NS) 121, 123 (CP, Hamilton 1934).

[11] Cleveland v Piskura, 145 OS 144, 60 NE(2d) 919 (1945).

discretion, but reviewing courts are generally not free to impose them if the agencies have not chosen to grant them. This is not to say necessarily that there are no circumstances which would ever justify a court in overturning agency action because of a failure to employ procedures beyond those required by the statute. But such circumstances, if they exist, are extremely rare.[12]

As intimated in the foregoing passage, participatory rights in the rulemaking context now flow primarily from administrative procedure statutes. These statutes are sufficiently comprehensive that they adequately address most situations, and due process alone has been an infrequent basis for according participatory rights.

It is textbook law that the "fundamental requisite of due process of law is the opportunity to be heard."[13] The hearing must be "at a meaningful time and in a meaningful manner."[14] The Ohio Supreme Court has recognized that due process requires a "reasonable opportunity to be heard."[15]

Precisely what process is "due" in the constitutional sense when an agency undertakes rulemaking is unclear. Notice and an opportunity to present comments are generally regarded as the minimum procedures which will satisfy due process. This conclusion is supported by federal court decisions that have imposed such requirements independent of the Administrative Procedure Act.[16]

1.04 Adoption of rules under RC 111.15

In addition to the adoption of rules under RC Chapter 119, non-Administrative Procedure Act agencies adopt rules pursuant to RC 111.15. RC 119.01 defines "agency" for the purposes of the Administrative Procedure Act. The definition limits "agency" to those agencies specifically named and any agency function "specifically made subject to sections 119.01 to 119.13 of the Revised Code." When RC 119.01 and 111.15 are read together, it appears that any agency with rulemaking authority not specifically named in RC 119.01 and not specifically made subject to RC Chapter 119 must adopt its rules in accordance with RC 111.15.

However, the requirements of RC 111.15 address filing and review of rules, not how a filed rule is developed. Moreover, RC 111.15 does not provide for input by persons potentially affected by a rule. Briefly, RC 111.15 requires the filing of copies of a proposed rule with the Clerk of the Senate, the Secretary of State, and the Director of the Legislative Service Commission at least sixty days prior to adoption. Any substantive changes to

---

[12]Vermont Yankee Nuclear Power Corp v Natural Resources Defense Counsel, 435 US 519, 524, 98 SCt 1197, 55 LEd(2d) 460 (1978).
[13]Grannis v Ordean, 234 US 385, 394, 34 SCt 779, 58 LEd 1363 (1914).
[14]Armstrong v Manzo, 380 US 545, 552, 85 SCt 1187, 14 LEd(2d) 62 (1965); Goldberg v Kelly, 397 US 254, 267, 90 SCt 1011, 25 LEd(2d) 287 (1970).
[15]New York Central RR Co v PUCO, 130 OS 548, 548, 200 NE 759 (1936).
[16]See Independent Broker-Dealers' Trade Assn v SEC, 442 F(2d) 132 (DC Cir 1971), cert denied 404 US 828, 92 SCt 63, 30 LEd(2d) 57 (1971); Caramico v Secretary of Housing & Urban Development, 509 F(2d) 694 (2d Cir NY 1974).

the proposed rule must also be filed. The proposed rule is subject to review by the Joint Committee on Agency Rule Review (JCARR) in accordance with RC 119.03. The legislative review process is provided for both under RC Chapter 119, as to those agencies subject to it, and under RC 111.15, as to those agencies not subject to RC Chapter 119. The Legislative Service Commission is covered by RC 111.15 and not RC Chapter 119. That section, however, incorporates the rule invalidation provisions of RC 119.03(I).[17]

CROSS REFERENCES

See Text 1.05(E)

1.05 The formal and informal aspects of the Ohio rulemaking process

RC 119.03 and RC 119.04 establish the procedure which any agency subject to RC Chapter 119 must follow in the adoption, amendment, and rescission of rules.[18] Failure to comply with RC Chapter 119 in the rulemaking process will result in the rule being invalid.[19]

RC 119.03 sets forth the specific procedure which must be followed in the adoption, amendment, or rescission of a rule. In actuality, the statute requires two separate proceedings which occur concurrently. One is the proceeding by which the promulgating agency gives public notice and holds a public hearing on the proposal. The other is a proceeding whereby the General Assembly, through the Joint Committee on Agency Rule Review (JCARR), has an opportunity to invalidate a rule which it determines is improper under the circumstances.[20]

(A) Prenotice procedures

Generally, before a rule reaches the first formal step in the rulemaking process, much informal activity will have been undertaken within, and sometimes without, the agency. There are several primary causes for an agency to propose a rule. Frequently, new rules are proposed because they have been mandated by statute. More often, however, the rule is proposed because the agency sees a problem which the rule can alleviate and has some statutory authority upon which to base such a rule. Although the authority selected may be weak, no one will normally contest the rule unless it causes direct, substantial harm.

If an agency is unable to find any statutory authority at all upon which to base a desired rule, it might issue a memorandum, bulletin, circular, or other document announcing a particular policy position with hopes of achieving substantial compliance. Such announcements, of course, do not require statutory authority; however, in many instances they achieve the regulator's desired effect.

---

[17]See Text 1.05(E), Legislative oversight of rulemaking.
[18]References to proposing or adopting a rule may include a new rule, an amendment to a rule, or a rescission or repeal of a rule, unless the text indicates otherwise.
[19]RC 119.02.
[20]RC 111.15(D) incorporates the JCARR procedure of RC 119.03.

Often the regulated business or industry suggests a rule to the agency. The regulated industry may discover problems which are particularly burdensome and which in its view require regulation.

The substantive language of proposed rules originates from various sources. Of course, a large proportion of it no doubt results from original drafting done within the agency by the staff members most intimately familiar with the subject area. Frequently, model rules proposed by national associations or regulators or similar groups of governmental policymakers provide the basis for the development of a rule. Similarly, new rules are often based on regulations adopted in other states where similar problems were experienced. This approach offers the advantage of knowing how well the proposal worked in those jurisdictions.

After an agency begins to formulate a proposed rule, many informal communications between the representatives of the agency and representatives of those affected by the rule should take place. Frequently, a regulatory agency informally communicates its intention to adopt particular rules to the industries, businesses, and groups which the agency expects will be most affected. The purposes for such communications include (1) verifying that the agency's proposal would be meaningful and worthy of adoption; (2) putting such groups on preliminary notice that such proposals are being considered within the agency; and (3) benefiting from the preliminary comments and technical expertise possessed by those outside the agency.

Agencies often contact their counterparts in other states when they appear to have similar problems or when they have a positive relationship with the counterpart and respect for its technical competence. Occasionally, proposed rules being considered in preliminary form within an agency touch upon politically sensitive areas which necessitate a political analysis (e.g., review by the Governor's staff before the rule is noticed for hearing).

When the matters to be regulated are highly technical and complex, agencies will seek out technicians from the groups and businesses ultimately to be regulated in order to obtain their views. As in the legislative process, those from the private sector who provide early, informal advice to regulators must be credible. If they are not, the agency will not accord them an early opportunity to comment in the future.

If the industry or group generally regulated by the agency initiates consideration of a rule to resolve a problem it identifies, frequently that industry or group will draft a proposal to submit to the agency. Instead of simply stating the problem, the industry may expedite the process by also offering a solution.

(B) Initial filing and public notice of proposed rule

RC 119.03(B) requires the agency promulgating the rule to file the full text of the proposed rule with the Secretary of State and the Director of the Legislative Service Commission. At the same time, RC 119.03(H) also requires that two copies be filed with the JCARR along with one copy of the rule summary and fiscal analysis prepared according to RC 121.24 or RC 127.18 or both.

RC 127.18(B) requires that a fiscal analysis of a proposed rule contain the following: (1) the name, address, and telephone number of the promulgating agency; (2) a citation to the statute under which the rule is being adopted; (3) the administrative code section number of the proposed rule; (4) an estimate in dollars of the increase or decrease in revenues or expenditures caused by the rule; (5) a citation to the appropriation authorizing any expenditure caused by the rule; and (6) any other information the JCARR prescribes. The analysis must be made on the form prescribed by the JCARR, and the JCARR must review the fiscal effect of each proposed rule.

The text of any substantive revision of the initial proposal and a copy of the rule summary and fiscal analysis must also be promptly filed with each of the above three agents and a revised fiscal analysis filed with the Senate Clerk. A hearing must be held no sooner than thirty days after the initial filing, and no order may be issued prior to sixty days after the initial filing is completed.

Printed copies of the text must be available at the agency's office for at least thirty days prior to the hearing. The copies must be provided without charge to any person affected by the proposal.

RC 119.03(A) requires the agency to give "reasonable public notice" at least thirty days before the date set for a hearing. The notice must include a statement of the agency's intention to adopt a rule, a synopsis of the rule or a general statement of the subject matter to which it applies, a statement of the reason or purpose of such rule, and the date, time, and place of the hearing. Each agency is required by RC 119.03(A)(4) to have a rule which sets forth in detail the method that the agency will follow in giving public notice as to adoption of rules. That public notice rule must require the agency to give a copy of the public notice to anyone who requests it and pays the cost of copying and mailing. The methods used for notification established by the agency in its public notice rule may include, but are not limited to, mailing notices to all subscribers on a mailing list or mailing notices in addressed, stamped envelopes provided by the person requesting the notice.

Thus, someone whose work involves frequent contact with a particular agency might inquire about the possibility of placing his name and address on a rulemaking notice list. If available, this method of notice increases the probability of learning of proposed rules well in advance of the hearing and adoption.

Although the statute does not require the filing and public notice to occur simultaneously, the effect of the time limitations on filing, notice, and hearing is to make concurrent filing and notice both practical and efficient.

(C) Availability of supporting documentation

There is no express statutory right in Ohio to gain access to the documentation which is contained in the state agency's files and upon which a proposed rule is based. Some argue that the express right to comment on proposed rules, orally or in writing, at the public hearing pursuant to RC 119.03(C) necessarily implies a right of access to the agency's supporting files, because background information may be of substantial value in preparing a meaningful, critical analysis of the rule proposed.

It may also be argued that RC 149.43, which states that all public records shall be made available to any member of the general public at all reasonable times for inspection and that copies shall be available at cost upon request, creates a right of access to the agency's supporting files.

RC 149.43(A)(1) defines "public record" as

> any record *required to be kept* by any governmental unit, including, but not limited to, state, county, city, village, township, and school district units, except medical records, records pertaining to adoption, probation, and parole proceedings, trial preparation records, confidential law enforcement investigatory records, and records the release of which is prohibited by state or federal law. (Emphasis added.)

However, the question arises whether supporting documents relating to a proposed rule, which are in the agency's possession but are not presented at the public hearing, are "public records" within the definition in RC 149.43 and, therefore, must be open to the public. The Ohio Supreme Court, in *Dayton Newspapers, Inc v Dayton*,[21] somewhat expanded the statutory definition in finding that a record is " 'required to be kept' by a governmental unit where the unit's keeping of such record is necessary to the unit's execution of its duties and responsibilities."

Thus, whether supporting documents are public records and required to be open under RC 149.43 depends on the type of documents involved. If they are of a type "required to be kept" either by specific statute or as an incident of the agency's discharge of a duty imposed by law, then those documents are required to be open for public inspection. However, if the documents were acquired by the agency other than in the process of or for the purpose of discharging its statutory duties, they likely would not be required to be available for public inspection.[22]

(D) Comment and hearing

RC 119.03(C) requires the agency to conduct a public hearing,[23] not sooner than thirty days after notice is given and copies of the proposal are made available.[24] The hearing must be held on the date and at the time and place designated in the notice. Any person affected by the proposal may appear; be represented by an attorney; present his position, arguments, and contentions, orally or in writing; offer and examine witnesses; and present evidence tending to show that the proposed rule would be unreasonable or unlawful. While this provision of RC 119.03 may be read to allow only

---

[21]Dayton Newspapers, Inc v Dayton, 45 OS(2d) 107, 107, 341 NE(2d) 576 (1976).

[22]See OAG 80-096 for full discussion of the "required to be kept" issue.

[23]Rules adopted by the Department of Taxation or the Bureau of Employment Services are effective without the hearing ordinarily required by RC 119.03 if the statutes pertaining to the agency give a specific right of appeal to the Board of Tax Appeals or to a higher authority within the agency or to a court, and also give the appellant a right to a hearing on such appeal. RC 119.03(G).

[24]RC 119.03(A), (B).

opponents of the proposed rule to comment, in practice all who have positive comments to offer are also permitted to express their views.

The agency determines the admissibility of evidence, but the person affected by a ruling may make an objection and may proffer evidence ruled inadmissible. Such a proffer must be made a part of the hearing record. A stenographic record of the proceedings, including all testimony and rulings, must be made at the expense of the agency. Finally, the agency may administer oaths and affirmations in any rules hearing.

Frequently, the agency will be represented at the hearing by several of its staff members who are most familiar with the subject area in question, and upon the conclusion of a witness' remarks, the staff members will be given the opportunity to question the witness. The Ohio Supreme Court has now determined, at least in dictum, that the "offer and examine" language of RC 119.03(C) grants no right to "cross-examine" witnesses.[25]

Finally, the hearing officer will often announce at the conclusion of a hearing that for a specified period of time the record will remain open in order that additional written comments may be received and made a part of the record.

(E) Legislative oversight of rulemaking

RC 119.03(I) sets forth the procedure whereby the Joint Committee on Agency Rule Review (JCARR), a committee of the General Assembly established by RC 101.35, may review a proposed rule.[26] An agency may hold the required public hearing while the JCARR is considering the proposal but may not issue an order adopting a proposed rule until the JCARR has taken final action, or the time specified for the action has run, generally when the initial filing is made with the JCARR under RC 119.03(H).

The JCARR may, upon the concurrence of a majority of its members, recommend to the General Assembly the adoption of a concurrent resolution invalidating all or a part of a proposed rule for any of the following reasons: (1) the agency has exceeded its statutory authority in proposing the rule; (2) the proposed rule conflicts with another rule adopted by the same or a different agency; (3) the proposed rule conflicts with the legislative intent in enacting the statute under which the agency proposed the rule; or (4) the agency has failed to prepare a complete and accurate summary and fiscal analysis of the proposed rule.[27] At hearings before the JCARR, the committee has refused to hear testimony on the merits of the rule and has strictly limited the testimony to matters bearing on the above reasons.

The House and Senate may then adopt a concurrent resolution stating which specific proposed rule, or part thereof, is to be invalidated. The General Assembly must adopt the resolution before the sixtieth day after the

---

[25]Sterling Drug, Inc v Wickham, 63 OS(2d) 16, 406 NE(2d) 1363 (1980).

[26]Rules required to be adopted verbatim pursuant to federal law or rule are specifically exempted from legislative review by RC 119.03(H)(2).

[27]RC 119.03(I).

initial filing of the original text, or before the thirtieth day after the filing of a revised version, whichever is later.[28]

However, there are two exceptions to this sixty-day time limit. First, if, between the time the JCARR recommends the adoption of a concurrent resolution and the expiration of the sixty-day period, the House or the Senate does not hold five floor sessions with recorded roll call votes disclosing a majority of the members present, the time is extended until that house has held five such floor sessions. Second, if the rule was filed with the JCARR on or after the first day of December of any year, it will be carried over for legislative review to the next succeeding regular session of the General Assembly. The rule is then subject to legislative review and invalidation "as if it were the original version of a proposed rule ... that had been filed with the joint committee for the first time on the first day of the session."[29] This extension to the sixty-day limit, when it occurs, also delays the date on which the agency may issue an order adopting the rule, discussed below.

Within five days of the adoption of a resolution to invalidate a proposal, the Senate Clerk must send the agency, the Secretary of State, and the Director of the Legislative Service Commission a certified copy of the resolution and a certification of the effective date. During the same General Assembly, the agency may not adopt any version of a rule which has been invalidated unless the General Assembly adopts a concurrent resolution allowing the agency to conduct or continue rulemaking proceedings.[30]

To help correct any misunderstanding or misinterpretation of a failure of the General Assembly to act regarding a particular rule, note the last paragraph of RC 119.03(I):

> *The failure of the general assembly to invalidate a proposed rule,* amendment, rescission, or part thereof under this section *shall not be construed as a ratification of the lawfulness or reasonableness of the proposed rule,* amendment, rescission, or any part thereof *or of the validity of the procedure by which the proposed rule,* amendment, rescission, or any part thereof *was proposed or adopted.* (Emphasis added.)

The legislative veto may be subject to constitutional infirmity as violating the separation-of-powers doctrine.[31]

(F) Promulgation of final rules

If the General Assembly does not adopt a resolution to invalidate a proposed rule within the prescribed time, the agency may issue an order adopting the rule, so long as the order is issued not sooner than sixty days

---

[28]*Id.*
[29]*Id.*
[30]*Id.*
[31]See, e.g., Consumer Energy Council v Federal Energy Regulatory Comm, 673 F(2d) 425 (DC Cir 1982), affirmed sub nom Process Gas Consumers Group v Consumer Energy Council, 463 US 1216, 103 SCt 3556, 77 LEd(2d) 1402 (1983); Alaska v A.L.I.V.E. Voluntary, 606 P(2d) 769 (Alaska 1980); Opinion of the Justices to the Governor, 384 Mass 840, 429 NE(2d) 1019 (1981); State ex rel Barker v Manchin, 279 SE(2d) 622 (W Va 1981).

after the initial filing of the proposed rule. At that time the agency must designate an effective date, which may not be sooner than ten days after the final form of the proposed rule is filed as required by RC 119.04.[32]

RC 119.04 requires two copies of the final version to be filed with the Secretary of State and the Director of the LSC before the rule can become effective. Two copies of the rule must also be filed with the JCARR, unless the rule is one to which RC 119.03(H) does not apply. The rule, as filed, must be numbered in accordance with the system of the Ohio Administrative Code and be submitted in compliance with the rules of the LSC. The rule must clearly state the effective date and expiration date, if known, and must contain a full statement of the rule as adopted.[33] If the Director of the LSC gives an agency written notice pursuant to RC 103.05 that a filed rule is not in compliance with LSC rules, the agency has thirty days to comply.

Before the effective date, the agency must make a reasonable effort to inform those affected by the action and must have copies of the full text available to those who request it.[34]

Upon filing the final rule, the chairman of the JCARR is required to compare the final rule with the original proposed rule. If he finds that the final rule contains a substantive revision from the proposed rule, he must notify the agency, the Secretary of State, and the director of LSC. The JCARR must again review the rule under its standards for review discussed above. JCARR may suspend the entire rule or any part of it. Within the same time limits as a proposed rule calculated from the date of filing in final form, the House of Representatives and Senate may adopt a concurrent resolution invalidating the rule or any part of it. The action or inaction of the General Assembly has the same effect as if taken with respect to a proposed rule.[35]

(G) Emergency rules

Pursuant to RC 119.03(F), the procedure set out in RC 119.03 may be suspended by written order of the Governor when the agency so requests and the Governor determines that an emergency requires that the rule become effective immediately. A copy of the Governor's order must be filed with the Secretary of State, the Director of the LSC, and the JCARR. Upon that filing, the procedure under RC 119.03 is suspended and, upon the agency's compliance with the filing requirements of RC 119.04, the rule becomes effective. The effectiveness of the rule terminates at the end of ninety days, unless, before the expiration of the ninety-day period, the agency complies with the requirements of RC 119.03.

(H) Record

RC 119.03(C) contains the following requirement: "At the hearing, the testimony, rulings on the admissibility of evidence, and proffers of evidence

---

[32] RC 119.03(D).
[33] RC 119.04(A)(2).
[34] RC 119.03(D).
[35] RC 119.031.

shall be recorded by stenographic means. Such record shall be made at the expense of the agency."

Also, as noted earlier, agencies may admit evidence into the record, or they may refuse to admit such evidence. In the latter event, the person offering the evidence should proffer on the record of the hearing.[36]

While the Ohio Administrative Procedure Act does not expressly provide interested persons the right of access to the records accumulated by the agency, Ohio agencies often permit the inspection of such records. In addition, access to the stenographic record may be forced by use of the Ohio Public Records Act as it clearly is a "record required to be kept" under RC 149.43.[37] Finally, the hearing record should be available by subpoena in an action for a declaratory judgment, where a justifiable controversy exists and the proper interpretation of a rule to which the record is related is at issue.

1.06 Judicial review

(A) Procedure for review

Former RC 119.11, which created a right of appeal to the court of common pleas from the making, revising, or rescinding of administrative rules by an agency subject to RC Chapter 119, was declared unconstitutional in *Rankin-Thoman, Inc v Caldwell*.[38] The court found that "the review of proceedings of administrative officers and agencies, authorized by Section 4(B), Article IV of the Ohio Constitution, contemplates quasi-judicial proceedings only."[39] The court then found that RC 119.11, which speaks to an appeal from "an order of an agency in adopting, amending, or rescinding a rule," particularly when read with RC 119.12, which gives a specific right of appeal from the quasi-judicial determinations of an administrative agency, was intended to give a right of appeal from the quasi-legislative proceedings of state administrative officers and bodies and was, therefore, unconstitutional. In the wake of *Rankin-Thoman*, there is presently no provision for direct appellate review of administrative rulemaking under RC Chapter 119.

However, in *Burger Brewing Co v Liquor Control Comm*,[40] the Ohio Supreme Court specifically recognized the availability of declaratory relief "where the action is within the spirit of the Declaratory Judgment Act, a justiciable controversy exists between adverse parties, and speedy relief is necessary to the preservation of rights which may otherwise be impaired or lost."

---

[36]See Text 1.05(D), Comment and hearing.
[37]See Text 1.05(C), Availability of supporting documentation.
[38]Rankin-Thoman, Inc v Caldwell, 42 OS(2d) 436, 329 NE(2d) 686 (1975).
[39]*Id*. Ohio law with respect to appellate review has developed tortuously. A detailed analytical discussion of this development through 1976 can be found in Brubaker and Northrup, *Appellate Review of Administrative Rulemaking in Ohio—Prospects for Revival*, 37 Ohio St L J 471 (1976).
[40]Burger Brewing Co v Liquor Control Comm, 34 OS(2d) 93, 93, 296 NE(2d) 261 (1973).

In *Union Camp Corp v Whitman*[41] and *Williams v Akron*,[42] the court recognized the availability of appellate review in the courts of appeal.[43] The court's reasoning was based on the absence of the term "proceedings" in section 3(B)(2), Article IV of the Ohio Constitution, which provides, "Courts of appeals shall have ... such appellate jurisdiction as may be provided by law to review and affirm, modify, or reverse final orders or actions of administrative officers or agencies." The court found the semantic distinction persuasive, holding in *Williams* that the above-quoted constitutional provision authorizes grants of jurisdiction to the courts of appeal for review of administrative action, "irrelative of the fact that it is an appeal from an administrative rulemaking action."[44] The court further noted that the appeal must present a justiciable controversy.

Both *Union Camp* and *Williams* involved appeals of rulemaking actions of the Ohio Environmental Protection Agency (EPA) taken pursuant to the provisions of RC Chapter 3745.[45] RC 3745.06 expressly provides for the appeal of decisions of the Environmental Board of Review (an administrative agency, the sole function of which is to review actions of the Director of the Environmental Protection Agency) to the Court of Appeals of Franklin County. It is clear that courts of appeal have only such appellate jurisdiction "as may be provided by law," and RC 3745.06 represents such a legislative provision with respect to environmental regulations in Ohio. There is no comparable statutory provision in RC Chapter 119.

(B) Standard of judicial review

In the case of agencies whose rulemaking may be appealed to courts of appeal, either directly or through intermediate administrative bodies, one must examine the organic statute to determine the standard of review. For example, RC 3745.06 provides that the court shall affirm the order appealed from it if it finds the order is supported by "reliable, probative and substantial evidence and is in accordance with law." The organic statute may also allow the court of appeals to take additional evidence.[46]

One challenging a rule by declaratory judgment has the burden of proving the rule unreasonable or unlawful. If the adoption of the rule depends upon the agency finding certain jurisdictional facts, one challenging the rule must

---

[41] Union Camp Corp v Whitman, 42 OS(2d) 441, 329 NE(2d) 690 (1975).

[42] Williams v Akron, 54 OS(2d) 136, 374 NE(2d) 1378 (1978).

[43] In Zangerle v Evatt, 139 OS 563, 41 NE(2d) 269 (BTA 1942), the Ohio Supreme Court determined that the General Assembly could not confer appellate jurisdiction on the Supreme Court over "quasi-legislative," i.e., rulemaking, actions of administrative agencies, because quasi-legislative actions were not "proceedings" within the meaning of O Const Art IV, § 2(B)(2)(c).

[44] Williams v Akron, 54 OS(2d) 136, 136, 374 NE(2d) 1378 (1978).

[45] Note that declaratory judgment may not be available to review Ohio Environmental Protection Agency rulemaking. Clearly, declaratory judgment is not available to review rules of that agency once an adjudication proceeding has been initiated. Warren Molded Plastics, Inc v Williams, 56 OS(2d) 352, 384 NE(2d) 253 (1978); State ex rel Williams v Bozarth, 55 OS(2d) 34, 377 NE(2d) 1006 (1978).

[46] See, e.g., RC 3745.06.

prove the nonexistence of those facts by a "preponderance of substantial, reliable and probative evidence upon the whole of the record sufficient to overcome" the presumption that the factual conclusions of the agency were made upon sufficient evidence.[47]

(C) Common issues in judicial review of rulemaking

Failure of an agency subject to the Administrative Procedure Act to comply with the procedural requirements of RC Chapter 119 for the adoption of rules is generally good cause to invalidate a rule.[48] Rules may also be challenged on the grounds of being arbitrary and unreasonable, an abuse of discretion, or unauthorized by statute.

(1) Consistency requirement of RC 119.03

RC 119.03 requires:

> In the adoption, amendment, or rescission of any rule, an agency shall comply with the following procedure:
>
> (A) Reasonable public notice shall be given at least thirty days prior to the date set for a hearing, in the manner and form and for the length of time as the agency determines and shall include:
>
> . . .
>
> (2) A synopsis of the proposed rule, amendment, or rule to be rescinded or a general statement of the subject matter to which the proposed rule, amendment, or rescission relates;
>
> . . .
>
> (D) After complying with divisions (A), (B), (C), and (H) of this section, and when the time for legislative review and invalidation under division (I) of this section has expired, the agency may issue an order adopting the proposed rule or the proposed amendment or rescission of the rule, consistent with the synopsis or general statement included in the public notice. At that time the agency shall designate the effective date of the rule, amendment, or rescission, which shall not be earlier than the tenth day after the rule, amendment, or rescission has been filed in its final form as provided in section 119.04 of the Revised Code.

In *Buckeye Power, Inc v Whitman*,[49] the Environmental Board of Review (EBR) addressed at length problems associated with public notice requirements when rules as finally adopted do not conform with the proposed regulations. The rulemaking proceedings appealed in *Buckeye* were preceded by the following notice in twelve newspapers in the state:

> Notice is hereby given that the Ohio Environmental Protection Agency intends to consider renumbering and revising Chapter AP-3 of the existing air pollution control regulations and alter the limiting final compliance date for sulfur dioxide in EP-32-03:
>
> (1) Control of Sulfur Dioxide; (2) Separate Treatment of Small Gray Iron Foundry Cupolas; (3) Redefinition of "Combustible Refuse."[50]

---

[47]Sterling Drug, Inc v Wickham, 63 OS(2d) 16, 16, 406 NE(2d) 1363 (1980).
[48]RC 119.02.
[49]Buckeye Power, Inc v Whitman, 74 OO(2d) 442 (EBR 1974).
[50]*Id.* at 452.

The EBR found that "the public notice was in extraordinarily broad and vague terms" and stated that it was "unable to see what could *not* be covered in regulations concerning sulfur dioxide where the notice says simply 'control of sulfur dioxide.' "[51]

The EBR concluded that if the director chooses to give a general statement of the subject matter rather than a synopsis of proposed rules, then the standard for determining consistency becomes the proposed regulations filed with the Secretary of State. On that basis, when the EBR compared the proposed and finally adopted versions of the regulations involved in *Buckeye*, RC 119.03 was found to have been violated. As the EBR stated:

> No person ... could have had the least clue as whether the consistency provisions of RC 119.03(D) were complied with, if they did not compare the proposed regulations as filed with the Secretary of State and what was finally adopted. To conclude otherwise ... would allow the Director to publish some vague and uninformative public notice with which any regulations ultimately finally adopted would be in conformity and to give no regard as to the proposed regulations filed with the Secretary of State as needing to have any consistency with what he finally adopts as his regulations.[52]

Thus, rules preceded by vague and uninformative published notice should be nullified even if they are consistent with the proposed rules, because such notice is inadequate to put affected persons on guard that the agency was planning action which could affect them.

(2) Adequacy of rulemaking documentation

An increasingly emphasized tenet of administrative law is that all persons who may be affected by agency rulemaking must be given adequate notice and information in order to make the right to participate and comment on proposed rules genuine and meaningful. This right to comment in Ohio is assured by RC 119.03(C).

The right of an interested party to comment and participate in a hearing on proposed rulemaking is a nullity unless the information necessary to understand the proposed rule and its derivation is available in the record *prior* to the expiration of the comment and hearing period. This proposition was recognized in *Mision Industrial, Inc v EPA*,[53] where, in the course of reviewing USEPA rulemaking action, the court stated:

> Whether defined as part of the actual [implementation plan] revision itself or merely a work paper, the [computer] print-out was the type of relevant documentation which should have been made available before the public hearing so as to maximize the opportunity for intelligent comment and debate.... Where documents of this sort are withheld ... prejudice should be assumed unless its absence can be fairly inferred from the record.

Failure of an agency to meet this burden is detrimental to all persons affected by adoption of the agency rules, who are invited more to "guess" at

---

[51]*Id.* at 455.
[52]*Id.*
[53]Mision Industrial, Inc v EPA, 547 F(2d) 123, 127-28 (1st Cir PR 1976).

the basis for the substance of the agency's proposed decision rather than to "comment" thereon. The agency's frustration with participatory rights is detrimental to proponents as well as opponents of the rules finally adopted. A rule adopted by an unlawful procedure prejudices everyone and benefits no one.

(3) Rules in conflict with or unauthorized by statute

Rules may be promulgated for the purpose of administering existing laws but may not add or subtract from the legislative enactment. Thus, rules adopted by administrative agencies are invalid where they are clearly in conflict with an enabling statute or any constitutional provision.

For example, where the General Assembly required that the basis for computing a worker's compensation benefits would be the *average* weekly wage of an injured employee, a rule of the Industrial Commission which provided that the *full* weekly wage should be the basis for compensation was void as being in conflict with the statute.[54]

(4) Rules must be reasonable

Rules must reasonably carry out the statutory authority of the agency. For example, in *Stouffer Corp v Bd of Liquor Control*,[55] the Supreme Court held that a rule of the Board of Liquor Control that froze the number of liquor permits available to a municipality without regard to population changes was unreasonable.

In *Sterling Drug, Inc v Wickham*,[56] although the court did not couch its rationale in terms of reasonableness, the court held that the challenger to the rules proved by a preponderance of substantial and probative evidence the nonexistence of certain facts which were a prerequisite to adoption of the rule. In other words, the agency acted unreasonably in finding those facts in order to adopt the rule.

CROSS REFERENCES

See Whiteside, Ohio Appellate Practice, Text 21.08, 21.09

1.07 Emerging issues

(A) Rulemaking docket

Of central importance to the rulemaking function is the documentation of the decision-making process. Proper management of the rulemaking record is critical to both effective public participation and meaningful judicial review of agency rulemaking. Unfortunately, Ohio law has yet to deal with certain basic issues concerning the rulemaking record such as (1) what documentation of the agency's legal conclusions, factual assumptions, and policy choices must be disclosed to the public at the initiation of a rulemak-

---

[54]State ex rel Kildow v Industrial Comm, 128 OS 573, 192 NE 873 (1934).
[55]Stouffer Corp v Bd of Liquor Control, 165 OS 96, 133 NE(2d) 325 (1956).
[56]Sterling Drug, Inc v Wickham, 63 OS(2d) 16, 406 NE(2d) 1363 (1980).

ing public comment period;[57] (2) how information or argument submitted by the public or by the agency itself during the comment period is to be "docketed" in the rulemaking proceedings; and (3) to what extent the agency can augment the record after it has been closed to the public.

RC 119.03 prescribes the procedure for rulemaking by most state agencies in Ohio. RC 119.03(A) to (C) contain the rulemaking record requirements imposed upon Ohio agencies subject to the Ohio Administrative Procedure Act. RC 119.03(A) addresses the reasonable public notice which must be given and includes requirements for a statement of the agency's intention to consider a rule, a synopsis of the proposal, a statement of the underlying reason or purpose, and the date, time, and place of a hearing. RC 119.03(B) requires that the full text of the proposed rule shall be filed with the Secretary of State not later than sixty days before promulgation and copies of the proposal shall be made available to the public for thirty days prior to the public hearing. Failure to comply with the availability requirement does not, however, provide grounds for invalidation of the rule. RC 119.03(C) provides that

> any person affected by the proposed action of the agency may appear [at the hearing] and be heard in person, by his attorney, or both, may present his position, arguments or contentions, orally or in writing, offer and examine witnesses, and present evidence tending to show that the proposed rule, amendment or rescission, if adopted or effectuated, will be unreasonable or unlawful.

RC 119.03(C) further provides that a stenographic record of the testimony and rulings on the admissibility of evidence at the hearing shall be made at the expense of the agency. The written materials submitted and evidence admitted, as well as the proffers of evidence the agency refuses to admit, constitute the rulemaking record for RC Chapter 119 rulemakings.[58]

Because the treatment of the concept of the rulemaking record in Ohio statutory and case law is somewhat limited, it is useful to examine an area of federal law for insight into the proper management of the rulemaking record. The most detailed statutory treatment of rulemaking record management is section 307(d) of the Clean Air Act,[59] which was added by the 1977 amendments to the Act. For the most part, section 307(d) has displaced the Federal Administrative Procedure Act with respect to rulemaking under the Clean Air Act.

In this regard, Ohio law is somewhat similar to its federal counterpart. RC Chapter 3745 governs appeals of both rulemaking and adjudicative

---

[57]See Text 1.05(C), Availability of supporting documentation, for discussion of what may or may not be a public record and thus required to be disclosed on request under RC 149.43.

[58]The decision in Ohio State Federation of Licensed Nursing Homes v Public Health Council, 113 App 113, 172 NE(2d) 726 (Franklin 1961), affirmed by 172 OS 227, 174 NE(2d) 251 (1961) supports this view of the rulemaking record for purposes of judicial review. It should be noted, however, that the term "record" or "rulemaking record" is not defined in RC Ch 119.

[59]42 USC 7607(d)(3).

actions of the Ohio Environmental Protection Agency. While the provisions of the Ohio Administrative Procedure Act are specifically incorporated into the various Ohio environmental statutes, RC Chapter 3745 departs from RC Chapter 119 in that it provides a direct appeal to the court of appeals (after exhaustion of administrative remedies) from agency rulemaking action.

Paragraph (3) of Section 307(d) of the Clean Air Act provides as follows:

> [N]otice of proposed rulemaking ... shall be accompanied by a statement of its basis and purpose (the proposed rule) and shall ... also state the docket number, the location ... of the docket, and the times it will be open to public inspection. The statement of basis and purpose shall include a summary of—
>
> (A) the factual data on which the proposed rule is based; (B) the methodology used in obtaining the data and in analyzing the data; and (C) the major legal interpretations and policy considerations underlying the proposed rule.
>
> ...
>
> All data, information, and documents referred to in this paragraph on which the proposed rule relies shall be included in the docket on the date of publication of the proposed rule.

Section 307(d) specifies the procedure to be followed in building the record during the public comment period. The docket must be kept open for inspection by the public, and comments which are submitted must be promptly added to the docket. Opportunities for oral presentations and rebuttals are specifically provided for.

In paragraph (6), the agency is cautioned that "the promulgated rule may not be based (in part or whole) on any information or data which has not been placed in the docket as of the date of such promulgation." Post hoc rationalizations for purposes of judicial review are therefore statutorily proscribed. As summarized by Professor Kenneth Culp Davis: "The record for review is limited to the notice and materials accompanying it, the written comments, the transcript of public hearings, material added during the comment period, the statement of basis and purpose, and the agency's response to written submissions."[60]

The section 307(d) proscription against post hoc rationalization was recognized by the court in *American Petroleum Institute v Costle*,[61] in which documents placed in the record after secondary standards had been signed but before publication in the Federal Register were ordered removed. With regard to the need for full candor from the regulatory agency during the comment period, the following statement of the First Circuit Court of Appeals is instructive: "Where documents ... are withheld, especially in circumstances suggesting something less than good faith, ... prejudice should be assumed unless its absence can be fairly inferred from the record."[62]

---

[60]1 Davis, *Administrative Law Treatise* 493 (2d ed 1978).
[61]American Petroleum Institute v Costle, 609 F(2d) 20 (DC Cir 1979).
[62]Mision Industrial, Inc v EPA, 547 F(2d) 123, 127-28 (1st Cir PR 1976).

It remains to be seen whether Ohio courts will follow the federal lead.

(B) The right to petition for rulemaking

There is no explicit statutory provision under Ohio law to enable an "outsider" to initiate or petition for rulemaking proceedings. However, there is a basis for a constitutional right to petition the government for the "redress of grievances,"[63] which logically encompasses the right of an interested citizen to request the consideration, adoption, modification, or repeal of agency rules.

Many administrative agencies in Ohio initiate rulemaking proceedings at the suggestion of those affected or to be affected by their rules. As a practical matter, this makes a great deal of sense. The primary function of an administrative agency is to supply the details necessary to effectively implement a general legislative objective. Those who will be subject to such agency rules tend to possess a broad knowledge of the subject of regulation, and their input can assist the agency in the most appropriate development of its regulatory program.

Federal law is much clearer on the subject. Section 4(e) of the Administrative Procedure Act[64] specifically provides, "Each agency shall give an interested person the right to petition for the issuance, amendment, or repeal of a rule." This statutory implementation of the basic constitutional right to petition the government has been recognized by the courts.[65]

A recent decision of the Franklin County Court of Appeals, *Youngstown Sheet & Tube Co v Maynard*,[66] addresses the right to petition for rulemaking in Ohio. The Ohio Environmental Board of Review had vacated the Ohio EPA's hazardous waste rules because of the absence of a provision authorizing petitions for rule changes. Such a provision had been requested by commenters before the Ohio EPA and was included in related federal rules. The court held that failure of the Ohio EPA to adopt such a provision was appealable but went on to uphold the agency. The court reasoned that any duty on the part of the Ohio EPA to include a right to petition for rulemaking had to have a basis in the enabling legislation passed by the General Assembly, and the court found none. And, while the court found that the failure to include such a rule was not unreasonable, the implication is left that agencies in their discretion may receive and act upon petitions to change their rules.

The court in *Youngstown* did not address the possible application of the constitutional right to seek "redress of grievances." However, the decision has not been appealed and, as such, it casts some doubt on the "right" in Ohio to petition for rulemaking absent an express grant by the General Assembly.

---

[63] US Const Am 1; O Const Art I, § 3.
[64] 5 USC 553(e).
[65] See, e.g., Joseph v US Civil Service Comm, 554 F(2d) 1140 (DC Cir 1977).
[66] Youngstown Sheet & Tube Co v Maynard, No. 83 AP-1014 (10th Dist Ct App, Franklin, 6-7-84)

(C) Relationship between rulemaking and adjudication

When a rule is adopted under RC 119.03, it has the force and effect of law, binding both persons affected by it and the agency. If the agency has jurisdiction to enforce the rule, as by revoking a license under RC 119.07 to RC 119.09, it is bound by the rule, subject only to its discretion to hold it invalid as not in compliance with law. That is, the rule is not merely advisory such that the agency may depart from it in making the adjudication order.[67]

When a statute authorizes an agency to define a crime by rule and imposes criminal sanctions for violation of the rule, enforcement of the rule accordingly depends upon the statutory imposition of a penalty. In the absence of a penalty, the rule would be of no effect.[68]

Even in the realm of civil enforcement, the statute giving the agency its jurisdiction may be framed or interpreted to preclude an adjudication leading to an order without the authority of a prior rule. The advocate representing the agency may need to argue that the statute does not require that its rulemaking jurisdiction be exercised as a condition precedent to exercise of its adjudicative jurisdiction. The regulated party's position obviously is the contrary. The language of a statute that confers both forms of power may resolve this issue by express provision.

The General Assembly has the following options to resolve this problem:

(1) To vest in the same agency both rulemaking and adjudicative power, with or without prescribing a sequence by which adjudication depends upon the existence of a prior rule;

(2) To vest in the agency rulemaking power but to vest adjudicative power either in another agency or (as in the case of crimes) in the courts; or

(3) To vest the agency with initial jurisdiction to adjudicate, without rulemaking power.

The last model suggests, if not compels, the conclusion that the agency has no sublegislative discretion and though it may be authorized to bind the courts on issues of fact, all other issues are issues of law for the reviewing court. If the agency may only make rules, its rules will bind the courts if made within the procedural and substantive boundaries of its discretion (as more fully elaborated above), and its rules will also bind another agency having adjudicative jurisdiction.

The first model raises the question whether an agency, vested with both rulemaking and adjudicative power without a specific statutory requirement that rules be adopted before enforcement, has implied discretion to develop policy having the effect of rules by adjudication on a case-by-case basis.

---

[67]State ex rel Wichman v Cleveland Police Relief Fund Bd of Trustees, 150 OS 280, 80 NE(2d) 842 (1948). See O Const Art I, § 18.

[68]State v Messenger, 63 OS 398, 59 NE 105 (1900).

Ohio law casts doubt on the existence of this discretion.[69] Ohio appears to favor an internal separation of agency powers. "Rules" based on case law are merely interpretations of the statute and thus are not in nature sublegislative. Accordingly, rulemaking can be accomplished only quasi-legislatively by formal promulgation after compliance with RC 119.03.

On the other hand, if this discretion exists, it seems almost certain to be available to the agency only to the extent that its exercise can be justified. What form the justifications might take is not clearly foreseeable, but the agency's advocate may encounter difficulty in arguing that there was no prior rule because the adjudicative issues were novel and the agency lacked experience to make a rule.[70] Similarly, the advocate of the regulated party may not be able to persuade the court that the order being challenged really represents new sublegislative policy rather than a straightforward application of the policy the General Assembly had already embodied in the statute. Although resolution of a legislative issue is not necessarily self-identifying, the agency will undoubtedly bear the brunt of justification for not having foreshadowed the order by a rule if the court perceives the agency's position as innovative either in terms of its "rules" or those apparent from the statute. That the Ohio Supreme Court will adopt the relatively free choice available to federal agencies, having both adjudicative and sublegislative powers, seems unlikely.

The Ohio Supreme Court has latitude to adopt this internal separation-of-powers principle, although it may follow the United States Supreme Court, which reads congressional statutes as conferring a choice on the agency whether to proceed first by rule.[71] That is, such choice is consistent with due process of law. What may not be in accordance with due process is a sudden turn by the agency in making policy that appears arbitrary and capricious to the reviewing court, even if it is not otherwise in excess of the policy-making power or authority delegated by statute.[72]

CROSS REFERENCES

See Text 1.05(C)

---

[69]Blue Cross of Northwest Ohio v Superintendent of Insurance, 40 App(2d) 285, 319 NE(2d) 212 (Franklin 1973).

[70]*Id.*

[71]See, e.g., NLRB v Wyman-Gordon Co, 394 US 759, 89 SCt 1426, 22 LEd(2d) 709 (1969).

[72]See State ex rel Homan v Bd of Embalmers & Funeral Directors, 135 OS 321, 21 NE(2d) 103 (1939).

Chapter 3

Adjudication

By Editorial Subcommittee of the
Administrative Law Committee of the
Ohio State Bar Association

3.01 Introduction
3.02 Institution of adjudication proceedings
3.03 Parties
3.04 Intervention
3.05 Prehearing procedure
3.06 Adjudication hearings
3.07 Posthearing procedures
3.08 Findings, decisions, and agency orders
3.09 Nature and effect of agency actions
3.10 Administrative appeal and review
3.11 Judicial review of administrative action

3.01 Introduction

(A) Definition of adjudication

"Adjudication" is defined in RC 119.01(D) of the Administrative Procedure Act (APA) as

> the determination by the highest or ultimate authority of an agency of the rights, duties, privileges, benefits, or legal relationships of a specified person, but does not include the issuance of a license in response to an application with respect to which no question is raised, nor other acts of a ministerial nature.

The distinctions between rulemaking, adjudication, and acts of a ministerial nature become important when considering whether an adjudication hearing is required under RC 119.06 et seq., or in determining whether a party is entitled to judicial review under RC 119.12.[1]

The rationale behind exemption of the issuance of licenses "with respect to which a question is raised" and other ministerial acts from the definition of adjudication is obviously sound. Without this provision, applications for barbers' licenses, drivers' licenses, and all other licenses and permits necessary for commerce and trade in this state could be interminably delayed by a backlog of adjudication hearings which no agency could handle. Questions are raised by the language "to which no question is raised." A person with a legitimate question involving the issuance of a license should notify the issuing agency of this concern prior to issuance and should request an adjudication hearing, although he may have to overcome challenges to his standing to raise questions.

Another question raised by the definition of "adjudication" is, what is a license? Although the term "license" is defined in RC 119.01(B), that

---

[1] See General Motors Corp v McAvoy, 63 OS(2d) 232, 407 NE(2d) 527 (1980).

definition does not definitively resolve the question. In many instances agency approval or authority is required to do certain things.[2] Is the grant of agency authority the issuance of a license as that term is used in the APA? Courts have not established any uniform rules to aid in determination of this issue. Only a review of cases cited in reference to a specific agency and a specific grant of authority can provide guidance in answering this question.[3]

(B) Adjudication distinguished from rulemaking

The right to appeal may depend upon classification of an agency action as "adjudication" or as some other form of administrative activity such as rulemaking or ministerial activity. In a series of cases the Ohio Supreme Court has differentiated between rulemaking (quasi-legislative action of an agency) and adjudication (quasi-judicial activity of an agency), holding that section 4(B), Article IV of the Ohio Constitution gives the court of common pleas jurisdiction to review the quasi-judicial but not the quasi-legislative actions of an agency.[4] Agencies often develop policies of general application through adjudication as well as through formal rulemaking.[5]

CROSS REFERENCES

See Text 1.06, Ch 5

3.02 Institution of adjudication proceedings

RC 119.06 provides that no adjudication order shall be valid unless an opportunity for a hearing is given before the order, except in the case of an adjudication order (1) revoking a license where required by statute pursuant to the judgment of a court, or (2) suspending a license where a statute specifically permits the suspension without a hearing. In addition, RC 119.06 provides an exception to the prior hearing requirement if the rules of the agency or the statutes pertaining to such agency specifically give a right of appeal to a higher authority within such agency or to another agency and also give the appellant a right to a hearing on such appeal. However, when a statute permits the suspension of a license without a prior hearing, any agency issuing an order pursuant to such statute shall afford the person to whom the suspension is issued a hearing upon request.[6] The Ohio Supreme Court has summarized the law in *Ohio Boys Town, Inc v Brown*:[7] "If . . . a permit is denied, the applicant must be afforded an opportunity for a prior

---

[2] See State v Hipp, 38 OS 199, 7 WLB 309 (1882).

[3] See Home Savings & Loan Assn v Boesch, 41 OS(2d) 115, 322 NE(2d) 878 (1975).

[4] Rankin-Thoman, Inc v Caldwell, 42 OS(2d) 436, 329 NE(2d) 686 (1975); Burger Brewing Co v Liquor Control Comm, 34 OS(2d) 93, 296 NE(2d) 261 (1973); Fortner v Thomas, 22 OS(2d) 13, 257 NE(2d) 371 (1970); Zangerle v Evatt, 139 OS 563, 41 NE(2d) 369 (BTA 1942).

[5] See Text 1.06, Judicial review, and Text Ch 5, Miscellaneous Judicial Review of Agency Action, for discussion of this distinction.

[6] RC 119.06. See General Motors Corp v McAvoy, 63 OS(2d) 232, 407 NE(2d) 527 (1980).

[7] Ohio Boys Town, Inc v Brown, 69 OS(2d) 1, 7, 429 NE(2d) 1171 (1982).

hearing under R.C. 119.06 unless the application is void on its face, does not present enough information to allow its issuance, or denial is not contested by the applicant."

In those cases in which RC 119.06 requires an administrative agency to afford an opportunity for a hearing prior to the issuance of an order, pursuant to RC 119.07, the agency must give notice to the party, informing him of his right to such hearing. RC 119.07 further provides that such notice shall be given by registered mail, return receipt requested. The notice must specify the charges or other reasons for the proposed action, and the law or rule directly involved, and must include a statement informing the party that he is entitled to a hearing if he requests it within thirty days of the time of mailing the notice. RC 119.07 also directs the administrative agency to inform the party about the nature of the adjudication hearing, including his right to appear in person or by his attorney; to present his position, arguments, or contentions in writing; and to present evidence and examine witnesses appearing for and against him. The specific notice requirements are necessary to provide adequate opportunity to prepare for the hearing.[8] Adequate notice of a hearing constitutes an essential part of the due process right to be heard.[9]

Upon receipt of a request for an adjudication hearing pursuant to RC 119.07, the agency must immediately set the date, time, and place for such hearing. The hearing shall commence within fifteen days, unless the agency and the party otherwise agree. Either the agency or the party may move to continue the hearing.[10] Frequently, the agency will send its first notice of the hearing with a continuance of that hearing. If the party requests in writing, the agency may designate the place of the hearing as the county seat of the county in which the party resides or a place within fifty miles of the party's residence.[11]

The various administrative agencies in Ohio have adopted their own particular rules implementing the foregoing statutory sections. For example, the Ohio Environmental Protection Agency has promulgated rules which prescribe the procedure for requesting adjudication hearings before that agency. OAC 3745-47-13(B) requires that all requests for adjudication hearings shall be in writing and shall state (1) the questions to be considered at the requested hearing; (2) the specific findings, orders, or actions of the agency objected to; and (3) the reasons why such provisions of the proposed action are contested. Failure to comply with these requirements constitutes a "default." The same rule also provides for a request that the hearing be held at a specific time or place.[12]

---

[8] Keaton v State, 2 App(3d) 480, 2 OBR 606, 442 NE(2d) 1315 (Franklin 1981).
[9] Tripodi v Liquor Control Comm, 21 App(2d) 110, 255 NE(2d) 294 (Jefferson 1970).
[10] RC 119.09.
[11] RC 119.08.
[12] See Text 11.02, Ohio Environmental Protection Agency.

In summary, the Ohio APA specifically gives an affected person the right to request and have an adjudication hearing before an agency denies an application for a license or permit or revokes the license or permit. Actions denying the application for or revoking such permit or license will not be valid unless the administrative agency gives the affected person the opportunity to request an adjudication hearing. However, in certain instances a statute may allow an administrative agency to suspend a license. In such case, while the suspension is effective, the administrative agency must nevertheless afford the person to whom the order is issued a hearing upon request.

CROSS REFERENCES

See Text 11.02

See Whiteside, Ohio Appellate Practice, Text 23.03

3.03 Parties

The particular statute under which an administrative proceeding is brought will determine who may or must be parties to the proceeding. RC 119.01(G) defines "party" as the person whose interests are subject to an adjudication by an agency.

In a licensing hearing, "party" usually includes the staff of the agency issuing the license as well as the applicant. The agency rules may require the staff to file a written report prior to commencement of a hearing, outlining its position with regard to issues which may exist. An assistant attorney general will usually serve as legal counsel for the staff.

3.04 Intervention

The Ohio APA contains no specific provisions regarding intervention in adjudication proceedings. However, party status may often be achieved through compliance with intervention requirements contained in specific statutes or agency rules.

The statutory requirements for intervention may differ between classes of intervenors. Public officials who have an interest in a matter to be adjudicated may need only to timely file a "notice" of intervention, with little discretion left to the agency to reject the notice. However, other persons may be required to file a timely "petition for leave" to intervene, which shall only be granted upon a showing of "good cause."

At times, members of the public at large or public interest groups will seek intervenor status. However, there are presently no reported Ohio cases under the APA discussing the rights of intervenors.[13] A number of courts have endorsed the "private attorney general" concept as justifying intervention by those who have no direct personal or economic interest in an agency

---

[13] For a federal case discussing a related standing issue with respect to the FCC, see Office of Communication of United Church of Christ v FCC, 359 F(2d) 994 (DC Cir 1966).

decision but who are seeking to protect and promote the "public interest." However, agency rules often provide for consolidation of petitions and briefs to avoid multiplicity of parties and duplication of effort.

To encourage public participation in administrative proceedings, agencies frequently publish public participation handbooks which describe in easy-to-understand language the steps necessary to achieve intervenor status and which contain model intervention petitions.

3.05 Prehearing procedure

(A) Pleadings and motions

The statute or agency rule governs the manner in which a proceeding before an administrative body is instituted. In some agencies jurisdiction will be invoked only by complaint or application by an interested person, while in others the agency will institute the proceedings on its own initiative.[14] As stated by Professor Kenneth Culp Davis: "The most important characteristic of pleadings in the administrative process is their unimportance. And experience shows that unimportance of pleadings is a virtue."[15]

Procedures to be followed before administrative agencies are not generally those required in civil actions.[16] The procedure for most Ohio licensing agencies is prescribed by RC Chapter 119. While the technical rules of a judicial hearing are not required to be strictly observed in administrative hearings, it is the duty of administrative tribunals to permit a full hearing on all subjects pertinent to the issue and to base their conclusions upon competent evidence. Such a result can best be accomplished by substantial adherence to the rules observed in court hearings.[17]

(B) Discovery: availability of agency files

Neither the federal nor the Ohio APA contains provisions for prehearing discovery, nor do the federal or Ohio Rules of Civil Procedure apply to federal or state administrative proceedings. Therefore, in the absence of statutory or agency rules, procedures for discovery are not normally available in administrative hearings. However, lack of administrative discovery is a concept that has become difficult to support. For example, the California Supreme Court in a "common law" holding, *Shively v Stewart*,[18] stated that an agency must provide prehearing discovery even in the absence of a statutory requirement.[19]

In 1970, the permanent United States Administrative Conference recommended to agencies that a discovery system be adopted, the most important feature of which would be the "emphasis upon the prehearing conference as

---

[14]RC 4907.08, for example, authorizes the Public Utilities Commission to investigate any railroad it believes is violating an Ohio law.
[15]1 Davis, *Administrative Law Treatise* 523 (1958).
[16]In re Milton Hardware Co, 19 App(2d) 157, 250 NE(2d) 262 (Franklin 1969).
[17]Bucyrus v Ohio Dept of Health, 120 OS 426, 166 NE 370 (1929).
[18]Shively v Stewart, 65 Cal(2d) 475, 421 P(2d) 65, 55 Cal Rptr 217 (1966).
[19]See also 1 Davis, *Administrative Law Treatise* 391-93 (Supp 1970).

a device for directing parties to exchange their evidentiary exhibits and witness lists."[20] Accordingly, it is not uncommon today to find that agencies have adopted rules providing for discovery and prehearing conferences.

The rules of the Power Siting Commission provide that parties shall cooperate in conducting discovery procedures with a view to accomplishing full and complete disclosure of all relevant facts.[21] The rules further provide that if the hearing officer finds that forms of discovery from the Ohio Rules of Civil Procedure are desirable for just, prompt, and efficient administration of the hearing, additional discovery may be authorized.[22] Since Ohio agencies subject to RC Chapter 119 are authorized to issue subpoenas and take depositions of witnesses,[23] discovery somewhat equivalent to that under the Rules of Civil Procedure can be accomplished.

Although there is little Ohio case law on the subject, a number of federal court opinions have been rendered defining the extent of discovery which can be had against governmental agencies. One of the earliest of these opinions, *United States v Reynolds*,[24] a Tort Claims Act case, upheld the United States Air Force's claim of privilege in not making available certain reports on the ground that they contained military secrets. In the absence of privilege, the government, like any other party, is subject to discovery.[25]

It has been held in a New York private litigation case, *Stratford Factors v New York State Banking Dept*,[26] that "where a claim of privilege is made, there must be an appropriate basis for the assertion thereof; and whether there is or not will be for the court to determine."[27]

(C) Continuances and postponements

Under RC 119.09, an agency may postpone or continue any adjudication hearing upon application of any party or upon its own motion. The grant or denial of a continuance is a matter within the sound discretion of the administrative agency.[28] An agency's refusal to grant a continuance will be affirmed unless it appears, after considering the whole record, that the agency abused its discretion and the complaining party was prejudiced by the refusal.[29]

An administrative agency should hear matters pending before it without unreasonable delay and with due regard to the rights and interests of all parties before it.[30]

---

[20] 1 Davis, *Administrative Law Treatise* 392 (Supp 1970).
[21] OAC 4906-7-07(B).
[22] OAC 4906-7-07(C).
[23] RC 119.09.
[24] United States v Reynolds, 345 US 1, 73 SCt 528, 97 LE 727 (1953).
[25] *Id.*
[26] Stratford Factors v New York State Banking Dept, 10 AD(2d) 66, 70, 197 NYS(2d) 375 (1960), appeal dismissed by 202 NYS(2d) 1027 (1960).
[27] See also 1 Davis, *Administrative Law Treatise* 391 (Supp 1970).
[28] Levitt v Cleveland, 22 Misc 54, 256 NE(2d) 631 (CP, Cuyahoga 1970).
[29] Meneley v Carpenter, 70 Abs 593, 129 NE(2d) 516 (App, Montgomery 1954).
[30] State ex rel Columbus Gas & Fuel Co v PUCO, 122 OS 473, 172 NE 284 (1930).

(D) Prehearing conference

Although the APA makes no specific reference to holding prehearing conferences,[31] agencies often use such conferences to narrow issues, identify witnesses, submit documents, and obtain admissions and stipulations. Prehearing conferences have become a valuable tool to reduce delay and expense in the conduct of administrative hearings. Agreements made at such conferences are generally embodied in a prehearing conference report and made part of the record. Of course, counsel may often negotiate such agreements without resort to a prehearing conference.

(E) Prehearing orders

When justified by the urgent need to protect the public welfare and safety, administrative agencies may issue an order prior to a hearing.[32]

CROSS REFERENCES

See Jacoby, Ohio Civil Practice, Text Ch 35

3.06 Adjudication hearings

(A) Burden of proof and presumptions

It is implicit throughout the Ohio APA that the party asserting the affirmation of an issue in an adjudication hearing bear the burden of proof.[33]

Courts have recognized several presumptions regarding the conduct of administrative proceedings. One such presumption is that of regularity of administrative action. The United States Supreme Court in *United States v Chemical Foundation*[34] has broadly held, "The presumption of regularity supports the official acts of public officers and, in the absence of clear evidence to the contrary, courts presume that they have properly discharged their official duties."[35]

A second presumption (the so-called "mental processes" rule) is that the manner, extent, and understanding of evidence by the decision-makers in administrative hearings will not be examined by reviewing courts. This presumption is part of the broader one of "administrative regularity."[36] In *Taub v Pirnie*,[37] the New York Court of Appeals made reference to the presumption when it stated: "And in ascertaining whether an 'informed' decision has been made, the courts accord the decision the presumption of regularity to

---

[31] Cf, 5 USC 556(c) (The federal APA contains specific authority for prehearing conferences.).

[32] See New York Central RR Co v PUCO, 157 OS 257, 105 NE(2d) 410 (1952).

[33] Goodyear Synthetic Rubber Corp v Dept of Industrial Relations, 76 Abs 146, 122 NE(2d) 503 (CP, Franklin 1954). The federal APA specifically places the burden of proof upon "the proponent of a rule or order." 5 USC 556(d).

[34] United States v Chemical Foundation, 272 US 1, 14-15, 47 SCt 1, 71 LEd 131 (1926).

[35] See also 2 Davis, *Administrative Law Treatise* § 11.06 (1958).

[36] Cf, General Motors Corp v McAvoy, 63 OS(2d) 232, 407 NE(2d) 527 (1980).

[37] Taub v Pirnie, 3 NY(2d) 188, 195, 144 NE(2d) 3, 165 NYS(2d) 1 (1957).

which it is entitled . . . and refrain from probing 'the mental processes of the . . . [deciding officer] in reaching his conclusions.' "[38]

(B) Witnesses

In an adjudication hearing under the Ohio APA, an agency may call such witnesses as it desires and may call any party to testify as upon cross-examination.[39] Depositions of residents or nonresidents may be taken by the agency in the manner prescribed for civil actions in the common pleas court.[40] A witness cannot be compelled to answer immaterial or irrelevant questions.[41] In *Brook Park v Cuyahoga County Budget Comm*,[42] the Ohio Supreme Court approved a procedure used by certain administrative agencies whereby questions to be propounded to witnesses appearing before the board were put in writing and submitted to the board. These questions were then asked by the board which, with the hearing examiner, had the sole authority to cross-examine the witnesses.

For purposes of efficiency, prefiled testimony may be substituted for direct examination of witnesses. When used, the prefiled testimony is commonly furnished to all parties several days or weeks prior to the date the witness is scheduled to testify so that at the time the witness appears, cross-examination immediately commences. An agreement by the parties to use this procedure is usually made at the time of a prehearing conference.

(C) Order of presentation of witnesses

The witnesses of the party having the burden of proof are generally the first to testify. The order of the remaining witnesses may be determined during a prehearing conference. During this conference, the order of rebuttal testimony may also be discussed and determined. The Ohio Environmental Protection Agency follows a procedure in which objectors to the issuance of permits are required to proceed first in an adjudication hearing even though the party seeking the permit has the burden of proof.

(D) Use of hearing examiners

Under the Ohio APA, the agency may appoint a qualified referee or examiner to conduct an adjudication hearing, giving the referee all the powers and authority of the agency.[43] The referee must be admitted to the practice of law in Ohio and have such other qualifications as the agency requires. The agency has a great deal of latitude in setting requirements for referees. Referees employed by the state presumably must have the qualifications of their job classification established pursuant to RC 124.14. In the case of referees employed as independent contractors, the authors know of no

---

[38] See also 2 Davis, *Administrative Law Treatise* § 11.06 (1958).
[39] RC 119.09.
[40] *Id.*
[41] Board of Tax Appeals v Zangerle, 32 Abs 486, 5 OSupp 246 (CP, Cuyahoga 1940).
[42] Brook Park v Cuyahoga County Budget Comm, 16 OS(2d) 119, 243 NE(2d) 77 (BTA 1968).
[43] RC 119.09.

instance in which specific "other qualifications" have been formally established. Some agencies, without specific authority to do so, have begun to designate their referees as "administrative law judges." This does not appear to be appropriate terminology, because RC 119.09 limits the referee to making a recommendation to the agency rather than rendering a judgment. Furthermore, pursuant to Article IV of the Ohio Constitution, only the General Assembly may create judgeships.[44] Some agencies use the term "hearing examiner."

The regulations of an agency may set forth the authority and duties of referees.[45] Generally, the referee is responsible for conducting a hearing in such a manner as to prevent unnecessary delay, maintain order, and insure the development of a clear and adequate record. More specific duties include the following:

(1) Administering oaths and examining witnesses;

(2) Making rulings on admissibility of evidence;

(3) Making rulings on procedural motions;

(4) Holding prehearing conferences; and

(5) Requiring parties to file briefs and recommended findings of fact and conclusions of law.[46]

Referees are also required by RC 119.09 to submit to the agency and parties a written report setting forth findings of fact and conclusions of law and a recommendation of the action to be taken by the agency.

(E) Objections

The party offering evidence that an agency refuses to admit should state the nature of the evidence and the facts proposed to be proved thereby.[47] No particular form of words is necessary either to sustain or overrule an objection. The agency need only make plain its disposition of the objection and whether an answer to the questions is expected or required.[48]

(F) Rules of evidence

RC 119.09 provides that agencies must pass upon the admissibility of evidence but does not attempt to formulate standards of admissibility. In some instances, the particular statute outlining the authority of the agency will make reference to this question. However, as a general rule, administrative agencies are not bound by the same rules of evidence applied in the courts, although they have a duty to base their conclusions upon competent evidence. The court in *Bucyrus v Ohio Dept of Health*[49] also noted, "[S]uch result can better be accomplished by a substantial adherence to the rules observed in hearings in court." As stated by Professor Davis:

---

[44]State ex rel Keeler v Levine, 19 App(3d) 113, 19 OBR 201 (Franklin 1984).
[45]E.g., OAC 4906-1-16 of the Power Siting Board.
[46]RC 119.09.
[47]*Id*.
[48]Slagle v Ohio, 366 US 259, 81 SCt 1076, 6 LEd(2d) 277 (1961).
[49]Bucyrus v Ohio Dept of Health, 120 OS 426, 430, 166 NE 370 (1929).

> The direction of movement on evidence problems throughout the legal system, in the judicial process as well as in the administrative process, is toward (1) replacing rules with discretion, (2) admitting all evidence that seems to the presiding officer relevant and useful, and (3) relying upon "the kind of evidence on which responsible persons are accustomed to rely in serious affairs."[50]

The hearsay rule is relaxed in administrative proceedings, particularly where a statute dispenses with rules of evidence. In any event, relevant hearsay testimony not objected to has some probative value.[51] The sufficiency of hearsay to support a finding is judged by taking into account the convincing quality of the particular hearsay or lack thereof, the opposing evidence or lack thereof, and the circumstances.[52] Exhibits offered are subject to objections or motions to strike. Oral arguments supporting or opposing those motions are generally permitted by the referee who may reserve judgment and require written memoranda to be submitted.

Just as a court has knowledge of which it may take judicial notice, an administrative agency has knowledge of which it will often take administrative notice. The extent to which Ohio administrative agencies may apply their own official or expert knowledge depends on the circumstances of the particular case.[53] Even when an agency is justified in taking administrative notice of particular facts, the opponent is not prevented from disputing those facts with evidence. An administrative agency cannot sustain a decision where the particular or evidentiary facts of which the agency took administrative notice and on which it rested its conclusion are not only unknown but also unobtainable. The statutory review provided for such decision limits the reviewing court to the record made below.[54]

(G) Transcripts

RC 119.09 does not require a stenographic record at a hearing except where the record may be the basis of an appeal to a court. In such a case, a stenographic record of testimony, evidence, and rulings on admissibility must be made at the expense of the agency. However, agency rulings may provide that a stenographic record will be made only on request of a party.

Where an order is made without a stenographic record of a required hearing, the party, on request, must be granted a hearing or rehearing to make a record for appeal.[55]

CROSS REFERENCES

See Whiteside, Ohio Appellate Practice, Text 23.04

---

[50] 2 Davis, *Administrative Law Treatise* 250 (1958). In his 1970 supplement, Professor Davis indicates that the movement continues toward admitting evidence in administrative proceedings without considering jury-trial rules.

[51] Shearer v Ohio Medical Bd, 91 App 277, 97 NE(2d) 688 (Franklin 1950), appeal dismissed by 91 App xlvi (1951).

[52] 2 Davis, *Administrative Law Treatise* § 14.11 (Supp 1970).

[53] Ohio Bell Telephone Co v PUCO, 301 US 292, 57 SCt 724, 81 LEd 1093 (1937).

[54] *Id.*

[55] RC 119.09.

3.07 Posthearing procedures

(A) Briefs and proposed findings

The Ohio APA makes no reference to the subject of briefs or proposed findings of fact or conclusions of law. The practitioner must, therefore, consult individual agency procedural rules with respect to the necessity for briefs and proposed findings. Informal guidelines for practice before each agency will often determine when, and in what form, briefs or proposed findings should be submitted.

Briefs should conform in length and format to the agency's rules and the instructions of the agency or the referee.[56]

(B) Hearing referee's report

A referee must submit a written report to the agency setting forth his findings of fact and conclusions of law, together with a recommendation of the action to be taken by the agency. Within five days of his filing the report, a copy of the report and recommendation must be served by registered mail upon the party or his representative.[57] Some agency rules contain time limitations within which the referee is required to file his report and recommendation.[58]

It is not an absolute requirement that the person who prepares the referee's report has actually heard the evidence, so long as that person has reviewed the record of the proceeding.[59]

(C) Objections to the referee's report

RC 119.09 provides that a party may, within ten days of receipt of a copy of the referee's report and recommendation, file with the agency written objections. RC 119.09 further provides that no recommendation be approved, modified, or disapproved until the expiration of ten days after the service of the report and recommendations of the referee upon parties to the adjudication hearing. In this manner the Ohio APA attempts to insure that a party's objections to the report shall be considered by the agency before it acts upon the referee's recommendation.

An administrative agency may grant extensions of time to the parties within which to file objections to the referee's report.[60] The agency may also order additional testimony to be taken or permit the introduction of further documentary evidence.

---

[56] See, e.g., Rule of Proceedings of the Power Siting Board, OAC 4906-7-16; Rule of the Environmental Board of Review, OAC 3746-5-17.

[57] RC 119.09.

[58] See, e.g., OAC 3745-47-24 (Forty-five-day limit upon the Ohio EPA referee to issue report.).

[59] Laughlin v PUCO, 6 OS(2d) 110, 216 NE(2d) 60 (1966).

[60] RC 119.09.

3.08 Findings, decisions, and agency orders

(A) Necessity for written findings by the agency

The Ohio APA does not specifically require that, in making its decision, an administrative agency make written findings of fact or conclusions of law. RC 119.09 requires only that if an agency decides to modify or disapprove the recommendations of a referee, it must include in the record of its proceedings the reasons for any modification or disapproval. However, most, if not all, agencies will be required to make specific findings of fact and conclusions of law for reasons other than the specific requirements of the APA.

First, an agency's enabling legislation will often require that an agency act only upon the basis of standards established by the legislature.[61] Second, constitutional requirements of due process generally require administrative agencies to support their decisions with findings of fact and conclusions of law.[62]

(B) Requirements for support in the record for agency findings

An agency order will be upheld on appeal only if the order is supported by reliable, probative, and substantial evidence and is in accordance with the law.[63] This requirement leads to the principle that an administrative decision in an adjudication hearing must be supported by some evidence in the record of the proceeding.[64] An administrative agency functions as a fact-finder and can accept or reject evidence as it sees fit. The agency is not limited to accepting the evidence of either one side or the other but may accept only part of the evidence of a party in reaching its decision.[65]

Generally, when an agency or administrative officer makes a finding and determination which is not supported by substantial evidence, the action of the agency or official is considered arbitrary, capricious, and an abuse of discretion.[66]

(C) Recording agency decisions and orders

RC 119.09 specifically requires an agency to enter an adjudication order on its journal. There is, however, no general requirement that an agency publish or index its decisions for the convenience of the public. Agency practice in this regard varies widely.

---

[61] See Meneley v Carpenter, 70 Abs 593, 129 NE(2d) 516 (App, Montgomery 1954).

[62] A. Dicillo & Sons, Inc v Chester Zoning Bd of Appeals, 59 Abs 513, 98 NE(2d) 352 (CP, Geauga 1950).

[63] RC 119.12.

[64] Bloch v Glander, 151 OS 381, 86 NE(2d) 318 (BTA 1949).

[65] East Ohio Gas Co v PUCO, 133 OS 212, 12 NE(2d) 765 (1938).

[66] State ex rel Beck v Hummel, 150 OS 127, 80 NE(2d) 899 (1948); A. Dicillo & Sons, Inc v Chester Zoning Bd of Appeals, 59 Abs 513, 98 NE(2d) 352 (CP, Geauga 1950).

Because all adjudication orders must be entered in a journal, it is commonly recognized that an agency speaks or acts only through those entries.[67] The absence of a journal entry in the agency's records will invalidate a purported agency order.[68] The record of an administrative agency should be reduced to writing and should clearly show the agency's findings and orders.[69]

There is no general rule with respect to how detailed an agency's findings must be. In Ohio, agencies vary widely in this respect. Some agencies, such as the Industrial Commission, make only limited findings of ultimate facts and conclusions. Other agencies, such as the Environmental Protection Agency, prepare detailed findings. The legal sufficiency of particular agency findings will depend upon the circumstances as well as the necessity and reasonableness of preparing detailed findings.

RC 119.09 requires an agency to serve upon an affected party a copy of its adjudication order and a statement of the time and method by which an appeal may be perfected. RC 119.07 provides that where a statute permits the suspension of a license without a prior hearing, notice of the agency's order must be sent to the party by registered mail, return receipt requested.

CROSS REFERENCES

See Whiteside, Ohio Appellate Practice, Text 23.08

3.09 Nature and effect of agency actions

(A) Generally

An adjudication order is not final until it has been approved and confirmed by an agency and entered upon its record of proceedings. A final order must also be served upon an affected party and a copy mailed to the party's attorney or representative of record.[70]

No one rule governs the effective date of appealable agency orders or acts. The statutes that create the right of appeal generally will determine what agency orders or acts are regarded as final and when the effective dates of such orders commence. For example, RC 4151.35 permits an appeal to the Mine Examining Board of the "finding" of the chief of the division of mines upon a report of a mine inspector. It is not always clear, however, what act or failure to act may result in an appealable order.[71]

---

[67]State ex rel Cundiff v Industrial Comm, 128 OS 636, 193 NE 345 (1934); Wittenberg v Bd of Liquor Control, 52 Abs 65, 80 NE(2d) 711 (App, Franklin 1948).
[68]See Wittenberg v Bd of Liquor Control, 52 Abs 65, 80 NE(2d) 711 (App, Franklin 1948).
[69]Simmons v Industrial Comm, 134 OS 456, 17 NE(2d) 751 (1938).
[70]RC 119.09.
[71]In re Appeal of Peabody Coal Co, Nos. 79AP-592, 79AP-593 (10th Dist Ct App, Franklin, 12-20-79) (Court found an informal opinion letter to be an appealable adjudication order pursuant to RC 119.12.).

(B) Rehearings

Administrative agencies are not necessarily required to rehear or reconsider their decisions. However, agencies do possess the power, for good cause, to vacate and set aside their decisions prior to the actual initiation of an appeal.[72] Upon a showing that facts previously found do not exist, an administrative agency has inherent power to revoke an order previously made.[73]

Principles of estoppel are applicable to administrative agencies and will, under certain circumstances, preclude an agency from subsequently modifying or vacating its order.[74]

(C) Nunc pro tunc entries

Because administrative agencies have the responsibility to maintain control over their records and make certain that they accurately reflect agency actions, agencies may correct errors in their records which were made through mistake or inadvertence,[75] even though the time for making an original entry has passed.[76] However, nunc pro tunc orders may not be used to correct errors of judgment. Instead, these orders are restricted to placing upon the record evidence of quasi-judicial actions actually taken and supply omissions of a clerical nature.[77]

(D) Res judicata effect of agency orders

In the past, the courts have not consistently applied the doctrine of res judicata.[78] Today, however, the general rule is that quasi-judicial agency orders operate as res judicata with respect to the parties and issues involved.[79]

3.10 Administrative appeal and review

Administrative appellate review of adjudication orders is available either within certain agencies or before other administrative bodies. Administrative review is an actual appellate proceeding before a quasi-judicial body composed of members of an administrative agency. This appellate review is to be distinguished from a request for reconsideration by the original decision-maker or from proceedings before a decision-maker after preliminary findings have been made by a hearing officer.

Members of appellate review boards often have a certain expertise in the particular administrative field in which they perform their function. In fact,

---

[72]National Tube Co v Ayres, 152 OS 255, 89 NE(2d) 129 (BTA 1949).

[73]Industrial Comm v Dell, 104 OS 389, 135 NE 669 (1922).

[74]State ex rel Simmons v Wieber, 45 Abs 590, 68 NE(2d) 134 (App, Cuyahoga 1944), affirmed by 145 OS 121, 60 NE(2d) 687 (1945).

[75]Helle v PUCO, 118 OS 434, 161 NE 282 (1928).

[76]State ex rel Wuebker v Bockrath, 152 OS 77, 87 NE(2d) 462 (1949).

[77]Haba v Cuff, 201 NE(2d) 343 (App, Summit 1963), appeal dismissed by 176 OS 374, 199 NE(2d) 736 (1964), cert denied sub nom Cuff v Van Bogart, 379 US 964, 85 SCt 883, 13 LEd(2d) 558 (1965).

[78]4 Davis, *Administrative Law Treatise* § 21.2 (2d ed 1983).

[79]Handler v Dept of Commerce, 14 Misc 9, 233 NE(2d) 147 (CP, Montgomery 1967).

applicable statutes may require that members of a board, or at least some of the members, have a particular background or educational degree. For example, members of the Environmental Board of Review must have technical experience and familiarity with environmental matters.[80] Often, there is no requirement that appellate board members be attorneys.

Where provided, an appeal to an administrative review board or body will normally constitute a prerequisite of obtaining later judicial review. Administrative appeals normally must be exhausted before an appeal will lie to either the common pleas court or a court of appeals.

For example, a decision of the administrator of the Bureau of Employment Services on reconsideration of an unemployment compensation claim *must* be appealed to the Board of Review before it may be appealed to the court of common pleas.[81]

The type of review to be conducted by an administrative appellate body may vary depending on the procedures conducted at the lower administrative level. In some cases, a fact-finding hearing may be conducted so that the reviewing board can make a de novo determination of the matter. Such fact-finding may be necessary to comport with traditional notions of due process where a regulated party's rights have been determined by the agency without opportunity for a hearing. In cases where a hearing is held prior to making the initial decision at the lower administrative level, the administrative review body may conduct only an appellate review. The scope of review may vary between these two extremes depending upon the particular agency and the proceedings surrounding the initial determination of the adjudication order.

The formality of procedures in conducting an administrative appeal will vary from agency to agency. For some agencies, the procedures are set forth in statutes, and extensive rules of procedure have been adopted.[82] For others, the administrative appeal may be set forth only by an administrative rule, with few or no procedural rules to guide the parties. In these agencies, informal, unwritten procedures may also be used. In some cases, the administrative review function is seldom used, often resulting in a lack of procedural rules to be followed in appeals and a lack of precedent to guide the administrative review board.

An example of a highly formalized administrative review body is the Environmental Board of Review. Appeals to this body are specifically circumscribed by RC 3745.04 and RC 3745.05. The board has an active docket, has adopted elaborate rules of procedure,[83] and has developed a considerable body of precedent. The Environmental Board of Review hears appeals from actions of the Director of the Ohio Environmental Protection Agency.[84] The board must conduct a hearing if no hearing was held before

---

[80]RC 3745.02.
[81]RC 4141.28. See Text 7.07, Appeals to court.
[82]OAC 4901.
[83]OAC 3746.
[84]RC 3745.04.

the lower agency and must provide for a de novo review of the record where a hearing was held below.[85] In contrast, the Mine Examining Board, despite express statutory authority,[86] to date has adopted no rules of procedure and has no formal docketing of appeals cases.

CROSS REFERENCES

See Text 7.07, 11.03

3.11 Judicial review of administrative action

(A) Right to review

The right to judicial review of adjudication orders issued by administrative agencies derives from both constitutional and statutory provisions. Concepts of due process require, at a minimum, the right to judicial review of the lawfulness and constitutionality of administrative actions when administrative agencies act upon judicial matters such as adjudicating the rights of an individual or a business.

Section 4 of Article IV of the Ohio Constitution authorizes the legislature to provide for review of administrative proceedings in the courts of common pleas. RC 119.12 grants a general right to judicial review to "any party adversely affected" by an agency order issued pursuant to an adjudication. Orders adjudicating the rights of licensees or applicants for licenses may generally be appealed to the court of common pleas of the county in which the licensee is located, although licensing decisions rendered by the Liquor Control Commission must be appealed to the Franklin County Court of Common Pleas.[87] Most other adjudication orders issued by Ohio agencies are also appealable to the Franklin County Court of Common Pleas.

Statutory enactments dealing with particular agencies may also grant a right of judicial review of agency adjudication orders.[88] Such statutes may specify the courts in which appeals are to be brought and may limit the right to review, subject to constitutional limitations, by providing that certain determinations are within the exclusive jurisdiction of an agency and are not to be reviewed by the judiciary. Alternatively, a statute may leave certain determinations to the discretion of a particular administrative agency. In such a case, judicial review is limited to a consideration of the scope of permissible agency action and the possible abuse of agency discretion.

(B) Limitations on right to review

(1) Primary jurisdiction

Courts will not involve themselves in issues which are within the jurisdiction of an administrative agency before the agency has had an opportunity to consider the matter.[89] This policy is commonly known as the doctrine of

---

[85] RC 3745.05. See Text 11.03, Environmental Board of Review.
[86] RC 4151.14.
[87] RC 119.12.
[88] See, e.g., RC 3745.06.
[89] Silverstein v Bd of Liquor Control, 67 Abs 1 (CP, Franklin 1953).

"primary jurisdiction" or of "prior resort." The authors have found no Ohio law establishing how a court must handle a question of primary jurisdiction in the absence of a statutory mandate that would deprive the court of original jurisdiction. The authors believe that courts, when invoking the policy, should retain jurisdiction but stay the action and direct the parties to first present the issues to the responsible administrative agency. The underlying policy for the doctrine of primary jurisdiction is twofold: the court receives the benefit of the agency's expertise on review, and the doctrine promotes uniform application of the pertinent statute or regulation.

Without a direct statutory mandate, invocation of the doctrine is discretionary, and counsel may argue that its application should be limited to cases where the underlying policies would be furthered. If, for example, the case presents an issue of the constitutionality or reasonableness of administrative regulations, or if the controlling issue does not involve matters within the special expertise of the agency, the underlying policy of the doctrine would not be furthered and consequently the doctrine need not be invoked.[90]

The doctrine of primary jurisdiction relates to whether the administrative agency has had the opportunity to consider the issue in the first instance and is to be distinguished from the doctrine requiring the exhaustion of administrative remedies, which involves full utilization of available administrative appellate procedures before applying to the court for relief from an agency decision.

(2) Timing: final order

RC 119.12 provides for appeal from administrative "orders" entered pursuant to an adjudication. RC 2506.01 of the Administrative Appellate Procedure Act provides for review of "every final order, adjudication, or decision" of administrative bodies of state subdivisions. Orders relating to discovery, provisional orders, or orders denying motions to dismiss are ordinarily held not to be final and are thus not appealable.[91]

No statutory provision is made for review of preliminary or procedural orders, but counsel may analogize to decisions which have authorized review of preliminary orders when necessary to prevent injustice. Counsel may also note section 15(a) of the Revised Model State Administrative Procedure Act,[92] which provides that a preliminary, procedural, or intermediate agency act or ruling is immediately reviewable if review of the final agency decision would not provide an adequate remedy.

---

[90]Cleveland Electric Illuminating Co v Cleveland, 50 App(2d) 275, 363 NE(2d) 759 (Cuyahoga 1976), cert denied 434 US 856, 98 SCt 175, 54 LEd(2d) 127 (1977).

[91]See Roxy Musical Bar, Inc v Bd of Liquor Control, 1 App(2d) 480, 205 NE(2d) 118 (Franklin 1963), appeal dismissed by 176 OS 415, 199 NE(2d) 878 (1964); Lakis v Bd of Liquor Control, 120 App 163, 201 NE(2d) 605 (Franklin 1963), appeal dismissed by 175 OS 221, 192 NE(2d) 776 (1963).

[92]Reprinted in 2 Cooper, *State Administrative Law*, Appendix (1965). Note, however, that the Uniform Law Commissioners' Model State Administrative Procedure Act, in its 1981 revision, does not give a clear right interlocutory review. The 1981 Act is reprinted in 2 Koch, *Administrative Law and Practice,* Appendix VII (1985).

The determination of whether a particular order is final, and thus perhaps appealable, should first involve analysis of the organic statute of the particular agency. If the statute does not define "final order," such a definition is available in the Appellate Procedure Act.[93] Regarding political subdivisions, however, RC 2506.01 expressly excludes certain decisions from the ambit of "final order, adjudication, or decision."

The finality requirement avoids entangling courts in the administrative process before the administrative agency has had an opportunity to resolve the matter. Without specific statutory directives, the court should determine "finality" by weighing the hardship to the appellant of delaying judicial consideration. If the question is legal rather than factual and does not involve agency discretion, there is usually little reason to delay review.

The "mailing of the notice of the agency's order" pursuant to RC 119.12 and "journal entry" of the final order pursuant to RC 2506.01 and RC 2505.07 begin the time running for filing a notice of appeal. An appellant must move without delay to perfect the appeal. A party wishing to appeal an order of an administrative agency should first look to the organic statute of that agency to determine the time limits for filing a notice and the forum in which an appeal may be filed. If the organic statute is silent on the matter, the party should consult either RC 119.12 or RC 2506.01 and RC 2505.07, depending upon the agency. If all of the above statutes are silent with respect to the time limit for filing and the forum for appeal, an affected party may consult the Appellate Procedure Act.

(3) Exhaustion of administrative remedies

Once an administrative body becomes involved in the controversy, one must exhaust the administrative proceedings available before turning to the courts for relief.[94] This doctrine, known as "exhaustion of administrative remedies," allows the administrative agency to exercise its discretion and expertise without disruption and to correct its own errors. The courts can use the agency's expertise and the record when reviewing the decision. In addition, the agency, by correcting its own errors, may obviate the necessity for judicial review.

The requirement of exhaustion of administrative remedies is the rule rather than the exception. In determining if exhaustion is required in a particular case, first review the statute pertaining to the agency to see if it provides for exclusive administrative procedures. If administrative appeal is not specifically mandated by the organic statute, then look to the policies underlying the doctrine and, if those reasons are absent, argue that immediate judicial review should be granted.

If resolution of a particular issue requires neither agency expertise nor the exercise of administrative discretion, and if the interest of the party in immediate judicial review outweighs the agency's interest in uninterrupted administrative proceedings, exhaustion should not be required. Likewise, if

---

[93]RC 2505.02.
[94]State ex rel Lieux v Westlake, 154 OS 412, 96 NE(2d) 414 (1951).

the agency is unable to provide an effective and adequate remedy, the courts generally will not require a party to pursue it.[95] To be effective and adequate, the remedy should be available within a reasonable time.

If the agency has clearly acted in excess of its statutory authority, the courts may intervene.[96] In the ordinary case, however, the agency should be afforded the opportunity to construe its own statute or regulations and to discover any errors and amend the decision of its own volition.

If the court finds that exhaustion would be burdensome or oppressive, exhaustion should not be required.[97] Administrative relief would be considered unduly expensive if the agency required the party to incur excessive expenditures in order to obtain simple relief, such as the requirement that a party submit complete plans and specifications to determine a setback line before the agency will entertain an application for a location permit.[98]

Finally, if the party can show that exhaustion would be futile, it should not be required. For example, if the agency's actions are patently discriminatory or if the agency has indicated that it has no intention of changing a past policy of questionable legality, exhaustion is futile. Similarly, exhaustion is normally futile if the sole question before the agency is the constitutional validity of a statute or ordinance.

(C) Forms of review

(1) Appeal

The statutes should be an appellant's first source for answers to questions regarding the form which a notice of appeal should take. Among the relevant statutes, the first to be studied should be the statute pertaining to the particular agency, which often expressly authorizes and delineates an exclusive method for review of adjudicative determinations. Where a particular method of review is provided by the organic statute, a petitioner ignores it in favor of an alternate method at great risk.[99]

The Ohio Administrative Procedure Act provides for judicial review of adjudicative determinations of certain state agencies. The Appellate Procedure Act, RC Chapter 2505, and the Administrative Appellate Procedure Act, RC Chapter 2506, together provide for judicial review of administrative decisions of state and local political subdivisions.[100]

RC 2505.03 states that "when provided by law, the final order of an administrative officer, tribunal, or commission may be reviewed as provided in sections 2505.04 to 2505.45, inclusive, of the Revised Code, unless otherwise provided by law." The Appellate Procedure Act applies when other

---

[95]See Weinberger v Salfi, 422 US 749, 95 SCt 2457, 45 LEd(2d) 522 (1975).
[96]Leedom v Kyne, 358 US 184, 79 SCt 180, 3 LEd(2d) 210 (1958).
[97]Gates Mills Investment Co v Pepper Pike, 59 App(2d) 155, 392 NE(2d) 1316 (Cuyahoga 1978).
[98]Burt Realty Corp v Columbus, 21 OS(2d) 265, 257 NE(2d) 355 (1970).
[99]Eggers v Morr, 162 OS 521, 124 NE(2d) 115 (1955).
[100]Vlad v Cleveland Bd of Zoning, 111 App 70, 164 NE(2d) 797 (Cuyahoga 1960).

provisions for appeal are not available and also when a statute pertaining to an agency provides for appeal of administrative decisions but does not specify the procedure for the appeal.

The Administrative Appellate Procedure Act provides for review by common pleas courts of final orders or decisions of officers, tribunals, authorities, boards, bureaus, commissions, departments, or other divisions of any political subdivision of this state.[101] The order or decision must have been made by the agency or division acting in its quasi-judicial rather than legislative capacity.

Section 4(B), Article IV of the Ohio Constitution provides that common pleas courts shall have such powers of review of proceedings of administrative officers and agencies as may be provided by law. The review is limited to quasi-judicial proceedings.[102] Further statutory relief is provided by the Declaratory Judgment Act.[103]

(2) Other forms of relief

Other forms of relief, such as declaratory judgment, prohibition, and mandamus, may be available to review certain aspects of adjudication proceedings, but they are more commonly used to review other types of administrative proceedings.[104]

(D) Scope of review

As with most other matters pertaining to judicial review, the scope of review depends in significant degree upon the language of the statutes pertaining to the particular agency involved. The Ohio Constitution guarantees judicial review of agency determinations to prevent arbitrariness. The review is to be substantial and adequate.[105]

Reviewable issues include (1) exceeding of statutory jurisdiction by an agency; (2) agency compliance with procedural requirements (i.e., its own organic statute and regulations; the APA, if applicable; and due process); (3) action which is arbitrary, capricious, unreasonable, or an abuse of discretion; and (4) administrative determination obtained by fraud, bad faith, or mistake. The issues involving procedure, allowable discretion, or reasonableness can be decided only after review of the agency's underlying statute.

Procedural regularity is reviewable. Procedural requirements are found in the federal and state constitutions, the agency's organic statute, miscellaneous statutes such as the Administrative Procedure Act and, at times, the agency's own regulations. Common procedural problems involve lack of, or insufficient, notice to affected parties, failure to hold required hearings, and failure to afford affected parties required or reasonable procedural safe-

---

[101] RC 2506.01.
[102] Rankin-Thoman, Inc v Caldwell, 42 OS(2d) 436, 329 NE(2d) 686 (1975).
[103] See Text 5.03, Declaratory judgments.
[104] See Text 5.02, Mandamus; Text 5.03, Declaratory judgments; Text 5.04, Prohibition.
[105] Hocking Valley Railway Co v PUCO, 100 OS 321, 126 NE 397 (1919).

guards during adjudication hearings. The rule of prejudicial error is applied to these issues.

While review is to be substantial and adequate, the courts are not free to substitute their own judgment for that of the agency.[106] This restriction particularly applies to matters involving review of issues that are within the agency's area of expertise. Agencies, however, may not act unlawfully, unreasonably, or in any other manner constituting an abuse of discretion.[107]

If a reviewing court determines that an agency has exceeded its statutory authority, it may reverse the agency's determination. Courts may also review agency adjudications to determine if they are arbitrary, capricious, or unreasonable.[108]

A court's power to review questions of fact varies with the language in the statute governing review of the particular agency's decision. However, inasmuch as every administrative decision must have evidence to support it to prevent it from being arbitrary or unreasonable, review must necessarily include inquiry into the evidence underlying the administrative decision. The degree of evidentiary inquiry is determined by the standard of review applicable to the particular agency and the particular issues. In some cases it is sufficient if any supportive or substantially supportive evidence exists; in others, review may include full inquiry into the credibility of witnesses and the relative weight of the evidence. For agencies to which the Ohio APA applies, courts will review whether the decision is supported by substantial, probative, and reliable evidence.[109]

Review pursuant to the Ohio APA could be described as a combination of legal and factual review. In order to determine whether an agency decision is supported by "substantial, probative, and reliable evidence," the authors believe that the courts necessarily have authority to inquire into the credibility of witnesses and into the probative nature of particular evidence. The requirement of substantiality authorizes some inquiry into the weight of the evidence supporting the determination.

(E) Review on record versus de novo review

Whether judicial review will involve a de novo hearing or merely a review of the record depends on the agency in question, the nature of the controversy, and the statute under which review is afforded. Generally, review will be on the record made during the administrative proceeding.

RC 119.12, pertaining to judicial review of adjudicative determinations by certain state agencies, provides for the introduction of additional evidence with leave of the court. The statute specifies, however, that "[u]nless otherwise provided by law, in the hearing of the appeal the court is confined to the

---

[106]Dudukovich v Lorain Metropolitan Housing Auth, 58 OS(2d) 202, 389 NE(2d) 1113 (1979); Farrand v Ohio Medical Board, 151 OS 222, 85 NE(2d) 113 (1949).
[107]Co-operative Legislative Committee of Transportation Brotherhoods v PUCO, 150 OS 270, 80 NE(2d) 846 (1948).
[108]RC 2506.04.
[109]RC 119.12.

record as certified to it by the agency." Leave for admission of additional evidence is to be given when the court is "satisfied that such additional evidence is newly discovered and could not with reasonable diligence have been ascertained prior to the hearing before the agency." The underlying policy is that if the court allows the introduction of evidence not brought before the agency, the court will be substituting its judgment for that of the agency.[110]

If there is reason to believe that a fair hearing was not conducted by the administrative body, or that the particular administrative body did not have the necessary powers to conduct an adequate hearing, the appellant should be allowed to introduce additional evidence. RC 2506.03 specifically allows the introduction of additional evidence in cases involving these and certain other similar circumstances.

Reviewing courts should be sensitive to arguments by appellants that the record as certified is insufficient to permit adequate court review of the decision or that there was good cause for not introducing particular evidence at the administrative level. If the petitioners can show that the administrative body improperly refused to consider certain evidence, the court should exercise its discretion in favor of allowing introduction of the evidence on review.[111]

CROSS REFERENCES

See Text 5.02 to 5.04

See Whiteside, Ohio Appellate Practice, Text 23.05, 23.08, 23.11, 23.12

---

[110] Powell v Young, 148 OS 342, 74 NE(2d) 261 (1947).
[111] 2 Cooper, *State Administrative Law* 624 (1965).

Chapter 5

Miscellaneous Judicial Review of Agency Action

By Editorial Subcommittee of the
Administrative Law Committee of the
Ohio State Bar Association

5.01 Introduction
5.02 Mandamus
5.03 Declaratory judgments
5.04 Prohibition
5.05 Collateral attack

5.01 Introduction

Judicial review of rulemaking and adjudication has been previously discussed.[1] A writ of mandamus may be used to force commencement of an agency adjudication, but it will not normally be used to review an adjudication order. The remedy of mandamus is included in this section because it is normally used to review other types of agency actions.

Writs of prohibition will technically issue only to prohibit the exercise of unauthorized judicial power. However, as noted in the discussion of administrative adjudications, courts have occasionally defined "judicial" rather broadly.[2]

Declaratory judgments were discussed previously in the context of rulemaking,[3] but the discussion below applies to review of a broader range of agency action.

Collateral attack is a catchall. It is beyond the scope of this handbook to detail all aspects of legal actions against the government, but the forms of action discussed below may be helpful as a starting point for the practitioner.

CROSS REFERENCES

See Text 1.06, 3.11, 5.04

---

[1] See Text 1.06, Judicial review; Text 3.11, Judicial review of administrative action.
[2] See State ex rel Newell v Brown, 162 OS 147, 122 NE(2d) 105 (1954). See also Text 5.04, Prohibition.
[3] See Text 1.06(A), Procedure for review; Text 1.06(B), Standard of judicial review.

5.02 Mandamus

An action in mandamus may be brought to compel government officials to perform nondiscretionary administrative acts which they have refused to perform, where the refusal violates an established legal right.[4]

Mandamus is an extraordinary writ, and the party seeking it must establish that (1) the government official has a legal duty to perform the requested act; (2) a beneficial interest has been injured by the failure to perform;[5] and (3) alternative statutory or administrative remedies are unavailable.

While it is sometimes written that a writ of mandamus will not issue if the requested act is discretionary, there is some authority in Ohio that mandamus may be available in cases involving abuse of discretion.[6] An example of an appropriate situation for the writ of mandamus is an agency refusal to institute proceedings which it has a duty to institute.[7]

5.03 Declaratory judgments

Declaratory judgments in Ohio are governed by RC Chapter 2721. While there must be a real and justifiable controversy and a need for speedy relief to preserve the rights of parties,[8] RC 2721.02 does not require that a petitioner have no other relief available.

Some courts have apparently viewed declaratory judgments involving agencies or administrative agencies as collateral actions and have therefore been reluctant to exercise discretion in favor of accepting such actions when the petitioners have available to them administrative or statutory remedies. In theory, if the controversy does not involve complicated or technical factual questions, the courts should not require exhaustion of administrative remedies nor deny judgments for declaratory relief because of alternate administrative or statutory remedies. Case law on the subject is mixed.[9]

The declaratory judgment could be an effective method for obtaining relief in cases involving administrative adjudication. The uncertainty occasioned by the reluctance of some courts to accept discretionary jurisdiction over cases involving administrative adjudication prevents the declaratory judgment action from constituting a more effective form of review.

---

[4]State ex rel Wright v Morrison, 80 App 135, 75 NE(2d) 106 (Hamilton 1947).
[5]State ex rel Moskowitz v Dickerson, 172 OS 551, 179 NE(2d) 48 (1961).
[6]State ex rel Marble Cliff Quarries Co v Morse, 154 OS 459, 96 NE(2d) 297 (1951).
[7]See State ex rel Michaels v Morse, 165 OS 599, 138 NE(2d) 660 (1956). See also State ex rel Federated Department Stores, Inc v Brown, 165 OS 521, 138 NE(2d) 248 (1956) (Writ of procedendo brought to compel performance of an agency's duty where the agency had refused to hear a case which it had a duty to hear.).
[8]Gannon v Perk, 46 OS(2d) 301, 348 NE(2d) 342 (1976); Burger Brewing Co v Liquor Control Comm, 34 OS(2d) 93, 296 NE(2d) 261 (1973).
[9]2 Cooper, *State Administrative Law,* 636-40 (1965).

5.04 Prohibition

Where there is no provision for review of an agency adjudication and that action exceeds the agency's statutory authority, a writ of prohibition may issue.[10] A writ may not issue if administrative or statutory review of the offending administrative action is available.[11]

There are a number of hurdles involved in maintaining an action for prohibition. The agency's action must be shown to be other than purely ministerial.[12] This requirement is eased by the courts' willingness sometimes to define "judicial" to include acts whose judicial attributes are not readily apparent.[13]

In Ohio not only will a writ of prohibition not issue if administrative or statutory remedies are available, but also it will not issue if the party could have obtained the necessary relief by bringing an action to enjoin the offending acts.[14]

5.05 Collateral attack

Collateral attack is a tool to be used primarily when alternate modes of judicial review are unavailable. Methods that are sometimes used to collaterally attack an administrative declaration include (1) an action for damages,[15] (2) a suit for an injunction,[16] and (3) a defense of an enforcement action by attacking the original administrative determination.[17]

Where adequate statutory methods for review of a particular agency determination are available, courts will not look favorably on a common-law collateral attack. Injunctive relief is an equitable remedy and consequently should not be employed if there are adequate legal remedies available. State courts have refused to grant injunctions to restrain the enforcement of administrative orders unless it was shown that the orders were void, that there was no other available remedy, and that the threatened injury was both irreparable and substantial.[18]

The major disadvantage of an injunction when compared to declaratory relief is that injunctive relief requires a showing of irreparable injury. A lower level of harm is necessary in an action for a declaratory judgment. In

---

[10]State ex rel Nolan v ClenDening, 93 OS 264, 112 NE 1029 (1915).

[11]State ex rel Geyer v Collopy, 152 OS 485, 90 NE(2d) 370 (1950).

[12]State ex rel Ohio Power Co v Franklin County Regional Planning Comm, 158 OS 496, 110 NE(2d) 415 (1953).

[13]See, e.g., State ex rel Newell v Brown, 162 OS 147, 122 NE(2d) 105 (1954).

[14]State ex rel Timken Roller Bearing Co v Industrial Comm, 172 OS 187, 174 NE(2d) 249 (1961); State ex rel Masterson v Racing Comm, 164 OS 312, 130 NE(2d) 829 (1955).

[15]Meyer v Parr, 69 App 344, 37 NE(2d) 637 (Hamilton 1941) (dicta).

[16]Green v State Civil Service Comm, 90 OS 252, 107 NE 531 (1914); Rankin-Thoman, Inc v Caldwell, 42 OS(2d) 436, 329 NE(2d) 686 (1975).

[17]Copperweld Steel Co v Industrial Comm, 143 OS 591, 56 NE(2d) 154 (1944) (dicta), appeal dismissed by 324 US 780, 65 SCt 1006, 89 LE 1363 (1945).

[18]2 Cooper, *State Administrative Law* 633 (1965).

addition, relief afforded in granting an injunction is more draconian than a declaratory judgment on the same issue. The difference is particularly evident in rulemaking proceedings, where an injunction may entirely preclude enforcement of the regulation whereas declaratory relief may allow continued, but narrower, application of the rule.

Chapter 7

Board of Review of the Ohio Bureau of Employment Services

By John W. Maurer, Esq.

7.01	Introduction
7.02	General hearing procedure
7.03	Liability hearings
7.04	Benefit and eligibility notice hearings
7.05	Conduct of hearings
7.06	Applications to institute further appeals
7.07	Appeals to court

CHARTS

7.08	Organizational chart, Unemployment Compensation Board of Review
7.09	Procedural chart, Bureau of Employment Services

7.01 Introduction

The referees of the Unemployment Compensation Board of Review hear cases involving unemployment compensation in Ohio. The Board consists of three members appointed by the governor serving staggered six-year statutory terms.[1] The referees appointed by the Board are civil service employees and must be licensed to practice law in Ohio. No person representing a claimant in any case heard by this Board or its referees may charge fees in excess of ten per cent of the amount of benefits involved in the case.[2] No such restriction exists on fees charged employers. Unemployment compensation hearings are open to the public.[3]

CROSS REFERENCES

Unemployment compensation board of review, OAC Ch 4146

Unemployment compensation; employment services, RC Ch 4141

7.02 General hearing procedure

This Board's proceedings are not governed by the Ohio Administrative Procedure Act (APA) found in RC Chapter 119.[4] Rules governing the conduct of adjudicatory proceedings of the Board of Review may be found in OAC 4146-1 to 4146-27. Copies of the rules are available from the Bureau of Employment Services and the Board and are provided upon request.[5]

---

[1] RC 4141.06.
[2] OAC 4146-19-03.
[3] OAC 4146-7-02(C).
[4] RC 119.01(A).
[5] OAC 4146-27-02.

Ohio's Rules of Civil Procedure do not apply to this Board. It is not bound by any common law or statutory rules of evidence or procedure.[6] Although objections based upon fundamental evidentiary principles may be made, the practitioner should avoid objections based upon technical or obscure evidentiary points. All testimony is taken under oath and is mechanically recorded. No other record of the hearing is allowed.[7]

Since the Unemployment Compensation Division of the Bureau of Employment Services serves both as a repository of payroll tax and as a distributor of income, two primary types of disputes lead to hearings which are conducted by the Board's referees. These are generally referred to as liability hearings[8] and benefit hearings.[9] A third, less common matter is an appeal to the Board by an employer adversely affected by a Bureau decision regarding the validity of an eligibility notice. Eligibility notices are submitted by a "base period or subsequent employer of a claimant who has knowledge of specific facts affecting such claimant's right"[10] to receive benefits for any continued claim.[11]

Any person whose interests are affected by a reconsidered decision of the Bureau may appeal to the Board by filing a timely written notice with the Board or with any state, federal, or Canadian agency charged with the duty of accepting unemployment claims.[12] When particularly complex circumstances are involved in a case, the administrator of the Bureau may refer a timely request for reconsideration of an initial determination to the Board. Such request shall then constitute an appeal to the Board.[13] All appeals must contain certain basic information[14] and must be filed within fourteen calendar days of the issuance of the agency decision,[15] except for liability appeals which must be filed within thirty calendar days.[16]

In *UAW v Giles*,[17] the court discussed distinctions between the issuance and receipt of agency decisions and the failure of the agency to toll the fourteen-day period for claimants who never received the notice. This case permanently restrains the Bureau and Board from failing to allow interested parties the opportunity to establish that they did not receive timely notice of adverse decisions and provides that, upon such a showing, a hearing on the merits be provided.

Most initial appeals are assigned to a referee who normally both hears and decides the case. Liability appeals and any other appeal specifically

---

[6] OAC 4146-7-02.
[7] OAC 4146-7-01.
[8] OAC 4146-23.
[9] OAC 4146-7.
[10] RC 4141.28(E).
[11] *Id.*; OAC 4146-21.
[12] OAC 4146-5-01.
[13] *Id.*
[14] *Id.*, OAC 4146-21-03, OAC 4146-23-02.
[15] OAC 4146-13-01.
[16] *Id.*
[17] UAW v Giles, No. C 81-415 (ND Ohio, 7-2-82).

retained are within the initial jurisdiction of the Board.[18] Liability appeals and allowed appeals from referee decisions[19] are customarily heard by a senior referee for and on behalf of the Board.[20] The senior referee may recommend a decision to the Board, but the Board makes its own decision. Hearings in which testimony is taken are seldom conducted before the appointed Board.

CROSS REFERENCES

See Whiteside, Ohio Appellate Practice, Text 35.02

7.03 Liability hearings

A senior referee conducts liability hearings for and on behalf of the Board to decide appeals from Bureau reconsideration decisions that involve employer contributions. The issues in these hearings may include (1) an employer's liability for contributions to the unemployment fund; (2) the assigned contribution rate (expressed as a percentage of payroll); (3) refunds; (4) seasonal employment issues; and (5) benefit charges to an employer's account.[21] Benefit charge hearings arise when a base period employer other than the most recent separating employer wishes to protest charges to its unemployment account. Hearings regarding benefit charges may be initially assigned to a referee rather than retained by the Board and are customarily so assigned. The Bureau and the employer are the only interested parties in these hearings.

As in any situation involving a taxing statute, the appellant-employer bears the burden of proof. The file containing the decision appealed from and underlying documentation is certified without employer comments to the Board by the agency upon appeal. It is to be considered as part of the record and contains only the findings of the agency.[22] If the employer makes no appearance at the hearing and fails within ten days to show good cause for nonappearance, a decision will be issued based upon the available record.[23]

An attorney member of the Bureau staff will normally attend such liability hearings; however, since the Bureau's case is presented in the file itself, the attorney usually takes little active part. The agency representative is given the opportunity to question any employer-witness and to present additional testimony or exhibits not already found in the file. All exhibits, caselaw, and testimony stating the employer's case must be presented by the employer at the liability hearing to be considered. The Board normally conducts all liability hearings in Franklin County.

---

[18] OAC 4146-3-01. See Text 7.03, Liability hearings.
[19] OAC 4146-25-01.
[20] OAC 4146-3-02.
[21] OAC 4146-23-01.
[22] RC 4141.28(J); OAC 4146-23-03.
[23] OAC 4146-23-05.

7.04 Benefit and eligibility notice hearings

The Board conducts benefit and eligibility notice hearings at various hearing locations, usually within the appellant's county of residence or in a contiguous county. The time and place of hearing must be convenient to the interested parties.[24] When a party requests that a hearing be scheduled in the evening because he is employed during the day, a hearing must be scheduled during hours that the party is not employed.[25]

When the appellee resides or is located out of state or out of county, a "split hearing" may be scheduled.[26] Such hearing occurs when testimony is taken from witnesses at more than one location. When a party is unable to attend at all locations, cross-examination may be conducted by prior submission of written questions. A party may review the complete record of the initial hearing, upon request, before the subsequent hearing. The review may be conducted at any regularly established hearing location within the state during normal working hours. Proceedings may be scheduled at other times and places in cases where special scheduling is necessary to give any interested party a reasonable opportunity for a fair hearing.[27] Upon the request of a party and approval of all parties, testimony may be taken by means of a telephone conference hearing.

The interested parties to a benefit hearing include the Bureau, one or more employers, and the claimant or claimants who are one or more employees or former employees of the employer. These three are also the parties in eligibility hearings brought about by valid eligibility notices and when a separation issue is heard. In cases involving only a claimant's eligibility for a continued claim for benefits, the employer is not a party. In cases involving validity of eligibility notices, the claimant is not a party,[28] as the only issue to be determined in these proceedings is whether the notifying employer meets the requirements for becoming an interested party.[29]

The Bureau is seldom represented at benefit hearings, except for those cases involving allegedly fraudulent applications for determination of benefit rights or fraudulent claims for benefits. When the Bureau is represented in a fraud hearing, the member of the Bureau's investigative staff who conducted the actual fraud investigation will customarily appear and testify. In fraud cases the Bureau carries a burden of proof that approaches the level of clear and convincing evidence.[30] Although fraud is being considered in such cases,

---

[24] OAC 4146-5-04.
[25] RC 4141.28(J)(3).
[26] OAC 4146-5-04.
[27] Id.
[28] OAC 4146-21-04.
[29] OAC 4146-21-02.
[30] See Powell v Administrator, Bureau of Employment Services, No. L-84-079 (6th Dist Ct App, Lucas, 7-27-84) (The court held that the common-law elements of fraud, including knowledge of the statement, must be proven.); Tatman v Administrator, Bureau of Unemployment Compensation, No. 1203, at 7 (12th Dist Ct App, Clermont, 7-13-83) (There must be "fraudulent misrepresentation with the object of obtaining benefits to which [the claimant] was not entitled."); In re McKenzie, No.

civil proceedings are not governed by such labels of proof as would be found in criminal proceedings.

CROSS REFERENCES

See Whiteside, Ohio Appellate Practice, Text 35.03

7.05 Conduct of hearings

In all hearings, the Board or referee is not restricted to the issue or issues raised on appeal. The Board or referee may consider any issue within the jurisdiction of the Bureau but must grant a continuance in the event any party is unprepared to proceed upon a newly raised issue.[31]

In hearings where separation is at issue, the burden of proof falls generally upon the party initiating the separation. The claimant carries the burden when a resignation is involved. The employer has the burden in a discharge or suspension situation. The party or a witness for the party initiating the separation will normally testify first. If the parties are in dispute as to the type of separation, questioning will normally begin with the party that the Bureau has determined to be the final initiator of the separation.

Usually, the referee will question the party or witness to elicit the basic facts of the dispute. The referee will then allow further questioning by the party's representative or allow voluntary submission of evidence and testimony by unrepresented parties and then allow questioning by the opposing party or its representative. The referee has a duty to aid the unrepresented party.[32] Testimony and cross-examination of the parties is permitted for the purpose of obtaining relevant facts or discrepancies in testimony not previously elicited by the referee's questioning. Each party has opportunity to submit and to examine exhibits during the hearing and may give closing arguments upon completion of testimony.[33]

Referee hearings are normally scheduled at forty-five-minute intervals. If extensive testimony is expected, advance notice of such expectations given to the Board will allow the Board's administrative staff to allow additional time for the hearing. Subpoena requests should be submitted at the earliest possible time, ideally with the appeal itself. Notice of hearing is mailed seven calendar days prior to the hearing, and subpoenas not requested prior to receipt of the hearing notice are often not received by those persons subpoenaed with sufficient time to allow them to attend.

In the event a hearing is not completed in the allotted time, the referee uses his own discretion as to continuing the hearing or reassigning the

---

19586 (CP, Jackson, 1-18-72) ("A finding by the Board which amounts to a finding of fraud should not be based upon inference and supposition."). Cf Hepner v Board of Review, 11 OO(3d) 144 (App, Cuyahoga 1978) (In a case not involving fraud, the court stated that the board must "reach a reasonable decision supported by relevant, probative evidence.").
[31]OAC 4146-5-03.
[32]OAC 4146-7-02.
[33]*Id.*

matter. When a case is reassigned, the Board attempts to reassign the case to the referee that began the hearing but may reassign it to any referee.[34] It is a responsibility of the referee to whom a case is reassigned to review the recording of the previous referee's hearing prior to conducting the subsequent hearing. In the event a split hearing has been scheduled, the referee that conducted the initial hearing will decide the case, unless interested parties from each side of the matter appear at a subsequent hearing. When both parties appear before a referee at some course of the hearing process, the Board will customarily assign the decisional responsibility to that referee who has had the opportunity to judge the credibility of both parties.

Failure of appellant or his representative to appear at a benefit hearing will cause the appeal to be dismissed, if a showing of good cause for failure to appear is not made within ten days.[35] When the nonappearing appellant is a claimant unable to appear solely because of his current employment, the Board will allow fourteen days to show such cause. The parties may, in writing, waive their right to hearing, thereby allowing the Board or referee to obtain necessary evidence on its own and to then issue a benefits decision on the record before it.[36] The referee would then normally issue a decision based upon any written stipulations and on the record certified to the Board by the Bureau.

Cases in which identical factual circumstances are considered, such as labor disputes, plant closings, shutdowns, etc., may be consolidated into what is commonly called a "mass appeal." The Board will make a single record and will consider evidence or stipulations introduced in one case as introduced in the other cases.[37]

The Board and its referees have subpoena powers.[38] Failure to comply with a duly issued and served subpoena may result in contempt proceedings.[39]

7.06 Applications to institute further appeals

The Board may allow or disallow "further appeals" from referee decisions. In the event that the Board allows a further appeal, it may affirm, modify, or reverse a referee's decision with or without further hearing. Further hearing, conducted by a senior referee, will be allowed where the appellee at the referee hearing, now the appellant, shows good cause for having failed to appear at the initial hearing, or where the record is silent or incomplete or appears to be erroneous on a material point, or when it appears that a fair hearing was not afforded by the referee.[40]

---

[34] OAC 4146-3-01.
[35] OAC 4146-7-02(F).
[36] OAC 4146-7-02(A).
[37] OAC 4146-7-02(E).
[38] OAC 4146-15-01.
[39] OAC 4146-15-03.
[40] OAC 4146-25-02(B).

CROSS REFERENCES

See Whiteside, Ohio Appellate Practice, Text 35.04

7.07 Appeals to court

A party may appeal the Board's disallowance of further appeals of referee's decisions to the court of common pleas in the county in which the appellant resides, if a benefit appeal, or to the Franklin County Court of Common Pleas in the case of a liability appeal, in the same manner in which Board decisions are appealed to courts of common pleas.[41]

The court may allow briefs with argument to be filed. However, the court is restricted to the record submitted to it upon appeal, which includes the file and a transcript of the hearing testimony. No de novo hearing is held.[42] The court may affirm, reverse, modify, or remand for further hearing.

The referee or Board is considered the trier of fact and as such is the judge of witness credibility.[43] The court will not disturb a benefits decision of the referee or Board unless the decision is held to be unlawful, unreasonable, or against the manifest weight of the evidence.[44] In liability cases the court may affirm if it finds the decision or order is supported by reliable, probative, and substantial evidence. The court may not impose a higher evidentiary standard upon review than that standard to which the Board and its referees are held.[45]

CROSS REFERENCES

See Text 3.11

See Whiteside, Ohio Appellate Practice, Text 35.05 to 35.11

---

[41] RC 4141.28(O). See Text 3.11, Judicial review of administrative action.
[42] Kilgore v Bd of Review, 2 App(2d) 69, 206 NE(2d) 423 (Jackson 1965).
[43] Bohannon v Board of Review, No. 42773 (8th Dist Ct App, Cuyahoga, 3-5-81).
[44] Leach v Bd of Review, 3 App(2d) 314, 210 NE(2d) 395 (Franklin 1963).
[45] Simon v Lake Geauga Printing Co, 69 OS(2d) 41, 430 NE(2d) 468 (1982).

CHARTS

7.08 Organizational chart, Unemployment Compensation Board of Review

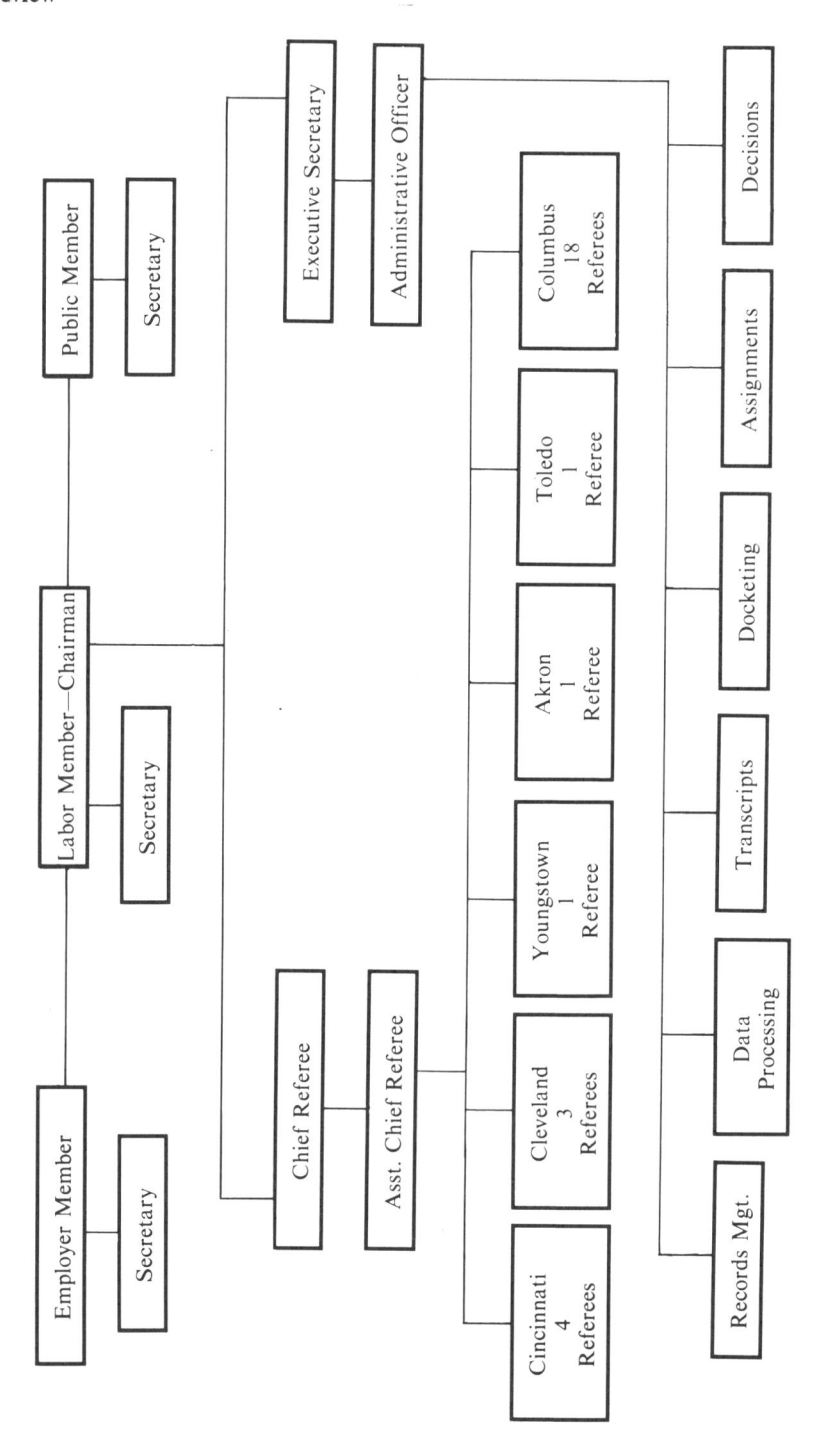

7.09 Procedural chart, Bureau of Employment Services

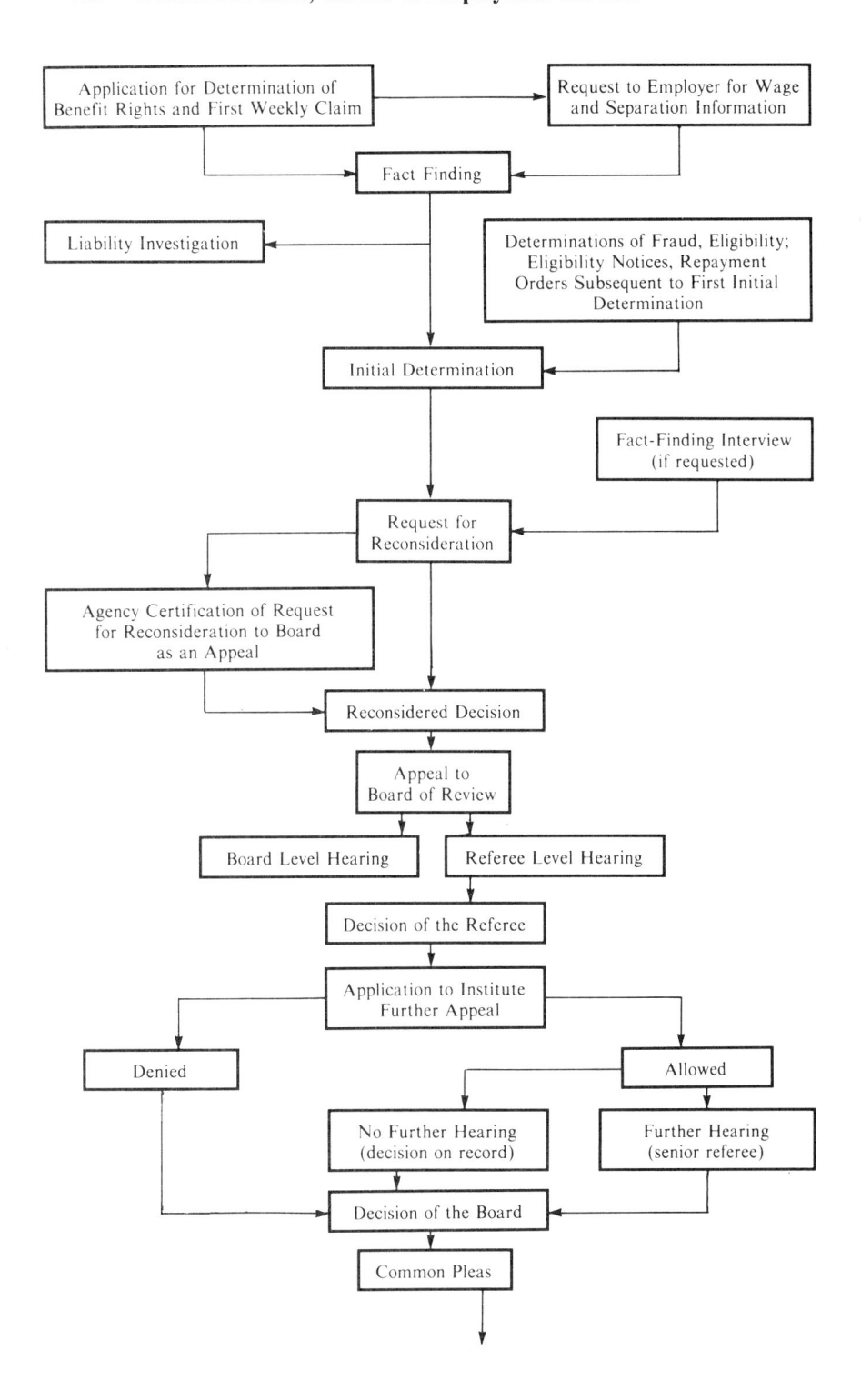

```
┌─────────────────────────────┐        ┌─────────────────────────────┐
│ Application for Determination│───────▶│ Request to Employer for Wage│
│ of Benefit Rights and First │        │  and Separation Information │
│        Weekly Claim         │        └──────────────┬──────────────┘
└──────────────┬──────────────┘                       │
               │         ┌──────────────┐             │
               └────────▶│ Fact Finding │◀────────────┘
                         └──────┬───────┘
                                │
     ┌────────────────────┐     │     ┌─────────────────────────────┐
     │ Liability          │◀────┤     │ Determinations of Fraud,    │
     │ Investigation      │     │     │ Eligibility; Eligibility    │
     └────────────────────┘     │     │ Notices, Repayment Orders   │
                                │     │ Subsequent to First Initial │
                                │     │ Determination               │
                                │     └──────────────┬──────────────┘
                                ▼                    │
                         ┌──────────────────┐        │
                         │ Initial Determination│◀───┘
                         └──────┬───────────┘
                                │            ┌──────────────────────┐
                                │            │ Fact-Finding Interview│
                                │            │   (if requested)      │
                                │            └──────────┬───────────┘
                                ▼                       │
                         ┌──────────────────┐           │
                         │ Request for       │◀─────────┘
                         │ Reconsideration   │
                         └──────┬────────────┘
          ┌─────────────────────┤
          ▼                     │
┌──────────────────────────┐    │
│ Agency Certification of  │    │
│ Request for Reconsideration│  │
│    to Board as an Appeal │    │
└──────────┬───────────────┘    │
           │                    ▼
           │           ┌──────────────────────┐
           └──────────▶│ Reconsidered Decision│
                       └──────────┬───────────┘
                                  ▼
                       ┌──────────────────────┐
                       │    Appeal to         │
                       │  Board of Review     │
                       └──┬─────────────────┬─┘
                          ▼                 ▼
              ┌─────────────────────┐  ┌─────────────────────┐
              │ Board Level Hearing │  │ Referee Level Hearing│
              └─────────────────────┘  └──────────┬──────────┘
                                                  ▼
                                       ┌─────────────────────┐
                                       │ Decision of the Referee│
                                       └──────────┬──────────┘
                                                  ▼
                                       ┌─────────────────────┐
                                       │ Application to Institute│
                                       │    Further Appeal   │
                                       └──┬───────────────┬──┘
                        ┌─────────────────┘               │
                        ▼                                 ▼
                 ┌──────────┐                      ┌──────────┐
                 │  Denied  │                      │ Allowed  │
                 └─────┬────┘                      └─────┬────┘
                       │         ┌─────────────────┐    │
                       │         │ No Further Hearing│◀──┤
                       │         │ (decision on record)│ │
                       │         └──────────┬──────┘    ▼
                       │                    │      ┌─────────────────┐
                       │                    │      │ Further Hearing │
                       │                    │      │ (senior referee)│
                       │                    │      └────────┬────────┘
                       ▼                    ▼               ▼
                              ┌─────────────────────┐
                              │ Decision of the Board│
                              └──────────┬──────────┘
                                         ▼
                              ┌─────────────────────┐
                              │    Common Pleas     │
                              └──────────┬──────────┘
                                         ▼
```

Chapter 9

Division of Securities, Ohio Department of Commerce

By William A. Carroll, Esq.

9.01 Introduction
9.02 The Securities Act and the division
9.03 Securities registration as a licensing procedure

FUNCTIONS OF THE DIVISION OF SECURITIES SPECIFICALLY SUBJECT TO THE APA BY STATUTE

9.04 Rulemaking
9.05 Dealer and salesman licensing
9.06 Proceedings under RC 1707.13
9.07 Proceedings under RC 1707.23
9.08 Hearings before the division
9.09 Administrative appeal
9.10 Miscellaneous division proceedings

CHARTS

9.11 Organizational chart, Division of Securities
9.12 Adjudication process/Enforcement, Division of Securities
9.13 Adjudication process/Registration procedure, Division of Securities

9.01 Introduction

This chapter discusses practice before the Division of Securities (the Division), insofar as it concerns hearings involving (1) licensing functions of the Division and (2) enforcement functions of the Division to the extent that the administrative process is invoked.

For purposes of this chapter, it is assumed that the practitioner is conversant with the provisions of the Ohio Administrative Procedure Act (APA) as codified in RC Chapter 119.[1] The administrative activities of state government are heavily influenced, although not completely governed, by the Ohio APA.

Significantly, the Ohio APA applies only to an "agency." RC 119.01(A) indicates that an "agency" is confined to (1) rulemaking or adjudication functions of specifically enumerated state departments or commissions, which do not include the Division of Securities; (2) functions of any "administrative" entity specifically made subject to RC Chapter 119; and (3) the "licensing" function of any "administrative" entity.

---

[1] See Text Ch 1, Rulemaking; Text Ch 3, Adjudication.

The Division is not one of the enumerated agencies and is therefore subject to the APA only to the extent provided by (1) its operative statute, RC Chapter 1707 (the "Securities Act"), and (2) its exercising one or more licensing functions.

The Division is "specifically subject" to the Ohio APA in rulemaking under RC 1707.20(D), in the licensing of dealers or salesmen of securities under RC 1707.22, and in adjudication hearings on "takeover bids" under RC 1707.041(B)(4). However, the principal function of the Division is the supervision of the securities industry by the registration of securities,[2] the registration of transactions in securities,[3] and the exercise of statutory enforcement responsibilities.[4]

The registration of securities or of a security transaction constitutes a license or a licensing function as defined in RC 119.01(B), which definition includes "any license, permit, certificate, commission, or charter issued by any agency." Although this proposition has not been definitively tested in the courts, it has not been seriously questioned. Similarly, any action by the Division to suspend or revoke a registration involves a "licensing function" subject to the Ohio APA.

CROSS REFERENCES

See Text Ch 1, Ch 3

Securities, RC Ch 1707

9.02 The Securities Act and the Division

Statutorily and historically, the Division differs from other state agencies in which the hearing process is a necessary, primary, or omnipresent function. The principal activity of many agencies is conducting hearings and settling controversies between two adversary parties,[5] or that of making factual or legal determinations via the hearing process.[6] The Division, on the other hand, becomes involved in the hearing process only when there is a dispute involving the registration of a new security or securities transaction, the suspension or revocation of an existing registration, or the denial or suspension of a dealer's or salesman's license. The majority of the Division's day-to-day activities are conducted without resort to the hearing process.

Many of the technical safeguards provided by the Ohio APA to a litigant appearing before the Division are more illusory than real. The situation results partially from the legislative history of securities regulation in Ohio, coupled with the fact that certain terms used in the Securities Act do not have a recognized judicial definition.

---

[2] RC 1707.05, RC 1707.08 to RC 1707.10.
[3] RC 1707.06, RC 1707.08, RC 1707.091.
[4] RC 1707.13, RC 1707.19, RC 1707.23 to RC 1707.27.
[5] E.g., employer-employee in the Bureau of Workers' Compensation.
[6] E.g., ratemaking in the Public Utilities Commission of Ohio.

The Securities Act had its genesis in a 1929 state effort to curb securities marketing abuses rampant in the predepression years of the 1920's.[7] The 1929 legislation was not the first Ohio legislative effort affecting the securities industry. 1914 House Bill 46, effective 5-19-14, primarily concerned the licensure of securities dealers, interdiction of securities fraud, and a modified regulatory procedure requiring the issuance or refusal of a certificate authorizing "disposal" upon an appearance that the disposal was not on "*grossly unfair terms.*" (Emphasis added.) This is the first time that this phrase appeared in Ohio securities law. Of even more interest is that 1914 House Bill 46 replaced 1913 House Bill 357, effective 8-4-13, which was of substantially similar import, except that the standard for denying a disposal certificate was that of "unfair terms." The Ohio Securities Act antedated substantial securities legislation on the federal level, notably the federal Securities Act of 1933 and the Securities Exchange Act of 1934. An examination of Ohio's Amended Senate Bill 12 of the 88th General Assembly, effective 7-23-29, discloses that a substantial and indeed surprising amount of its content is preserved in the current Ohio Securities Act.

The conceptual approach of the Ohio legislation is quite different from that of the federal legislation. The federal act requires adequate (meaning complete) disclosure of the securities and security transactions subject to federal jurisdiction.[8] Theoretically, the Securities Exchange Commission (SEC) does not pass upon the merits of an offering as a precondition to registration. The distinction between disclosure and regulation does become somewhat blurred on the federal level, particularly when the SEC exercises its rulemaking power in defining and refining (not necessarily rewriting) federal securities legislation.

Under the Ohio Securities Act, the consideration of the merits of the offering is a precondition to certain registrations[9] and a cause for the suspension or revocation of virtually all Ohio registered security offerings.[10] The basic statutory standard for Ohio's regulatory authority is the administrative determination that "the proposed offer or disposal of securities is not on *grossly* unfair terms."[11] This is not the only statutory yardstick, but the other criteria involving "fraud" or "deception" are terms of comparative legal art that have been the subject of judicial definition in a securities law context as well as other contexts. Logically, the administrator who finds that the proposed issue or issuance is merely "unfair," but not "grossly unfair," is legally required to issue an appropriate registration order, particularly in light of the legislative history noted above. However, various administrators have applied the "not grossly unfair" standard as tantamount to (1) not fraudulent; (2) a

---

[7]Query: Why did the legislature within a period of one year (apparently by design) further circumscribe the administrator's discretion by adding the word "grossly"?
[8]15 USC 77h.
[9]RC 1707.09.
[10]RC 1707.13.
[11]RC 1707.09, RC 1707.13. (Emphasis added.).

potentially good investment, as opposed to a poor one; and (3) a "fair, just and equitable offering."[12]

The statutory standard appears to mean whatever the current securities commissioner says it means. Even under the same commissioner, it is common to find proposed issues that appear to be substantially indistinguishable, but some have been registered and others have not. Such inconsistency is encouraged by the lack of a recognized definition of the "not grossly unfair" standard in statute, administrative rule, or case law. In turn, this definitional lack is largely caused by the nature of the securities industry itself.

The securities industry is volatile. Historically, a substantial portion of the issues qualified by the Division consist of federally registered offerings that still require qualification under "blue sky" procedures in Ohio, as well as in other states. The mere statement by the Division that the offering is unacceptable as "grossly unfair" will usually result in the withdrawal of the application. By the time the legal issues involved could be tested via the administrative process, with or without a court appeal, the issue usually would be moot in a practical sense. Dealers and underwriting groups which register numerous offerings on a regular basis exhibit a marked reluctance to offend the Division lest future offerings be prejudiced.

Since July 20, 1978, Ohio has permitted registration by coordination with certain federal offerings. RC 1707.091 provides for concurrent effectiveness of federal and state registrations with a simplified application procedure. However, this procedure provides for the Division inter alia to advise the applicant "whether the division then contemplates the institution of a proceeding" under RC 1707.13 or RC 1707.23. This activates the application of the grossly unfair standard and, conceivably, the advent of adverse Division reaction, in the face of which the offeror will perhaps withdraw his application, deeming discretion to be the better part of valor, as in the case of a registration pursuant to RC 1707.09.

Even with comparatively small intrastate offerings, the same principle applies. By the time a final judicial determination is made, the financial and business posture of the offeror undoubtedly will have changed. Statements that were true at the time of the application and upon which the ultimate decision, administrative or judicial, is predicated are no longer applicable. The necessary revisions to reflect the current status may well result in a new "grossly unfair" determination, and the whole process may start again. This process can be repeated endlessly.

Consequently, the lawyer should first exhaust his informal approaches to the registration referees. However, lest the lawyer overzealously seek to extract concessions from the referee, the lawyer should realize that approval of the registration provides no safe harbor from liability, civil or criminal, under state or federal securities law.

---

[12]This is the standard incorporated in blue sky legislation in other states. See, e.g., Cal Corporations Code 25140; Mo Rev Stats 409.306; Minn Stat 80A.13.

9.03 Securities registration as a licensing procedure

If the lawyer deems it necessary or advisable to test an adverse reaction to a registration application, the lawyer should invoke the appropriate provisions of the Ohio APA for initiating a hearing on a license denial.[13] The lawyer should request a determinative (adverse) order and request a hearing under the Ohio APA.

In preparing for the hearing, the lawyer may use a number of tactics. First, the lawyer can subpoena all division records relative to the filing including memoranda, intraoffice communications, and notations. However, communications between the Attorney General and the Division may not be discoverable, as they may be subject to the attorney-client privilege.[14]

Second, the lawyer may, pursuant to the Ohio APA, request an independent attorney as referee. Although the Ohio APA permits a Division employee to be appointed as referee, an objection should be made to such an appointment on the ground of prejudice. Such an objection would be particularly appropriate where an examination of subpoenaed material discloses the in-house referee's involvement in the initial decisional process.

Third, the attorney should examine all published division policy statements, particularly the *Ohio Securities Bulletin*, published from May 1973 to January 1975. These publications contain pronouncements of administrative principles variously denominated as "Policy Developments," "Regulatory Standards," "Written Policy Guidelines," with further reference to "Unwritten Policies," "Interpretive Opinions," and "Illustrative Rulings." The principles announced in the *Ohio Securities Bulletin* have not been reduced to rules adopted pursuant to the Ohio APA. If the attorney finds a pronouncement favorable to the qualification of his issue, he should argue that it is a persuasive expression of the agency's expertise, in the nature of collateral estoppel. If the attorney is confronted with an adverse pronouncement, he should object that the Division is applying a rule that has not been adopted pursuant to the Ohio APA.

CROSS REFERENCES
See Text Ch 3

FUNCTIONS OF THE DIVISION OF SECURITIES SPECIFICALLY SUBJECT TO THE APA BY STATUTE

9.04 Rulemaking

Rulemaking has been discussed previously.[15] In *Fortner v Thomas*,[16] the court reviewed the practice by persons aggrieved with agency rulemaking of

---
[13] See Text Ch 3, Adjudication.
[14] RC 1707.12 provides that persons having a direct economic interest in the transaction have a right to review "information obtained by the division" but not investigatory records or trial preparation records.
[15] See Text Ch 1, Rulemaking.
[16] Fortner v Thomas, 22 OS(2d) 13, 17, 257 NE(2d) 371 (1970).

using RC 119.11 as a vehicle for "challenging the lawfulness of an administrative regulation in a vacuum—of obtaining judicial review of a quasi-legislative proceeding." The court held that RC 119.11 may not be used to obtain such review of quasi-legislative actions of administrative agencies. Now, counsel may only be called upon to make a record in a rule adoption hearing when the client is immediately and adversely affected by the proposed rule of rescission. If the Division adopts a harmful rule, the proper recourse is an original declaratory judgment action in common pleas court. Assuming the criteria established in *Burger Brewing Co v Liquor Control Comm*[17] are met, the record (while not serving the same function as in the Ohio APA appeal) might well prove valuable as an aid in discovery, as a source of admissions by the Division, and as material for cross-examination.

CROSS REFERENCES

See Text Ch 1

9.05 Dealer and salesman licensing

The statutory requirements for licensure, as well as the grounds for refusal, revocation, or suspension of a license, are specifically set forth in RC 1707.15, RC 1707.16, and RC 1707.19. The procedures for hearing, appeal, and determination of venue on appeal are essentially the same as those procedures used in the licensure of other occupations and professions under RC Title 47.

The tactics used in the administrative litigation of a securities registration may also be helpful in the licensure context.[18] In addition, unlike in the registration process, the practitioner may be confronted with a rule or regulation purportedly adopted pursuant to the Ohio APA. The regulation may purport to define or refine the statutory grounds for refusal, revocation, or suspension of a license. If the rule is at all relevant to the case, the attorney should determine whether the requirements of RC 119.03 were strictly complied with when the rule was adopted. If the requirements were not met, the rule is invalid.[19] The lawyer should carefully check compliance with the requirements of RC 119.03 in its statutory posture as of the time the rule was adopted. RC 119.03 has been amended a number of times in recent years.[20]

CROSS REFERENCES

See Text Ch 1, 9.03

---

[17]Burger Brewing Co v Liquor Control Comm, 34 OS(2d) 93, 296 NE(2d) 261 (1973).

[18]See Text 9.03, Securities regulation as a licensing procedure.

[19]RC 119.02. See Text Ch 1, Rulemaking.

[20]1984 S 239, eff. 1-1-85; 1984 H 244; 1983 H 291; 1981 H 694, H 1; 1979 H 204, H 657, S 8; 1978 S 321; 1977 S 43, H 25, H 257; 1976 H 317; 1969 H 1.

9.06 Proceedings under RC 1707.13

RC 1707.13 permits, without a hearing, the suspension of a registration, a license, or an issuer's selling rights, predicated on the commission of certain enumerated violations which the Division finds. A mandatory hearing within ten days is the only constitutional safeguard against the unreasonable exercise of this power of suspension. The most important provision of the statute is that "following such hearing the division *shall* either confirm or revoke such suspension." (Emphasis added.) This provision, coupled with the provision for early hearing, insures the constitutionality of RC 1707.13.

In the hearing under RC 1707.13, the Division will try to establish a prima facie case. The Division should also establish the existence of a clear, present, and continuing injury, damage, or threat to the public weal that justifies the exercise of the Division's power to terminate the lawful conduct of the issuer's business. If the Division fails in the latter endeavor, the practitioner should note the omission on the record after the Division has rested its case.

At the conclusion of the hearing, the lawyer should demand an immediate decision. If the Division makes a decision within a suitable time, and if the decision on the merits is adverse, the lawyer may apply to the court for a suspension of the agency's order, pursuant to RC 119.12. However, the Division may not make a decision, relying on the fact that the Ohio APA provides no time limit for the submission of a referee's report and the ultimate decision of the agency. This lack of a time limit effectively continues the administrative suspension indefinitely.

It is advisable to appear at the hearing with a complaint and ancillary papers prepared for an original action for a temporary restraining order, preliminary injunction, and permanent injunction. After the Division manifests its intention to refrain from acting in a timely manner, the lawyer may, on the record, serve notice that he will apply as soon as possible for a temporary restraining order under Civil Rule 65(A). The attorney should then file the action and argue the cause before a judge. While the record of the administrative hearing will not be available at this juncture, forceful oral representation should be made that the requisite "clear and present continuing injury" was not established at the hearing. The attorney should try to put this contention on the record before a court reporter. The assistant attorney general may or may not dispute the contention. If he does not dispute it, the court may be inclined to grant the temporary restraining order. If the assistant attorney general does dispute it and if the court, despite the hardships which will result as enumerated in an affidavit supporting the temporary restraining order, is still indisposed to grant relief, the lawyer's posture on the argument for preliminary injunction (at which time he will have acquired the administrative hearing record) will be immensely improved. This procedure assumes, of course, that the administrative record does fail to establish a "clear and present continuing injury."

The argument to be made to the court is simple. Acting both as judge and adversary, the Division has, without hearing, effectively exercised the drastic power equivalent to injunction under circumstances in which a court would be reluctant to so act. Having interrupted the issuer's business activities for at least ten days (to obvious financial damage and detriment), the Division may be reluctant to acknowledge that its original findings were erroneous. Thus, the lawyer should assume from the outset that eventual recourse to the courts will be necessary.

Perhaps recognizing that the courts have in recent years expanded personal civil liability of public officers and employees,[21] the Division has recently implemented RC 1707.13 by issuing a "Notice of Opportunity for Hearing," in the nature of an order to show cause, rather than an ex parte suspension order. This presuspension hearing procedure is preferable to all parties. The Division does not assume an initial position from which it may be embarrassed into retreating, and the respondent is not prejudiced by a unilateral forced cessation of business activity. Meanwhile, the due process assurances, inherent in the hearing and appeal provisions of the Ohio APA, are preserved.

There are circumstances where the rather drastic remedy of an ex parte order under RC 1707.13 might be indicated; however, any securities law transgressor who is so flagrantly and continuously depredating the public would probably give scant heed to the Division order. In short, the ex parte suspension can be infinitely damaging to the vast number of legitimate licensees but is ineffectual as far as the true criminal activist is concerned.

9.07 Proceedings under RC 1707.23

RC 1707.23 is a mixture of procedural and penal provisions. In its initial form, RC 1707.23 was essentially procedural, detailing investigative powers of the Division, including, inter alia, the power to (1) require "any person" to file statements or reports relative to securities sales; (2) subpoena and examine witnesses; and (3) initiate criminal proceedings. However, in 1978, the General Assembly amended RC 1707.23 by adding subdivision (H). This subdivision purports to grant the Division authority to require "person or persons to cease and desist from the acts or practices appearing to the division ... to constitute violations of Chapter 1707 of the Revised Code." The distinction between RC 1707.23(H) and a summary suspension under RC 1707.13 is that the former apparently applies to both unlicensed and licensed persons. In any event, the Division has so interpreted it and applied it. The lawyer should be aware, however, that RC 1707.23(H) is constitutionally questionable as a violation of the doctrine of separation of powers.[22]

---

[21]Tcherepnin v Franz, 570 F(2d) 187 (7th Cir Ill 1978), cert denied sub nom First Natl Bank & Trust Co v Berke, 439 US 876, 99 SCt 214, 58 LEd(2d) 190 (1978). RC 9.87, enacted less than two years later, in effect provides a public officer or employee with a taxpayer-funded indemnity to the extent of one million dollars per occurrence, insuring against liability "incurred in the performance of his duties."

[22]See Sylvania Home Telephone Co v PUCO, 97 OS 202, 119 NE 205 (1918); New Bremen v PUCO, 103 OS 23, 132 NE 162 (1921).

In view of its application to unlicensed persons, the proceedings under RC 1707.23(H) arguably are not governed by the Ohio APA.[23] However, the Division has proceeded on the theory that the Ohio APA is applicable and has issued to unlicensed alleged transgressors a "Notice of Opportunity for Hearing" and, after an adverse determination, has advised them of their rights of appeal pursuant to RC 119.12.

If confronted with a "cease and desist" proceeding directed against his client, the lawyer, in addition to the measures previously mentioned, should raise jurisdictional and constitutional questions at the outset of the hearing. The Division may recognize the validity of such objections and summarily terminate the proceeding. If the Division persists in proceeding as if the Ohio APA were applicable, the procedural tools suggested above should be employed. An appeal under RC 119.12 is a potential method to test the legal questions involved. The notice of appeal should be filed within the ten-day limitation of RC 2505.07(B), which automatically brings it under the fifteen-day limitation of RC 119.12.

CROSS REFERENCES

See Text 9.01

9.08 Hearings before the Division

Hearings before the Division range from extremely informal to highly formal. How a lawyer arrives at his initial confrontation with the Division depends on the circumstances of the case and the disposition of the commissioner. On the informal (nonrecord) level, the lawyer should adjust his approach according to the letter, subpoena, order, proposed order, or other notice received by the client. If the Division issues an order affecting the client, and if the lawyer then avails himself of the opportunity to make a record as provided by the Ohio APA, the case will receive special attention rather than being heard on an assembly-line basis. The attorney should not neglect the use of discovery and subpoena.[24] In a proper case it may even be necessary to subpoena the commissioner. The request will probably be denied, and rightfully so, since the commissioner, although acting through a surrogate referee, is the ultimate arbiter of the proceeding. The attempt to subpoena, however, coupled with the denial of record, will lay the groundwork for expansion of the record after appeal to the common pleas court, on the basis that the testimony is newly discovered and was not ascertainable before the hearing.[25]

The enforcement section of the Division (headed by the statutory office of attorney inspector),[26] the investigative personnel of the Division, and the assistant attorney general assigned to the Division are all devoted to proving the Division right in its initial determination. The arbiter of this crucial issue

---

[23]See Text 9.01, Introduction (See the discussion on the definition of agency.).
[24]See Text 9.03, Securities registration as a licensing procedure.
[25]RC 119.12.
[26]RC 1707.36.

is the commissioner as head of the Division. He was responsible for the order against the client originally. Under these circumstances, the practitioner should anticipate an adverse decision. The Division is concerned with establishing that there is "reasonable, substantial and probative evidence" to support its decision. How this standard will be applied on the initial appellate level depends largely upon the approach taken by the common pleas court. The court may find (and the Division will urge) that the standard is tantamount to a scintilla of competent evidence. It may use the equivalent of the burden of proof in a civil case. Note that the evidentiary standard has an important additional qualification that it be "in accordance with law." The only way the lawyer can achieve a favorable decision at the Division level is to make a record in which the Division's posture, on the facts or on the law, is so unsupportable that its exposure to judicial scrutiny would subject the Division to administrative embarrassment. Thus, the lawyer must prepare and try his case and make his record with the same care that he would employ in any civil action.

Stipulations of fact, issues, and the precise nature of Division allegations, if not clearly defined in the paperwork that initiated the proceeding, may be the subject of an informal prehearing conference[27] should the Division be disposed to grant it. The Division should be cooperative in this regard in the interests of judicial, or rather, quasi-judicial, economy. In the unlikely event of a refusal to hold a prehearing conference, the lawyer should be prepared to delineate at the record hearing those areas in which his case has been prejudiced by the failure or refusal of the Division to grant the prehearing conference necessary to a fair presentation of the case. Thus, where appropriate, the lawyer should formally or informally avail himself, at least by letter request, of whatever discovery may be necessary to try the case.[28]

In a rules hearing conducted on August 22, 1984, the Division proposed to adopt a new rule, OAC 1301:6-3-12, which apparently limited the comprehensive scope of RC 1707.12, at least as interpreted in an unreported decision of the Franklin County Court of Common Pleas. After the hearing, the proposed rule was withdrawn by the Division.

CROSS REFERENCES

See Text 3.05(D), 9.03

9.09 Administrative appeal

In order to bring the case into court, the attorney must follow the procedural requirements for an administrative appeal.[29] Subject to local rule, the lawyer should draft his appeal brief with the same care and in the same form

---

[27]See Text 3.05(D), Prehearing conference.

[28]See RC 1707.12 which provides that persons having a direct economic interest in the transaction have a right to review information obtained by the division but not investigatory records or trial preparation records.

[29]RC 119.12. See also Text 3.10, Administrative appeal and review.

as a brief in the court of appeals. Specific and comprehensive assignments of error should be raised.

Admittedly, the Rules of Appellate Procedure, by virtue of Appellate Rule 1, apply only to the various courts of appeal in Ohio. Initially, this requirement indicates a similar limitation on Appellate Rule 12(A), which provides in pertinent part, "All errors assigned and briefed shall be passed upon by the court in writing, stating the reasons for the court's decision as to each such error." However, RC Chapter 2505 applies to all appeals and by its terms encompasses administrative appeals to the common pleas courts, including "proceedings whereby one court reviews ... a cause determined by ... an administrative officer, tribunal, or commission."[30] RC 2505.21 embodies the requirement of Appellate Rule 12(A) to the extent that all assignments of error shall be passed upon by a reviewing court. Since RC 2502.01 and RC 2505.21 cover an area which is not "in conflict" with the Rules of Appellate Procedure, i.e., administrative appeals to common pleas courts, these sections apply to such an appeal.

The rationale of Appellate Rule 12(A) (or RC 2501.21, in an administrative appeal) was forcefully noted by the Ohio Supreme Court in *State v Jennings*:[31]

> Thus, it is clear that the Court of Appeals should rule on all errors assigned. Furthermore, the court should give the reasons for its decision on each assignment of error. Reasons for a decision are necessary—otherwise all parties concerned must speculate on the obstacles, legal or other, which need be overcome in an appeal to this court.

To the lawyer bringing the appeal, the advantage of the strict application of the statute in this respect is obvious, particularly if the case lends itself to additional appeals.

CROSS REFERENCES

See Text 3.10

See Whiteside, Ohio Appellate Practice, Text 15.01

9.10 Miscellaneous Division proceedings

The Division may apply directly to the courts for a contempt order in the event of noncompliance with Division subpoenas or with reporting requirements of RC 1707.23;[32] for an injunction against certain securities violations;[33] and for receivership where the violations result in material prejudice to the holder or purchaser of securities.[34]

To the extent that implementation of these sections involves investigative procedures employed by the Division under RC 1707.23, the subject has

---

[30] RC 2505.01(A).
[31] State v Jennings, 69 OS(2d) 389, 433 NE(2d) 157 (1982).
[32] RC 1707.24.
[33] RC 1707.25, RC 1707.26.
[34] RC 1707.27.

already been discussed.[35] Original actions in the common pleas court are beyond the scope of this chapter.[36] Knowledge of local rules, practices, procedures, and customs is of the utmost importance in common pleas courts.

CROSS REFERENCES

See Text Ch 5, 9.07

---

[35]See Text 9.07, Proceedings under RC 1707.23.
[36]See Text Ch 5, Miscellaneous Judicial Review of Agency Action.

73   Division of Securities, Ohio Department of Commerce T 9.11

CHARTS

9.11   Organizational chart, Division of Securities

```
                        Commissioner of Securities
                                  |
          ┌───────────────────────┼───────────────────────┐
          |                       |                       |
                           Deputy Commissioner
                                  |
                            Enf. Research

          ┌───────────────────────┼───────────────────────┐
    Administrative Manager   Attorney Inspector    Registration Administrator
          |                       |                       |
    Supv. of Reg. Exams   Enforcement Adm. Mgr.      Registration

    Broker/Dealer Supv.

    Office Manager
          |
     Fiscal Office
```

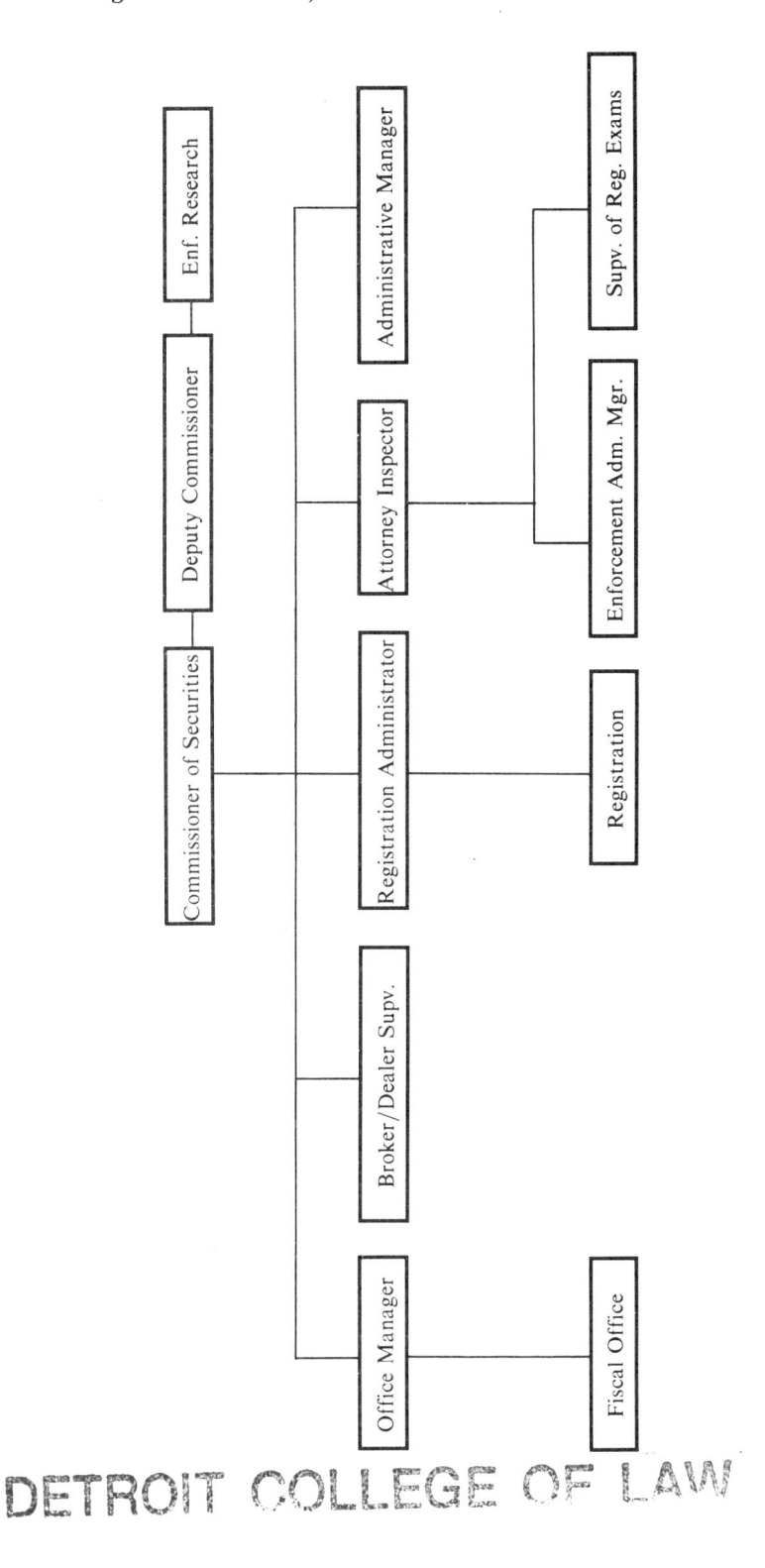

DETROIT COLLEGE OF LAW

9.12 Adjudication process/Enforcement, Division of Securities

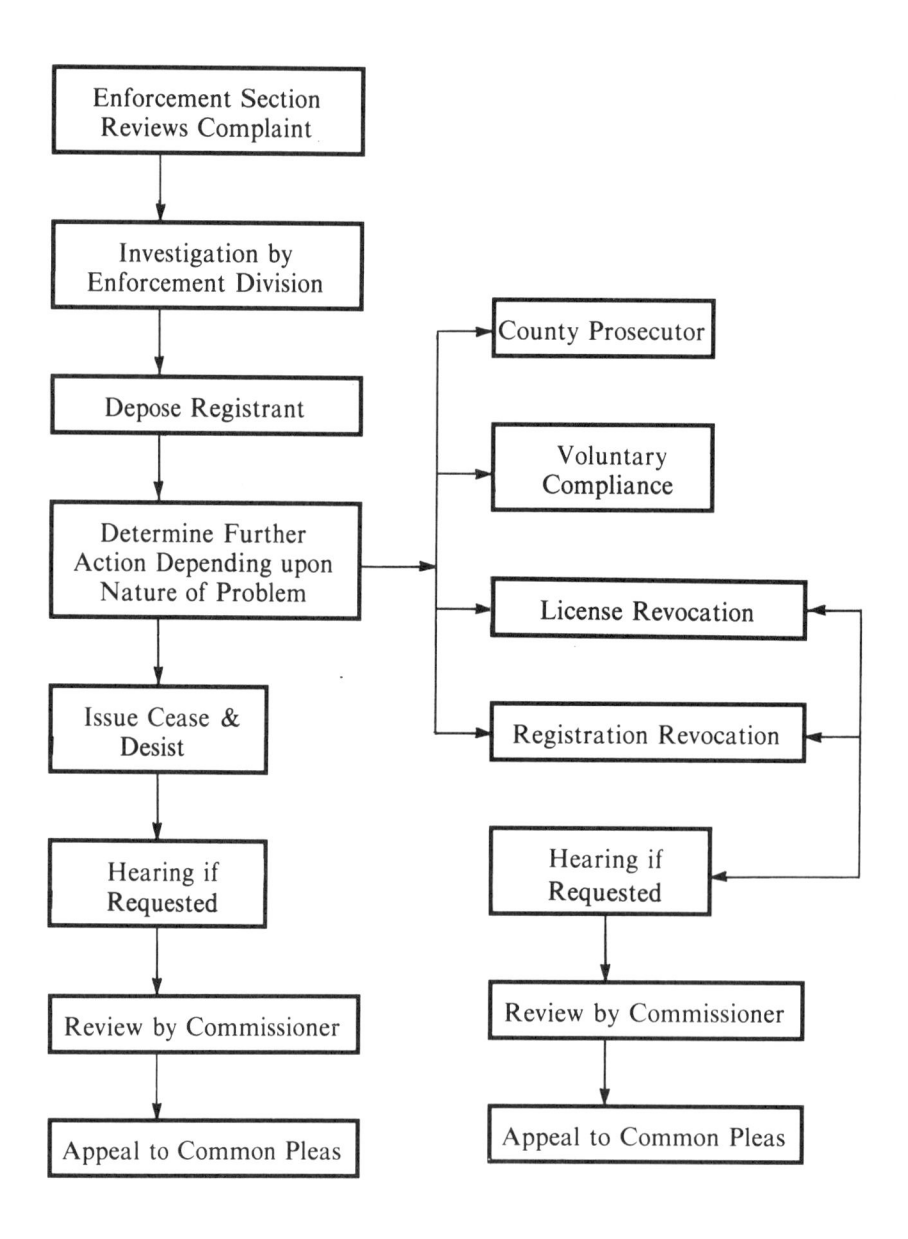

```
┌─────────────────────┐
│ Enforcement Section │
│  Reviews Complaint  │
└──────────┬──────────┘
           ↓
┌─────────────────────┐
│   Investigation by  │
│ Enforcement Division│
└──────────┬──────────┘
           ↓
┌─────────────────────┐              ┌──────────────────┐
│   Depose Registrant │         ┌──→ │ County Prosecutor│
└──────────┬──────────┘         │    └──────────────────┘
           ↓                    │
┌─────────────────────┐         │    ┌──────────────────┐
│  Determine Further  │         ├──→ │     Voluntary    │
│ Action Depending upon├────────┤    │    Compliance    │
│  Nature of Problem  │         │    └──────────────────┘
└──────────┬──────────┘         │
           ↓                    │    ┌──────────────────┐
┌─────────────────────┐         ├──→ │ License Revocation│←─┐
│   Issue Cease &     │         │    └──────────────────┘  │
│      Desist         │         │                          │
└──────────┬──────────┘         │    ┌──────────────────┐  │
           ↓                    └──→ │Registration Revocation│←┤
┌─────────────────────┐              └─────────┬────────┘  │
│     Hearing if      │                        ↓           │
│     Requested       │              ┌──────────────────┐  │
└──────────┬──────────┘              │    Hearing if    │──┘
           ↓                         │    Requested     │
┌─────────────────────┐              └─────────┬────────┘
│ Review by Commissioner│                      ↓
└──────────┬──────────┘              ┌──────────────────┐
           ↓                         │Review by Commissioner│
┌─────────────────────┐              └─────────┬────────┘
│Appeal to Common Pleas│                       ↓
└─────────────────────┘              ┌──────────────────┐
                                     │Appeal to Common Pleas│
                                     └──────────────────┘
```

9.13 Adjudication process/Registration procedure, Division of Securities

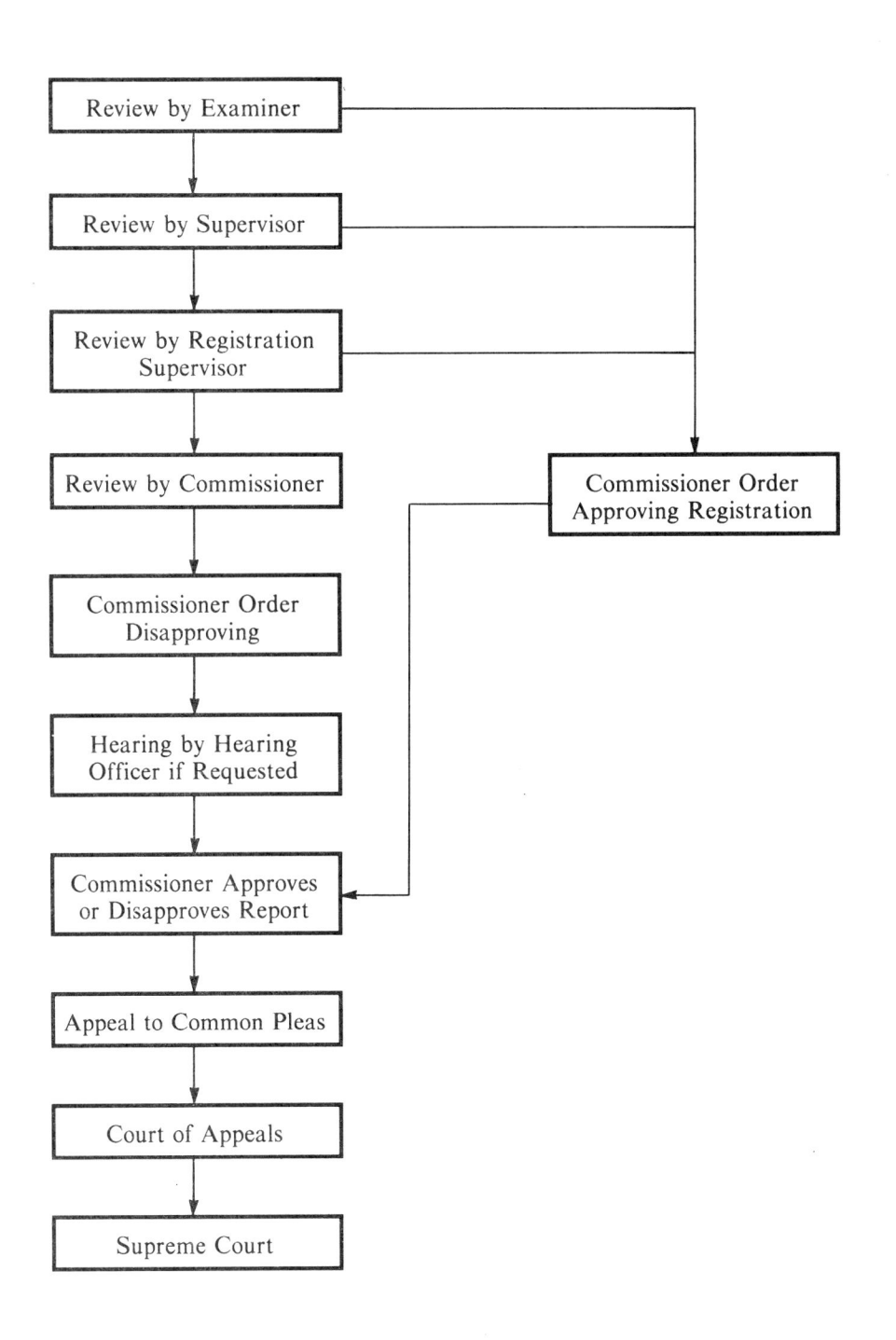

```
┌──────────────────────┐
│  Review by Examiner  │───────────────────────────┐
└──────────┬───────────┘                           │
           ▼                                       │
┌──────────────────────┐                           │
│ Review by Supervisor │───────────────────────────┤
└──────────┬───────────┘                           │
           ▼                                       │
┌──────────────────────┐                           │
│ Review by Registration│                          │
│     Supervisor       │───────────────────────────┤
└──────────┬───────────┘                           │
           ▼                                       ▼
┌──────────────────────┐        ┌──────────────────────────┐
│ Review by Commissioner│       │   Commissioner Order     │
└──────────┬───────────┘        │  Approving Registration  │
           ▼                    └──────────────────────────┘
┌──────────────────────┐
│  Commissioner Order  │
│     Disapproving     │
└──────────┬───────────┘
           ▼
┌──────────────────────┐
│  Hearing by Hearing  │
│ Officer if Requested │
└──────────┬───────────┘
           ▼
┌──────────────────────┐
│ Commissioner Approves│◄───────
│ or Disapproves Report│
└──────────┬───────────┘
           ▼
┌──────────────────────┐
│ Appeal to Common Pleas│
└──────────┬───────────┘
           ▼
┌──────────────────────┐
│   Court of Appeals   │
└──────────┬───────────┘
           ▼
┌──────────────────────┐
│    Supreme Court     │
└──────────────────────┘
```

Chapter 11

Ohio Environmental Protection Agency, the Environmental Board of Review, and the Hazardous Waste Facility Board

By Russell S. Frye, Esq. and Martin H. Lewis, Esq.

11.01 Introduction
11.02 Ohio Environmental Protection Agency
11.03 Environmental Board of Review
11.04 Hazardous Waste Facility Board

CHARTS

11.05 Organizational chart, Environmental Protection Agency
11.06 Organizational chart, Environmental Board of Review
11.07 Organizational chart, Hazardous Waste Facility Board
11.08 Adjudication process, Environmental Protection Agency
11.09 Adjudication process, Hazardous Waste Facility Board

11.01 Introduction

Three primary state agencies with which the practitioner with an environmental problem in Ohio may come into contact are the Ohio Environmental Protection Agency (Ohio EPA), the Environmental Board of Review (EBR), and the Hazardous Waste Facility Board (HWFB). This chapter will discuss the statutory and regulatory provisions germane to the administrative procedures of these agencies and will provide some insight into the uncodified, but equally important, routine practices of these agencies.

CROSS REFERENCES

Procedural rules, OAC Ch 3745-47
General appellate procedure, OAC Ch 3746-5
Hearings, OAC Ch 3746-7
Appeal from an adjudication hearing, OAC Ch 3746-9
Decisions by the board, OAC Ch 3746-11
Appeal to the courts, OAC Ch 3746-13

Air pollution control, RC Ch 3704
Solid and hazardous wastes, RC Ch 3734
Environmental protection agency, RC Ch 3745
Safe drinking water, RC Ch 6109
Water pollution control, RC Ch 6111

11.02 Ohio Environmental Protection Agency

RC Chapter 3745 creates the Ohio EPA and sets forth its general authority. The Ohio EPA administers four programs: (1) air pollution;[1] (2) water

---
[1] RC Ch 3704.

pollution;[2] (3) safe drinking water;[3] and (4) solid and hazardous waste.[4] These statutes authorize the director of the agency to take certain actions which then trigger formal administrative procedures.

These actions can be categorized under three broad headings: permit and plan approvals, enforcement orders, and rulemaking. The types of permits and plan approvals issued by the director include permits to install (1) a system for the disposal of sewage, industrial wastes, or other wastes; (2) a solid waste disposal facility; and (3) a new source of air pollutants. Another type of permit under the national pollutant discharge elimination system (NPDES) governs discharges of pollutants into waters of the state while other permits allow an air contaminant source. Two types of plan approvals are found, either for the construction of a public water supply system or for the installation and construction of treatment works for sewage disposal or the treatment of industrial waste.

The director may issue enforcement orders in all permit and plan approval programs. In addition, the director may issue an order as a result of an investigation of a verified complaint pursuant to RC 3745.08. The statute for each of the programs authorizes the director to issue rules pursuant to RC Chapter 119.[5]

The director issues permits or orders as proposed, draft, or final actions.[6] A final action is issued without the opportunity for an adjudication hearing. It becomes final immediately upon issuance and is appealable within thirty days to the EBR. A proposed action does not become final upon issuance but allows thirty days in which one can request an adjudication hearing. A draft action results in a public hearing, rather than an adjudication hearing, before becoming final. After public discussion, the director will then issue this action as a final action, appealable to the EBR. In *White Consolidated Industries v Nichols*,[7] the "draft action" provision of the rules was challenged on the basis that it did not provide the opportunity for an adjudication hearing as provided by RC 119.06. The Franklin County Court of Appeals, however, upheld the rule, citing it as an exception to the RC 119.06 requirements.[8]

During the mid and late 1970's, the Ohio EPA issued virtually every action as a final action, with no opportunity for an adjudication hearing. However, this trend ended in 1980 with the decision in *General Motors Corp v McAvoy*.[9] There, the Ohio Supreme Court held that a permit denial must be issued as a proposed action in order to conform to the requirements of RC Chapter 119. The court in dicta, however, stated that no requirement existed

---

[2]RC Ch 6111.
[3]RC Ch 6109.
[4]RC 3734.01.
[5]See generally Text Ch 1, Rulemaking.
[6]OAC 3745-47-05.
[7]White Consolidated Industries v Nichols, No. 82AP-505 (10th Dist Ct App, Franklin, 6-23-83).
[8]*Id.*
[9]General Motors Corp v McAvoy, 63 OS(2d) 232, 407 NE(2d) 527 (1980).

for a proposed action to be issued when a permit is granted. The court did not address the issue of whether an enforcement order should be issued in proposed or final form.

In response to this decision, the Ohio EPA began to issue proposed actions for permit denials or revocations. The Ohio EPA also began, in limited instances, to issue proposed actions in granting permits for controversial projects, such as a solid waste disposal facility.

Orders, with the exception of orders to fluoridate public water supply systems under RC 6109.14, and hazardous waste emergency orders under RC 3734.13(B), are usually issued as final actions with no opportunity for an adjudication hearing. RC 6109.14 requires the director to provide for a hearing. An emergency order issued under RC 3734.13(B) becomes effective immediately and remains in effect for ninety days; however, any person who is issued an order must be afforded the opportunity for a hearing to be held as soon as possible after the issuance of the order. On the basis of the hearing, the director may continue, revoke, or modify the order.

For many years, the director issued a proposed order as a result of an investigation of a citizen's verified complaint, filed under RC 3745.08, if the director found "probable cause" that a violation of a statutory and/or regulatory provision was occurring. Prior to 1980, when RC 3745.08 was amended, the director, upon a finding of "probable cause," either conducted a hearing and issued an order or referred the matter to the Attorney General's office.

This section was amended in 1980 to delete the "probable cause" language.[10] Under the statute currently in effect, the director, after investigation, must determine whether the alleged violation has occurred, is occurring, or will occur. Depending on this determination, the director will either dismiss the complaint, enter an order with the opportunity for a hearing, or refer the matter to the Attorney General. As a matter of policy, the director has not been issuing orders but has been referring the cases to the Attorney General's office for enforcement action if a determination is made that a violation has occurred, is occurring, or will occur.

Verified complaints remain an important mechanism in bringing environmental problems to the Ohio EPA's attention and have frequently been filed by attorneys for both private citizens and industry. Individuals will often contact the Ohio EPA about a particular environmental problem, but often this contact does not result in a formal investigation. However, the filing of a verified complaint triggers an investigation and a formal statutory procedure.

The Ohio EPA conducts its rulemaking pursuant to RC 119.03. The agency usually provides an extensive opportunity for public reaction and public comment before adopting a rule. Usually the agency solicits comments and then holds a public hearing. Notice of the issuance of proposed rules is given through the Ohio EPA Weekly Review (an EPA publication

---

[10] 1980 S 284, eff. 8-7-80.

available by subscription on payment of an annual fee),[11] notices in newspapers of large circulation, and mailings to interested parties and groups.[12] The director adopts rules as a final action, appealable to the EBR.

In *Middletown v Nichols,*[13] the Court of Appeals for Franklin County held that the Ohio EPA need not, under RC 119.03, disclose to the public the scientific and support data for proposed rules nor the ex parte comments from other agencies. The court also held that the Ohio EPA need not provide a new comment period if the final adopted rules substantially differ from the proposed rules. It is too early to predict what effect, if any, this recent decision will have on agency rulemaking.

Because most actions are issued as final rather than as proposed actions, the adjudication process is being used less frequently. However, a review of Ohio EPA's procedural rules is helpful for those who do become involved in the adjudication process.[14] Ohio EPA's procedural rules are contained in OAC 3745-47. Key provisions of these rules are as follows:

OAC 3745-47-05 provides for the issuance of draft or proposed actions by the director of the Ohio EPA. As discussed above, a proposed action gives an indication of the director's proposal to act in a certain manner.[15] This proposed action becomes final on the date specified but not until thirty days after the issuance of the proposal. Within that time, any aggrieved or adversely affected party may request an adjudication hearing on the proposal. In contrast, a draft action does not give rise to the rights for a formal adjudication hearing but only gives the right to public comment and eventually for EBR review. To conform with federal law, the director issues NPDES permits in draft form only.

Pursuant to OAC 3745-47-13(E), a party who does not request an adjudication hearing on a proposed action is "deemed to have consented to the proposed action" and to have "waived all rights to a hearing." The Franklin County Court of Appeals, however, in *Campbell v Maynard,*[16] held that this provision is invalid. A party who does not request a hearing on a proposed action still has the statutory right to appeal to the Environmental Board of Review, with the appeal limited to the record.

OAC 3745-47-11 sets forth the requirements for filing of papers and service. This rule includes service requirements and methods for computing time, the number of copies to be filed, and other similar procedural details.

OAC 3745-47-15 provides for intervention of parties in an adjudication hearing. This rule sets forth the criteria to be applied by the referee in deciding whether a party should be allowed to intervene.

---

[11] See RC 3745.07.
[12] OAC 3745-49-01.
[13] Middletown v Nichols, 9 App(3d) 135, 9 OBR 199, 458 NE(2d) 886 (Franklin 1983).
[14] See generally Text Ch 3, Adjudication.
[15] OAC 3745-47-03(M).
[16] Campbell v Maynard, 19 App(3d) 41, 19 OBR 107, 482 NE(2d) 990 (Franklin 1984).

OAC 3745-47-20 provides for discovery. It states that discovery should be conducted in the same manner and to the same extent as prescribed in the Ohio Rules of Civil Procedure. This rule also makes special provisions for examination of governmental materials.

OAC 3745-47-21 sets forth the procedures to be followed during the administrative hearing. Especially significant is the provision in OAC 3745-47-21(A) that "[t]he referee shall admit all relevant and material evidence, except evidence that is unduly repetitious, even though inadmissible under the rules of evidence applicable to judicial proceedings." This section also provides for judicial notice, the procedure for filing proposed findings and orders, for briefing schedules, etc.

OAC 3745-47-23 states the burden of proof at adjudication hearings. OAC 3745-47-23(A)(1) provides, "The burden at all hearings with respect to applications, permits, licenses, variances, and certificates shall be upon the applicant to prove entitlement to the permit, license, variance, or certificate." OAC 3745-47-23(A)(2) provides, "The agency shall bear the burden of proof at all adjudication hearings relating to proposed modifications initiated by the agency, proposed revocations, proposed orders, and findings and notice of hearing under section 3745.08, 6109.14, or 6111.32 of the Revised Code."

OAC 3745-47-24 provides that the referee shall submit to the director a written report setting forth findings of fact, conclusions of law, and recommendations of the action to be taken by the director. This report is to be filed within forty-five days of the filing of the adjudication hearing transcript by the hearing clerk or, where a posthearing briefing schedule has been established, within forty-five days of the date set for completion of briefing. A copy of the report and recommendations of the referee is mailed to all parties or their attorneys. Each party has the opportunity to file written objections to the report and recommendations within ten days of receipt of the report.

Pursuant to OAC 3745-47-26, the director shall take action upon the report and recommendation of the referee not later than sixty days after the submission of objections to the hearing referee's report and recommendation. The director may adopt either the report of the referee as a whole or only parts of the report, or he may entirely disapprove the report. The director then issues a final action appealable to the EBR.

The Ohio EPA has recently created a "modified procedure" for hearing.[17] The purpose of this procedure is to allow an adjudication hearing to be conducted through written rather than oral testimony.

The above procedures summarize the administrative procedures of the Ohio EPA as set forth in its rules. However, it is important to note some general practices of the Ohio EPA that are not codified in the rules and, in some instances, may conflict with the rules.

---

[17]OAC 3745-47-10 to OAC 3745-47-31, eff. 6-30-81.

The adjudication process is extremely slow. Often several months or even years elapse from the time a hearing request is filed to the time that a hearing is held. There may be several prehearing conferences and long drawn-out discovery proceedings and settlement discussions before hearing. Once a hearing is held and completed, it may take months for a hearing referee to write his report and recommendation. It often takes the director several months to issue a decision. Although the rules establish certain times in which the referee or director must act, these time frames are routinely ignored.

The referees at the Ohio EPA are full-time employees of the agency rather than outside referees under contract. The referees have the reputation for fairness and objectivity even though they are often slow in issuing their opinions. The referees, as in many other administrative agencies, are very flexible regarding the admissibility of evidence. Hearsay, opinion, and cumulative evidence are routinely admitted into the record. However, evidence that is obviously irrelevant or immaterial is excluded.

The hearings, however, are conducted in a fairly formal manner. They are recorded by a stenographer. Transcripts are routinely made and are available at cost to the parties.

The referees strongly encourage informal discovery and cooperation among the parties in discovery. As a general rule, hearing referees do not appreciate discovery battles, overly technical arguments, or recalcitrance in discovery either by agency personnel or by the private parties. The referees encourage an open free-flow of information in discovery.

The referees are also quite lenient regarding intervention. Hearing referees traditionally view the criteria for intervention set forth in the rule very liberally. Rarely is a request for intervention denied. This policy is especially of concern to a permittee, when various citizens seek to intervene to challenge the issuance of a permit.

Although referees at the EPA are full-time employees of the agency, by no means are their decisions dictated by a blind, favorable attitude toward agency practices. Hearing referees will often issue reports and recommendations changing or overruling the proposed action. Usually, the director of the EPA concurs with the referee's decision.

CROSS REFERENCES

See Text Ch 1, Ch 3

See Whiteside, Ohio Appellate Practice, Text Ch 27
See Jacoby, Ohio Civil Practice, Text Ch 35

11.03 Environmental Board of Review

All final decisions of the director are appealable to the EBR pursuant to either RC 3745.04 or RC 3745.07. RC 3745.04 authorizes "[a]ny person who was a party to a proceeding before the director" to participate in an appeal to the EBR for an order "vacating or modifying the action of the director of the environmental protection agency or local board of health[18] or ordering the director or the board of health to perform an act."

The EBR has exclusive, original jurisdiction over any matter which may, under RC 3745.04, be brought before it. Action is defined as

> the adoption, modification, or repeal of a rule or standard, the issuance, modification, or revocation of any lawful order other than an emergency order, and the issuance, denial, modification, or revocation of a license, permit, lease, variance, or certificate, or the approval or disapproval of plans and specifications pursuant to law or rules adopted thereunder.[19]

Third-party appeals are authorized by RC 3745.07 which states, in part:

> If the director issues, denies, modifies, revokes, or renews a permit, license, or variance without issuing a proposed action, an officer of an agency of the state or of a political subdivision, acting in a representative capacity, or any person who would be aggrieved or adversely affected thereby, may appeal to the environmental board of review within thirty days of the issuance, denial, modification, revocation, or renewal.

RC 3745.07 is often invoked by a third party, such as a citizens' group, to challenge the issuance of a permit, such as to a solid waste disposal facility.

One of the major issues involving RC 3745.04 and RC 3745.07 is the exclusivity of the EBR's jurisdiction. There have been at least four Ohio Supreme Court cases which firmly establish the exclusivity of the EBR's jurisdiction.[20] Although there is much debate among environmental lawyers regarding the wisdom of these decisions, a lawyer, when faced with an objectionable regulation, permit, or order, must advise his client to appeal to the EBR. Even if the lawyer attempts to attack the director's action in another forum, he must file at the EBR to preserve his client's rights.

One of the rationales for granting the EBR exclusive, original jurisdiction over actions of the director of the Ohio EPA is that the EBR members are supposed to be selected by the Governor, with the advice and consent of the Senate, on the basis of their expertise in environmental matters.[21] The three members of the board are each chosen for a six-year term. Pursuant to RC 3745.02, at least one member must be an attorney.

The EBR's administrative procedures are set forth in OAC 3746. The more important sections will be discussed below. These rules have the reputation of being confusing, redundant, and ambiguous.

---

[18]Solid, as opposed to hazardous, waste facilities are usually licensed by the local board of health rather than the EPA.

[19]RC 3745.04.

[20]State ex rel Maynard v Whitfield, 12 OS(3d) 49, 12 OBR 42, 465 NE(2d) 406 (1984) (Collateral attack upon a denial of a license.); Warren Molded Plastics, Inc v Williams, 56 OS(2d) 352, 384 NE(2d) 253 (1978) (Collateral attack upon director's regulation.); State ex rel Williams v Bozarth, 55 OS(2d) 34, 377 NE(2d) 1006 (1978) (Collateral attack upon the director's application of regulations.); and Cincinnati ex rel Crotty v Cincinnati, 50 OS(2d) 27, 361 NE(2d) 1340 (1977) (Collateral attack upon a director's order.).

[21]RC 3745.02.

OAC 3746-5-02 delineates the parties in the proceeding before the EBR. The person appealing to the Board is the "appellant," and the director or any party substantially supporting the action from which the appeal is taken is the "appellee." For example, if an order is issued and then appealed to the EBR, the person to whom the order is issued is the "appellant," and the director is the "appellee." However, if a permit is issued by the director and is then appealed by a third party, the third party is known as the "appellant," and the permittee and the director are both known as the "appellee."

OAC 3746-5-03 requires that every party substantially supporting the director's decision be joined as a party appellee. If the appellant fails to join the proper parties, the Board will do so sua sponte.

OAC 3746-5-06 to OAC 3746-5-10 describe the requirements for a notice of appeal. The appeal must be filed with the Board within thirty days after notice of the director's action. The notice of appeal must set forth assignments of errors, why the appeal is taken, what action is being appealed, the facts essential for review, and the relief sought on appeal.

OAC 3746-5-12 relates to the certification of the record. Within seven days after receiving the appeal, the director must certify to the Board a record of the proceedings from which the appeal arose. In actual practice, however, certification of the record may take weeks. In a case where an adjudication hearing was held, the certified record would include the transcript of the adjudication hearing and all information submitted into evidence at the hearing. Where no adjudication hearing was held, the record would include all documents, correspondence, etc., which form the basis for the decision of the director.

The EBR is authorized to hold both de novo hearings and arguments on the record depending on whether there was a hearing below. OAC 3746-7-01 describes the situations in which the Board will hold a de novo hearing. For instance, the Board shall hold such hearing if the director issued a final action without holding an adjudication hearing.

OAC 3746-9-01 sets forth the procedures for the hearing before the Board when an adjudication hearing was held by the Ohio EPA. In this instance, a de novo hearing is not held but rather the Board will hold a hearing in the form of oral arguments. There is, however, a provision for the submission of newly discovered evidence.[22]

OAC 3746-5-13 and OAC 3746-5-15 authorize the Board to grant stays of the director's action pending appeal. The filing of an appeal does not automatically suspend or stay the action appealed from; one must apply to the Board for a stay pursuant to OAC 3746-5-13 and OAC 3745-5-15. However, "[e]xcept for compelling reasons justifying a stay, a stay shall be denied."[23] If a stay is granted, the hearing is expedited and held within a matter of days.

---

[22]OAC 3746-9-02.
[23]OAC 3746-5-13.

OAC 3746-5-23 sets forth the evidentiary rules of the Board. The rules provide that written testimony may be submitted, provided the witness is present and sworn. This rule does not state what evidence is admissible but states that the Board shall pass upon the admissibility of evidence.

OAC 3746-5-30 sets forth the burden of proceeding at an EBR hearing. This rule places the burden of proceeding upon the party appealing the action of the director except when the director has (1) issued an order to a party to take an affirmative act toward abatement; (2) revoked a license or permit; or (3) sought to engage in activity objected to as harmful.[24] However, at least one EBR decision places the burden of proceeding on the party appealing the director's order.[25] The party with the burden of proceeding must present a prima facie case. If a prima facie case is presented, then the burden of proof shifts to the other party.

For example, if a permit is granted and appealed by a third party, the third party must present a prima facie case that the director was unreasonable or unlawful in granting the permit. Once this prima facie case is presented, the permittee has the burden of proving entitlement to its permit.

Although the Board discusses the burden of proof and proceeding at every hearing, this issue, to an extent, does not have much impact on how the Board rules. Traditionally, the Board has put emphasis on the "scope of review" in arriving at its decision.

The Board has subpoena powers which are set forth in OAC 3746-7-07 to OAC 3746-7-09. Both parties have the right to ask the Board to issue subpoenas. However, the Board, in its discretion, may refuse to issue a subpoena on the grounds of materiality and relevance. No subpoena shall be issued to any person in the decision-making process unless there is a showing of bad faith or improper behavior by that person.[26]

OAC 3746-7-15 provides for depositions. The Board may compel attendance at depositions.

OAC 3746-13-01 provides that decisions of the EBR must be appealed to the Court of Appeals of Franklin County or "if the appeal arises from an alleged violation of a law or regulation, to the court of appeals in the district in which the violation was alleged to have occurred." Consistent with RC 3745.06, there is no appeal to the court of common pleas.

Many of the general practices of the EBR are different from those of the Ohio EPA. Whereas the administrative process is very slow at the Ohio EPA, it can move quickly at the EBR. The EBR prides itself on expeditiously moving its docket. Immediately upon appeal, the case is set for a prehearing conference, which usually is held within a few weeks. At the prehearing conference a briefing schedule and hearing date are set. The hearing date will usually be only a few months after the prehearing conference.

---

[24]OAC 3746-5-30(B).
[25]Truck world, Inc v McAvoy, EBR 80-3 (6-10-80).
[26]OAC 3746-7-08.

Although continuances are granted, the Board is very reluctant to grant them, absent an important reason. The Board renders its decisions very quickly. Often the EBR will express from the bench, at the conclusion of the hearing, its intent on how to rule. The Board will instruct the prevailing party to prepare findings of fact, conclusions of law, and a final order and file these within approximately three weeks of the conclusion of the hearing.[27] Approximately a month thereafter, the Board will issue its final decision. Therefore, most cases are disposed of within approximately a six-month period after the notice of appeal is originally filed.

The Board, viewing itself as the protector of the public interest against governmental abuses, treats virtually any piece of paper which is filed as a notice of appeal, even if it does not meet the requirements set forth in the rules. If any document filed purports to be, or resembles, a notice of appeal, the Board will docket it as a notice of appeal and then order an amended notice of appeal to be filed to conform with the rules. However, it will almost never dismiss the appeal because the form is not correct.

The Board strongly encourages settlement. Usually at the prehearing conference, it will suggest that the parties meet at the conclusion of the prehearing conference or at some other time to engage in settlement discussions. The Board also requires that joint settlement reports be filed prior to the hearing to apprise it of what progress is being made.

Although the rules provide for the granting of a stay, the EBR almost never grants a stay. In the history of the EBR only a few stays have been granted. To convince the Board to stay an action, one must show immediate, irreparable harm and be prepared to go to hearing within a few days.

Practitioners before the Board often are presented with a case in which there are only questions of law and no factual issues. In such an instance, the natural inclination is to file a motion for summary judgment. The Board, however, does not have a rule providing for the filing of this type of motion, and it is unlikely that they would grant it.

The Board takes its responsibility to provide a de novo hearing very seriously. The Board, especially its chairman, strongly believes that the director should not issue final actions without the opportunity for an adjudication hearing. At virtually every hearing the Board raises this topic, even though the Ohio Supreme Court has held that an opportunity for an adjudication hearing is only necessary when a permit is denied. However, because of its strong opinion on this issue, the Board is very insistent that the parties be allowed to present and conduct a de novo evidentiary hearing.

This attitude also encompasses the Board's rulings on evidentiary issues. The Board is extremely liberal about the admissibility of testimony and exhibits no matter how irrelevant, incompetent, or cumulative they might be. Because the Board has much experience with these types of cases, it can discern what evidence is probative and what is not. Nevertheless, it will allow all evidence.

---

[27] OAC 3746-11-04.

The Board also allows narrative testimony and leading questions on direct. In general, the hearings are informal. Typical trial-court demeanor is not appreciated by the Board.

No stenographic records are kept of the hearings; rather, the hearings are taped. A transcript is made only if requested and/or in the event of an appeal. The Board is quite aggressive in probing the salient issues of the case during the hearing. This attitude in turn triggers extensive questioning by the Board. In fact, often the members will ask more questions of witnesses than the attorneys ask. Often these questions will go beyond the witnesses' direct testimony and the witnesses' expertise.

Similarly, hearings consisting of oral arguments frequently turn into a several-hour, free-flowing discussion among the attorneys and Board members. Rarely are oral arguments confined to fifteen or twenty minutes for each side as is customary in the courts.

In preparing a case, the practitioner often is inclined to call the director or another policymaker as a witness. The Board has, in the past, allowed the director to testify but only within limited parameters. Usually it will not require the director to testify.

The Board allows and encourages discovery among the parties. Like Ohio EPA referees, the EBR likes to see a cooperative attitude in discovery matters and a free flow of information. Board members become perturbed if they feel that any party, especially the government, is withholding any pertinent information or is recalcitrant in discovery matters. The Board will not hesitate to issue discovery-type orders if the parties cannot resolve their differences themselves.

The filing of comprehensive briefs is very important to the Board. It also benefits the parties. As stated above, the Board is well versed in technical issues but not that well versed in the law. Therefore, the legal issues should be precisely defined and expounded in the briefs, along with a detailed discussion of the pertinent facts.

The EBR may either vacate, modify, or affirm the director's action. It was found in the early 1980's, as a result of an informal survey by the Board itself, that the Board modified or vacated the director's actions in approximately forty-seven per cent of the cases heard. Of that percentage, however, the great majority were modifications rather than vacations. In addition, many of these modifications are minor modifications.

In the three years since the Board's informal survey, a move toward settlement of issues and cases has developed within the Ohio EPA, which removes some of the prior need for modifications of the director's actions. This tendency toward settlement has reduced the level of modifications to where the majority of the director's actions are now affirmed.

The Board is sensitive about curbing what it feels is unreasonable or unlawful decision-making by the director. However, it does not vacate more cases or make more major modifications because it feels constrained, probably unduly so, by a narrow scope of review.

RC 3745.05 requires the Board to affirm the director's action if it finds, after hearing, that it was lawful and reasonable or if it finds the action unreasonable or unlawful, to vacate or modify the action. The Franklin County Court of Appeals in *Citizens Committee to Preserve Lake Logan v Williams*,[28] also commonly known as the "Lake Logan" case, stated that " 'unreasonable' means that which is not in accordance with reason, or that which has no factual foundation." The EBR has consistently read this decision to affirm the director's action if there is *any* valid factual foundation for the director's action. Because of this reading, very few cases are vacated.

The Board, in assessing the factual foundation for the director's action, looks beyond the certified record to all the evidence produced at the hearing. This could be quite confusing for the practitioner unfamiliar with the EBR's practice. In other words, there could be a grossly inadequate certified record, yet the director's actions still could be affirmed because the state, at the hearing, supplies abundant evidence which supports the reasonableness of the director's action, even though that evidence may have been generated after the action. On the other hand, the appellant also has the opportunity to present additional evidence to support its position and is not confined to the certified record in preparing its case.

When the Board does not hold a de novo hearing but holds an oral argument on the record, the Board decides the case based on the record. However, because the Board has heard so many similar cases, it is inevitable that its decisions will reflect the members' knowledge of the subject matter.

As stated previously, decisions of the EBR are appealable pursuant to RC 3745.06 to either the Franklin County Court of Appeals or a court of appeals where the violation took place.

CROSS REFERENCES

See Jacoby, Ohio Civil Practice, Text Ch 35

11.04 Hazardous Waste Facility Board

The Hazardous Waste Facility Board (HWFB) was created in late 1980 pursuant to RC 3734.05. The purpose of this board is to approve or disapprove applications for hazardous waste facility installation and operation permits. Although the Ohio EPA continues to review applications for hazardous waste facilities, the actual permit is issued by the HWFB, not the Ohio EPA.

The Board is composed of the director of environmental protection who serves as chairperson, the director of natural resources, the chairman of the Ohio water development authority, one chemical engineer, and one geologist. Both the chemical engineer and geologist are employed by a state university

---

[28] Citizens Committee to Preserve Lake Logan v Williams, 56 App(2d) 61, 70, 381 NE(2d) 661 (Franklin 1977).

and are appointed by the Governor with the advice and consent of the Senate for a term of two years.[29]

The Board is given the power to promulgate rules regarding its procedure and is given the authority to conduct both public hearings and adjudication hearings on applications for hazardous waste installation and operation permits. The Board has the power to hire referees who preside at adjudication hearings and then make reports and recommendations to the full Board for its action.

The Board presently has a staff consisting of an executive director, several lawyers and engineers, plus a public information officer and clerical help. The Board staff provides for public hearings and adjudication hearings, reviews applications, and advises the Board.

The Board meets once a month for a regularly scheduled meeting. It is very difficult to generalize about the procedure of the Board. First of all, only two adjudication hearings have been held, both in front of referees. Second, new procedural rules have been proposed but not yet finalized. These rules are currently subject to much controversy and comment and may be substantially changed.

In addition, the Governor recently signed Substitute House Bill 506,[30] which is a comprehensive revision of the hazardous waste program. Although its impact is much more substantive than procedural, this bill will undoubtedly have an impact on the conduct of Board hearings and the adjudication process, such as the procedures for permit modifications and renewals.

---

[29] RC 3734.05.
[30] 1984 H 506, eff. 8-1-84.

CHARTS

11.05 Organizational chart, Environmental Protection Agency

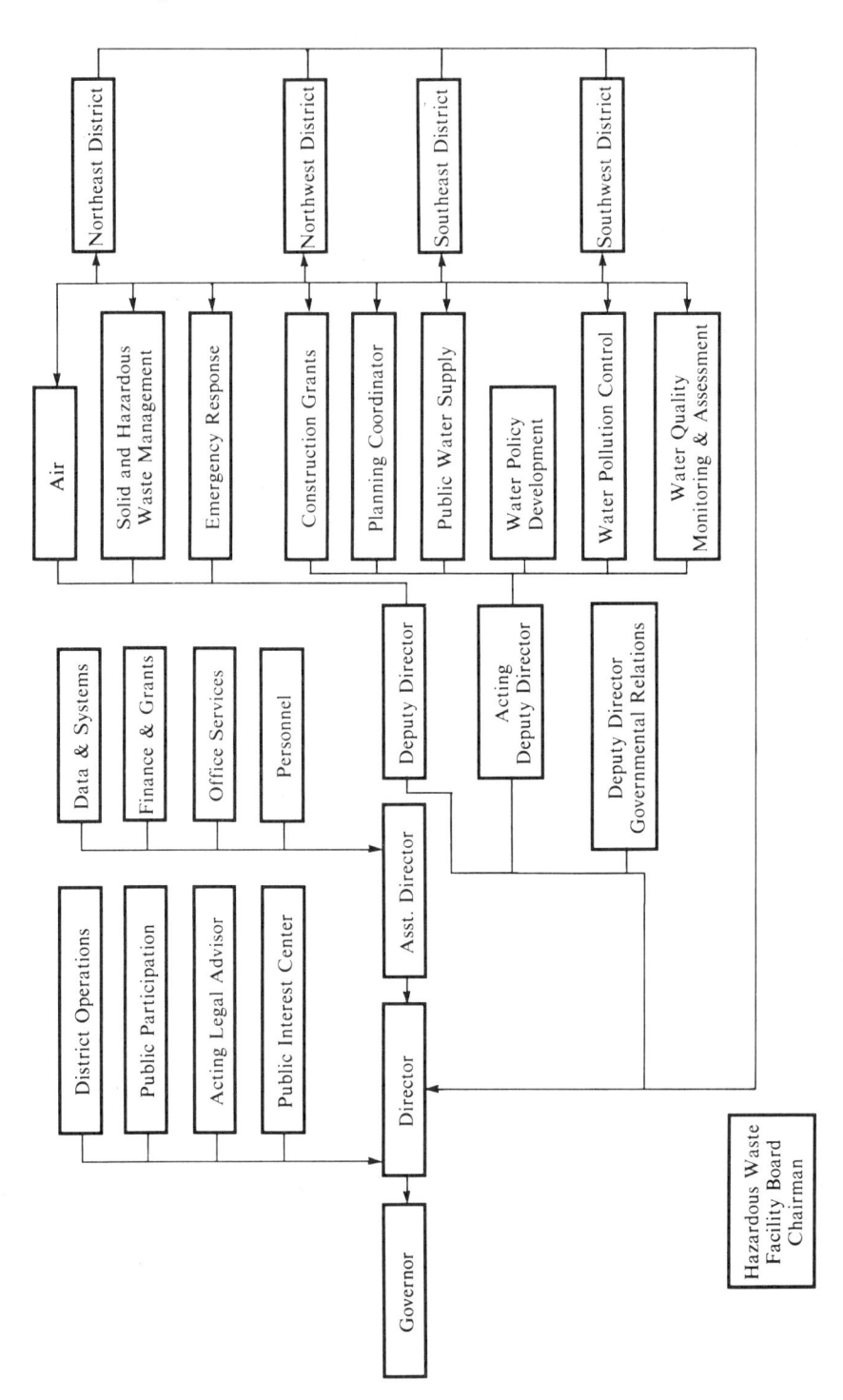

11.06 Organizational chart, Environmental Board of Review

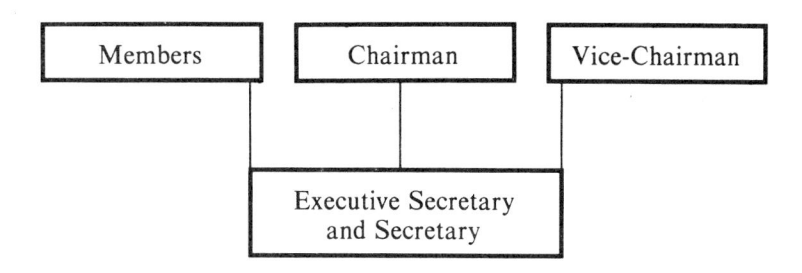

```
┌──────────┐   ┌──────────┐   ┌──────────────┐
│ Members  │   │ Chairman │   │ Vice-Chairman│
└────┬─────┘   └────┬─────┘   └──────┬───────┘
     │              │                │
     └──────┬───────┴────────┬───────┘
            │                │
         ┌──┴────────────────┴──┐
         │  Executive Secretary │
         │     and Secretary    │
         └──────────────────────┘
```

11.07 Organizational chart, Hazardous Waste Facility Board

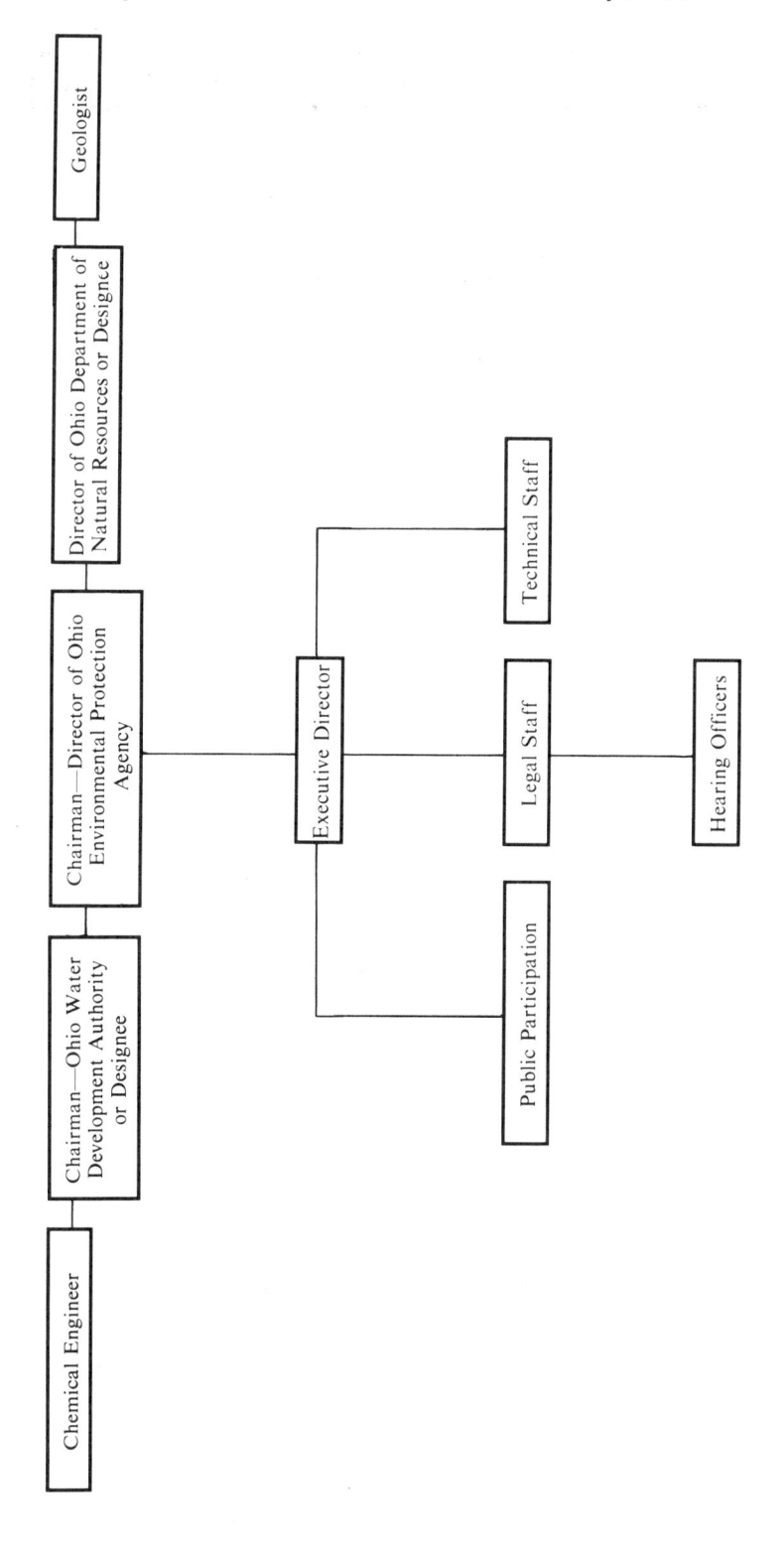

```
                          Geologist
                              |
         Director of Ohio Department of
         Natural Resources or Designee
                              |
                                           ┌── Technical Staff
         Chairman—Director of Ohio         |
         Environmental Protection ──── Executive Director ──── Legal Staff ──── Hearing Officers
         Agency                            |
                              |            └── Public Participation
         Chairman—Ohio Water
         Development Authority
         or Designee
                              |
                       Chemical Engineer
```

11.08 Adjudication process, Environmental Protection Agency

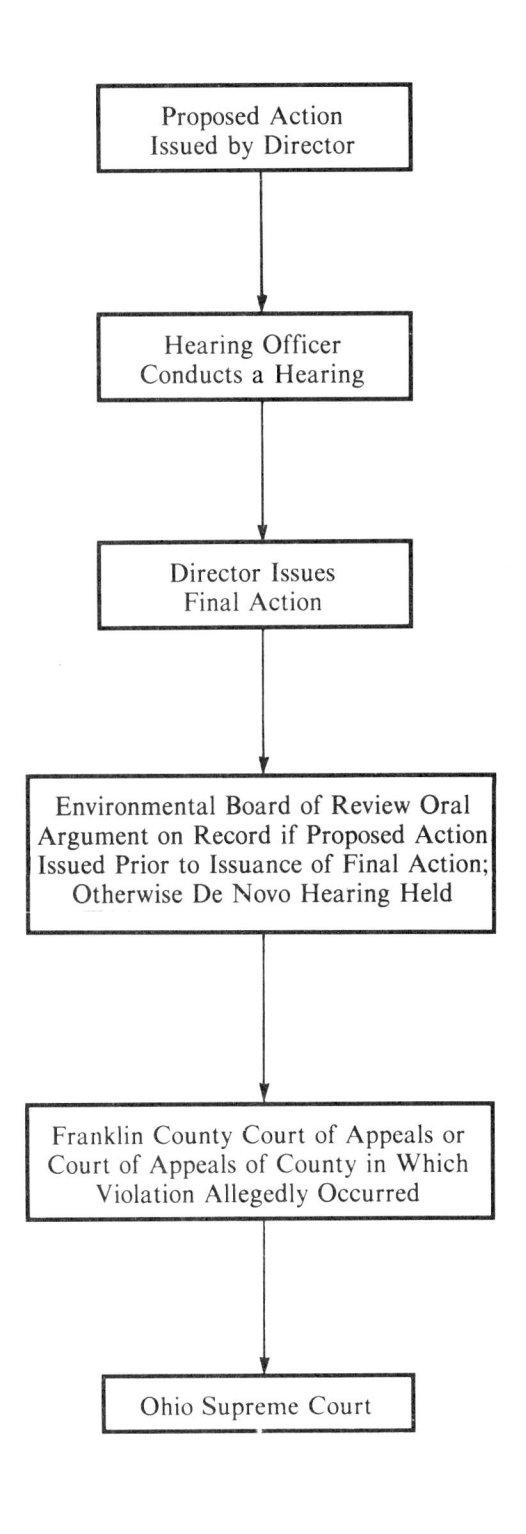

```
┌─────────────────────────┐
│    Proposed Action      │
│   Issued by Director    │
└───────────┬─────────────┘
            │
            ▼
┌─────────────────────────┐
│     Hearing Officer     │
│   Conducts a Hearing    │
└───────────┬─────────────┘
            │
            ▼
┌─────────────────────────┐
│     Director Issues     │
│      Final Action       │
└───────────┬─────────────┘
            │
            ▼
┌───────────────────────────────────────────┐
│  Environmental Board of Review Oral       │
│  Argument on Record if Proposed Action    │
│  Issued Prior to Issuance of Final Action;│
│  Otherwise De Novo Hearing Held           │
└───────────────────┬───────────────────────┘
                    │
                    ▼
┌───────────────────────────────────────────┐
│  Franklin County Court of Appeals or      │
│  Court of Appeals of County in Which      │
│     Violation Allegedly Occurred          │
└───────────────────┬───────────────────────┘
                    │
                    ▼
        ┌─────────────────────┐
        │  Ohio Supreme Court │
        └─────────────────────┘
```

11.09 Adjudication process, Hazardous Waste Facility Board

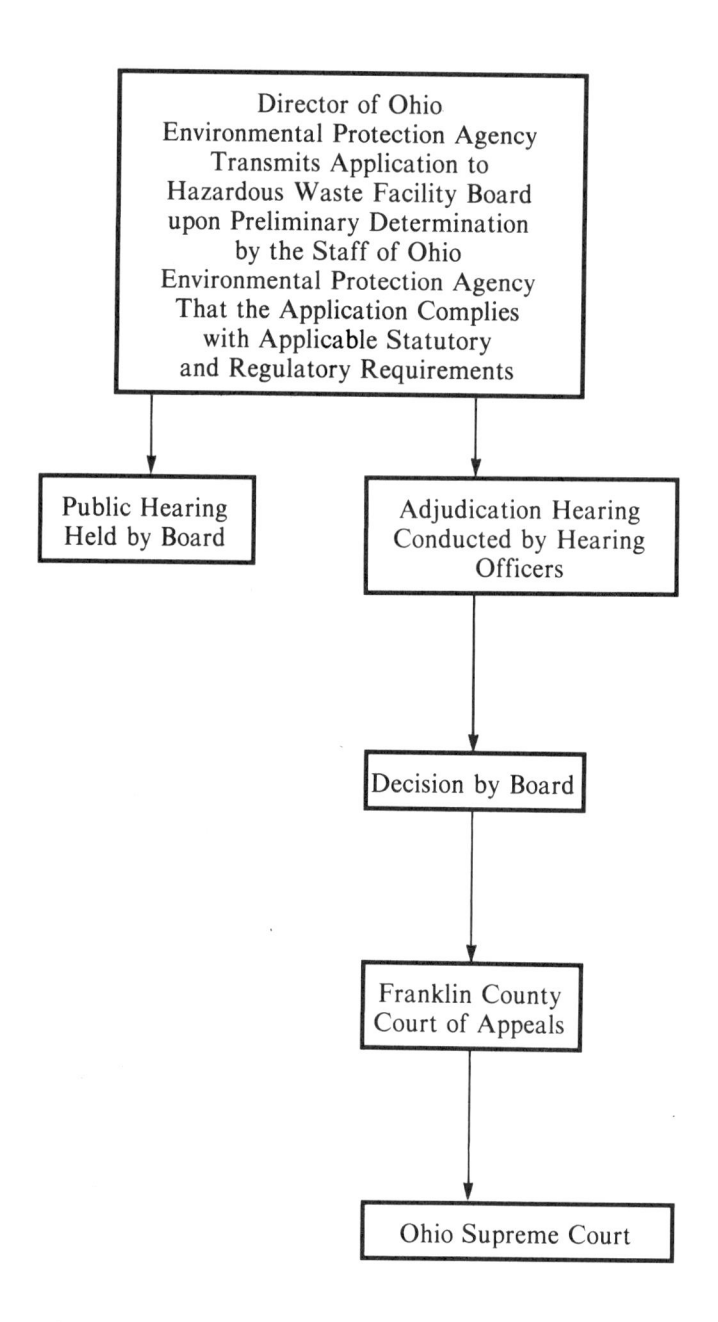

```
┌─────────────────────────────────┐
│     Director of Ohio            │
│ Environmental Protection Agency │
│    Transmits Application to     │
│   Hazardous Waste Facility Board│
│   upon Preliminary Determination│
│       by the Staff of Ohio      │
│ Environmental Protection Agency │
│  That the Application Complies  │
│    with Applicable Statutory    │
│    and Regulatory Requirements  │
└─────────────────────────────────┘
         │                │
         ▼                ▼
┌─────────────────┐  ┌─────────────────────┐
│ Public Hearing  │  │ Adjudication Hearing│
│ Held by Board   │  │ Conducted by Hearing│
│                 │  │      Officers       │
└─────────────────┘  └─────────────────────┘
                              │
                              ▼
                     ┌─────────────────┐
                     │ Decision by Board│
                     └─────────────────┘
                              │
                              ▼
                     ┌─────────────────┐
                     │ Franklin County │
                     │ Court of Appeals│
                     └─────────────────┘
                              │
                              ▼
                     ┌─────────────────┐
                     │Ohio Supreme Court│
                     └─────────────────┘
```

Chapter 13

Ohio Department of Human Services

By Robert L. Mullinax, Esq.

13.01 Introduction
13.02 RC Chapter 119 hearings for providers
13.03 Reconsideration process for hospital prospective payments
13.04 State hearing procedures for applicants and recipients

CHARTS

13.05 Organizational chart, Department of Human Services
13.06 Adjudication process/Chapter 119 proceedings, Department of Human Services
13.07 Adjudication process/State hearing process, Department of Human Services

13.01 Introduction

The Ohio Department of Human Services (ODHS)[1] is the state agency responsible for the operation of all public assistance programs including Medicaid, Aid to Dependent Children, General Relief, and food stamps. It also has certain responsibilities for social services, adoption, assistance, foster care licensing and maintenance, child day care licensing, adult protective services, child abuse and neglect services, refugee assistance, and child support enforcement. The Ohio public assistance programs are administered by eighty-eight county departments of human services under the supervision of the ODHS.

The responsibilities of ODHS involve two distinct groups of people affected by departmental actions: those who receive assistance and services and those who provide services. Due to the nature of issues raised by these two distinct interests, separate administrative hearing systems are provided. The ODHS Office of Legal Services administers both provider and recipient hearings on behalf of the director. Attorney referees conduct provider hearings, which are of two types: (1) provider appeals pursuant to RC Chapter 119 and (2) reconsideration procedures for hospitals under the prospective reimbursement system. Recipient hearings are the responsibility of the Bureau of State Hearings, which is supervised by the Office of Legal Services. Recipient hearings are conducted by nonattorney hearing officers who are from the five ODHS district offices.

Each hearing system operates independently under its own set of administrative rules. All hearings involve a very complex framework of regulations and administration and may involve issues of federal, state, and county rules, regulations, and administrative procedures. As a result, practice before the ODHS has become very specialized.

---
[1] Formerly Ohio Department of Public Welfare.

CROSS REFERENCES

State hearings, OAC Ch 5101:1-35
General information, OAC Ch 5101:3-1
Coverage and limitations; hospital services, OAC Ch 5101:3-2
Adjudication hearings, OAC Ch 5101:3-50
Fair hearings, OAC Ch 5101:4-9

Medical assistance programs, RC Ch 5111

13.02 RC Chapter 119 hearings for providers

An adjudication order pursuant to RC Chapter 119 is required whenever ODHS proposes to take any action based upon a final fiscal audit of a Medicaid provider or proposes to enter, refuses to enter, suspends, terminates, or refuses to renew a provider agreement with a Medicaid provider.[2] Furthermore, ODHS orders revoking, suspending, or taking other action relating to licenses of other providers must also be made pursuant to RC Chapter 119.[3] These other providers include providers of child day care services,[4] child foster care services,[5] and adult foster care.[6]

The appropriate ODHS bureau sends providers proposed adjudication orders by registered mail, return receipt requested. Adjudication orders include the reasons for the action, the laws or rules involved, and a notice of the right to a hearing if a request is made within thirty days of the notice.

Hearing requests are made to the Ohio Department of Human Services, Office of Legal Services. When a request is received, the Office of Legal Services determines whether it is timely. If the request is untimely, a letter denying the hearing request will be sent to the provider or attorney. After the denial letter is mailed, the Department will issue a final and binding adjudication order adopting and ratifying the allegations contained in the original notice and will implement the proposed action.[7] If the hearing request is timely, the Office of Legal Services will assign a docket number to be used by all parties on briefs, motions, and other written communications. The docket number contains the year and sequence of the receipt of the hearing request and identifies the ODHS bureau which proposed the action. At this time, ODHS assigns the referee, who is an attorney appointed by the director to conduct adjudication hearings and may be employed by or under contract to the Department.[8]

The Office of Legal Services will then notify the provider or representative of the name of the referee and the date, time, and place of the adjudication hearing. Although ODHS will schedule the hearing for a date seven to

---

[2] RC 5111.06; OAC 5101:3-1-57. See Text Ch 3, Adjudication.
[3] RC 119.06.
[4] RC 5104.02, RC 5104.03.
[5] RC 5103.03.
[6] RC 5103.31.
[7] OAC 5101:3-50-11.
[8] RC 119.09.

fifteen days after the hearing request,[9] ODHS usually will, upon its own motion and in the same notice, postpone the adjudication hearing and schedule a prehearing conference.[10] ODHS will send a copy of this notice to the Attorney General who then assigns a lawyer to represent ODHS.[11]

The prehearing conference will generally be scheduled two to three weeks after the hearing request is received. The referees are reluctant to grant continuances, but if there is a scheduling conflict, the referee may reschedule the prehearing conference to a date before the originally scheduled date if all parties agree.

Both the provider and assistant attorney general representing the Department are required to submit a prehearing questionnaire prior to the scheduled conference. This questionnaire, enclosed with the scheduling notice, requires the identification of specific issues of fact and law, exhibits, witnesses, and requests for discovery. While the questionnaire may be amended after the prehearing conference to include more specific information, counsel for the parties should make every effort to provide specific information prior to the prehearing conference.

The prehearing conference is an informal forum designed to provide for the resolution and narrowing of issues of fact and law. It usually takes less than one hour. Representatives of the ODHS bureau responsible for the proposed action attend the conference and are generally familiar with the details of the case and the documents upon which the action is based. Requests for discovery will usually be resolved in an informal manner at this time, while audit work papers, copies of rules, and other documents are made available at a mutually agreeable time. It is generally best to review the documents before requesting copies as the Department requires payment, at cost, for all copies produced.

All requests for formal discovery and prehearing briefing should be made at the prehearing conference. While not binding, the Ohio Rules of Civil Procedure serve as a guide to the prehearing proceedings. However, as a practical matter, the referee will establish a schedule for conducting discovery and the submission of briefs at the conference.

The referee will also establish a date for the final adjudication hearing and set a date for the submission of final hearing statements. Unless special circumstances exist, or prehearing discovery or briefing requires a longer time, the final hearing will be held approximately thirty days after the prehearing conference. The final hearing statements should state issues of fact and law to be presented at the hearing, as well as list proposed witnesses and exhibits, and state any stipulations of the parties.

After the conference, the referee will issue a prehearing order. All agreements reached and dates established should be included in the order, with any other requirements set by the referee for the orderly conduct of the

---

[9] RC 119.07, RC 119.08.
[10] RC 119.09.
[11] RC 119.10.

proceedings. This order is a part of the record. Additional prehearing orders may be issued as the referee deems necessary, especially when the parties brief issues of law before the hearing.

Most hearing requests are resolved informally through settlement negotiations prior to the final hearing. Only ten per cent of hearings requested are resolved through an adjudication hearing. Liberal use of informal discovery, access to ODHS staff, and a general departmental willingness to resolve disputes contribute to the settlements. The formal nature of the adjudication hearing, the complex issues, and the possibility that the hearing will last several days are also major reasons why settlement frequently occurs prior to the hearing. Final adjudication hearings range from one-half to five days with the majority lasting one or two days.

A stenographic record is made of all ODHS hearings at the agency's expense.[12] The stenographer will generally mark exhibits prior to the hearing and administer oaths or affirmations. Hearing transcripts customarily may be secured directly from the stenographer.

The Department is represented by the same assistant attorney general who appeared at the prehearing conference. The RC Chapter 119 coordinator or an equivalent person from the relevant ODHS bureau will usually represent the director at the hearing. The provider may be represented "by an attorney or by such other representative as is lawfully permitted to practice before the agency in question."

Brief opening statements by both parties are encouraged. The Department will present its case first, and both parties are provided a full opportunity to cross-examine the opposing party's witnesses. Both parties may call rebuttal witnesses. Formal rules of evidence do not apply to these proceedings; however, the Ohio Rules of Civil Procedure and the Ohio Rules of Evidence are used as guidelines by the referee on any motions or objections made by a party.[13] If the referee refuses to admit evidence, the party offering the evidence shall make a proffer thereof.[14]

While neither the Ohio Revised Code nor the Ohio Administrative Code addresses burden of proof in ODHS hearings, generally accepted administrative law principles apply. A party asserting the affirmative of an issue has the burden of proof.[15] In effect ODHS will have the burden of proving the finding upon which the proposed adjudication order is based while the provider has the burden of proving the issues it affirmatively asserts. However, any audit report, report of examination, exit conference report, or report of final settlement issued by the Department and entered into evidence is considered prima facie evidence of what it asserts.[16]

---

[12] RC 119.09.
[13] OAC 5101:3-50-22.
[14] RC 119.09; OAC 5101:3-50-22.
[15] Am Jur 2d: 2, Administrative Law § 391.
[16] OAC 5101:3-50-22.

At the conclusion of the hearing, the referee will determine whether posthearing briefs will be requested and the dates for submission of briefs and replies. Most parties and referees request posthearing briefs containing proposed findings of fact and conclusions of law in addition to arguments which the party wishes to advance.

After the receipt of posthearing briefs and the transcript, the referee will issue a written report containing findings of fact, conclusions of law, and recommendations.[17] This written report is filed with the ODHS Office of Legal Services, which mails a copy to the provider or counsel within five days of receipt.[18]

Within ten days of receipt of the referee's written report, the provider may file written objections with the ODHS Office of Legal Services.[19] An extension of time to file objections may be granted for good cause at the discretion of the chief legal counsel. The objections should not be a reargument of the entire case but should be directed at those particular sections of the referee's written report that the provider believes are incorrect. All supporting arguments of law and fact are to be included in the objections when filed.

Additional testimony or evidence may be taken as directed by the chief legal counsel. The referee's written report, all timely filed objections, and any additional evidence shall be considered in issuing the final adjudication order. Any modifications or disapproval of the hearing referee's recommendations will be explained when the final order is issued by the director. ODHS orders are appealable, pursuant to RC 119.12, to the Franklin County Court of Common Pleas. The provider must give notice of the appeal to the Office of Legal Services within fifteen days of the mailing of the final order of adjudication to the provider.[20]

CROSS REFERENCES

See Text Ch 3

13.03 Reconsideration process for hospital prospective payments

A specialized system for hospitals has been established by OAC Chapter 5101:3-2 for reconsideration of decisions made by ODHS regarding Diagnosis Related Groups (DRG) prospective payments. The new reconsideration procedures were effective October 1, 1984; therefore, to date there has been no experience with this new system. However, a general outline of how the reconsideration process is expected to work may be helpful.

Determinations made by ODHS regarding payments, necessity and delivery of services, proper application of rules relating to setting peer group rates, committed capital costs, and most other determinations and rule applications in the operation of the DRG prospective payment system are subject

---

[17] OAC 5101:3-50-24(A).
[18] OAC 5101:3-50-24(B).
[19] RC 119.09.
[20] OAC 5101:3-50-27.

to the reconsideration process.[21] The ODHS administrative rules establishing the reconsideration process require an understanding of the complex and technical prospective payment system for hospitals. The issues determined by the specific actions made or proposed by ODHS are whether (1) a hospital must first seek a review by a medical review entity or resubmit corrected billing data;[22] (2) ODHS provides a notice and opportunity for a hearing before the proposed action;[23] (3) a "special appeal" is provided for hospitals serving a disproportionate number of low income patients or for rehabilitative and neonatal specialty services;[24] and (4) the issue is not appealable.[25] Regardless of any special procedural requirements imposed by the rules relating to the specific actions, all reconsideration requests are to be made in writing to the Office of Legal Services, should state the specific reasons for the request, and should summarize the supporting documents.[26] All supporting documents are attached to the reconsideration request.[27]

All reconsideration requests received from a particular hospital during specified reconsideration periods will be consolidated for review. The reconsideration periods are as follows: October 1, 1984 through December 31, 1984; January 1, 1985 through June 30, 1985; July 1, 1985 through December 31, 1985; and every six months thereafter.[28] The ODHS Deputy Director for Medicaid Administration will review all requests and supporting documents received from a particular hospital during a reconsideration period. Within forty-five days of the end of the reconsideration period, the deputy director will prepare a written report indicating whether the initial determination is sustained, overruled, or amended and the reason for this decision. The hospital will then be given fifteen days to accept or reject each decision in this report. All decisions not accepted by the hospital will be scheduled for a hearing.[29]

All reconsideration hearings will be conducted by an attorney hearing officer. The hearings are to be informal; the rules of evidence and procedure do not apply. The hearing will be recorded for the benefit of the hearing officer;[30] however, the hospital and ODHS may agree to submit the entire case in writing.[31]

The hearing officer is required to issue findings of fact, conclusions of law, and recommendations. The hospital has fifteen days following receipt of the

---

[21] OAC 5101:3-2-0712(B).
[22] OAC 5101:3-2-0712(B)(2)(e), (C)(1)(b).
[23] OAC 5101:3-2-0712(C)(1)(b).
[24] OAC 5101:3-2-0712(E), (F) (Special appeals are to be submitted to the director of the ODHS.).
[25] OAC 5101:3-2-0712(G).
[26] OAC 5101:3-2-0712(C)(1).
[27] OAC 5101:3-2-0712(C)(4).
[28] OAC 5101:3-2-0712(C)(3).
[29] OAC 5101:3-2-0712(C)(4).
[30] OAC 5101:3-2-0712(C)(5), (6).
[31] OAC 5101:3-2-0712(C)(6)(e).

hearing officer's report to file written objections with the director of ODHS,[32] who issues the final administrative decision of the ODHS.[33]

13.04 State hearing procedures for applicants and recipients

Any action, failure to act, or delay in acting by a county department of human services (CDHS) may be contested by any applicant for or recipient of public assistance by requesting, in writing or orally, a state hearing.[34] A state hearing may also be requested to challenge the level of benefits awarded to the recipient. A lawyer or other representative may request the hearing but must show written authorization from the appellant.[35] Hearing requests may be made at either the local CDHS or through the ODHS Bureau of State Hearings.

A state hearing request must be received by the CDHS or ODHS within ninety days of the action being appealed. However, if the hearing is requested because of a proposed action to reduce or terminate benefits, the request must be received by the CDHS or ODHS within fifteen days of the date of the notice to insure continued benefits pending the hearing decision.[36] The payment of continued benefits may result in an overpayment if the appellant loses the appeal.[37] Retroactive benefits may be awarded to a prevailing appellant.

When a request is accepted, the ODHS Bureau of State Hearings will notify the appellant and authorized representative of the time and place for the hearing at least ten days in advance. All hearings are conducted at the local CDHS unless the appellant is physically unable to attend.[38]

Prior to the hearing, the CDHS prepares an "Appeals Summary," setting forth the position of the CDHS and the rules and evidence upon which it intends to rely.[39] By contacting the local CDHS, the appellant or representative may obtain a copy of the "Appeals Summary," relevant case records, and rules[40] at no charge.

The hearing is informal and conducted by a hearing officer, who usually is not a lawyer, from one of the five ODHS district offices.[41] The CDHS is most frequently represented by the appellant's caseworker, although in some counties it is represented by a specialized hearing representative.

---

[32] OAC 5101:3-2-0712(C)(7).
[33] OAC 5101:3-2-0712(C)(8).
[34] OAC 5101:1-35-01, OAC 5101:4-9-01. See also 45 CFR 205, 10(a)(5), 7 CFR 273.15(a).
[35] OAC 5101:1-35-03, OAC 5101:4-9-03(B).
[36] OAC 5101:1-35-04, OAC 5101:4-9-07.
[37] OAC 5101:1-35-07(F), OAC 5101:4-9-11(D)(2).
[38] OAC 5101:1-35-06, OAC 5101:4-9-09.
[39] OAC 5101:1-35-05(A), OAC 5101:4-9-05(B).
[40] OAC 5101:1-35-06(H), OAC 5101:4-9-05(C).
[41] OAC 5101:1-35-06(I), OAC 5101:4-9-09 (District offices are located in Canton, Cincinnati, Cleveland, Columbus, and Toledo.).

The CDHS presents its case first, which frequently consists of a summary of the facts and applicable rules along with copies of relevant documents. The appellant will testify briefly and present supporting documents. Even though no formal rules of evidence are applied, the appellant has the right to cross-examine and present testimony from other witnesses. The typical hearing lasts approximately thirty minutes.

The hearing decision must be based on the evidence presented at the hearing and the rules contained in the applicable ODHS manual.[42] Effective January 1, 1985, ODHS is tape-recording all state hearings; previously, the hearing officer's notes and written evidence were used to determine the contents of the hearing record.

An appellant who is dissatisfied with the hearing decision may address a written appeal to the Director, Ohio Department of Human Services. All arguments, including federal and state laws and regulations, and supporting evidence should be included in this appeal. A lawyer in the ODHS Office of Legal Services will review the written administrative appeal and the hearing record and will recommend to the director whether the initial hearing decision should be sustained, overruled, or modified. The decision of the director is final. There is currently no judicial review of state hearing decisions.[43]

Final administrative action must be taken within ninety days of the hearing request in all cases except those which involve solely food stamp issues. In food stamp cases, the hearing decision must be issued within sixty days of the request with an additional ten days allowed for compliance with the decision.[44]

While the above description gives some guidance to lawyers and other advocates representing applicants and recipients, it should be noted that there are specialized state hearing procedures for particular circumstances. Among these specialized procedures are the following: (1) food stamp fraud disqualification;[45] (2) Aid to Dependent Children overpayments;[46] (3) General Relief Medicaid Services;[47] (4) emergency assistance;[48] (5) the Primary Alternative Care and Treatment (PACT) Program;[49] (6) Preadmission Certification for Elective Inpatient Hospital Admission;[50] and (7) Client Monthly Reporting.[51] Representation of clients in state hearings has become

---

[42] OAC 5101:1-35-07, OAC 5101:4-9-11.

[43] Bolin v White, 51 App(2d) 92, 367 NE(2d) 63 (Franklin 1976); Lehew v Rhodes, 23 App(2d) 102, 261 NE(2d) 280 (Franklin 1970).

[44] OAC 5101:1-35-07(J)(1); 45 CFR 205.10(a)(16), 7 CFR 273.15(C)(1).

[45] OAC 5101:4-9-17; 7 CFR 273.16.

[46] OAC 5101:1-35-10.

[47] OAC 5101:1-35-15.

[48] OAC 5101:1-35-17.

[49] OAC 5101:1-35-19 to OAC 5101:1-35-23.

[50] OAC 5101:1-35-25, OAC 5101:1-35-27.

[51] A state support center for all local legal aid programs may provide assistance and materials in some public assistance cases. This support center is partially supported by the Ohio State Bar Association. For assistance, contact the Ohio State Legal Services Association, 155 North High Street, Columbus, Ohio 43215. Telephone (614) 221-2668 or 1-800-282-3586 (toll-free).

a specialized practice primarily involving legal aid attorneys and paralegals. More detailed information on these specialized procedures should be available from local legal aid programs.

CHARTS

13.05 Organizational chart, Department of Human Services

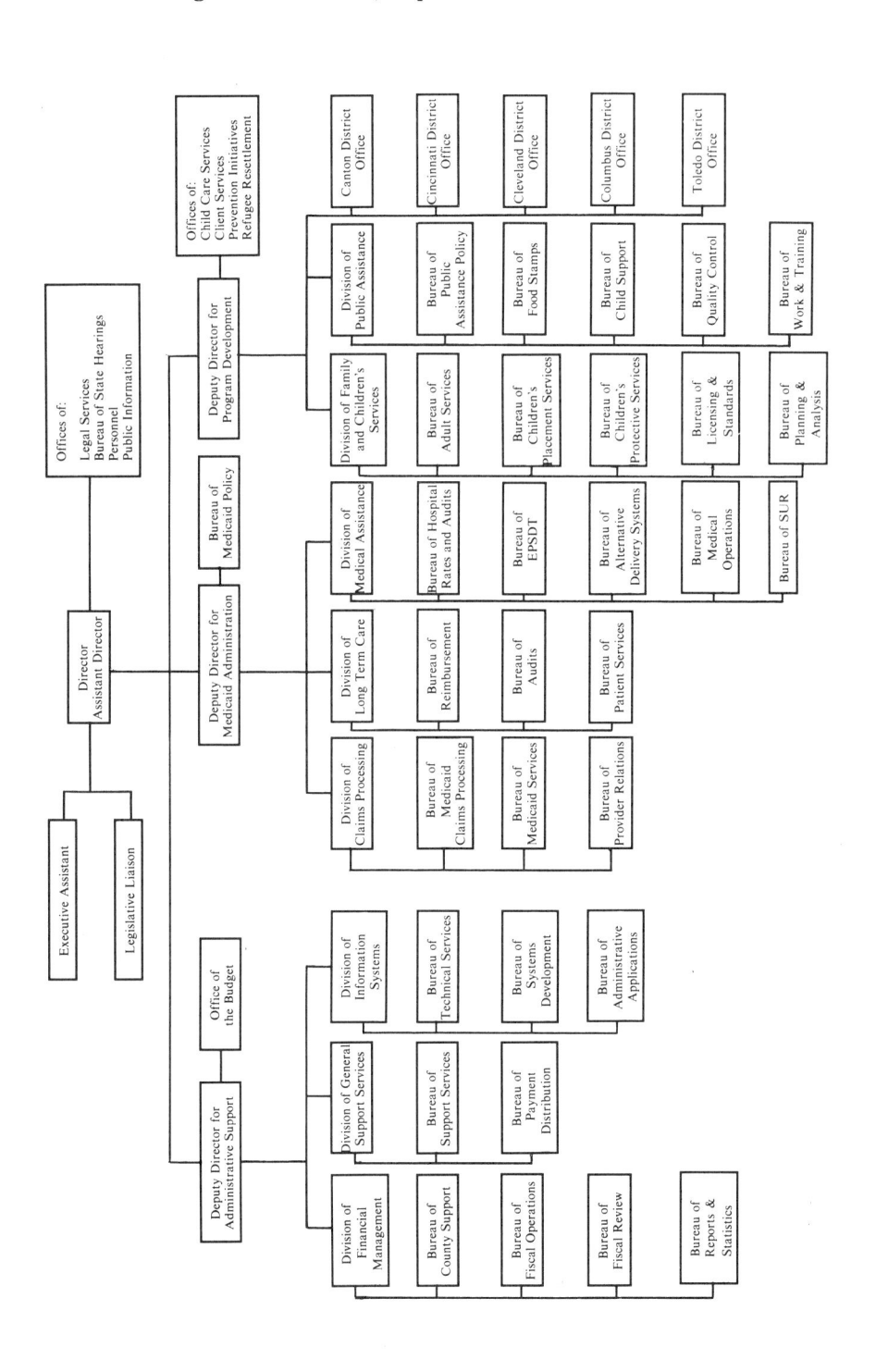

13.06 Adjudication process/Chapter 119 proceedings, Department of Human Services

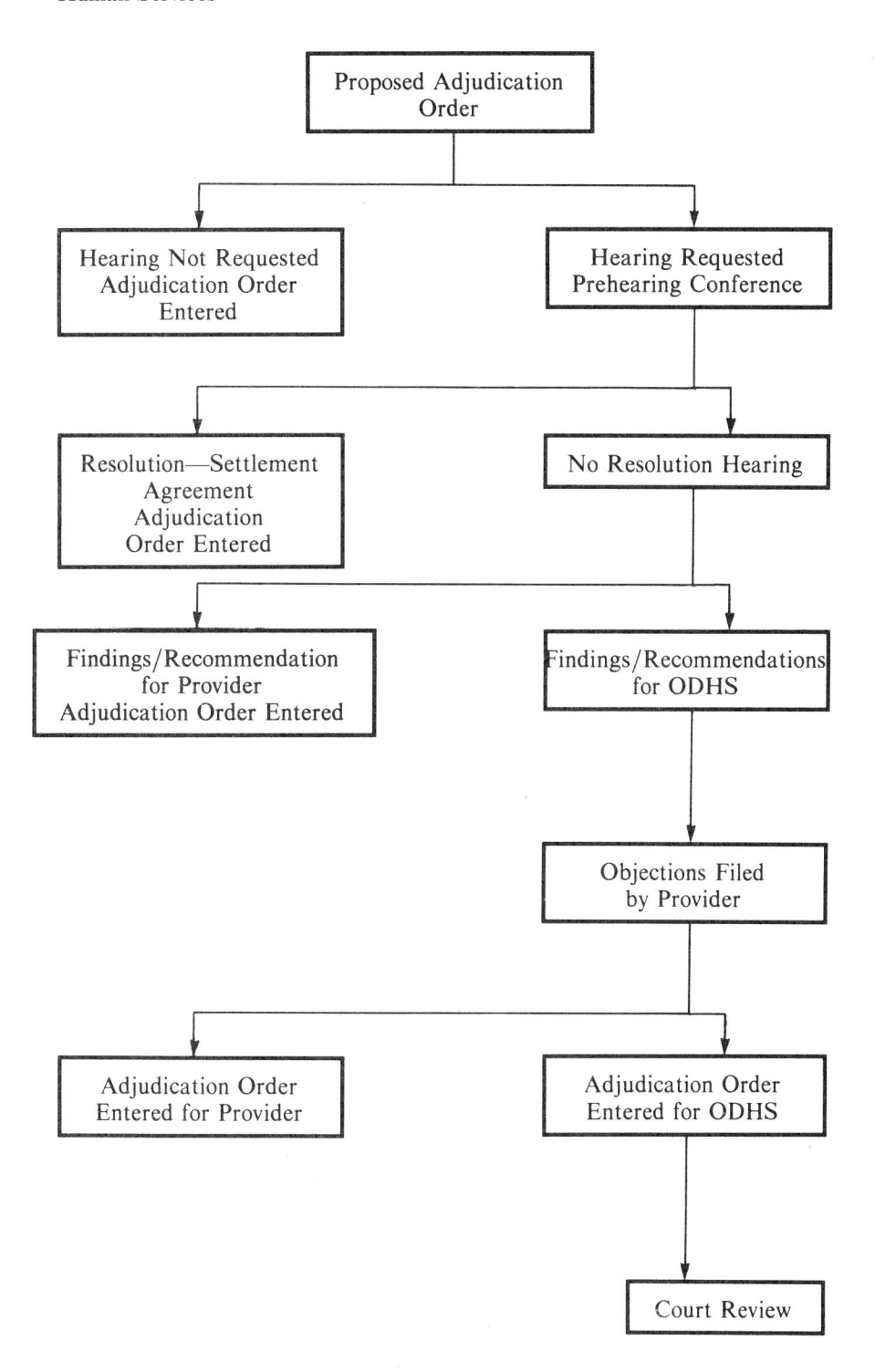

```
                    ┌─────────────────────┐
                    │ Proposed Adjudication│
                    │       Order          │
                    └──────────┬──────────┘
              ┌────────────────┴────────────────┐
              ▼                                 ▼
  ┌─────────────────────┐           ┌─────────────────────┐
  │ Hearing Not Requested│           │   Hearing Requested │
  │  Adjudication Order  │           │ Prehearing Conference│
  │       Entered        │           └──────────┬──────────┘
  └─────────────────────┘                       │
                         ┌─────────────────────┴────────┐
                         ▼                              ▼
              ┌─────────────────────┐      ┌─────────────────────┐
              │Resolution—Settlement│      │  No Resolution Hearing│
              │      Agreement       │      └──────────┬──────────┘
              │    Adjudication      │                 │
              │    Order Entered     │                 │
              └──────────┬──────────┘                 │
                         ▼                              ▼
              ┌─────────────────────┐      ┌─────────────────────┐
              │Findings/Recommendation│    │Findings/Recommendations│
              │     for Provider      │    │      for ODHS         │
              │  Adjudication Order   │    └──────────┬──────────┘
              │       Entered         │                │
              └─────────────────────┘                  ▼
                                          ┌─────────────────────┐
                                          │   Objections Filed   │
                                          │     by Provider      │
                                          └──────────┬──────────┘
                           ┌─────────────────────────┴────┐
                           ▼                              ▼
              ┌─────────────────────┐      ┌─────────────────────┐
              │  Adjudication Order  │      │  Adjudication Order  │
              │ Entered for Provider │      │   Entered for ODHS   │
              └─────────────────────┘      └──────────┬──────────┘
                                                      ▼
                                          ┌─────────────────────┐
                                          │     Court Review     │
                                          └─────────────────────┘
```

13.07 Adjudication process/State hearing process, Department of Human Services

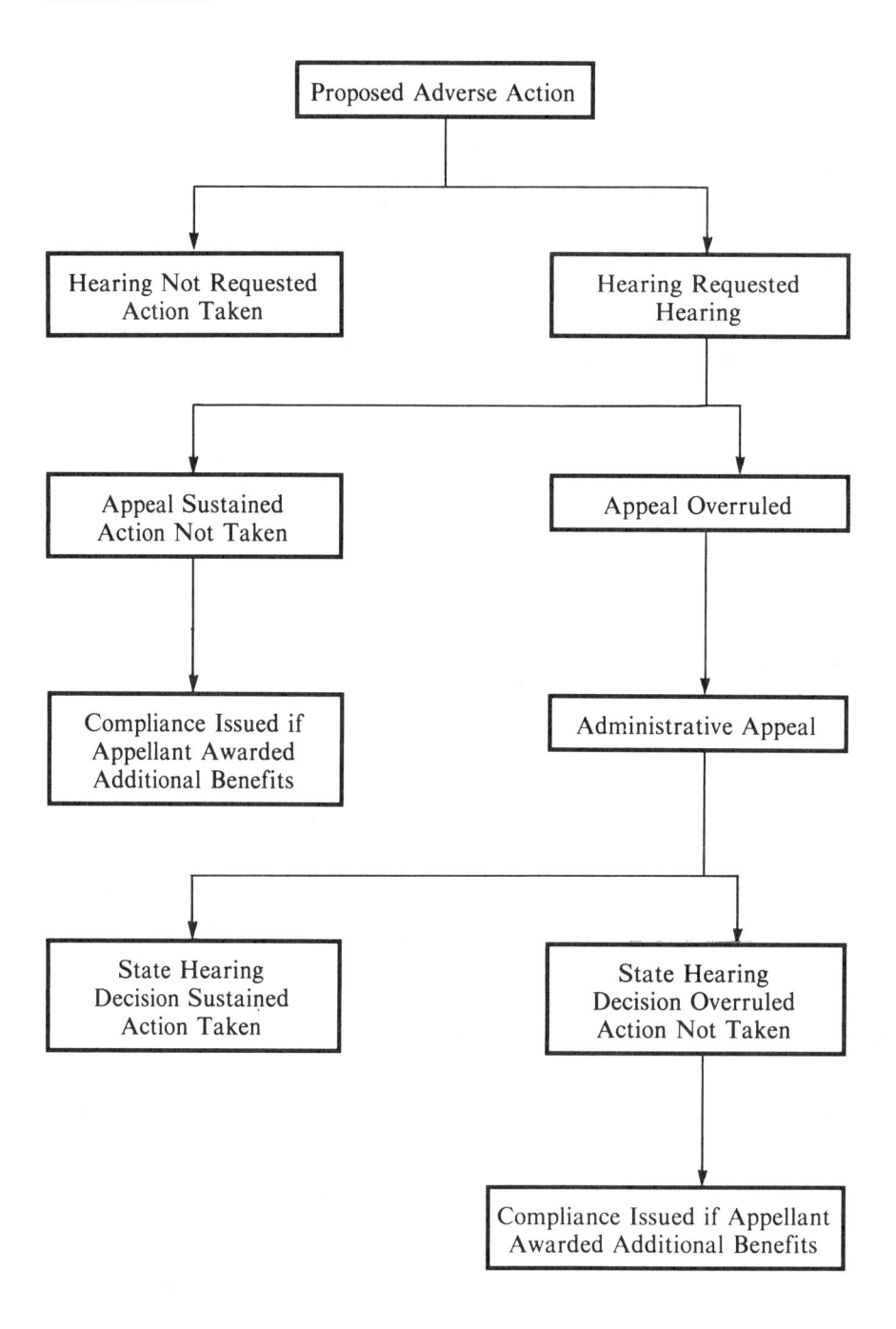

```
                    ┌──────────────────────┐
                    │ Proposed Adverse Action │
                    └──────────┬───────────┘
                               │
                ┌──────────────┴──────────────┐
                ▼                             ▼
      ┌───────────────────┐         ┌───────────────────┐
      │ Hearing Not Requested │     │ Hearing Requested │
      │   Action Taken    │         │      Hearing      │
      └───────────────────┘         └─────────┬─────────┘
                                              │
                              ┌───────────────┴───────────────┐
                              ▼                               ▼
                   ┌───────────────────┐           ┌───────────────────┐
                   │ Appeal Sustained  │           │  Appeal Overruled │
                   │ Action Not Taken  │           │                   │
                   └─────────┬─────────┘           └─────────┬─────────┘
                             ▼                               ▼
                   ┌───────────────────┐           ┌───────────────────┐
                   │ Compliance Issued if │        │ Administrative Appeal │
                   │ Appellant Awarded │           │                   │
                   │ Additional Benefits│          └─────────┬─────────┘
                   └───────────────────┘                     │
                                              ┌──────────────┴──────────────┐
                                              ▼                             ▼
                                    ┌───────────────────┐       ┌───────────────────┐
                                    │  State Hearing    │       │  State Hearing    │
                                    │ Decision Sustained│       │ Decision Overruled│
                                    │   Action Taken    │       │ Action Not Taken  │
                                    └───────────────────┘       └─────────┬─────────┘
                                                                          ▼
                                                            ┌───────────────────────────┐
                                                            │ Compliance Issued if Appellant│
                                                            │  Awarded Additional Benefits  │
                                                            └───────────────────────────┘
```

Chapter 15

Ohio Department of Liquor Control and the Liquor Control Commission

By Gary L. Jones, Esq.

15.01	Introduction
15.02	Acquisition of a new permit
15.03	Purchase of existing permit business
15.04	Closing authority and safekeeping
15.05	Violations and appeals

FORMS

15.06	Retail permit definitions/privileges

CHARTS

15.07	Organizational chart, Department of Liquor Control
15.08	Adjudication process, Department of Liquor Control

15.01 Introduction

RC Title 43 regulates the production, sale, and distribution of beer, wine, and spirituous liquors through the Department of Liquor Control. The various types of retail permits issued in Ohio and the corresponding annual fees are listed in the appendix.

Rulemaking power is vested primarily in the three-member Ohio Liquor Control Commission, which also holds hearings on all violations of the liquor law by permit holders.[1] In addition, the Commission hears appeals from any Department of Liquor Control action adverse to the interest of an applicant for or holder of a permit.[2]

CROSS REFERENCES

General provisions, OAC Ch 4301:1-1

Liquor control law, RC Ch 4301
Liquor permits, RC Ch 4303

15.02 Acquisition of a new permit

(A) Application

Application for a new liquor permit, as well as transfer of a liquor permit, is made on forms supplied by the Department of Liquor Control. Availability of new permits is regulated by a population quota system. Each city or township is allocated a certain number of each permit class, based upon its population. The Department maintains a record of available permits and

---

[1] RC 4301.03.
[2] *Id.*, RC 4301.28.

applications known as the "quota register."³ Quota information in a particular taxing district is readily available from the Department.

The local option status as to the sale of intoxicating liquor (whether the area is "dry") also affects the availability of a new permit.⁴ While the Department routinely verifies the local option status for any new application filed, preliminary information should be obtained from the county board of elections. Counsel should obtain this information in writing prior to the client's becoming obligated to a lease or purchase of property for the purpose of engaging in a liquor business.

Applications are processed by the Department in order of their filing date as permits become available. Acceptance of the application for an available quota opening should be verified before the applicant acts in reliance on the availability of the required permit. RC 4303.26 states that the department must act on an application within fifteen days. If a permit is available for a requested location, if the location is a completed structure, and if there are no objections as discussed below,⁵ the Department normally requires four to five weeks to act on the application.

(B) Objections to issuance of a new permit

Local legislative authorities and any school, church, library, public playground, or township park within 500 feet of the proposed permit premises are notified by the Department of Liquor Control of every pending permit and have thirty days in which to object. Objectors are entitled to a hearing on any objections to the issuance of the permit.⁶

Since this hearing procedure can require sixty to ninety days to complete, the possibility of an objection should be considered in determining the time required to obtain the new permit. Many churches and schools receiving notice routinely object to the issuance of the permit. Often the authorities in charge of the nearby church have been through the process before and know that they are not likely to succeed in their objection but feel the need at least to make the attempt on moral grounds.

Hearings on these objections are held by hearing officers of the Department of Liquor Control and tend to be somewhat informal. The objecting party presents evidence first. While the Ohio Rules of Evidence apply, the hearing officers prefer to admit most testimony to provide the objecting parties as complete a hearing of their views as possible. The applicant may then present evidence in rebuttal. Since the institution making objection has the option, these hearings are usually held in the county seat of the county of the applicant.⁷

The objection will not be sustained on merely moral grounds. To prevail, the objector must show secular reasons why the proposed permit would be a

---

³RC 4303.29; OAC 4301:1-1-64.
⁴RC 4301.32.
⁵See Text 15.02(B), Objections to issuance of a new permit.
⁶RC 4303.26.
⁷*Id.*

detriment to the community. On a new permit application, the objector faces a difficult task because there is generally no history to establish a detriment to the community; any such testimony should be (and generally is) discounted as speculative. The objector's burden is substantially lightened on a renewal application when there has been a history of prostitution, sales to minors, or other prohibited activity. However, on an annual renewal, only county commissioners, township trustees, or the legislative authority of a municipal corporation have the right to object.

If the objections are sustained and the application rejected, the applicant may appeal to the Liquor Control Commission.[8] The objecting parties must appear and present their objections at the Commission hearing held in Columbus. The notice of appeal must be filed with the Liquor Control Commission within thirty days of the Department's order.

15.03 Purchase of existing permit business

This chapter will not review all of the considerations in representing a client in the purchase of a business that holds a liquor permit. For most purposes, the purchase of a carry-out business or restaurant does not differ from the purchase of any other type of business; however, the acquisition of a going concern that also holds a liquor permit does contain some additional pitfalls. Initially, counsel should verify the status of the existing permit with the Department to determine if any violations or any other departmental action is pending against the permit.

The timing of the permit application is very important. Unless there are objections to the transfer (as in the case of a new application previously discussed),[9] the process can be expected to take a minimum of four to five weeks. The Department is normally more efficient than the six to eight weeks stated on the application. RC 4303.27 prohibits the operation of the permit business unless the owner or operator of the business is the permit holder. The Department takes the position that the permit holder must have at least a fifty per cent interest in the profits of the permit business; thus, the new owner may not operate for any period under the former owner's permit. The purpose of this internally developed policy is to preclude the leasing of a permit business.

Although the transfer should be accomplished simultaneously with the closing, in efforts to save legal fees clients frequently wait until the eve of closing before consulting an attorney about the transaction. Since it is too late to obtain a transfer before the new owner assumes operation of the business, a device known as a "management agreement" has been developed.

The management agreement generally provides that the new owner will operate the permit holder's business until the approval of the transfer application. The practitioner is still faced with the Department's policy that the

---

[8] RC 4301.28.
[9] See Text 15.02(B), Objections to issuance of a new permit.

permit holder must have at least a fifty per cent financial interest in the business.

The management agreement, regardless of its validity, involves serious risks to both the buyer and the seller of the business:

(1) The Department may refuse to approve the transfer;

(2) If the operator incurs violations before the transfer, the transfer will be impeded, or at least delayed, until the violations are resolved; or

(3) If, under the management contract, the prospective owner participates in the operation, the prospective owner may incur liability (including criminal liability) for the permit holder/seller, as the prospective owner may have no indicia of ownership prior to the actual transfer of the permit. Any and all violations are attributable to the permit holder.

By far the best practice has the lawyer involved in the transaction well in advance of the closing in order to accomplish the transfer simultaneously with the closing. The transfer may be accomplished in five to six weeks if all proceeds well (although it has been known to go faster in an emergency for a thoroughly experienced lawyer and for a client who can afford to pay for the lawyer's time). To insure a speedy application, the applicant must complete and timely submit the fingerprint cards. Of course, the entire application must be timely. The application approval is to some extent at the mercy of the local law enforcement agency from which the department obtains its report; therefore, the earlier the application is filed, the better.

Again, as for the application for a new permit,[10] any school, church, library, public playground, or township park within five hundred feet of the permit premises and the local legislative authority (usually the city council) have thirty days in which to object. The objection will delay the application at least sixty days until a hearing may be held and may prevent the transfer.

Unpaid state taxes, such as sales tax or unemployment taxes, that have been certified to the Department as due and owing will prevent the transfer of a liquor permit.[11] Additionally, the transferee of a liquor permit assumes successor liability for any unpaid sales taxes of the prior permit holder, whether certified at the time of transfer or not,[12] and for unpaid unemployment taxes.[13] A request for certificates of state tax release will identify most problems, and proper escrow arrangements should be provided in the agreement.

CROSS REFERENCES

See Text 15.02(B)

---

[10] See Text 15.02(B), Objections to issuance of a new permit.
[11] RC 4303.292(A)(1)(b).
[12] RC 5739.14.
[13] RC 4141.24(F).

15.04 Closing authority and safekeeping

The closing of a permit business for more than thirty days without proper notification to the Department of Liquor Control will subject the permit holder to citation before the Liquor Control Commission and possible permit revocation. If the closing is expected to be temporary, OAC 4301:1-1-16 requires the permit holder to submit an affidavit to the Department stating the reason for the closing and the period of time that the permit business will be closed, up to a period of 180 days. Upon request of the permit holder, the closing authority may be extended for good cause beyond the initial 180-day period.[14] The Department's refusal to extend the closing authority may be appealed to the Liquor Control Commission.

RC 4303.272 requires delivery of the permit to the Department upon destruction of the premises or termination of the permit holder's tenancy. This section also provides that the permit may be renewed only once while in safekeeping with the department unless reconstruction of the premises is underway or the building to which the permit is to be transferred is under construction or reconstruction.

15.05 Violations and appeals

The Department of Liquor Control maintains a full-time staff of agents trained in the investigation of violations of the Ohio liquor law. Since this staff is comparatively small in relation to the total number of permit holders, most enforcement action by the Department originates from complaints. Anonymous complaints are accepted, and strict confidentiality of the source of any complaint is maintained by the Department.

When a permit holder is cited by the Department for a violation of the liquor law, the violation notice, specifying the nature of the charge, is delivered to the permit holder or person in charge of the premises at the time of the violation.[15] Most of the less serious offenses, especially for a first-time offender, do not justify substantial investigation and hearing preparation. Each lawyer must decide on a case-by-case basis how much investigation to do. At a minimum, he should ask his client about the existence of aggravating circumstances. The more serious circumstances require factual investigation. The Commission considers particularly serious those cases resulting from gambling, nudity, and solicitation for prostitution. In matters such as these, the Commission makes a subjective decision, by considering such elements as whether the permit holder profited from criminal activity or engaged in prohibited activity on prior occasions. Commission rules[16] and case law[17] clearly provide that the Commission may reject the transfers and renewals on its own initiative.

---

[14] OAC 4301:1-1-16.
[15] *Id.*
[16] OAC 4301:1-1-12.
[17] State ex rel Jones v Bryant, 159 OS 59, 110 NE(2d) 912 (1953); Arvay v Bd of Liquor Control, 104 App 385, 149 NE(2d) 265 (Franklin 1957).

The liquor control section of the Attorney General's office sends a letter and questionnaire to the permit holder approximately two weeks after the notice of violation is issued. The questionnaire, not statutorily mandated, is used by the Attorney General as a scheduling tool. The permit holder should complete and return the questionnaire, because if he does not or if he admits the charge(s) against him, the assistant attorney general will not subpoena witnesses to the hearing before the Liquor Control Commission. If the attorney for the permit holder appears at the hearing with witnesses, the Commission will usually grant a continuance to allow the assistant attorney general to subpoena his witnesses. As a result, the lawyer leaves with nothing accomplished and must return at a later date. This is an inconvenience that should be avoided.

Depending upon the docket of the Liquor Control Commission, a hearing on the violation will usually be set for sixty to ninety days after the violation. The permit holder and counsel listed on the questionnaire have a right to receive no fewer than fifteen days' notice of this hearing.[18]

The notice of hearing before the Liquor Control Commission will specify the time of the hearing. However, a large number of cases are usually set for hearing at the same time. Counsel should sign in with the Commission bailiff in the rear of the hearing room and make contact with an assistant attorney general to review and discuss the case, although this discussion may be conducted by telephone in advance of the hearing.

Generally, violation cases are heard first. Due to its heavy calendar, the Commission splits the cases into two groups. One group of cases is heard by only one of the three commissioners in a different hearing room. This group of cases generally includes "no-shows" and unrepresented permit holders. The single commissioner conducts the hearing more informally and more privately than the two commissioners who conduct the other hearings.

The remaining two commissioners handle the violation cases in the main hearing room. The Commission faces a heavy hearing schedule on hearing days; accordingly, the commissioners appreciate the courtesy of brief presentations by the lawyers involved. Counsel should agree to stipulate undisputed facts. The Commission may attribute improper purpose to the client if the lawyer, acting on his client's behalf, becomes unduly and unreasonably contentious.

The cases are called before the Commission when the staff of the Attorney General's office determines that the permit holder and the necessary witnesses are available. This scheduling can best be compared to that of a very busy traffic court.

Most assistant attorneys general will allow counsel to read the department investigator's report supplied to the assistant attorney general. This report, supplemented by any conversation he has had with the permit holder's attorney and with the investigator, constitutes the total information the assistant attorney general has on the case. Often the prehearing consultation

---

[18] RC 119.07; OAC 4301:1-1-65(A).

will result in an agreement on the handling of the case that may eliminate the need for the client's personal appearance on the day of the hearing. If the case is resolved by an admission before the hearing, the lawyer may be able to convince the assistant attorney general to move the case to the beginning of the day's docket.

The assistant attorney general will usually discuss plea bargain offers. The plea bargain involves dropping one or more of multiple charges in exchange for an admission to one or more other charges. The assistant attorney general cannot agree to a given penalty, although he could agree to recommend a penalty. However, the assistant attorneys general will usually decline to agree even to a recommendation. The Commission is not bound by any recommendation. There is no opportunity for discussion with the Commission on the likelihood of the acceptance or rejection of a recommendation by counsel. Frequently, the assistant attorney general will hazard his nonbinding best guess on the penalty the Commission will likely impose.

The liquor control law was recently amended to allow the Commission to impose fines for violations.[19] Formerly, the Commission could impose only suspension or revocation as a penalty. Generally, the Commission provides a first offender on a violation of lesser seriousness the option of paying a fine or suffering a license suspension. The lawyer should keep in mind, however, that the Commission has the statutory authority to revoke licenses for liquor law violations.

In determining the penalty to impose, the Commission considers the seriousness of the violation, the violation history of the permit holder, the sophistication of the permit holder, and the circumstances of the violation. For example, on a violation resulting from the sale of alcoholic beverages to a minor, the Commission may consider whether the minor looks older than his age and whether the employer has disciplined the employee involved.

Accordingly, it is often advisable to offer an explanation in mitigation of the violation. The Commission generally appreciates a brief statement by the lawyer, rather than an evidentiary presentation of the mitigating circumstances. It is unusual for the assistant attorney general to object to such a statement of facts outside the information contained in the investigation report. Without an objection, no formal evidence is necessary.

After the commissioners complete the violation hearings, the three commissioners together (unless one is absent for the day) will hear the appeals from Department of Liquor Control orders. As with violation cases, the lawyer should contact the assistant attorney general before the hearing date to discuss the case. Often, a compromise of the appeal may be reached, subject to the concurrence of the Commission. Occasionally, there are remedies which the Department, represented by the assistant attorney general, would agree to recommend to the Commission but which the Department does not feel it has the authority to implement on its own.

---

[19]RC 4301.252 (1983 H 67, eff. 10-10-83).

For either a violation or an appeals hearing, the Commission may take evidence. The moving party presents the first case-in-chief which, in both violation hearings and administrative appeals, is done by the assistant attorney general. If formal evidence is taken, the witnesses are sworn and sit on a witness stand while they present their testimony. If requested, the Commission will grant a separation of witnesses. The witnesses may be cross-examined by the party not offering them. To prove a violation, the Commission requires direct testimony. Although the rules of evidence are not strictly enforced, the Commission prefers to decide contested facts on evidence that would be admissible in a court, rather than rely on the relaxed standards of evidence technically available in administrative hearings.

After evidence is taken, the Commission will allow argument. Again the Commission appreciates brief argument that is to the point of the issues. In violation cases and contested appeals, the Commission will not announce the decision and penalty at the hearing. The decision will be mailed to the client and his attorney within two to three weeks of the hearing. In administrative appeals in which the parties have agreed to the remedy, the Commission will normally express its concerns or concurrence at the hearing, subject to a written decision later mailed to the parties.

FORMS

15.06 Retail permit definitions/privileges

C-1	Beer only in original sealed containers for carry out only	$ 63.00
C-2	Wine and certain prepackaged mixed drinks in sealed containers for carry out only	$ 94.00
D-1	Beer only for on premises consumption or in sealed containers for carry out only	$ 125.00
D-2	Wine and certain prepackaged drinks for on premises consumption or in sealed containers for carry out	$ 188.00
D-3	Spirituous liquor for on premises consumption only until 1:00 A.M.	$ 400.00
D-3A	Extension of issued permit privileges until 2:30 A.M.	$ 500.00
D-4	Beer and any intoxicating liquor to members only, for on premises consumption only until 2:30 A.M.	$ 250.00
D-5	Spirituous liquor for on premises consumption only, beer and wine for on premises, or off premises in original sealed containers, until 2:30 A.M.	$1,250.00
D-5A	(Same as D-5) for hotel or motel with 50 or more rooms for transient guests	$1,250.00
D-5B	(Same as D-5) for enclosed shopping mall	$1,250.00
D-6	Sale of intoxicating liquor on Sunday between the hours of 1:00 P.M. and midnight	variable
F	Valid for beer only until 1:00 A.M.	$ 6.00

F-1	No specific permit language (allows "B.Y.O.B." by qualified national non-profit organization at Municipal Convention Center)	$ 63.00
F-2	Beer and any intoxicating liquor by glass or container on premises only until 1:00 A.M.	$ 63.00

CHARTS

15.07 Organizational chart, Department of Liquor Control

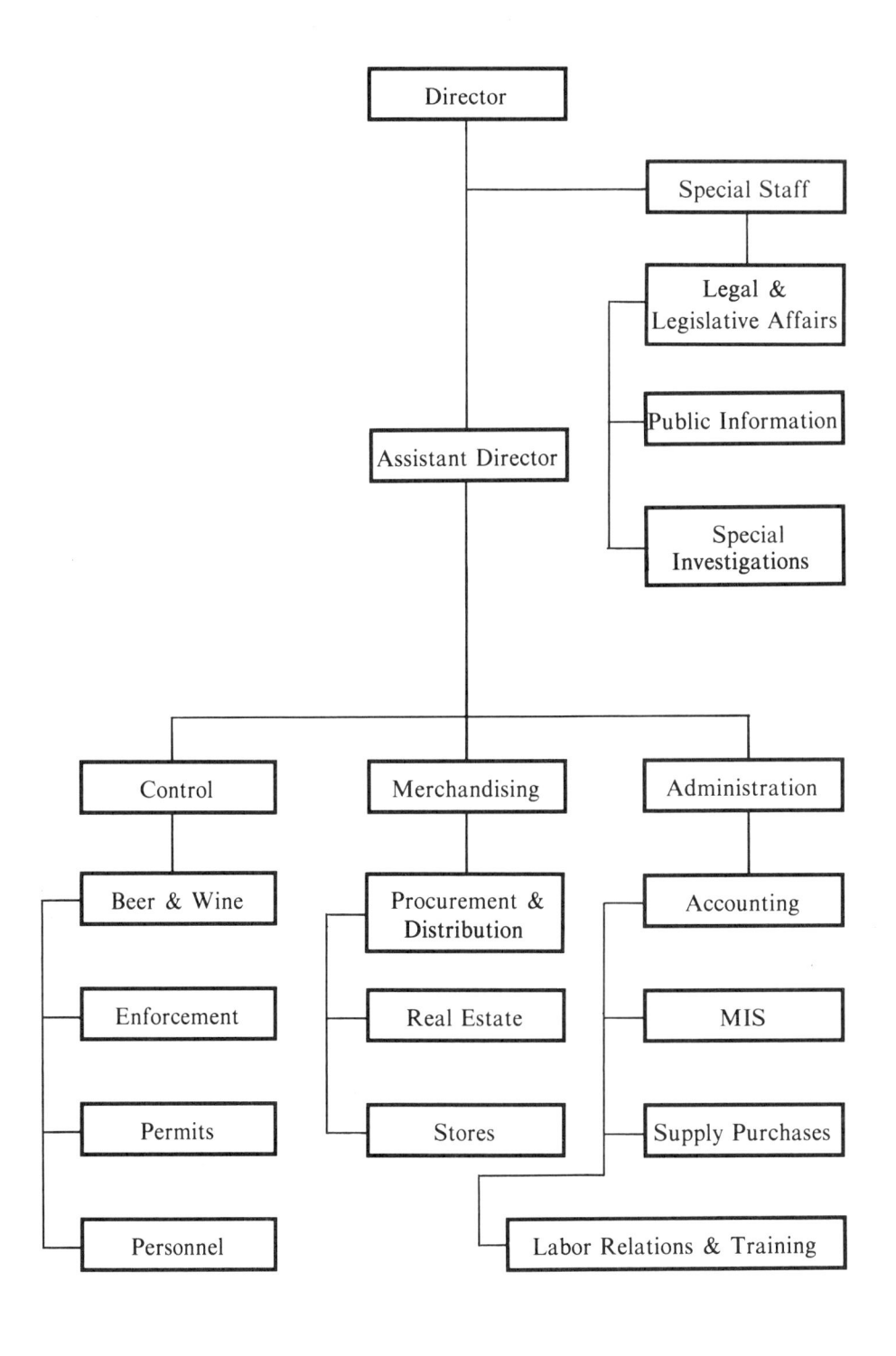

```
                            Director
                               |
                               |─────────── Special Staff
                               |                  |
                               |                  ├── Legal & Legislative Affairs
                               |                  |
                               |                  ├── Public Information
                               |                  |
                         Assistant Director        └── Special Investigations
                               |
          ┌────────────────────┼────────────────────┐
        Control           Merchandising        Administration
          |                    |                    |
        Beer & Wine      Procurement &           Accounting
          |              Distribution               |
        Enforcement           |                    MIS
          |                Real Estate              |
        Permits               |                 Supply Purchases
          |                 Stores                  |
        Personnel                             Labor Relations & Training
```

15.08 Adjudication process, Department of Liquor Control

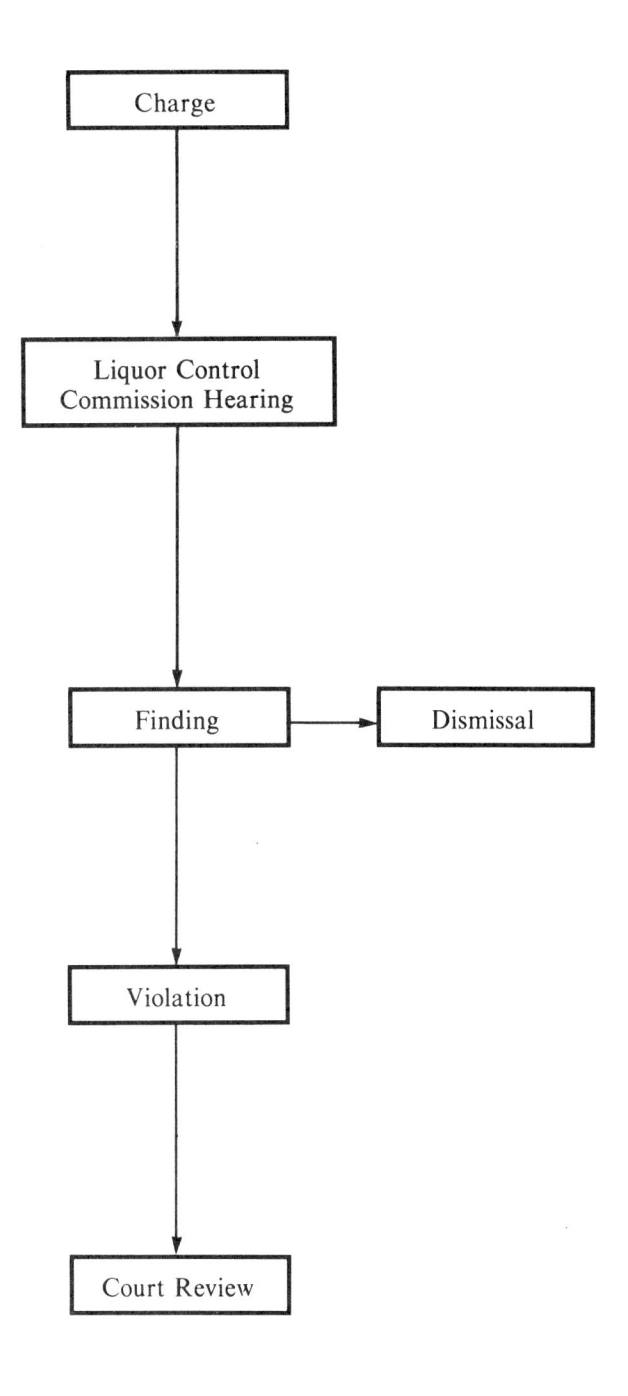

```
        ┌──────────┐
        │  Charge  │
        └────┬─────┘
             │
             ▼
   ┌───────────────────┐
   │  Liquor Control   │
   │ Commission Hearing│
   └─────────┬─────────┘
             │
             ▼
        ┌──────────┐      ┌───────────┐
        │ Finding  │─────▶│ Dismissal │
        └────┬─────┘      └───────────┘
             │
             ▼
        ┌───────────┐
        │ Violation │
        └─────┬─────┘
              │
              ▼
        ┌──────────────┐
        │ Court Review │
        └──────────────┘
```

Chapter 17

Public Utilities Commission of Ohio

By William S. Newcomb, Jr., Esq. and Sheldon A. Taft, Esq.

17.01 Introduction
17.02 Jurisdictional overview of the Commission
17.03 General hearing process
17.04 Specific types of nontransportation hearings
17.05 Motor carrier regulation
17.06 Other types of utilities

CHARTS

17.07 Organizational chart, Public Utilities Commission
17.08 Complaint proceeding, PUCO, RC 4905.26
17.09 Proceeding, PUCO, RC 4909.18
17.10 Motor carrier applications under RC Chapter 4921 or 4923, PUCO
17.11 Appellate process, PUCO

17.01 Introduction

RC 4901.02 creates the Public Utilities Commission of Ohio, consisting of five public utilities commissioners appointed by the Governor and selected from a list of qualified persons submitted to the Governor by a nominating council created by RC 4901.021. The legislation mandates specific areas of expertise as prerequisites for individuals to be considered by the nominating council and ultimately the Governor. The commissioners' terms are for five years. RC 4901.19 provides that the Commission may appoint "a secretary, attorney referees, experts, engineers, accountants, and such other officers as it may deem necessary." The offices of the Commission are located at 180 East Broad Street, Columbus, Ohio; except for certain transportation investigators and utility field inspectors, all employees are located in the Columbus office. The Commission's telephone number is (614) 466-3016.

CROSS REFERENCES

Rules of practice, OAC Ch 4901-1
Procedure on motor carrier cases, OAC Ch 4901-5

Public utilities commission—organization, RC Ch 4901
Public utilities commission—general powers, RC Ch 4905
Public utilities commission—railroad powers, RC Ch 4907
Public utilities commission—fixation of rates, RC Ch 4909
Public utilities commission—motor transportation companies, RC Ch 4921
Public utilities commission—private motor carriers, RC Ch 4923

17.02 Jurisdictional overview of the Commission

Practice before the Public Utilities Commission of Ohio ("Commission") is a specific type of administrative practice. The Commission is an administrative agency and, therefore, is constrained by precedents relating to practice before administrative bodies generally.[1] In addition, the Commission is subject to specific constraints imposed by statute or rule.

As with other administrative bodies, absent a legislative delegation of authority by the General Assembly, the Commission is without authority to act. Accordingly, reference must be had to the Commission's specific statutory powers described in RC Title 49. A general overview of the makeup of the Commission and its jurisdictional powers and duties is, therefore, helpful in understanding practice before the Commission.

RC 4905.05 extends the jurisdiction of the Commission to every public utility and railroad in the state of Ohio. RC 4905.02 defines a public utility as

> every corporation, company, copartnership, person, or association, their lessees, trustees, or receivers, defined in section 4905.03 of the Revised Code, including all telephone companies, but excepting such other public utilities as operate their utilities not for profit, such other public utilities as are owned or operated by any municipal corporation, and railroads as defined in sections 4907.02 and 4907.03 of the Ohio Revised Code.

Accordingly, except for the specific exceptions stated above and certain activities of utilities within municipalities, the Commission maintains its broad jurisdiction over all public utilities described in RC 4905.03. The legislature has granted the Commission supervisory power over all aspects of each public utility's activities.

For ease of administration in fulfilling its statutory obligations, the Commission has created the following various internal departments: (1) administration, (2) transportation, (3) public interest center, (4) legal, and (5) utilities. As mandated by statute, a section at the office of the Attorney General has been designated to serve as legal counsel for the Commission.[2] The various departments are further broken down as follows:

(1) Administration

    (a) Office Services

    (b) Docketing

    (c) Information Systems

    (d) Library

    (e) Word Processing

    (f) Fiscal

    (g) Personnel

(2) Transportation

    (a) Motor Carrier Regulation

    (b) Tariffs

    (c) Auditing

---

[1] See Text Ch 1, Rulemaking; Text Ch 3, Adjudication.
[2] RC 4901.17.

(d) Data and Research

   (e) Railroads

   (f) Enforcement

(3) Public Interest Center

(4) Legal

(5) Utilities

   (a) Compliance

   (b) Finance and Economics

   (c) Telecommunications

   (d) Accounts and Valuations

   (e) Rates and Tariffs

The legislative and media liaisons are staff positions located within the offices of the commissioners.

Information about a public utility may be obtained by contacting the appropriate department of the Commission. This will aid in obtaining a timely response. A good starting point is a utility company's tariff. RC 4905.30 mandates that all public utilities shall print and file with the Commission schedules known as tariffs which show rates, rentals, tolls, classifications, and charges for services of every kind furnished by the utility and, further, all rules and regulations affecting those services. These tariffs are all filed with the Commission and open to public inspection.[3] A public utility is limited to those activities authorized in its tariffs,[4] which must be approved by the Commission. In the event the inquiry with the Commission does not obtain a satisfactory result, the Commission's administrative legal process may be initiated.

The Commission is vested with the authority to conduct hearings on many difficult subjects. Pursuant to RC 4905.26, a hearing is initiated by a complaint relating to any "rate, fare, charge, toll, rental, schedule, classification, or service rendered, charged, demanded, exacted, or proposed to be rendered, charged, demanded or exacted."[5] The issue in such a hearing is whether the action complained of is unjust, unreasonable, unjustly discriminatory, unjustly preferential, in violation of law, inadequate, or unobtainable.

Other sections more specifically describe the hearing process utilized by the Commission in fulfilling its adjudicatory responsibilities. The general format for these hearings is outlined by the Commission in its rules of practice in OAC Chapter 4901-1. The same hearing procedures generally will apply notwithstanding the subject matter of the case; however, Commission rules do specify procedures for certain types of hearings. Examples of these differences are special rules relating to rate proceedings, transportation

---

[3] RC 4905.12.
[4] RC 4905.32.
[5] See generally Text Ch 3, Adjudication.

matters, fuel clause hearings, or other statutory proceedings. Generally, however, the rules are uniform and vary only in details such as intervention timing or testimony filing requirements. Therefore, it is helpful to understand the basic hearing process while keeping in mind that review of specific Commission rules is necessary, especially in hearings involving a specific matter.

CROSS REFERENCES

See Text Ch 1, 3

17.03 General hearing process

Any person may request a Commission hearing to adjudicate any controversy involving a public utility. While the specific subject matter of the proceeding may dictate various aspects of the hearing process, this section focuses on the general hearing process.

The General Assembly has empowered the Commission to hire attorneys to serve as attorney referees, who serve as administrative law judges or hearing officers on behalf of the commissioners. Because of the large volume of cases adjudicated by the Commission, it is physically impossible for the commissioners individually to hear cases; accordingly, the attorney referees fulfill this role on behalf of the Commission.

Since the commissioners and/or the attorney referees are fulfilling the role of administrative law judges, both RC 4903.081 and OAC 4901-1-09 prohibit a Commission member or attorney referee who is associated with a case from discussing the merits of the case once it has been assigned a formal docket number. This restriction applies to any party or intervenor to the proceeding unless all other parties and intervenors have been notified and given an opportunity to be present, or unless a full disclosure or the communication, insofar as it pertains to the subject matter of the case, has been made. Any violation of this law and/or the accompanying rule may, at the discretion of the commissioners, lead to the referee's or commissioner's removal from a particular case or other disciplinary action.

The Commission, pursuant to RC 4901.13, has adopted rules outlining procedures to be followed in the hearing process. While the substantive necessity for a hearing may be promoted by different statutory bases, the procedural steps of the hearing are quite consistent.

An action is initiated with the Commission by the filing of the requisite number of copies of the initial pleading with the Commission Docketing Division. The appropriate form, verifications, and other procedural considerations are specifically outlined in OAC 4901-1-11. Once an action has been filed with the Commission, a Commission entry will subsequently be issued directing the public utility to respond to the filing.[6] Pleadings are generally subject to the same content requirements in civil actions. The response in

---

[6] OAC 4901-9-01.

many instances will be in the nature of an answer or a motion.[7] If the Commission determines that a hearing is necessary, it will fix a time and place for the hearing which, unless otherwise ordered, will be at the Commission offices in Columbus.[8]

OAC 4901-1-12 provides that motions are to be accompanied by a memorandum in support. Memoranda contra are to be filed within fifteen days after the service of the motion, unless the Commission provides otherwise. Finally, a reply memorandum may be filed within seven days after service of a memorandum contra, unless the Commission orders otherwise. All pleadings must be filed with the Commission, served upon all parties (including all persons who have petitioned to intervene) no later than the date of filing, and must contain a certificate of service. OAC 4901-1-07(B) adds three days to the time of response to a motion or memorandum served by mail, and OAC 4901-1-07(A) provides that a response day falling on a holiday or weekend extends the response day to the following business day. The Commission, however, does not necessarily allow both rules to work together. If, by adding three days, the response date falls on a weekend, the Commission staff has informally interpreted the rules to require the response on the preceding business day. At the time of writing, the Commission has made no definitive ruling.

Persons affected by a Commission proceeding may intervene upon timely motion filed with the Commission and served on all parties.[9] Like any other motion, the request must be accompanied by a memorandum in support. The Commission may grant, qualify, or deny a motion to intervene and may require intervenors with substantially similar interests to consolidate their cases.[10]

Discovery necessary to facilitate preparation for participation in Commission proceedings is provided in OAC 4901-1-16 to OAC 4901-1-24.[11] Discovery tools available are interrogatories, requests for production of documents and things, permission to enter upon land or other property, depositions, and requests for admission. Discovery may begin immediately after a proceeding is commenced and should be completed expeditiously. In fact, unless otherwise ordered for good cause, discovery must be completed prior to the commencement of the hearing.

Pursuant to OAC 4901-1-14, rulings upon procedural motions or other procedural matters are to be reduced to writing and served upon all parties to the proceedings. Any party who is adversely affected by such a ruling may take an interlocutory appeal to the Commission, provided the appeal is certified by the legal director, attorney referee, or presiding hearing officer. An oral ruling issued during a public hearing or preliminary conference may also be subject to an interlocutory appeal by any adversely affected party.

---

[7]*Id.*
[8]OAC 4901-1-27.
[9]See generally Text 3.04, Intervention.
[10]OAC 4901-1-11.
[11]See generally Text 3.05(B), Discovery: availability of agency files.

The ruling is subject to appeal if it (1) grants a motion to compel discovery; (2) denies a motion for a protective order; (3) denies a motion to intervene; (4) terminates a party's right to participate in a proceeding; (5) refuses to quash a subpoena; or (6) requires the production of documents or testimony over an objection based on privilege.

The Commission is empowered by RC 4903.03 as well as OAC 4901-1-25 to issue subpoenas. To assist in conducting discovery as well as procuring witnesses for the hearing, OAC 4901-1-25(G) states that failure to obey a subpoena issued by the Commission, a commissioner, the legal director, or an attorney referee shall subject such person to relief as provided by RC 4903.02 or RC 4903.04.

OAC 4901-1-26 provides for prehearing conferences upon motion by the Commission or any party in order to resolve various issues. Upon completion of discovery and upon conclusion of the prehearing conference, if one is held, the Commission will, if issues still remain, schedule a hearing.

Hearings before the Commission, while administrative in nature, are considered formal, especially when compared to proceedings before public utility commissions of other states. The normal hearing format is outlined in OAC 4901-1-27. Prior to any legal arguments or presentation of witnesses, referees will usually prescribe a supplemental procedural format setting forth the order of presentation of witnesses, method of objection, order of cross-examination, etc. OAC 4901-1-29 directs that the testimony of experts, unless otherwise ordered, must be filed prior to the hearing. The timetable for such filings is dependent upon the nature or substance of the hearing. Direct expert testimony ordinarily must be filed no later than ten days prior to the commencement of the hearing. The expert witness is then presented at the hearing and specifically required to adopt his prefiled testimony. Cross-examination of the witness is then offered to the parties and the Commission. Nonexpert testimony need not be reduced to writing or filed prior to the hearing. Nonexpert witnesses may merely testify at the hearing, subject to cross-examination.

In a number of Commission proceedings, prior to the commencement of the formal hearing, the Commission will allow members of the public to give either sworn or unsworn statements. Sworn statements are subject to cross-examination and become part of the record, while unsworn statements are not subject to cross-examination and do not become part of the record.

At the conclusion of the direct portion of the proceeding, the matter of rebuttal testimony may be considered. While there is no specific rule mandating rebuttal testimony, OAC 4901-1-29(A)(2) provides that expert testimony (and presumably nonexpert testimony) offered in rebuttal may be presented in a manner establishing by the Commission or presiding hearing officer.

Briefs or memoranda may be required at any stage of a proceeding.[12] Oral arguments are sought by motion and may be authorized at any time during a

---

[12] OAC 4901-1-31.

proceeding, within the discretion of the Commission, the legal director, or an attorney referee.[13] Once the hearing is concluded, OAC 4901-1-31 provides that, upon motion of the Commission or any party, the Commission may permit or require the filing of briefs or memoranda. The nature and extent of the briefs or memoranda are within the discretion of the Commission, the legal director, or the attorney referee.

At the conclusion of the hearing and subsequent to the filing of briefs and reply briefs, OAC 4901-1-33 requires the attorney referee to prepare a written report of findings, conclusions, and recommendations, except in general emergency rate proceedings, fuel component proceedings, and purchased gas adjustment proceedings, or unless otherwise ordered by the Commission, or expressly waived by the parties. The report is filed with the Commission and served upon all parties. Any party may file exceptions to the report within twenty days after it is filed. Exceptions shall be stated and numbered separately and shall be supported by a memorandum. Any party may file a reply to another party's exceptions within fifteen days after service of those exceptions. RC 4903.09 states that at the conclusion of all filings relating to an referee's report, or in the event an referee's report is not applicable, the Commission must file an order stating "findings of fact and written opinions setting forth the reasons prompting the decision." The Commission's decision must be based upon the stated findings of fact.

Both RC 4903.10 and OAC 4901-1-35 allow the filing of a rehearing application by any party or any affected person, firm, or corporation from any order made by the Public Utilities Commission. RC 4903.10 specifies that after the Commission has issued an order, any party who has entered an appearance may apply for rehearing on any matter determined in the proceeding. The statute further indicates that in any uncontested proceeding, or by leave of the Commission, any affected person, firm, or corporation may make an application for rehearing, provided the Commission first finds that the applicant's failure to make a timely appearance was due to just cause and that the interests of the applicant were not adequately considered in the proceeding. OAC 4901-1-35 requires the filing of an application for rehearing within thirty days after the entry of the order upon the journal of the Commission. All applications for rehearing or applications for leave to filing an application for rehearing must be served upon all parties who have entered an appearance in the proceeding. The rule further states that any party may file a memorandum contra within ten days after the filing of the application for rehearing.

Pursuant to RC 4903.10, any application for rehearing must be in writing and set forth specifically the ground(s) upon which the applicant alleges the order to be unreasonable or unlawful. Unless the applicant has raised a ground in the application for rehearing, such applicant is precluded from raising the ground in any subsequent court appeal. Where an application for rehearing has been properly filed, the Commission may grant and hold such rehearing on the specified matters which it deems appropriate. Notice of a

---

[13]OAC 4901-1-32.

rehearing is given by registered mail to all parties who have entered an appearance in the proceeding. If the Commission does not grant or deny an application for rehearing within thirty days from the date of filing of the application, the application is denied by operation of law. In granting a rehearing application, the Commission shall specify the purpose for which it is granted and, further, specify the scope of additional evidence, if any, that will be taken; provided, however, it may not accept evidence that could have been ascertained with reasonable diligence at the original hearing. No time periods are established for completion of the rehearing.[14]

After a rehearing, the Commission may modify the original order if it determines that the order or any part thereof was unjust or unreasonable or should be changed; otherwise, the Commission must affirm the order. An order made after such a rehearing "shall have the same effect as an original order, but shall not affect any right ... arising from or by virtue of the original order prior to the receipt of notice by the affected party of the filing of the application for rehearing."[15]

A party aggrieved by a Commission order may appeal only to the Supreme Court of Ohio,[16] and such an appeal is a matter of right. No other court has the power to review, suspend, or delay any order of the Commission or to enjoin or interfere with the Commission or any public utilities commissioner in the official performance of his duties.[17] The appellant must commence the appeal by filing with the Commission a notice of appeal within sixty days after the date of denial of the application for rehearing by operation of law or by entry upon the journal of the Commission or, if rehearing is had, after the date of the order made after such rehearing.[18] The notice of appeal must be served, unless waived, upon the chairman of the Commission or, in the event of his absence, upon any commissioner, or by leaving a copy at the office of the Commission.[19] The court may permit any interested party to intervene by cross-appeal.[20]

RC 4903.16 states that an appeal to the Ohio Supreme Court from an order of the Commission "does not stay execution of such order unless the supreme court or a judge thereof in vacation, on application, and three days notice to the commission, allows such stay."[21] In such an event the applicant must execute an undertaking payable to the state in such amounts and manner as the Supreme Court may prescribe.

Once a notice of appeal has been served or a waiver of service has been obtained, RC 4903.21 provides that the Commission shall forthwith transmit to the clerk of the Supreme Court a transcript of the journal entries, the

---

[14]RC 4903.10.
[15]*Id.*
[16]RC 4903.12.
[17]*Id.*
[18]RC 4903.11.
[19]RC 4903.13.
[20]*Id.*
[21]RC 4903.12.

original papers or transcripts thereof, and a certified transcript of all evidence adduced upon the hearing before the Commission and the proceeding complained of, which documents are then filed with the Court. Appeals made to the Supreme Court are subject to the Rules of Practice of the Supreme Court of Ohio.

CROSS REFERENCES

See Text 3.04, 3.05(B)

17.04 Specific types of nontransportation hearings

The foregoing discussion gives a broad overview of the hearing process generally applicable to proceedings at the Commission. However, the subject matter of a particular hearing may alter the procedures to be followed in a specific case. It is impossible to address every hearing alternative, but a description of several representative types follows.

(A) Complaint proceeding

RC 4905.26 provides a mechanism for the filing of a complaint either by a person, firm, corporation, or upon the complaint of the Public Utilities Commission as such complaint relates to

> any rate, fare, charge, toll, rental, schedule, classification, or service, or any joint rate, fare, charge, toll, rental, schedule, classification, or service rendered[,] charged, demanded, exacted, or proposed ... or that any regulation, measurement, or practice affecting or relating to any service furnished by said public utility, or in connection with such service, is, or will be, in any respect unreasonable, unjust, insufficient, unjustly discriminatory, or unjustly preferential, or that any service is, or will be, inadequate or cannot be obtained.

This statute further allows any public utility to file a complaint affecting its own product or service. Upon the filing of the complaint, the statute provides that, if reasonable grounds for a complaint are stated, the Commission must set a time for hearing, notify the complainants and the public utility of the hearing date, and publish notice of the complaint and hearing date in a newspaper of general circulation in the county in which the complaint arose.

Upon the filing of the complaint, the general hearing process commences.[22] At the hearing the complainant bears the burden of proving its case.[23] Failure to sustain the burden will result in a dismissal of the complaint. Any ruling during the hearing or a final decision by the Commission may be appealed.[24]

(B) Rate increase application

RC Chapter 4909 addresses the fixing of rates for public utilities regulated by the Commission. Specifically, RC 4909.18 is the focal point for setting rates and states as follows:

---

[22] See Text 17.03, General hearing process.
[23] Grossman v PUCO, 5 OS(2d) 189, 214 NE(2d) 666 (1966).
[24] See Text 17.03, General hearing process.

> Any public utility desiring to establish any rate, joint rate, toll, classification, charge, or rental, or to modify, amend, change, increase, or reduce any existing rate, joint rate, toll, classification, charge, or rental, or any regulation or practice affecting the same, shall file a written application with the public utilities commission.

Since all utilities must file all of their rates with the Commission, the activity of any public utility must commence with a filing pursuant to this statute. If the Commission determines that an application filed pursuant to this section is not for an increase in rates, is for a new service or for the use of new equipment, it may permit the filing of the tariff and fix a time when the tariff schedules shall take effect. However, if the Commission concludes that the proposal may be unjust or unreasonable, it must set the matter for hearing and give notice of the hearing to the public utility as well as publish notice of the hearing in accordance with statutory requirements. At the hearing the applicant public utility will bear the burden of proof relating to the justness and reasonableness of its proposal. This hearing follows the general hearing procedures.[25]

If the application requests an increase in rates, it must be accompanied by exhibits showing the public utility's property used and useful in rendering service, complete operating statements, a statement of any income and expense, a statement of financial condition, a proposed notice for newspaper publication, and any other information required by the Commission.[26] Rules and forms known as the "Standard Filing Requirements" have been promulgated by the Commission to be used in filing an application. These requirements are listed in an appendix to OAC Chapter 4901-7 that is available from the Secretary of State or the Legislative Service Commission.[27] For smaller companies the Commission has lessened the burden of these filings. A review of the rules prior to filing is therefore appropriate to determine if the size of the applicant company will qualify it for lessened informational filing requirements.

The lessened filing requirements apply to electric and gas utilities with five hundred or fewer customers, telephone companies with five thousand or fewer main stations, and water and sewer companies with five thousand or fewer customers.

Upon the filing of an application for an increase under RC 4909.18, the Commission will order the public utility to publish a notice of the substance and prayer of the application.[28] The staff of the Commission then undertakes an independent investigation of the application leading to a written report known as a staff report,[29] which is filed with the Commission. A copy of the report is sent to the applicant, the mayor of any municipal corporation affected by the application, and to such other persons as the Commission deems interested. Parties then have thirty days to file objections to the staff

---

[25] See Text 17.03, General hearing process.
[26] RC 4909.18.
[27] OAC Ch 4901-7.
[28] RC 4909.19.
[29] *Id.*

report. If no objections are filed, the Commission will proceed with a hearing to consider the application and the staff report. If objections to the staff report are filed, the hearing will address matters raised in the application, the staff report, and objections raised by the interested parties. The issues are ordinarily defined by the objections to the staff report.

While parties may intervene in accordance with the rules,[30] intervention requests should be made as early in the process as possible since discovery timing, expert witness preparation, and testimony filings will occur as described below.

The actual hearing process will be similar to the general hearing process; however, the Commission has promulgated specific rules relating to the time of discovery,[31] the filing of testimony,[32] and other facets of the hearing in a rate case. These specific rate case procedures are necessitated to assure full and fair hearings consistent with the Commission's obligation under RC 4909.42 to issue an order within 275 days from the date of the utility's filing of the application. In the event such an order is not made, the public utility may implement the proposed increase upon the filing of an undertaking with the Commission. If the Commission has not entered a final order within 545 days from the filing date of the application, the public utility shall have no further obligation to refund amounts collected after the 545th day which exceed the Commission's final order.[33] Accordingly, timeliness of Commission hearings relating to rate case applications is critical.

In addition to the rate increase proceedings under RC 4909.18, RC 4909.34 provides a mechanism for a public utility to appeal a municipal ordinance setting a rate, price, or charge for service within its municipal corporation. The public utility has thirty days from passage of an ordinance to appeal the ordinance to the Commission. In reviewing the municipal ordinance rate, the Commission uses the procedural requirements set forth in RC 4909.18.

RC 4909.66 provides for the temporary amendment, alteration, or suspension of rates. This statute has been used generally to respond to emergency situations such as emergency rate case proceedings and actions taken during the natural gas shortage to implement curtailment programs, as well as actions to address preliminary matters prior to full Commission hearings. Action taken pursuant to this statute, however, is limited. In addressing a matter pursuant to RC 4909.16, the Commission may issue an emergency order prior to holding a hearing.[34] Hearings held pursuant to this statute follow the general hearing procedure.[35]

---

[30] See Text 17.03, General hearing process.
[31] OAC 4901-1-17.
[32] OAC 4901-1-29.
[33] RC 4909.42.
[34] Duff v PUCO, 56 OS(2d) 367, 384 NE(2d) 264 (1978).
[35] See Text 17.03, General hearing process.

(C) Gas and electric fuel clause hearings

(1) Electric fuel component ("EFC") rate hearings

RC 4905.301 requires that the Commission hold a hearing at least every six months to determine the fuel component portion of electric public utilities. In accordance with this statutory mandate, the Commission has enacted OAC Chapter 4901:1-11, specifying information needed as well as procedures to be followed in electric fuel component hearings. In connection with this process, RC 4905.66 requires an annual audit as well as monthly evaluations which are considered in the semiannual hearings. Intervention requests by parties should be made as quickly as possible if a party is to prepare adequately for the hearing and prefile expert testimony. Except to the extent modified by specific rules relating to EFC hearings, the general requirements for hearing apply.[36] The time between audit reports, hearing, and Commission order is, however, quite brief.

(2) Gas cost recovery ("GCR") hearings

As in the electric utility area, the Ohio legislature has mandated Commission review of the fuel procurement practices of gas or natural gas utilities. RC 4905.302 requires the Commission to establish a purchase gas adjustment clause to be implemented by gas companies and natural gas companies. The Commission must also establish investigative procedures and proceedings including, but not limited to, periodic reports, audits, and hearings. In accordance with this statute, the Commission has promulgated OAC Chapter 4901:1-14. Pursuant to the statutory mandates and the Commission rules, the Commission provides for annual audits as well as periodic reports and annual hearings to establish and review each gas company's and natural gas company's GCR rate. The hearings, except where modified by the specific Commission rules addressing the GCR, follow the general hearing procedures.[37] Again, any intervention should occur as quickly as feasible, so the intervenor will have sufficient time to complete discovery and prefile expert testimony.

CROSS REFERENCES

See Text 17.03

17.05 Motor carrier regulation

The Commission is charged with the responsibility of regulating motor transportation companies, both common and private, engaged in the business of providing or furnishing transportation service for hire. If a motor transportation company is offering its services to the public generally, as a common carrier, it is regulated under RC Chapter 4921. Private motor carriers, or as they are more commonly known "contract carriers," are regulated pursuant to the provisions of RC Chapter 4923.

---

[36] See Text 17.03, General hearing process.
[37] *Id.*

(A) Motor transportation company

RC Chapter 4921 delineates the qualifications for, and the requirements of, a motor transportation company. This chapter applies to motor transportation companies as defined by RC 4921.02. These are carriers that engage or propose to engage in the business of transporting persons or property, or the business of providing such transportation service, for hire. The business or service must be provided for the general public, directly or by lease or other arrangement, by motor-propelled vehicles over public highways. Before a carrier can engage in such activity, absent some statutory exemption as delineated in RC 4921.02, the carrier must apply for and obtain from the Commission authority to conduct its transportation movement.[38] The Commission has prescribed procedures and forms for any application for new authority, modified authority, or transfers of existing authority of motor transportation companies.[39]

Applicants for common carrier authority may seek either regular route authority or irregular route authority as these terms are defined in RC 4921.02(E) and (F). An application filed pursuant to RC Chapter 4921 must show that public convenience and necessity require the service requested in the application.[40] In considering such an application, the Commission must consider existing transportation facilities in the area for which the certificate is requested and must deny the application if it determines that the existing transportation facilities are reasonably adequate.[41] Because of this burden in an application for new authority, the applicant will, in all probability, face a difficult task. Carriers who hold existing authority will protest the application by stating that they already provide the needed service. The applicant then must show why such existing service is not adequate.

Applications for transfer of a certificate as well as applications for bus service authority are significant exceptions to applications for certificates.[42]

(B) Private motor transportation companies

The Commission also regulates each private motor carrier pursuant to RC Chapter 4923. This jurisdiction extends to carriers who engage in or propose to engage in the private carriage of persons or property, or both, or provide or furnish transportation service for hire in motor-propelled vehicles over public highways, unless such carriage is exempt under RC 4923.02. As with common carrier authority, the Commission has enacted OAC Chapter 4901-5 to prescribe proper forms and hearing procedures for contract carriage applications. RC 4923.05 and OAC 4901-5-05 require the filing of contracts between a private motor carrier and the shipper for whom the transportation service is to be rendered. The hearing process, except as specifically altered by the transportation section at OAC Chapter 4901-5, will be the same as

---

[38] RC 4921.07.
[39] OAC Ch 4901-5.
[40] RC 4921.10.
[41] *Id.*
[42] RC 4921.101, RC 4921.13.

outlined for general hearing procedures[43] and applies whether the application seeks a new contract, a modification of an existing contract, or a transfer of an existing contract.

The Commission has enacted specific hearing procedures for motor transportation proceedings, defined in OAC Chapter 4901-5. Except as distinguished by that chapter, the general rules and procedures of a Commission hearing apply.[44]

CROSS REFERENCES

See Text 17.03

17.06 Other types of utilities

The foregoing sections obviously do not address all the possible hearing scenarios before the Commission. Hearings may involve other types of utilities such as telegraph companies, pipeline companies, or railroads. However, these types of companies appear much less frequently before the Commission. For example, railroads are generally only involved in disputes about safety at crossings, since rate regulation of railroads has been largely, if not totally, preempted by federal legislation. Additionally, telegraph companies are not subject to the same rate procedures and jurisdictional requirements as outlined above for public utility rate increases. Therefore, preparations for a particular hearing should be made following a review of the individual applicable statutes as well as the accompanying Commission rules and regulations.

---

[43]See Text 17.03, General hearing process.
[44]*Id.*

CHARTS

Note: The following diagrams are meant to reflect only general outlines of procedures before the Commission. Each case may vary from the general diagram, and the statutes and Commission rules should be consulted in ascertaining procedures in a specific matter.

17.07 Organizational chart, Public Utilities Commission

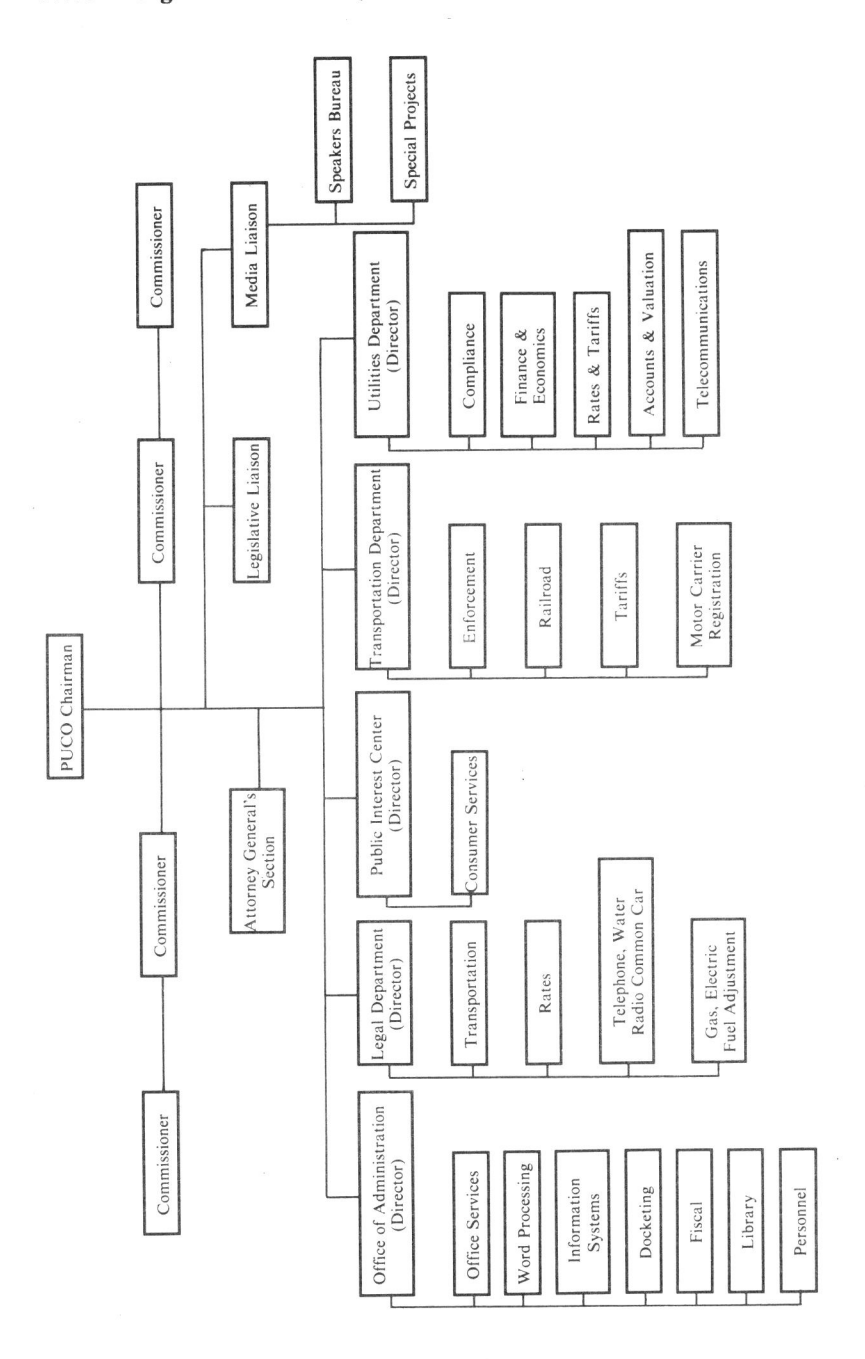

```
PUCO Chairman
├── Commissioner
├── Commissioner
├── Commissioner
├── Commissioner
├── Media Liaison
│   ├── Speakers Bureau
│   └── Special Projects
├── Legislative Liaison
├── Attorney General's Section
├── Utilities Department (Director)
│   ├── Compliance
│   ├── Finance & Economics
│   ├── Rates & Tariffs
│   ├── Accounts & Valuation
│   └── Telecommunications
├── Transportation Department (Director)
│   ├── Enforcement
│   ├── Railroad
│   ├── Tariffs
│   └── Motor Carrier Registration
├── Public Interest Center (Director)
│   └── Consumer Services
├── Legal Department (Director)
│   ├── Transportation
│   ├── Rates
│   ├── Telephone, Water Radio Common Car
│   └── Gas, Electric Fuel Adjustment
└── Office of Administration (Director)
    ├── Office Services
    ├── Word Processing
    ├── Information Systems
    ├── Docketing
    ├── Fiscal
    ├── Library
    └── Personnel
```

17.08 Complaint proceeding, PUCO, RC 4905.26

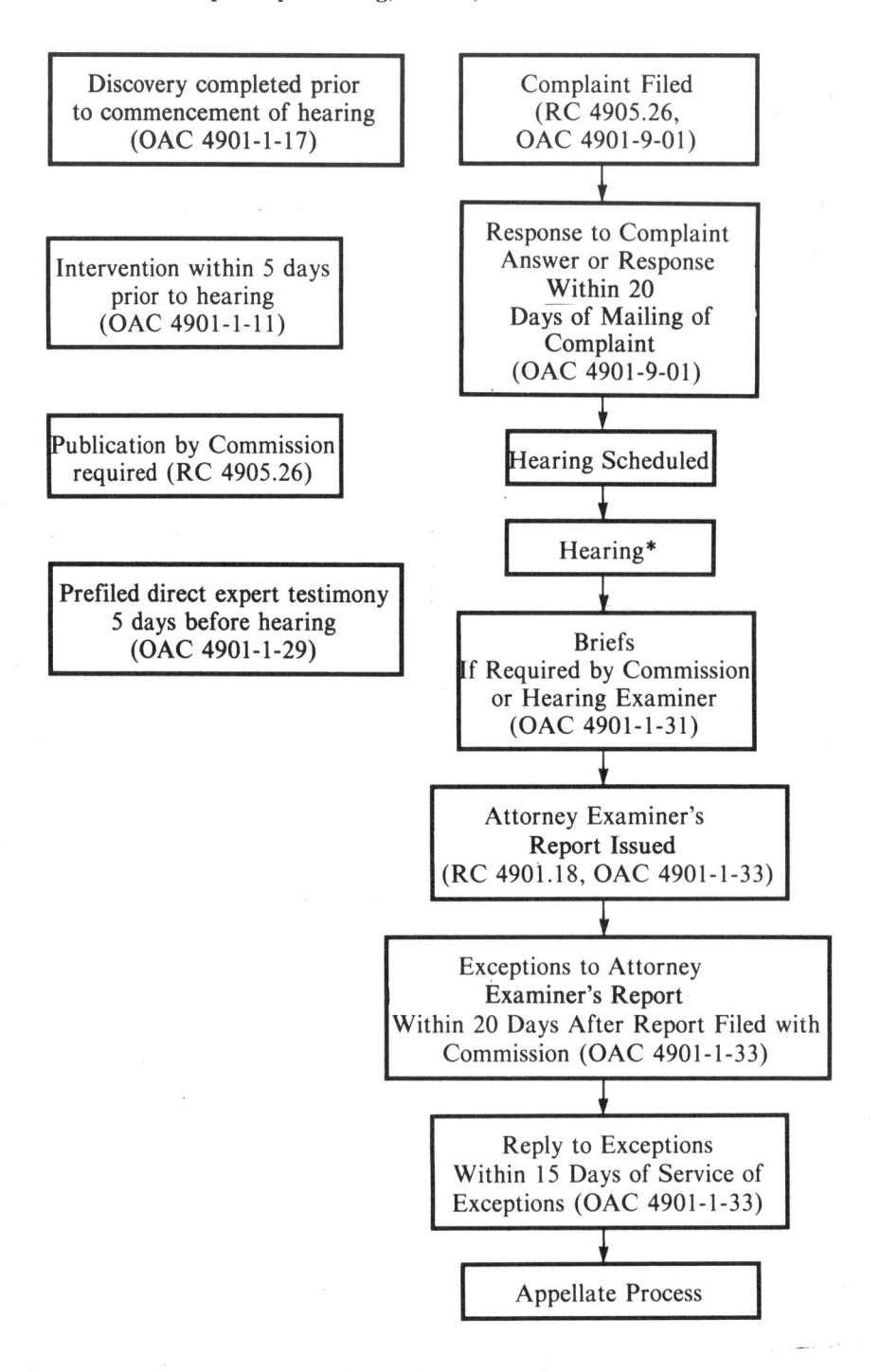

```
┌─────────────────────────┐          ┌─────────────────────────┐
│ Discovery completed prior│          │     Complaint Filed     │
│ to commencement of hearing│         │      (RC 4905.26,       │
│    (OAC 4901-1-17)      │          │     OAC 4901-9-01)      │
└─────────────────────────┘          └────────────┬────────────┘
                                                  │
                                                  ▼
                                     ┌─────────────────────────┐
┌─────────────────────────┐          │  Response to Complaint  │
│ Intervention within 5 days│         │    Answer or Response   │
│    prior to hearing     │          │       Within 20         │
│    (OAC 4901-1-11)      │          │  Days of Mailing of     │
└─────────────────────────┘          │       Complaint         │
                                     │    (OAC 4901-9-01)      │
                                     └────────────┬────────────┘
                                                  │
                                                  ▼
┌─────────────────────────┐          ┌─────────────────────────┐
│ Publication by Commission│          │    Hearing Scheduled    │
│  required (RC 4905.26)  │          └────────────┬────────────┘
└─────────────────────────┘                       │
                                                  ▼
                                     ┌─────────────────────────┐
                                     │        Hearing*         │
                                     └────────────┬────────────┘
┌─────────────────────────┐                       │
│Prefiled direct expert testimony│                ▼
│   5 days before hearing │          ┌─────────────────────────┐
│    (OAC 4901-1-29)      │          │         Briefs          │
└─────────────────────────┘          │If Required by Commission│
                                     │   or Hearing Examiner   │
                                     │    (OAC 4901-1-31)      │
                                     └────────────┬────────────┘
                                                  │
                                                  ▼
                                     ┌─────────────────────────┐
                                     │   Attorney Examiner's   │
                                     │      Report Issued      │
                                     │(RC 4901.18, OAC 4901-1-33)│
                                     └────────────┬────────────┘
                                                  │
                                                  ▼
                                     ┌─────────────────────────┐
                                     │  Exceptions to Attorney │
                                     │    Examiner's Report    │
                                     │Within 20 Days After Report Filed with│
                                     │ Commission (OAC 4901-1-33)│
                                     └────────────┬────────────┘
                                                  │
                                                  ▼
                                     ┌─────────────────────────┐
                                     │   Reply to Exceptions   │
                                     │Within 15 Days of Service of│
                                     │ Exceptions (OAC 4901-1-33)│
                                     └────────────┬────────────┘
                                                  │
                                                  ▼
                                     ┌─────────────────────────┐
                                     │    Appellate Process    │
                                     └─────────────────────────┘
```

*Note that Commission rulemaking proceedings may be conducted with comment only and without a hearing.

17.09 Proceeding, PUCO, RC 4909.18

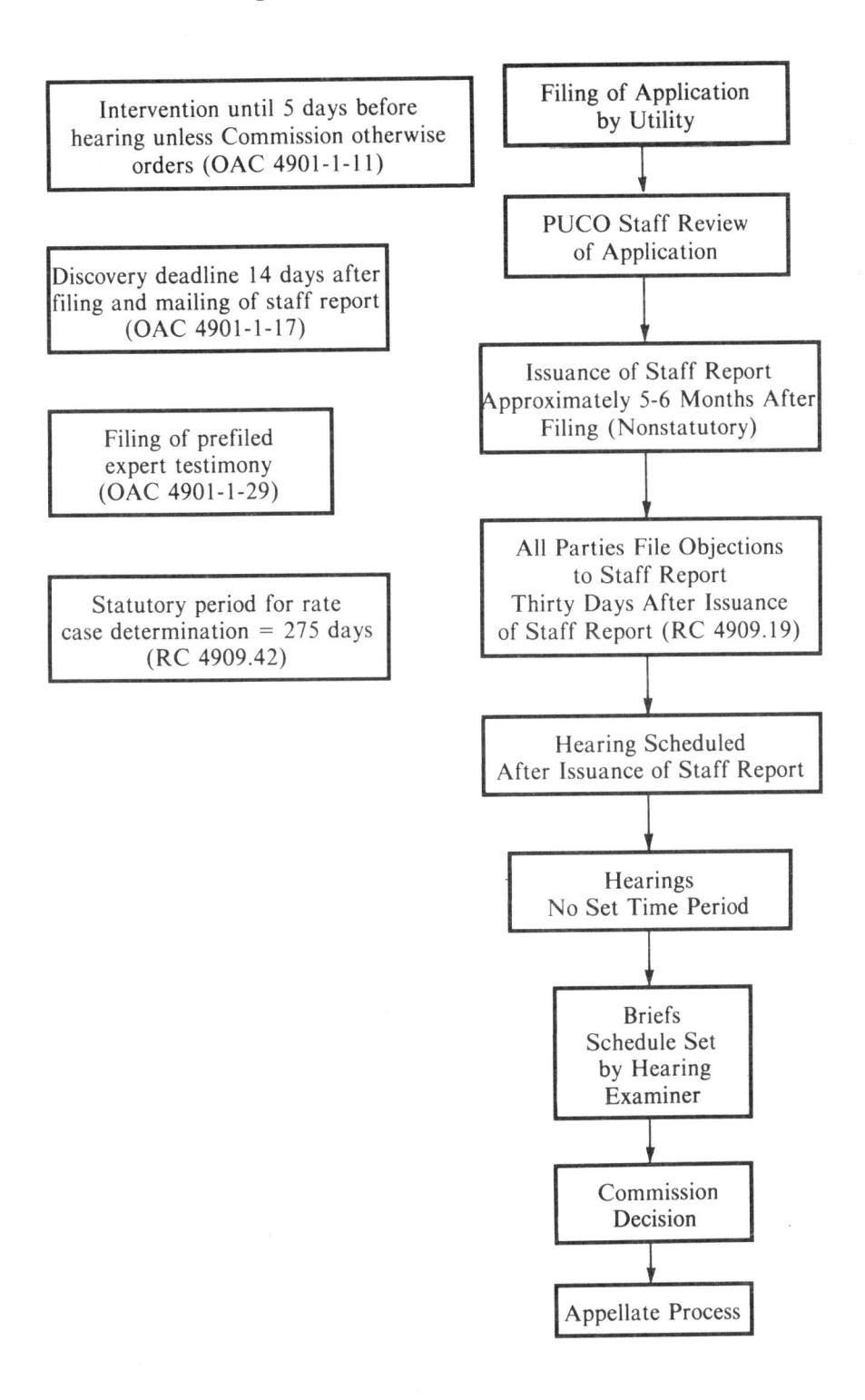

- Intervention until 5 days before hearing unless Commission otherwise orders (OAC 4901-1-11)

- Discovery deadline 14 days after filing and mailing of staff report (OAC 4901-1-17)

- Filing of prefiled expert testimony (OAC 4901-1-29)

- Statutory period for rate case determination = 275 days (RC 4909.42)

Flow:

1. Filing of Application by Utility
2. PUCO Staff Review of Application
3. Issuance of Staff Report Approximately 5-6 Months After Filing (Nonstatutory)
4. All Parties File Objections to Staff Report Thirty Days After Issuance of Staff Report (RC 4909.19)
5. Hearing Scheduled After Issuance of Staff Report
6. Hearings No Set Time Period
7. Briefs Schedule Set by Hearing Examiner
8. Commission Decision
9. Appellate Process

17.10 Motor carrier applications under RC Chapter 4921 or 4923, PUCO

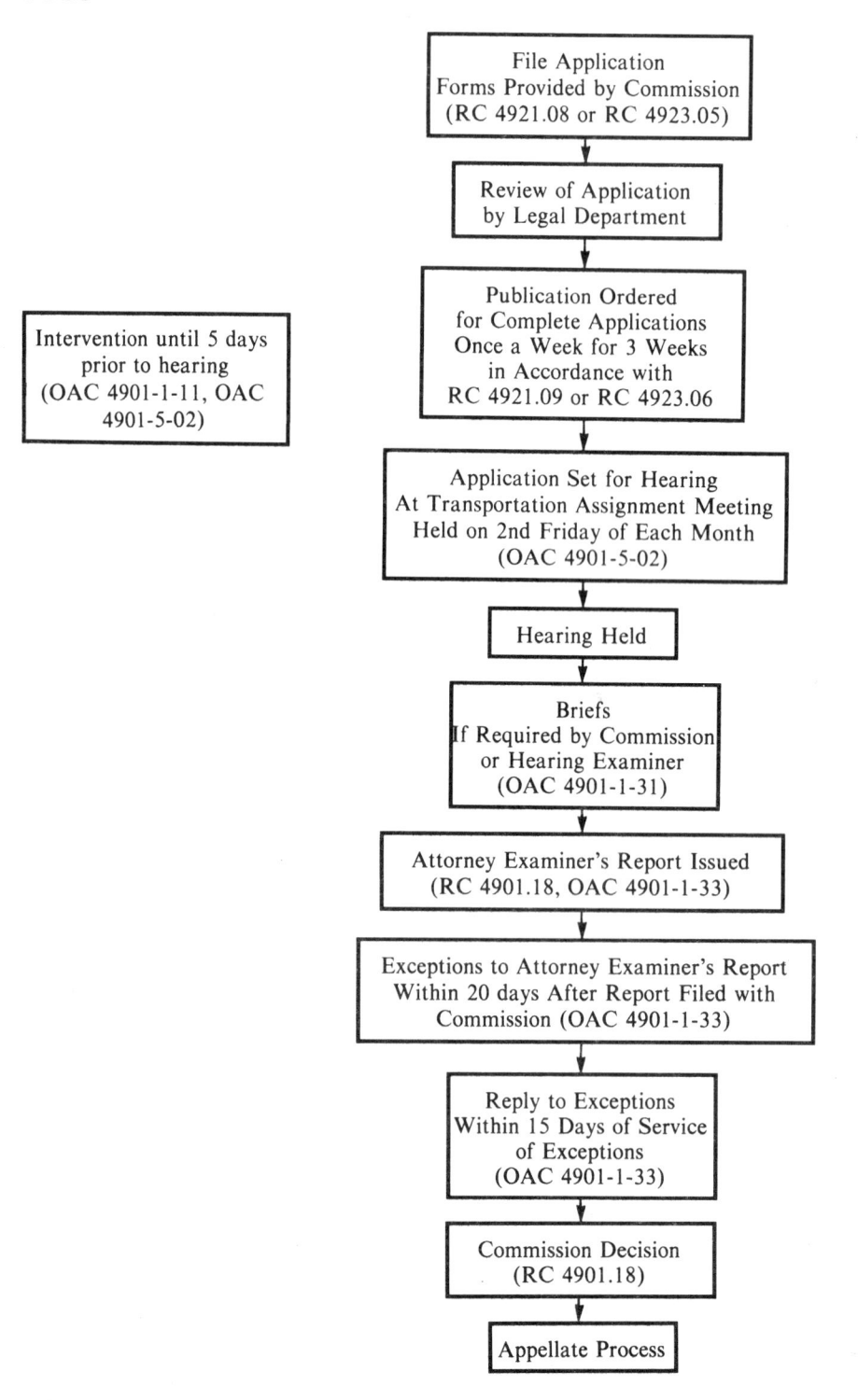

```
┌─────────────────────────────┐
│    File Application         │
│ Forms Provided by Commission│
│  (RC 4921.08 or RC 4923.05) │
└──────────────┬──────────────┘
               ▼
┌─────────────────────────────┐
│    Review of Application    │
│      by Legal Department    │
└──────────────┬──────────────┘
               ▼
┌─────────────────────────────┐
│    Publication Ordered      │
│ for Complete Applications   │
│  Once a Week for 3 Weeks    │
│     in Accordance with      │
│  RC 4921.09 or RC 4923.06   │
└──────────────┬──────────────┘
               ▼
┌─────────────────────────────┐
│ Application Set for Hearing │
│At Transportation Assignment │
│  Meeting Held on 2nd Friday │
│       of Each Month         │
│      (OAC 4901-5-02)        │
└──────────────┬──────────────┘
               ▼
┌─────────────────────────────┐
│       Hearing Held          │
└──────────────┬──────────────┘
               ▼
┌─────────────────────────────┐
│          Briefs             │
│ If Required by Commission   │
│     or Hearing Examiner     │
│      (OAC 4901-1-31)        │
└──────────────┬──────────────┘
               ▼
┌─────────────────────────────┐
│ Attorney Examiner's Report  │
│          Issued             │
│ (RC 4901.18, OAC 4901-1-33) │
└──────────────┬──────────────┘
               ▼
┌─────────────────────────────┐
│Exceptions to Attorney       │
│Examiner's Report Within 20  │
│days After Report Filed with │
│ Commission (OAC 4901-1-33)  │
└──────────────┬──────────────┘
               ▼
┌─────────────────────────────┐
│     Reply to Exceptions     │
│ Within 15 Days of Service   │
│       of Exceptions         │
│      (OAC 4901-1-33)        │
└──────────────┬──────────────┘
               ▼
┌─────────────────────────────┐
│     Commission Decision     │
│       (RC 4901.18)          │
└──────────────┬──────────────┘
               ▼
┌─────────────────────────────┐
│     Appellate Process       │
└─────────────────────────────┘
```

Intervention until 5 days prior to hearing (OAC 4901-1-11, OAC 4901-5-02)

17.11 Appellate process, PUCO

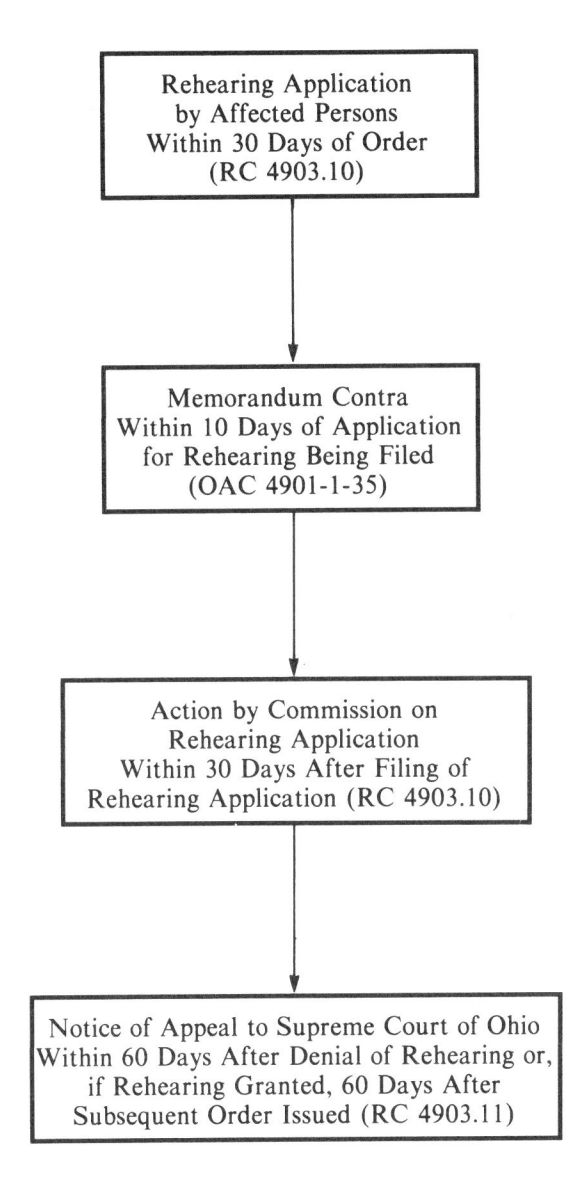

```
┌─────────────────────────────┐
│   Rehearing Application     │
│     by Affected Persons     │
│   Within 30 Days of Order   │
│        (RC 4903.10)         │
└─────────────┬───────────────┘
              │
              ▼
┌─────────────────────────────┐
│     Memorandum Contra       │
│ Within 10 Days of Application│
│  for Rehearing Being Filed  │
│       (OAC 4901-1-35)       │
└─────────────┬───────────────┘
              │
              ▼
┌─────────────────────────────┐
│   Action by Commission on   │
│    Rehearing Application    │
│ Within 30 Days After Filing of │
│ Rehearing Application (RC 4903.10) │
└─────────────┬───────────────┘
              │
              ▼
┌───────────────────────────────────────────┐
│ Notice of Appeal to Supreme Court of Ohio │
│ Within 60 Days After Denial of Rehearing or, │
│  if Rehearing Granted, 60 Days After      │
│  Subsequent Order Issued (RC 4903.11)     │
└───────────────────────────────────────────┘
```

Chapter 19

Ohio Department of Natural Resources

By Jay McKirahan, Esq.

19.01 Introduction
19.02 Division of Reclamation
19.03 Division of Oil and Gas
19.04 Practical considerations

FORMS

19.05 Notice of appeal, Reclamation Board of Review
19.06 Notice of violation, Division of Reclamation

CHARTS

19.07 Organizational chart, Department of Natural Resources
19.08 Procedural chart, Department of Natural Resources: Reclamation; Oil and Gas

19.01 Introduction

The Division of Reclamation and the Division of Oil and Gas are the primary regulatory bodies within the Ohio Department of Natural Resources (ODNR). In the last decade each has undergone major reorganization due to increasing concern over the potential for harm to the environment from the search for Ohio's subsurface wealth. The most significant changes have occurred in the increased strength of the enforcement authority and its administration by the two divisions. The legal practitioner should focus on how the law is being applied rather than what it says. Each division appears to be taking a stricter stance on procedural questions, and certain procedural peculiarities may catch the unwary. Reclamation, for example, is dismissing appeals that previously would have been processed, because of failure to follow procedures for submitting an appeal of a chief's order.

This chapter will analyze the changes that most affect the lawyer representing a miner, an oil and gas producer, or affected landowners who now have the right to appeal certain types of orders.

CROSS REFERENCES

Rules of practice, OAC Ch 1509-1
Meetings, OAC Ch 1513-3

Oil and gas, RC Ch 1509
Coal surface mining, RC Ch 1513
Other surface mining, RC Ch 1514

19.02 Division of Reclamation

Perhaps the most striking changes in regulatory enforcement in Ohio have taken place in the Division of Reclamation. Ohio has progressed from a position of no regulation in 1914, when coal strip mining first commenced in Ohio, to a role of leadership in mining reclamation standards. The most prominent changes have occurred since 1972, when the General Assembly passed one of the most comprehensive coal strip mining laws in the country.[1] The General Assembly later added a comprehensive law dealing with surface mining for other minerals.[2] Further, pursuant to RC 1513.35, effective September 1, 1981, the chief of the division may issue permits for underground coal mining.[3] Because of the latter provision, an understanding of the order and appeal procedure is critical not only for the lawyer who represents the miner but also for the lawyer who represents the landowner who may be affected by subsidence caused by an underground mine.

(A) Enforcement orders

The major enforcement tool of former RC 1513.02(D) was the chief's order notifying an operator of a violation and prescribing a time in which the violation must be corrected. However, as noted in a 1975 law review article, "The . . . disadvantage of the Chief's Order is that an operator can avoid compliance for a substantial period of time pending appeals, even where the violation is such that immediate action is required to avert environmental damage or damage to a third party."[4] The authors of that article suggested, "To better implement the provisions of Ohio Revised Code Chapter 1513 and to prevent serious environmental damage, the Chief should have the power of suspension of a license, i.e., the power to issue a cease and desist order."[5]

RC 1513.02(D) was amended in 1982. The Division of Reclamation now has the power to order the immediate cessation of coal mining activities and to order an operator to show cause why its permit should not be suspended or revoked. The Division is using both of these orders as powerful enforcement tools. These powers have developed because Ohio is now a deferral state; it has its own program to comply with the requirements of the Surface Mining Control and Reclamation Act of 1977.[6]

RC 1513.02 sets the basic standard for the issuance of enforcement orders and, in addition, creates three separate species of orders that the chief may issue. Subsection (D)(1) allows him to issue a cease and desist order when he determines that a condition exists that "creates an imminent danger to the health or safety of the public, or is causing or can reasonably be expected to cause significant, imminent environmental harm to land, air or water resources." Since this type of order remains in effect until the operator abates the condition, immediate administrative review is critical.

---

[1] RC Ch 1513 (1972 H 928, eff. 4-10-72). See Cryder, Faulk, and McKirahan, *Strip Mining: The Ohio Experience,* 4 Capital L Rev 169 (1975) for an explanation of this legislation and for an overview of strip mining law in Ohio.

[2] RC Ch 1514.

[3] RC 1513.07.

[4] Cryder, Faulk, and McKirahan, *Strip Mining: The Ohio Experience,* 4 Capital L Rev 169, 175 (1975).

[5] *Id.* at 192.

[6] 30 USC Ch 25.

RC 1513.02(D)(2) allows the chief to issue a "notice of violation" if the condition does not satisfy the imminent danger test. The notice of violation fixes a reasonable time for the operator to abate the condition. Although the notice is appealable, an operator must comply unless the Reclamation Board of Review grants temporary relief. If such relief is not applied for or is declined, and if the operator does not timely comply while an appeal is pending, the operator may be subjected to a civil penalty assessment.[7] RC 1513.02(D)(3) allows the chief to issue a show cause order before suspending or revoking a license, if the chief finds a pattern of violations of RC Chapter 1513.

Orders may involve persons other than the actual operator and include orders granting permits, approving partial and final reclamation, and approving partial and final release of a bond. Because landowners may now appeal these types of orders, counsel must keep abreast of developments in mining operations that may affect an absentee landowner and must be aware of the proper appellate procedure.

(B) Appeals to the Reclamation Board of Review

For both RC Chapters 1513 and 1514, appeals generally are governed by RC 1513.13. Rules are adopted pursuant to RC 1513.02. Although the statutory provisions generally establish the criteria for an appeal, counsel should become familiar with the Rules of the Reclamation Board of Review.[8] Effective November 1, 1984, new rules prescribe the content of appeals to the Reclamation Board of Review (RBR). Specifically, OAC 1513-3-04 mandates the content of a notice of appeal to the RBR. This is a major step forward. The RBR has changed from a long-established, but informal, practice concerning the contents or attachments required for an appeal to a policy of strict compliance with the rule on pain of dismissal of the appeal. No longer may an operator or his counsel file an appeal in form only and defer the content to the time of a hearing. If both form and content are not present at the outset, the appeal will probably be dismissed.

Another problem for counsel and the operator is the avoidance of the immediate effects of a cease and desist order or of a notice of violation with a short compliance time. The operator may comply with no questions asked; however, if the operator believes that the order is unfounded, relief is potentially available. Pending final review, RC 1513.13(C) allows the chairman of the RBR to grant temporary relief from an order. The new rules spell out the precise procedural process.[9] OAC 1513-3-08 requires compliance with RC 1513.13(C), OAC 1513-3-04, and "a detailed written statement setting forth the reasons why relief should be granted."[10] Counsel should contact the RBR in writing or by telephone to make emergency arrangements for the chairman of the RBR to consider the request for temporary relief.

---

[7] RC 1513.02(F).
[8] OAC 1513-3-01 et seq.
[9] OAC 1513-3-04.
[10] OAC 1513-3-08(B)(1).

Hearings on appeals are generally held within forty-five days of filing. However, cessation orders can be heard in thirty days pursuant to RC 1513.13. Scheduling is accomplished by writing or calling the RBR.

The practitioner should focus discovery efforts in two areas: first, the evidence used to support the order in issue, and second, the past records of the client, if the client's earlier activity may become an issue. As with many other administrative review bodies, the rules of evidence are generally relaxed, and hearings will usually take no more than one day.

(C) Appeals to the court of appeals

Another significant change in the appellate process is found in RC 1513.14. Originally, an appeal from an order of the RBR was first made to the Franklin County Court of Common Pleas. Now, however, the appeal is heard by the court of appeals for the county in which the activity in question is located. The court of appeals, when determining whether to grant temporary relief, is bound by the same criteria as the RBR as set forth in RC 1513.13. In the past, appellants commonly failed to file a copy of the notice of appeal with the RBR, although the filing was necessary to trigger the transmittal of the transcript of proceedings. To remedy this confusion, the new RBR rules specifically incorporate the Ohio Rules of Appellate Procedure.[11]

On balance, the substantive changes in the reclamation laws in the last fifteen years have not been as far-reaching as the enforcement and procedural changes outlined above. By carefully following the new procedures, operators and their counsel should be able to avoid errors when engaged in legal actions with the Division of Reclamation.

19.03 Division of Oil and Gas

Much of what has been said previously about the Division of Reclamation can be said for the Division of Oil and Gas. Initially neglected, recent regulatory enactments have been aimed at protecting surrounding land and ground water supplies as well as other environmental concerns.[12]

The law and regulations governing oil and gas are found in RC Chapter 1509 and OAC Chapter 1501. As with the Division of Reclamation, the most critical area of concern for the legal advisor is the administrative procedure regarding orders and notices.

(A) Appeals to the Oil and Gas Board of Review

RC 1509.03 authorizes the chief of the Division of Oil and Gas to issue enforcement orders. Appeals are governed by RC 1509.36 and OAC 1509-1-01 to OAC 1509-1-17. As with the Division of Reclamation, the location for

---

[11]OAC 1513-3-22.

[12]Two leading articles have traced the early history and later development of oil and gas law in Ohio: Meyers and Williams, *Petroleum Conservation in Ohio,* 26 Ohio St L J 591 (1965) and Emens and Lowe, *Ohio Oil and Gas Conservation Law—The First Ten Years (1965-1975),* 37 Ohio St L J 31 (1976).

filing the appeal is critical. OAC 1509-1-01 specifies the official address of the Oil and Gas Board of Review (OGBR): Oil and Gas Board of Review, Building "B," Fountain Square, Columbus, Ohio 43224.

All appeals must be timely filed at the official address. OAC 1509-1-03 specifies that filing of an appeal means actual delivery to the OGBR.

Although not as onerous as OAC 1513-3-04, OAC 1509-1-04 details specifically the necessary contents for a valid notice of appeal.[13]

Unlike the RBR rules, the OGBR rules do not address the question of temporary relief. RC 1509.36, however, provides some authority for temporary relief: "The filing of an appeal ... does not automatically suspend or stay execution of the order appealed from, but upon application by the appellant the board may suspend or stay execution pending determination of the appeal upon such terms as it deems proper."

The Board generally does not rule upon requested stays; however, the Division usually quietly acquiesces to a stay of some type. Extreme caution is urged for any operator or legal advisor because of the uncertainty of such a situation. More precise rules would help remedy the problem. If the OGBR is not going to rule on a request for temporary relief, counsel should request that the Division make a written commitment to some type of stay order. The necessity for a specific understanding is highlighted by RC 1509.33, which authorizes civil penalties for up to $2,500 for a violation of a rule or order. The Division considers each day of violation of an order as a separate violation so the monetary stakes can become incredibly high very quickly in the event of a misunderstanding about the existence or terms of a stay order. Until more precise rules are enacted, the operator and his counsel must rely on any written statements that can be obtained from the Division.

(B) Appeals to the court of common pleas

OGBR orders are appealed to the Franklin County Common Pleas Court pursuant to RC 1509.37. There is no automatic stay of the order pending appeal; however, stay may be granted in the discretion of the court in light of any hardship that might occur. There is no procedural rule adopted by the Division of Oil and Gas incorporating either the Franklin County Common Pleas Court Local Rules or the Ohio Rules of Appellate Procedure. Counsel should examine each before filing an appeal from an OGBR decision, to avoid dismissal of the filing as untimely.

CROSS REFERENCES

See Text 19.02(B)

19.04 Practical considerations

The highly technical aspects of strip and surface mining and oil and gas drilling are all dealt with in the various statutes and rules enacted for those purposes and are probably best left to engineering experts. Legal counsel

---

[13] See Text 19.02(B), Appeals to the Reclamation Board of Review.

should be involved whenever necessary to practice preventive law and to keep violations from occurring. It is symptomatic of such enterprises that violations of at least a technical nature will from time to time occur. The matters discussed above should alert counsel to the enforcement philosophies at work as well as the procedural processes and pitfalls which await. The watchword today is compliance—compliance in every respect—with the statutes and procedural regulations enacted to govern appeals. Only with such compliance can the administrative appeals before these two divisions be properly processed.

FORMS

19.05   Notice of appeal, Reclamation Board of Review

BEFORE THE RECLAMATION BOARD OF REVIEW

ABC COAL COMPANY,	)
ADDRESS	)
TELEPHONE	)
Appellant,	)
	)
-vs.-	)Case No.
	)
OHIO DEPARTMENT OF	)
NATURAL RESOURCES,	)
DIVISION OF RECLAMATION	)
FOUNTAIN SQUARE	)
COLUMBUS, OH 43224	) NOTICE OF APPEAL
Appellee	)

Appellant hereby appeals the decision of the Chief of the Division of Reclamation in Order No _____ which (here describe order or N.O.V.). Pursuant to Section 1513.13(C), Ohio Revised Code, Appellant requests that the Chairman of the Reclamation Board of Review grant temporary relief from said order by (here describe temporary relief sought) until such time as the entire Board of Review has heard this appeal.

The permit area to which this Order/N.O.V. relates is _____.

The grounds upon which review is sought are _____.

Appellant does/does not request the Reclamation Board of Review to review the area in question.

Appellant does/does not waive its right to have a hearing within the time set forth in Division (B) of Section 1513.13 of the Ohio Revised Code.

                                             _____
                                             Signature of Appellant
                                             or Authorized Representative

19.06 Notice of violation, Division of Reclamation

TO: _____ PERMIT NO: _____

ADDRESS: _____ DISCOVERY DATE:

_____   _____ , 19 ___

APPLICABLE STATUTE AND/OR RULE: _____

_____

DESCRIPTION OF VIOLATION: _____

_____

_____

_____

_____

(A) REMEDIAL ACTION & ABATEMENT TIME: _____

_____

_____ TIME: _____ a.m./p.m. DATE: _____ , 19 ___

(B) REMEDIAL ACTION & ABATEMENT TIME: _____

_____

_____ TIME: _____ a.m./p.m. DATE: _____ , 19 ___

SERVED TO: _____ BY: _____ TIME: ____ a.m./p.m. DATE: _____
                                Authorized
                                Representative

EXTENDED TO: ___ a.m./p.m. _____ , 19 ___   EXTENDED TO: ___ a.m./p.m. _____ , 19 ___

Served to: _____ Date: _____   Served to: _____ Date: _____

By: _____ Date: _____   By: _____ Date: _____

EXTENDED TO: ___ a.m./p.m. _____ , 19 ___   EXTENDED TO: ___ a.m./p.m. _____ , 19 ___

Served to: _____ Date: _____   Served to: _____ Date: _____

By: _____ Date: _____   By: _____ Date: _____

MODIFIED: _____ , 19 ___ To: _____ By: _____

NON-
COMPLIANCE: ___ a.m./p.m. _____ , 19 ___ To: _____ By: _____

  Cessation Order
  Issued? ___ yes ___ no.   If no, explain _____

VACATED: _____ , 19 ___ To: _____ By: _____

TERMINATED: _____ , 19 ___ To: _____ By: _____

CIVIL PENALTY ASSESSMENTS

This Notice of Violation may result in a *civil penalty assessment of up to $5,000.00 per day*. Each day of continuing violation may be deemed a separate violation for purposes of penalty assessments.

FAILURE TO COMPLY

Failure to comply with *any* remedial action required by this Notice of Violation, within the prescribed abatement time, may result in *CESSATION OF MINING* and a civil penalty assessment of at least *$750.00 PER DAY*, for each day the violation continues.

INSTRUCTIONS FOR APPEAL

Review of this Notice of Violation may be obtained by filing a notice of appeal with the Reclamation Board of Review, Ohio Department of Natural Resources, 1840 Belcher Drive, Suite 200, Columbus, Ohio 43224, *within thirty days* after receipt of this Notice of Violation, and by filing a copy of the notice of appeal with the Chief of the Division of Reclamation, Ohio Department of Natural Resources, Fountain Square, Building B, Third Floor, Columbus, Ohio 43224, *within three days* after filing the notice of appeal with the Board.

Further provisions governing the review of this Notice of Violation, including request for temporary relief, are found in section 1513.13 of the Revised Code and rule promulgated thereunder.

147 Ohio Department of Natural Resources T 19.07

CHARTS

19.07 Organizational chart, Department of Natural Resources

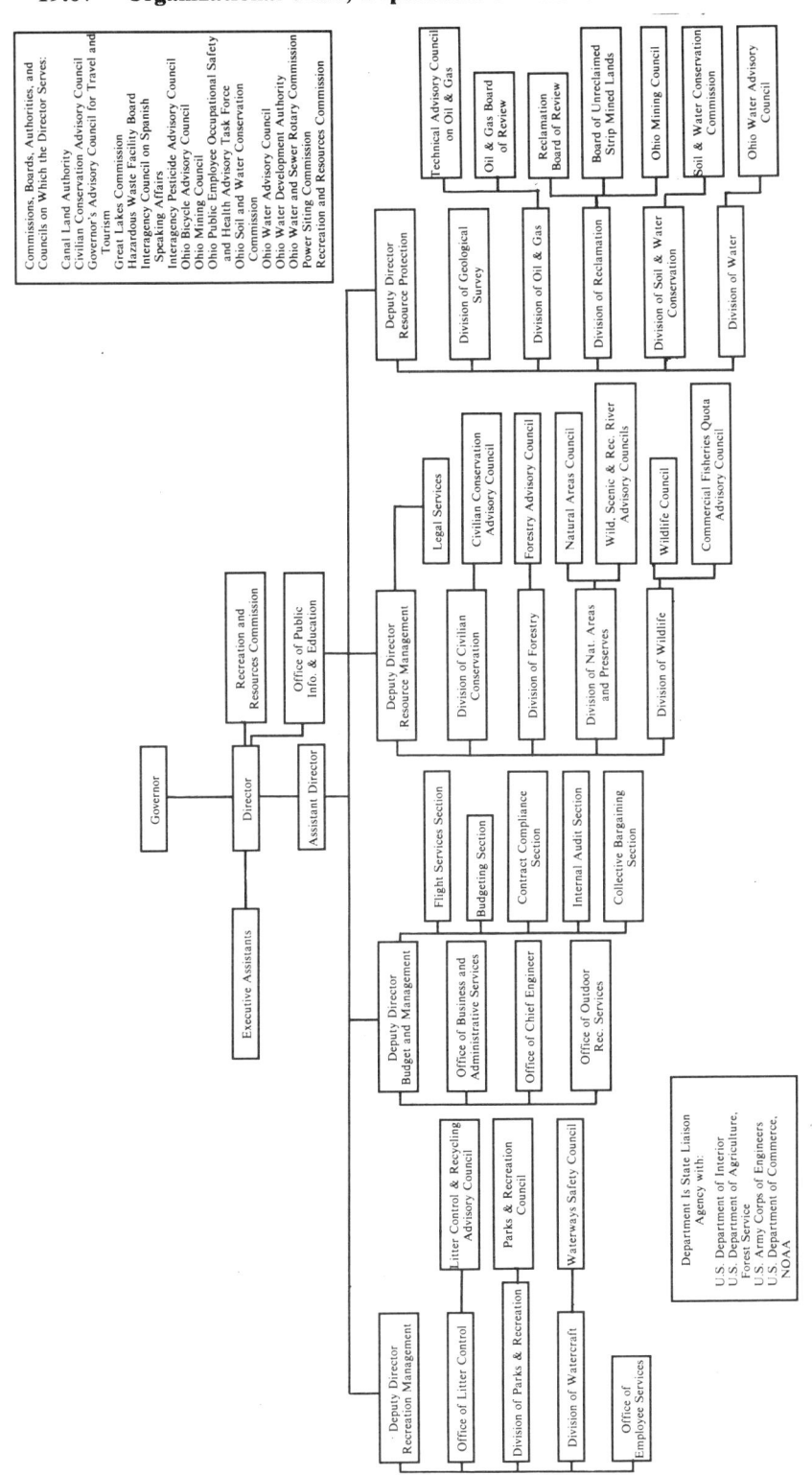

19.08 Procedural chart, Department of Natural Resources: Reclamation; Oil and Gas

Reclamation

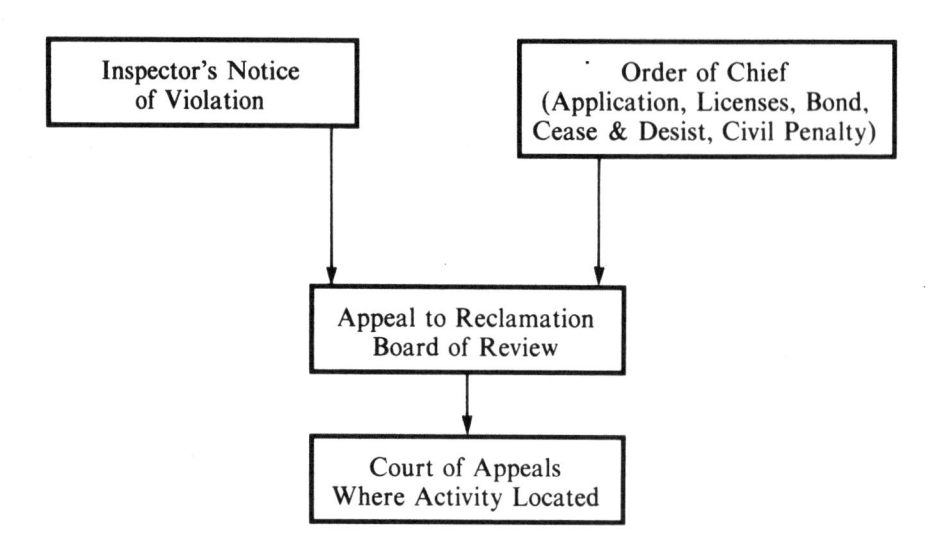

```
┌─────────────────┐      ┌──────────────────────────────┐
│ Inspector's Notice │      │       Order of Chief         │
│  of Violation    │      │ (Application, Licenses, Bond, │
│                 │      │  Cease & Desist, Civil Penalty)│
└────────┬────────┘      └──────────────┬───────────────┘
         │                              │
         └──────────────┬───────────────┘
                        ▼
              ┌──────────────────┐
              │ Appeal to Reclamation │
              │  Board of Review  │
              └─────────┬────────┘
                        ▼
              ┌──────────────────┐
              │  Court of Appeals │
              │ Where Activity Located │
              └──────────────────┘
```

Oil and Gas

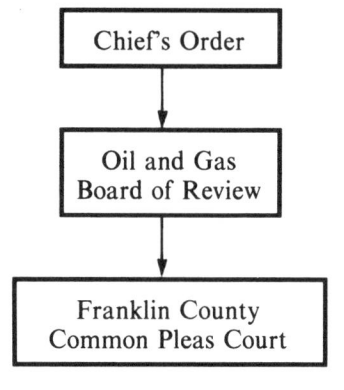

```
          ┌──────────────┐
          │ Chief's Order │
          └──────┬───────┘
                 ▼
          ┌──────────────┐
          │  Oil and Gas  │
          │ Board of Review │
          └──────┬───────┘
                 ▼
          ┌──────────────┐
          │ Franklin County │
          │ Common Pleas Court │
          └──────────────┘
```

Chapter 21

Guide to the Ohio Workers' Compensation System

By Gary W. Auman, Esq. and Michael F. Krall, Esq.

21.01	Introduction
21.02	The initial hearing
21.03	The administrative appeal process
21.04	Appeals to courts
21.05	Permanent partial disability hearings
21.06	"Handicap reimbursement" hearings
21.07	Hearings on specific safety requirements
21.08	Miscellaneous administrative proceedings

FORMS

21.09	Forms available from the Bureau of Workers' Compensation Office Services

CHARTS

21.10	Organizational chart, Bureau of Workers' Compensation
21.11	Organizational chart, Industrial Commission
21.12	Adjudication process, Industrial Commission

21.01 Introduction

To understand the procedures involved in workers' compensation practice in Ohio, a rudimentary knowledge of the framework of the Ohio Industrial Commission and the Ohio Bureau of Workers' Compensation is useful.

Private employers, as defined in RC 4123.01, may insure their workers' compensation responsibilities either by obtaining coverage through the state insurance fund administered by the Bureau of Workers' Compensation or by applying for the privilege of administering a program of "self-insurance," which is monitored by the Bureau of Workers' Compensation and the Industrial Commission.[1] An injured worker, whether employed by a state fund employer or a self-insuring employer, is entitled to the same rights and benefits. A self-insuring employer may certify (i.e., accept) claims and pay compensation and benefits directly to the injured worker.[2] A state fund employer may also certify a claim, but the claim will still be scrutinized by a Bureau of Workers' Compensation claims referee to determine compensability. If either the Bureau or the employer disputes compensability of a claim, a hearing is held before a district hearing officer (DHO) of the Industrial Commission.[3]

---

[1] RC 4123.35; OAC 4121-9-01 et seq.
[2] RC 4123.35.
[3] RC 4123.515.

The Bureau of Workers' Compensation and the Industrial Commission are separate entities with distinct legislatively mandated responsibilities in the administration of the Ohio workers' compensation program. The agencies' respective roles are myriad, and only some of their administrative functions will be discussed in this chapter.

The Bureau of Workers' Compensation may broadly be considered as the "bill-paying" agency with strictly administrative functions including the initial evaluation of claims. The Industrial Commission may properly be thought of as the adjudicatory body, although this characterization is a vast simplification. The two agencies share many functions as well as physical space in sixteen district offices across Ohio.[4]

Generally, the Industrial Commission's responsibility for adjudication of claims is handled through the use of district hearing officers, regional boards of review, staff hearing officers, and the five-member Industrial Commission itself. The hearing officer employees of the Industrial Commission must either be lawyers or have the experience necessary to make them knowledgeable in workers' compensation practices and procedures. District hearing officers exercise original jurisdiction over all partial disability compensation determinations made pursuant to RC 4123.57 and over all contested claim issues arising under RC Chapter 4123, except those for which the Industrial Commission has original jurisdiction.[5] Thus, the district hearing officers have jurisdiction over nearly all matters that would normally confront a workers' compensation practitioner, including (1) the allowance of a claim; (2) motions requesting additional conditions to be included in the claim; (3) applications to reactivate a claim; (4) problems concerning payment of medical bills; and (5) questions of continuing disability in a claim. The Industrial Commission, for example, has original jurisdiction over claims for violations of specific safety requirements[6] and applications for the final settlement of claims.[7]

The five regional boards of review created by RC 4123.14 constitute the appellate step between the decision of the district hearing officer and that of the Industrial Commission. Similar to the courts of appeals, each regional board serves a number of the Bureau's sixteen districts. Its members are appointed by the Governor, with the advice and consent of the Senate, and serve six-year staggered terms.[8]

One member of each board is classified as a representative of employers, one is classified as a representative of claimants, and the third member as chairman of the board must be admitted to the practice of law. RC 4123.14

---

[4]RC 4121.121; OAC 4121-3-01, OAC 4123-3-01 (The district offices are located in Akron, Bridgeport, Canton, Cincinnati, Cleveland, Columbus, Dayton, Hamilton, Lima, Logan, Mansfield, Portsmouth, Springfield, Toledo, Youngstown, and Zanesville.).
[5]RC 4121.34(B).
[6]RC 4121.131.
[7]RC 4123.65.
[8]RC 4123.14.

also directs the political composition of the Board, stipulating that no more than two members may belong to the same party.

The five-member Industrial Commission of Ohio has ultimate administrative authority over disputed workers' compensation claims. The members are appointed by the Governor with the advice and consent of the Senate for a term of six years. RC 4121.02 provides that two members of the Commission are designated as representatives of employers, two are designated as representatives of employees, and one is considered a representative of the public. The Industrial Commission retains exclusive jurisdiction to determine questions of permanent total disability,[9] lump sum awards,[10] final settlement of a claim,[11] appeals from regional boards of review,[12] and several other special types of problems arising in the workers' compensation system.[13]

Staff hearing officers serve as direct deputies of the five-member Industrial Commission and have original jurisdiction to consider matters over which the Industrial Commission itself has jurisdiction.[14]

One of the primary functions of the Industrial Commission is to provide an appropriate forum for the adjudication of contested claims.[15] Traditional notions of due process, the recognition of the highly specialized nature of workers' compensation practice, and a coincident belief that such disputes are best handled administratively have resulted in the evolution of a fairly complex structure of hearings.

When an employee asserts a claim, either with a self-insuring employer or with the Bureau of Workers' Compensation, the employer may certify and accept the claim as valid or reject the claim.[16] The Bureau of Workers' Compensation assigns a claim number and initiates the opening of a claim file, even when the claim is against a self-insuring employer who directly handles the bulk of the administration and paperwork. The claim file, located in the district office of the district in which the claimant resides, is freely accessible to the claimant, the employer, and their authorized representatives. Each bureau district office has a claim investigation unit responsible for obtaining the information the bureau claims referee requires to enable him to review the claim and either pay the appropriate compensation and benefits or dispute the claim[17] and docket it for a hearing before a district hearing officer.[18]

---

[9] RC 4121.35(B)(1).
[10] RC 4121.35(B)(2).
[11] RC 4121.35(B)(3).
[12] RC 4123.516.
[13] See, e.g., RC 4121.13 (Describing the powers and duties of the Industrial Commission.).
[14] RC 4121.35.
[15] RC 4121.131.
[16] OAC 4121-3-08(B).
[17] OAC 4123-3-09.
[18] RC 4123.515.

CROSS REFERENCES

Claims procedures, OAC Ch 4121-3
Claims procedures, OAC Ch 4123-3

Industrial commission, RC Ch 4121
Workers' compensation, RC Ch 4123

21.02 The initial hearing

When a claim is contested and therefore docketed for a hearing, the Industrial Commission notifies the claimant, employer, Bureau of Workers' Compensation administrator and their respective representatives of the time and place for the hearing at least fourteen days in advance.[19] All hearings before district hearing officers are conducted in the district in which the claimant resides.[20] The hearings are informal, quasi-judicial proceedings, at which the strict rules of evidence do not apply.[21] An interested party may have a court reporter present if the party notifies the Industrial Commission in writing and in advance. Although no formal guidelines presently exist regarding the use of court reporters, it is generally accepted practice for a party to provide the Industrial Commission hearing officer with ample advance notice of the intention to use a court reporter. In addition, a copy of the transcript is supplied to the state's file.

Nonparty witness testimony is occasionally utilized though not required. The claimant must establish the validity and compensability of his claim. His representative must be prepared to submit evidence on these issues; however, the testimony of the claimant himself is often sufficient to result in the district hearing officer's allowing the claim.[22] The law is to be construed liberally in favor of the claimant.[23]

Four to eight hearings are generally scheduled per hour. The district hearing officer is interested in the efficient presentation of the case. A claimant testifies briefly, subject to cross-examination; however, the remaining evidence generally consists of witness affidavits, doctor reports, and other documentary evidence. The practitioner should keep his questioning of the claimant brief, since the time constraints of the hearing schedule could detract from discussion of the law as applied to the available evidence.

A party dissatisfied with a decision of a district hearing officer may appeal as of right within twenty days of receipt of the officer's written order.[24] Appeal of the district hearing officer's order is accomplished by use of Form IC-12.[25] Like all other forms used by the Industrial Commission and the Bureau of Workers' Compensation, IC-12 is available free of charge at

---

[19] OAC 4121-3-09(C)(2) See also OAC 4121-3-30 (Hearings set on an emergency basis.).
[20] OAC 4121-3-09(C)(2).
[21] RC 4123.515.
[22] OAC 4121-3-09(B)(1) to (3).
[23] RC 4123.95.
[24] RC 4123.516.
[25] OAC 4121-3-18.

all Bureau of Workers' Compensation district offices.[26] An aggrieved party may submit a written statement in lieu of the form. The statement must be filed with the twenty-day period, and it must contain the names of the claimant and employer, the claim number, the date of the decision appealed from, and the fact that the appellant appeals therefrom as provided by law.[27]

CROSS REFERENCES
See Whiteside, Ohio Appellate Practice, Text 29.02

21.03 The administrative appeal process

Either the claimant or employer may appeal any decision of a district hearing officer.[28] The administrator of the Bureau of Workers' Compensation may appeal any decision involving a strict question of law or allegation of fraud, or one in which the employer was unrepresented at the district hearing.[29]

If no appeal is taken, the Bureau of Workers' Compensation (or the self-insuring employer) must carry out the provisions of the order.[30] An appeal of a district hearing officer's order, however, stays the payment of any compensation or benefits ordered until the appropriate regional board of review has heard the appeal and issued an order.[31]

No reason need be provided with the appeal filed from the order of a district hearing officer. The form used for the appeal requires the names of the parties, the claim number, identification of the party taking the appeal, the date that the appealing party received the order appealed, the date of the order appealed, and that portion of the order from which the appeal is taken (generally quoted in full).[32] Although no reasons need be stated to support the appeal, appeals taken for frivolous or vexatious reasons are discouraged.

The regional boards of review are three-member panels which meet periodically throughout regions encompassing three, four, or five districts. The Industrial Commission supplies a notice of hearing for district hearings. The hearings are informal. The appellant normally proceeds first and presents any evidence he feels is useful. The appeal hearing is considered a de novo hearing. The parties and the board members are not limited to any record from the district hearing.

Regional boards customarily do not announce their decisions at the conclusion of the hearing. The members may review the evidence, discuss the issues, and then vote in private. The regional boards are required by RC 4123.516 to issue their decisions within two months of the hearing or be able to demonstrate good cause for additional delay.

---

[26] OAC 4123-3-02, OAC 4123-5-12.
[27] OAC 4121-3-18.
[28] RC 4123.516; OAC 4121-3-18(A)(4).
[29] OAC 4121-3-18(A)(4).
[30] RC 4123.515.
[31] *Id.*
[32] See OAC 4121-3-18(A)(2).

As with district hearing orders, a party dissatisfied with the decision of the regional board may file a notice of appeal within twenty days of receipt of the order.[33] If the Industrial Commission decides not to hear the appeal from the regional board order, the order becomes a final order of the Industrial Commission[34] and may be appealed to a common pleas court.[35] The Industrial Commission may refuse to hear an appeal from an order of the regional board affirming the order of the district hearing officer but must hear an appeal as of right from a regional board order reversing the order of the district hearing officer and in other specified situations.

Pursuant to OAC 4121-3-18(A)(9), the situations specified in the rule include as follows: (1) the proof on file indicates the existence of an unusual legal, medical, or factual problem; (2) one of the parties failed or refused to supply needed material or factual proof within his knowledge; (3) it appears that a substantial injustice has been done to one of the parties; and (4) the proof on file indicates the possible existence of fraud.

An appeal accepted by the Industrial Commission will be heard by either the five-member Industrial Commission in Columbus or by a two-member panel of deputy commissioners, known as staff hearing officers, sitting in the appropriate region or in Columbus.[36] The appeal of a regional board order does not stay the effect of the order as does the appeal of a district hearing officer.[37] Where an order to the Bureau of Workers' Compensation or self-insuring employer to pay compensation or benefits is reversed by the Industrial Commission or its staff hearing officers, the employer may obtain from the statutory surplus fund reimbursement for the expenses caused by payment of the compensation.[38] The employer is thus not compelled to pursue a claimant for reimbursement.

CROSS REFERENCES

See Whiteside, Ohio Appellate Practice, Text 29.03

21.04 Appeals to courts

RC 4123.519 gives the limited jurisdictional basis upon which the claimant or employer may appeal a decision of the Industrial Commission to the common pleas court. This section specifically bars appeals of Industrial Commission decisions involving only the question of "extent of disability." Although the subject of many court decisions,[39] no clear definition of "extent of disability" exists. Because of the many types of issues the Industrial Commission may address, the practitioner must research the caselaw and use traditional legal analysis to determine whether his case is appealable to the

---

[33] RC 4123.516.
[34] *Id.*
[35] RC 4123.519.
[36] RC 4121.35.
[37] OAC 4121-3-18(A)(16).
[38] OAC 4121-3-18(A)(17).
[39] See, e.g., State ex rel Bosch v Industrial Comm, 1 OS(3d) 94, 1 OBR 130, 438 NE(2d) 415 (1982); Zavatsky v Stringer, 56 OS(2d) 386, 384 NE(2d) 693 (1978).

common pleas court. RC 4123.519 specifies that the appeal to common pleas court must be perfected within sixty days of receipt of the final order of the Industrial Commission.

If the decision of the Industrial Commission is not appealable to common pleas court, the practitioner should consider a petition for writ of mandamus. A mandamus action is typically filed directly with the Franklin County Court of Appeals. As is generally true of mandamus actions, the court will reverse or modify the Industrial Commission's action only if it finds that the Industrial Commission abused its discretion.[40]

For example, in *State ex rel Hutt v Frick-Gallagher Mfg Co*,[41] the Ohio Supreme Court held that the Industrial Commission abused its discretion by failing to find the claimant permanently and totally disabled. Two of the four medical reports relied on by the Commission stated that the claimant could not return to work (the dispositive issue in determining permanent and total disability), and the remaining two reports did not address this issue. Thus, there was no evidence in the record to support the Commission's finding.

The writ of mandamus was denied in *State ex rel Burdette v Dayton Walther Corp*.[42] There the Commission denied the claimant's motion to be declared permanently and totally disabled due to pulmonary silicosis. The Commission based this decision on one medical report stating that silicosis was not the total cause of the claimant's inability to return to work and on another report stating that the claimant could work in a pollution-free environment. There was, therefore, some substantial evidence in the record to support the Commission's finding, and the writ was properly denied.

The Ohio Supreme Court has held that an official's act is arbitrary, and consequently an abuse of discretion, when it is not founded on supportive evidence.[43]

CROSS REFERENCES

See Whiteside, Ohio Appellate Practice, Text 29.04 to 29.09

21.05 Permanent partial disability hearings

Forty weeks after the last payment of temporary total disability compensation to a claimant (or after the date of injury if no payment of compensation has ever been awarded), the claimant may file an application for the determination of permanent partial disability.[44] This is also known by its

---

[40]State ex rel Burdette v Dayton Walther Corp, 14 OS(3d) 29, 14 OBR 331, 470 NE(2d) 897 (1984).

[41]State ex rel Hutt v Frick-Gallagher Mfg Co, 11 OS(3d) 184, 11 OBR 497, 464 NE(2d) 1005 (1984).

[42]State ex rel Burdette v Dayton Walther Corp, 14 OS(3d) 29, 14 OBR 331, 470 NE(2d) 897 (1984).

[43]See, e.g., State ex rel Mitchell v Robbins & Myers, Inc, 6 OS(3d) 481, 6 OBR 531, 453 NE(2d) 721 (1983); State ex rel Wilms v Blake, 144 OS 619, 60 NE(2d) 308 (1945).

[44]RC 4123.57.

Industrial Commission form number as a "C-92." The forty-week "healing period" is designed to insure that any temporary disability has become permanent, because it is a permanent, residual impairment for which the claimant is to be compensated.

Upon application, the claimant will be scheduled for an examination by an Industrial Commission physician who will render an opinion as to the percentage of residual impairment resulting from the allowed condition in the claim.[45] Both the claimant's attorney and employer's representative may have the claimant examined by a physician of their choosing. The Industrial Commission rules allow an employer to have the claimant examined in accordance with certain guidelines within thirty days of receipt of the claimant's application for determination of permanent partial disability.[46]

After the examinations are completed, the Industrial Commission will docket the application and claim file and schedule the application for a hearing before a district hearing officer. The Industrial Commission gives notice of the hearing in the same manner as the original allowance hearing.[47] The commissioner schedules permanent partial disability hearings approximately twelve to an hour, because the only issue to be discussed at the hearing is the claimant's actual residual impairment. At this stage, the district hearing will not entertain any question of the compensability or the allowed conditions in the claim.

The hearing officer will evaluate the report of the Industrial Commission doctor and any reports from the claimant's and the employer's doctors. Normally at the conclusion of the hearing, the hearing officer will announce his decision of the percentage award, which, for payment purposes, is translated into weeks of compensation. For example, if a claimant is found to be five per cent permanently and partially impaired as a result of an industrial injury, he is awarded ten weeks of compensation at a rate set by RC 4123.57(B). The claimant may elect to receive this compensation in the form of a lump sum known as a "paragraph B award," or in the form of an impairment of earnings capacity known as a "paragraph A award." The latter could result in more compensation over a longer period of time subject to a statutory maximum. A paragraph A award contemplates that the employee has returned to work but due to the residual impairment cannot earn as much as before the injury.

A party may appeal the permanent partial disability decision of a district hearing officer by requesting reconsideration using Industrial Commission form C 88. The request must be filed within ten days of receipt of the order. A staff hearing officer of the Industrial Commission hears the request for reconsideration.[48] This hearing is the only available administrative review of a percentage of permanent partial disability determination award. The only recourse of a party dissatisfied with an order rendered on reconsideration is a

---

[45] OAC 4121-3-15(C)(3).
[46] OAC 4121-3-15(C)(2).
[47] RC 4123.57(A); OAC 4121-3-15(C)(4).
[48] RC 4123.57(B); OAC 4121-3-15(C)(6).

petition for writ of mandamus filed in the Franklin County Court of Appeals. Commission orders that award and determine only the extent of an individual's disability are not appealable to the common pleas court under RC 4123.519.

21.06 "Handicap reimbursement" hearings

"Handicap reimbursement" is one of the few procedures in which the Revised Code and the rules of the Ohio Industrial Commission provide an opportunity for employers to receive reimbursement from the Industrial Commission of money paid to claimants in workers' compensation claims. Handicap reimbursements are not intended as a bonus for complying with the law nor are they available to every employer in every workers' compensation claim.

In enacting the handicap reimbursement statute, RC 4123.343, the intent of the General Assembly was to encourage employers to hire handicapped employees by creating an incentive to the employer to hire and retain handicapped employees, rather than merely making it unlawful to discriminate against the handicapped. Pursuant to the handicap reimbursement provisions, RC 4123.343 and OAC 4121-3-28, employers in Ohio who hire an employee with a handicap that either causes or significantly increases the cost of a workers' compensation claim will be entitled to a reimbursement of a percentage of the cost of that claim. Reimbursement is through an actual dollar rebate for a self-insuring employer[49] and lowered premiums for a state fund employer.[50] The statute and rule enumerate twenty-five recognized handicaps for which an employer may seek handicap reimbursement.

The percentage of handicap reimbursement may be applied only against certain costs of the claim. A reimbursement may be received for temporary total benefits, permanent total disability benefits, or death benefits. Further, the reimbursement may be awarded for all medical costs that have accrued in the claim.[51] No reimbursement is awarded for permanent partial disability or impairment of earning capacity awards or for lump sum settlements. A handicap reimbursement award applies to all appropriate benefits paid in the claim, both before and after the award for as long as the claim is open.

To be eligible for handicap reimbursement, the employer must demonstrate that the injured employee was afflicted with one of the enumerated handicaps prior to sustaining an industrial injury and that the industrial injury would not have occurred or was aggravated by the preexisting handicap condition.[52] The employer also must notify the Commission of the existence of the handicap of each employee as soon as the employer becomes

---

[49] RC 4123.343(B); OAC 4121-3-28(I).
[50] RC 4123.343(B); OAC 4121-3-28(B).
[51] RC 4123.343(B).
[52] See RC 4123.343(D)(1), (2).

aware of it.[53] This preregistration requirement generally causes the employer the most difficulty.

Application for handicap reimbursement is made on Form IC-CHP-4. Pursuant to OAC 4121-3-28(I), a self-insured employer has five years from the date of injury to file an application for handicap reimbursement. How this administrative statute of limitations will be applied to an additional condition finally added to a claim more than five years after the original date of injury is unclear. The reimbursement application does not require great detail. The Industrial Commission is usually interested in the answer to only one question: Was prior notification made to the Industrial Commission of the preexisting handicap? If the answer is "No," the employer's representative must be prepared to explain to the hearing officer the reason for the employer's failure to notify the Commission and preregister the employee as a handicapped individual.

Upon the filing of an application for handicap reimbursement, the claim file is sent to the Columbus office of the Industrial Commission where the Commission dockets the claim on a special docket only for handicap reimbursement hearings. Normally the claimant does not attend the hearing. The notice of hearing states to the claimant that the decision made at the hearing will not in any way affect the claimant's benefits. Under RC 4121.39(A)(4), the administrator of the Bureau of Workers' Compensation is designated as the trustee of the surplus fund from which handicap reimbursements are paid. Therefore, the employer's representative can normally expect the assistant attorney general representing the administrator to oppose the application.

The hearing on an application for handicap reimbursement is before a staff hearing officer. At a handicap reimbursement hearing the employer's representative will present medical evidence to the hearing officer establishing (1) that the handicap preexisted the industrial injury; (2) that the handicap was involved in the disability caused by the industrial injury; and (3) the extent of that involvement. Upon conclusion of the hearing, the hearing officer generally will announce the amount of reimbursement that the employer will receive.

There is no appeal to the common pleas court from a handicap reimbursement hearing decision.[54] Only one internal appeal within the administrative agency is available. OAC 4121-3-28(H) provides the employer a right of appeal from the staff hearing officer's decision to the Industrial Commission. As in any appearance before the full Industrial Commission, the employer's representative should be certain that his case is well prepared and presented. When the employer appeals a handicap reimbursement decision, the administrator's representative will be notified of the appeal; therefore, the practitioner must remember that the staff hearing officers or the Industrial Com-

---

[53] RC 4123.343(C); OAC 4121-3-28(B)(5).

[54] RC 4123.519 (Only orders pertaining to injury and occupational disease claims may be appealed to the courts.).

mission may reduce the award rather than increase it. The appeal is a final appeal, subject only to the possibility of an action in mandamus.[55]

21.07 Hearings on specific safety requirements

Section 35, Article II of the Ohio Constitution provides:

> Such board [now Industrial Commission] shall have full power and authority to hear and determine whether or not an injury, disease or death resulted because of the failure of the employer to comply with any specific requirement for the protection of the lives, health or safety of the employees, enacted by the general assembly or in the form of an order adopted by such board, and its decision shall be final. ... When it is found, upon hearing, that the injury, disease or death resulted because of such failure by the employer, such amount as shall be found to be just, not greater than fifty nor less than fifteen per centum of the maximum award established by law, shall be added by the board, to the amount of compensation that may be awarded on account of such injury, disease, or death.

Pursuant to this constitutional provision and RC 4121.13, the Industrial Commission's Bureau for Prevention of Accidents and Diseases (commonly known as the Division of Safety and Hygiene) has promulgated in the Ohio Administrative Code the following safety standards to govern industry in Ohio:

(1) OAC 4121:1-1, Specific Safety Requirements for the Operation of Elevators

(2) OAC 4121:1-3, Specific Safety Requirements Relating to Construction

(3) OAC 4121:1-5, Workshops and Factories

(4) OAC 4121:1-7, Foundries

(5) OAC 4121:1-9, Steel Mills

(6) OAC 4121:1-11, Laundry Machinery and Operation; Drycleaning and Dyeing

(7) OAC 4121:1-13, Rubber and Plastic Industries

(8) OAC 4121:1-15, Potteries

(9) OAC 4121:1-17, Window Cleaning

(10) OAC 4121:1-19, Installation and Maintenance of Electrical Supply Lines and Transmission and Distribution of Electrical Power in Such Lines

When an employee suffers an industrial injury and he or his representative feels that the injury was caused by the employer's violation of a specific safety requirement, the employee may elect to file an application for an

---

[55]See, e.g., State ex rel Dover Corp v Industrial Comm, 13 App(3d) 430, 13 OBR 518, 469 NE(2d) 935 (Franklin 1984) (The court heard and allowed a writ of mandamus to vacate the Industrial Commission's order denying the relator-employer handicap reimbursement.).

additional award alleging violation of the specific safety requirement. The employee's application should provide a description of the incident or injury, the nature of the injury suffered, and a list of the specific safety requirements which the employee alleges were violated and which resulted in the injury.[56] This application must be filed by the employee within two years of the date of injury; there are no exceptions.[57] The defense of untimely filing should be stated by the employer in its answer to the application, which must be filed with the Industrial Commission within thirty days after receipt of the application.[58] The employer's attorney should treat the application for an additional award in the same manner as a complaint in a civil suit and should immediately initiate a fairly detailed and serious investigation of the equipment or circumstances involved in the alleged violation. A carefully drafted answer based on a thorough employer's investigation may serve the employer well by guiding the later Commission investigation.

After the answer to the application has been received by the Industrial Commission, the Industrial Commission's Division of Safety and Hygiene conducts an investigation.[59] Usually, several months after the filing of the answer, the Commission's investigator will appear unannounced at a company's facilities. The investigator will interview witnesses and will inspect and photograph any equipment alleged to be in violation of a specific safety requirement.

After receipt of the investigator's report, the employer and the claimant may submit any additional evidence that they feel should be before the Industrial Commission at the hearing. OAC 4121-3-20(D) limits to thirty days the time to submit this additional evidence; however, a party may request additional time. The Industrial Commission has historically been quite liberal in allowing a party as much time as the party deems necessary to submit all of its evidence. During the period for submitting additional evidence, the parties must evaluate the possibility of having a record hearing. If such a hearing is held, a transcript is made of evidence received and testimony taken.[60] If a record hearing is elected, the parties need not submit evidence before the hearing.

After the period for submitting additional evidence has closed, the Industrial Commission will set the application for additional award for a hearing. Unless a record hearing has been requested, no additional evidence other than testimony will be accepted at the hearing.[61]

At the hearing, held before a staff hearing officer in Columbus, both the claimant and the employer are usually present and represented by counsel. Testimony may be presented, but the major purpose of the hearing is to

---

[56] OAC 4121-3-20(A).
[57] *Id.*
[58] OAC 4121-3-20(C).
[59] OAC 4121-3-20(D).
[60] OAC 4121-3-20(D).
[61] *Id.*

provide the employer and the claimant an opportunity to present legal arguments on the application based upon the evidence.

To reach his determination, the hearing officer must go through a three-step process on each specific safety requirement allegedly violated. First, the officer must decide whether the specific safety requirement allegedly violated applies to the particular employer's industry and to the job at which the claimant was working when he was injured. If the staff hearing officer decides that the safety requirement allegedly violated applies to the industry and job, he must next determine whether there was actually a violation of a cited specific requirement. Once the hearing officer is convinced of both of these points, he must still determine whether the requirement violated was a direct cause of the claimant's injury.[62]

After the hearing, the staff hearing officer generally takes the matter under advisement and issues an order several weeks later. This order merely states whether the hearing officer has found a violation and, if so, what specific section of the safety requirement has been violated and what penalty the hearing officer has determined to assess.

If either party demonstrates that additional relevant evidence is available that was not considered at the hearing, the Industrial Commission will grant an appeal or a rehearing,[63] which is typically heard by another staff hearing officer. In some special cases or in extreme circumstances, the full five-member Commission may hear the appeal. Section 35, Article II of the Ohio Constitution declares the decision of the Industrial Commission to be a "final" decision; therefore, the decision on rehearing is not appealable to the common pleas court.[64] Consequently, the only remedy available to an aggrieved party is to seek a writ of mandamus, alleging an abuse of discretion on the part of the Industrial Commission.[65] In accordance with Section 3, Article IV of the Ohio Constitution, the Ohio courts of appeal are the courts of original jurisdiction for a writ of mandamus. The petition is filed as a complaint, and the complaint is filed in the Franklin County Court of Appeals pursuant to Civil Rule 3, which places venue in the county wherein the defendant (Industrial Commission) has its principal place of business. As in all such cases, the court of appeals is restricted to the record before the Industrial Comm and to the Industrial Commission's findings.

---

[62] See State ex rel Haines v Industrial Comm, 29 OS(2d) 15, 278 NE(2d) 24 (1972).

[63] OAC 4121-3-20(G).

[64] See, e.g., State ex rel Cleveland Railway Co v Atkinson, 138 OS 157, 34 NE(2d) 233 (1941) (Holding that the enabling legislation of the Bureau of Unemployment Compensation limited appeal of final orders of the Bureau, unless the statute expressly provided for an appeal.).

[65] See, e.g., State ex rel Harris v Industrial Comm, 12 OS(3d) 152, 12 OBR 223, 465 NE(2d) 1286 (1984) (Holding that mandamus will not lie to vacate an order of the Commission unless that order constitutes an abuse of discretion.).

21.08 Miscellaneous administrative proceedings

The Industrial Commission hearings previously discussed are the ones most commonly encountered by a practitioner in a workers' compensation case. However, there are numerous other types of hearings and issues which come before various hearing officers of the Industrial Commission.

One less common type of administrative proceeding is a hearing conducted pursuant to RC 4123.522. That section reads in pertinent part:

> The employee, employer and their respective representatives shall be entitled to written notice of any hearing, determination, order, award or decision, under the provisions of Chapter 4123. of the Revised Code.
>
> If any person to whom a notice is mailed shall fail to receive such notice and the industrial commission, upon hearing, shall determine that such failure was due to cause beyond the control and without the fault or neglect of such person or his representative and that such person or his representative did not have actual knowledge of the import of the information contained in such notice, such person may take the action afforded to such person within twenty days after the receipt of such notice of such determination of the industrial commission.

In essence, two Industrial Commission staff hearing officers consider such ".522 motions" in hearings having a format similar to other Industrial Commission hearings. Typically, these hearings are very brief as they address only one issue: whether the moving party may appeal even though the twenty-day appeal period has run. Occasionally, however, a legal argument arises, and many significant court decisions concerning this area of workers' compensation law have been rendered in recent years.[66] Historically, the staff hearing officers have liberally allowed late appeals, giving the party alleging nonreceipt of an order the benefit of any doubts.

An agreement among a claimant, employer, and, in the case of a state fund claim, the Bureau of Workers' Compensation on a figure for full and final settlement of a claim is subject to the approval of the Industrial Commission.[67] Hearings on applications for settlement are scheduled if some doubt exists as to the fairness of the settlement sum; however, applications are often approved without a formal hearing.

Finally, as already alluded to, the full five-member Industrial Commission reserves for itself hearings on applications for permanent and total disability. These hearings follow the basic Industrial Commission format but are more formal because of the seriousness of the question whether an injured worker is capable of continuing any substantial remunerative employment.

The practitioner should remember that he is dealing with an administrative agency which has a great deal of discretion. Anything requested by a claimant or an employer that causes the other party to object may result in

---

[66]See, e.g., Skiba v Connor, 5 OS(3d) 147, 5 OBR 313, 449 NE(2d) 775 (1983); State ex rel Nicodemus v Industrial Comm, 5 OS(3d) 58, 5 OBR 115, 448 NE(2d) 1360 (1983).

[67]RC 4123.64, RC 4123.65.

an Industrial Commission hearing. Such a miscellaneous hearing may be held by a district hearing officer, or one or more staff hearing officers, or by the Industrial Commission. In no case will a question first be heard by a regional board of review.

The Industrial Commission retains broad discretion to determine how to dispose of questions concerning a workers' compensation claim. The practitioner must remember that flexibility is the key to any good administrative agency. The Industrial Commission and the Bureau of Workers' Compensation attempt to be as accommodating as possible.

FORMS

21.09 Forms available from the Bureau of Workers' Compensation Office Services

C-1	State Fund—Lost Time Application
C-1A	Attending Physician's Report and Fee Bill
C-2	First Notice of Death
C-3	State Fund—Medical Only
C-5	Application for Widows Benefits (Death)
C-16	Hospital Fee Bill
C-17	General Fee Bill
C-19	Attending Physician's Fee Bill
C-35	Fee Bill Status Notification
C-47	Authorization for Medical Treatment
C-48	Disallowance of Medical Treatment
C-50	Application for Payment of Compensation and Medical Benefits
C-62C	Additional Information Request—Claimant
C-62E	Additional Information Request—Employer
C-74	Cides Error Tag
C-77	Address Verification
C-84	Physician's Report Supplemental
C-85A	Application to Reactivate Claim
C-86	Motion (Hrg. Request)
C-87	Undertaker's Certificate of Death and Cost Bill
C-94A	Wage Statement
C-102	Fee Bill Inquiry Response
C-108	Dentist's Report and Fee Bill
C-110	Exclusive Remedy Agreement—Ohio
C-112	Exclusive Remedy Agreement—Other States
C-116	Sole Proprietor Coverage
C-129	Review of Microfiche
C-151	Status Report
C-158	Request for Action from Representative
C-161	Request for Medical Authorizations
C-173	FBIS Reject Letter

C-174	Self-Insured Report Form
C-180	Code "77" Message Slip
C-181	Fee Bill Inquiry
C-230	Power of Attorney Form
CA-1	Change of Address
OD-1	Occupational Disease Claim Application
OIC 3012 (IC-2)	Application for Compensation for Permanent and Total Disability
OIC 3017 (IC-6)	Application for Compensation Accrued at Time of Death
OIC 3000 (IC-12)	Notice of Appeal
OIC 2016 (IC-20)	Nursing Fee Bill
OIC 3002 (IC-90)	Election
OIC 3023 (IC-92)	% Permanent Partial Application
OIC 3024 (IC-92A)	% Permanent Partial Increase Application
OIC 1029 (IC-CHP-2)	Update of Handicapped Employees Inventory
OIC 1012 (IC-CHP-4)	Application for Handicapped Reimbursement
OIC 3003 (IC-32)	Lump Sum Payment Application
OIC 3022 (IC-32A)	Lump Sum Payment of Attorney Fees
OIC 3016 (F-32)	Lump Sum Payment Invoice
OIC 3005 (L-102)	Lump Sum Settlement Application
R-1	Employer Attorney Authorization
R-2	Claimant Attorney Authorization
R-3	Request to Inspect Claim or Risk File

CHARTS

21.10 Organizational chart, Bureau of Workers' Compensation

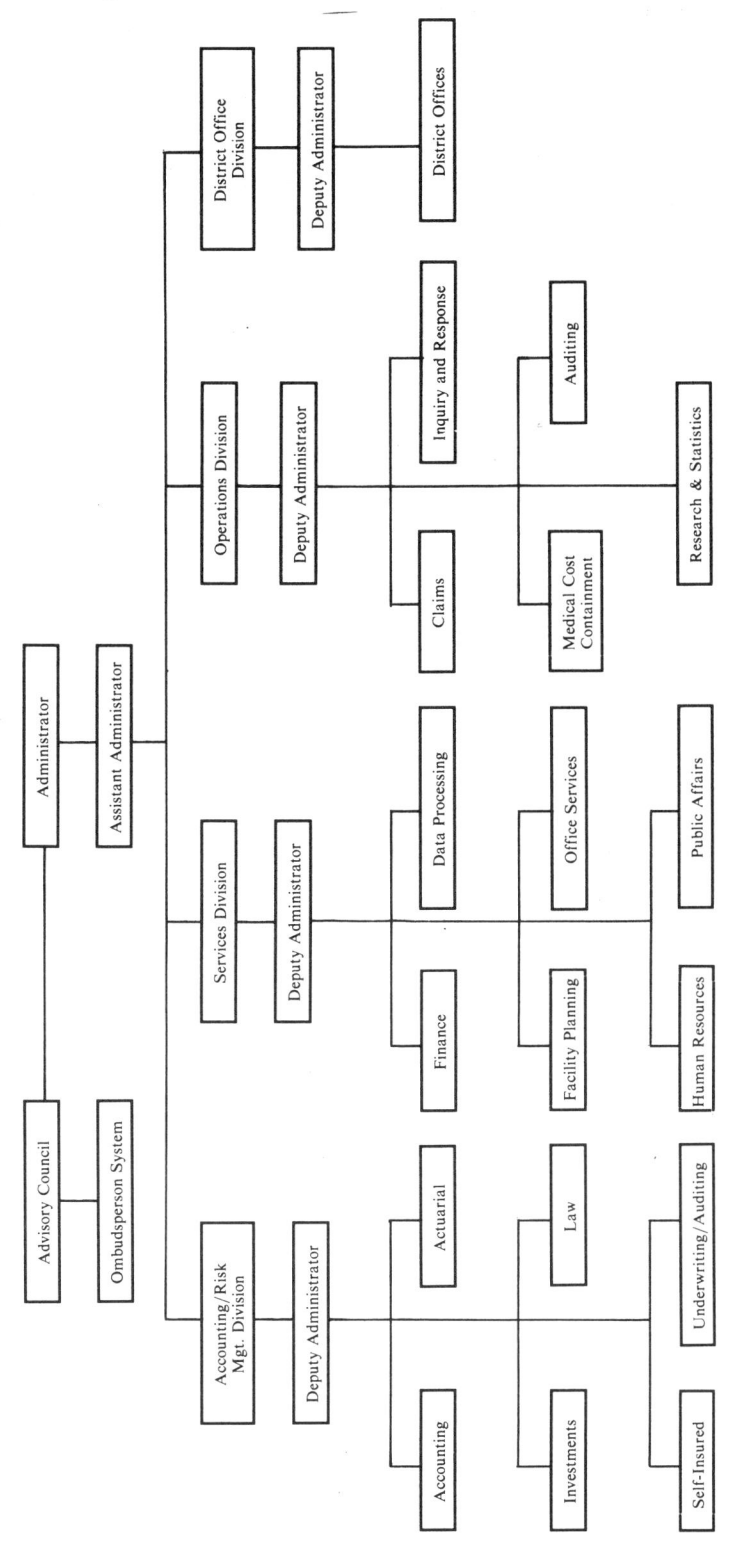

```
                                    Administrator
                                          |
                    +---------------------+---------------------+
                    |                     |                     |
            Advisory Council      Assistant Administrator
            Ombudsperson System           |
                                          |
    +-------------------+-----------------+-----------------+-------------------+
    |                   |                                   |                   |
Accounting/Risk    Services Division              Operations Division    District Office
Mgt. Division           |                                   |              Division
    |                   |                                   |                   |
Deputy Administrator  Deputy Administrator        Deputy Administrator   Deputy Administrator
    |                   |                                   |                   |
    +--Actuarial        +--Data Processing                  +--Inquiry and      +--District Offices
    +--Accounting       +--Finance                          |   Response
    +--Law              +--Office Services                  +--Claims
    +--Investments      +--Facility Planning                +--Auditing
    +--Underwriting/    +--Public Affairs                   +--Medical Cost
    |   Auditing        +--Human Resources                  |   Containment
    +--Self-Insured                                         +--Research & Statistics
```

21.11 Organizational chart, Industrial Commission

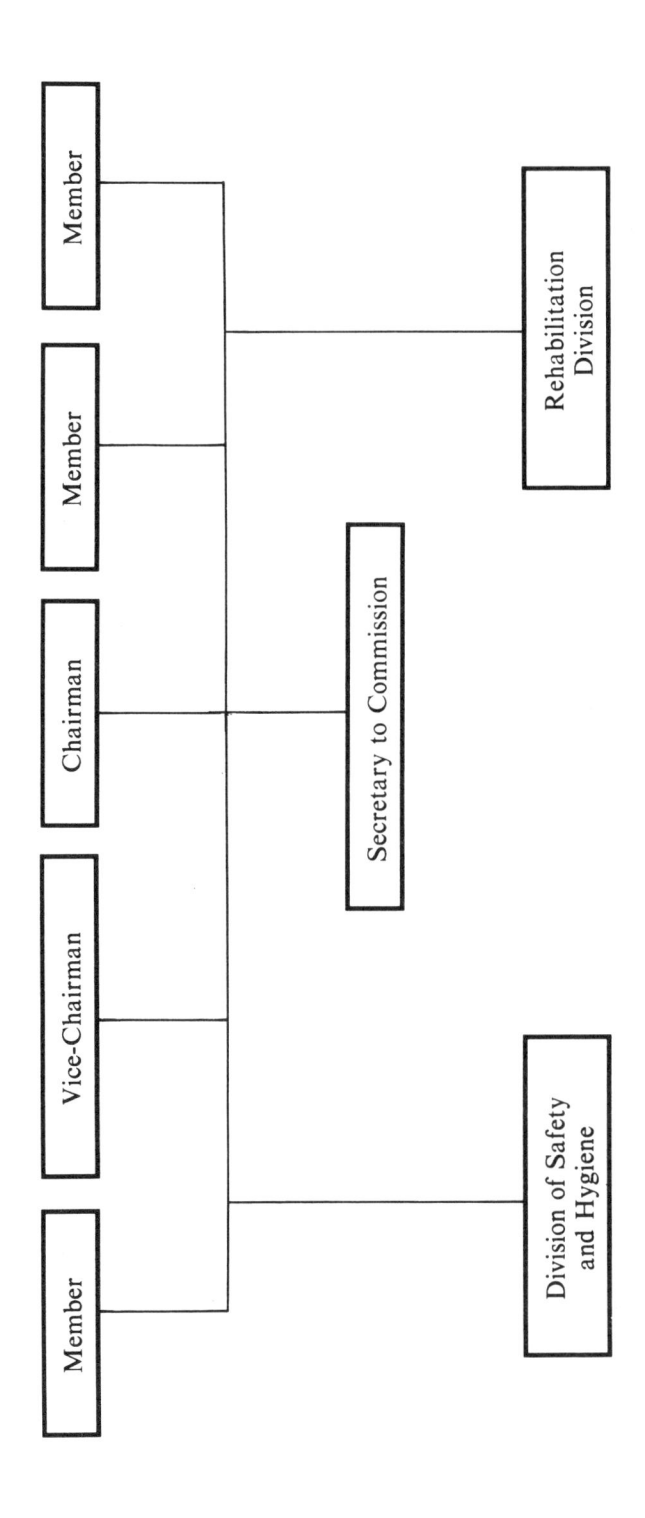

```
                    ┌──────────┐
                    │  Member  │
                    └────┬─────┘
                         │
                    ┌────┴─────┐                    ┌────────────────┐
                    │  Member  │────────────────────│ Rehabilitation │
                    └────┬─────┘                    │    Division    │
                         │                          └────────────────┘
                    ┌────┴─────┐                    ┌────────────────┐
                    │ Chairman │────────────────────│  Secretary to  │
                    └────┬─────┘                    │   Commission   │
                         │                          └────────────────┘
                    ┌────┴─────────┐
                    │ Vice-Chairman│
                    └────┬─────────┘
                         │                          ┌────────────────┐
                    ┌────┴─────┐                    │ Division of    │
                    │  Member  │────────────────────│ Safety and     │
                    └──────────┘                    │ Hygiene        │
                                                    └────────────────┘
```

21.12 Adjudication process, Industrial Commission

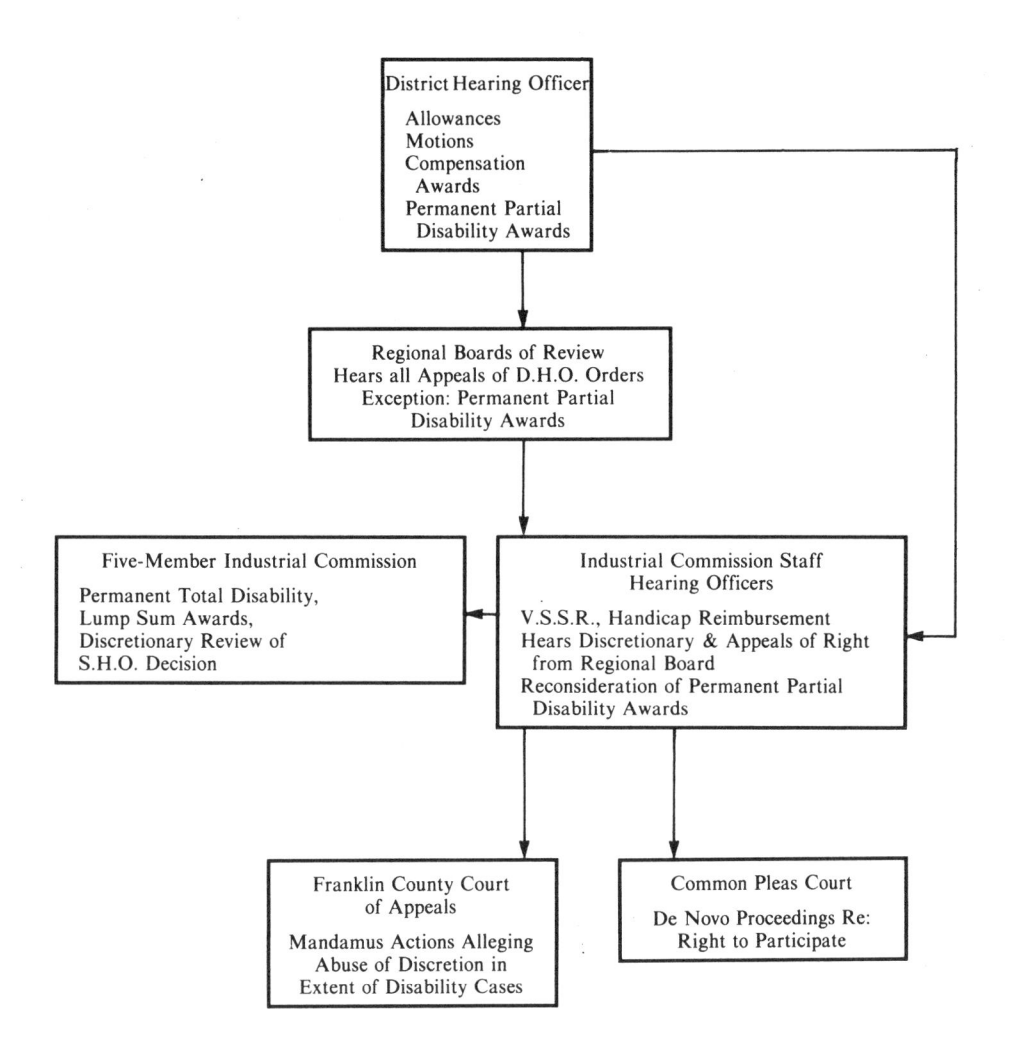

```
┌─────────────────────────┐
│ District Hearing Officer│
│                         │
│   Allowances            │
│   Motions               │
│   Compensation          │
│     Awards              │
│   Permanent Partial     │
│     Disability Awards   │
└─────────────────────────┘
            │
            ▼
┌─────────────────────────┐
│ Regional Boards of Review│
│ Hears all Appeals of D.H.O. Orders │
│ Exception: Permanent Partial │
│   Disability Awards     │
└─────────────────────────┘
            │
            ▼
┌──────────────────────────┐     ┌──────────────────────────────┐
│ Five-Member Industrial   │     │ Industrial Commission Staff  │
│ Commission               │◄────│ Hearing Officers             │
│                          │     │                              │
│ Permanent Total Disability,│   │ V.S.S.R., Handicap Reimbursement │
│ Lump Sum Awards,         │     │ Hears Discretionary & Appeals of Right │
│ Discretionary Review of  │     │   from Regional Board        │
│ S.H.O. Decision          │     │ Reconsideration of Permanent Partial │
│                          │     │   Disability Awards          │
└──────────────────────────┘     └──────────────────────────────┘
                                        │              │
                                        ▼              ▼
                        ┌──────────────────────────┐  ┌────────────────────┐
                        │ Franklin County Court    │  │ Common Pleas Court │
                        │ of Appeals               │  │                    │
                        │                          │  │ De Novo Proceedings Re: │
                        │ Mandamus Actions Alleging│  │   Right to Participate │
                        │ Abuse of Discretion in   │  │                    │
                        │ Extent of Disability Cases│ │                    │
                        └──────────────────────────┘  └────────────────────┘
```

Chapter 23

Afterword

By William A. Carroll, Esq.

In connection with research incident to the preparation of this book as well as research necessitated in litigating differences of legal opinion with agencies, the author, at least from the viewpoint of a superannuate, has been impressed by the relative infancy of the entire body of administrative law and procedure. For example, before the 1947 edition of West's *Decennial Digest*, there was no topical heading of "Administrative Law and Procedure." In a relatively brief period, however, agencies, with their concomitant impact on the legal, social, and political structure, have proliferated.

Practicing law in an environment that is increasingly regimented, increasingly government oriented, and increasingly monolithic tends to create a virtually unconscious assumption of the legality or correctness of the basic premises upon which agencies purport to perform their various functions. Thus, while the practitioner may vigorously and competently evaluate and contest the litigable facts in a case, he must not fail to explore thoroughly

(1) The facial constitutionality of the statute involved;

(2) The constitutionality of the statute involved as applied by the agency;

(3) The substantive validity of the rule or regulation involved, i.e., its legal consonance with the statute to which it relates or its effect of writing or rewriting the underlying legislation;

(4) Compliance with the requirements of the Ohio Administrative Procedure Act in adopting any rule relevant to the case; and

(5) Any other factor which a lawyer, thinking offensively rather than defensively, should explore.

Only after considering all of these issues should the practitioner make his ultimate decision whether to demand justice or beg for mercy. The first alternative is infinitely professionally fulfilling; the latter is often necessary.

In agency practice, it helps to know the agency personnel. It also helps to have an established reputation for straight shooting. The agency staff will generally help the lawyer unfamiliar with agency procedures. Thus, a telephone call to the department or, when applicable, to the assistant attorney general handling a case will generally yield dividends in assisting the lawyer in his journey through the unfamiliar maze.

The attitude with which the practitioner approaches the case and the attitude with which he regards the agency itself are fundamental to successful advocacy before an agency. In this respect the words of Justice Jackson, while not legally authoritative since they belong to a dissenting opinion, illustrate the proper attitude:

> Courts have differed in assigning a place to these seemingly necessary bodies in our constitutional system. Administrative agencies have been

called quasi-legislative, quasi-executive or quasi-judicial, as the occasion required, in order to validate their functions within the separation-of-powers scheme of the Constitution. The mere retreat to the qualifying "quasi" is implicit with confession that all recognized classifications have broken down, and "quasi" is a smooth cover which we draw over our confusion as we might use a counterpane to conceal a disordered bed.[1]

Thus, it behooves the lawyer having confidence in his cause to mount his white charger, couch his (albeit wilted) lance, enter the lists, and courageously joust with the awesome force of bureaucracy arrayed against him. To utterly mix the metaphor, should the practitioner in the guise of David best the formidable Goliath of government, more power to him. At least, he may emerge from the fray with head bloody but unbowed, better prepared to fight again.

---

[1] Federal Trade Commission v Ruberoid Co, 343 US 470, 487-88, 72 SCt 800, 96 LEd 1081 (1952) (Jackson, J., dissenting).

OHIO REVISED CODE
(Selected Provisions)

Chapter 101   General Assembly
Chapter 111   Secretary of State
Chapter 119   Administrative Procedure
Chapter 2506   Appeals from Orders of Administrative Officers, and Agencies

Chapter 101

General Assembly

101.35 Joint committee on agency rule review

There is hereby created in the general assembly the joint committee on agency rule review. The committee shall consist of five members of the house of representatives and five members of the senate. Within fifteen days after the commencement of the first regular session of each general assembly, the speaker of the house of representatives and the president of the senate shall each appoint the members of the committee from his house; not more than three of the members from each house shall be of the same political party. In the first regular session of a general assembly, the chairman of the committee shall be appointed by the speaker of the house from among the house members of the committee, and the vice-chairman shall be appointed by the president of the senate from among the senate members of the committee. In the second regular session of a general assembly, the chairman shall be appointed by the president of the senate from among the senate members of the committee, and the vice-chairman shall be appointed by the speaker of the house from among the house members of the committee. The chairman, vice-chairman, and members of the committee shall serve until their respective successors are appointed or until they are no longer members of the general assembly. When a vacancy occurs among the officers or members of the committee, it shall be filled in the same manner as the original appointment.

The committee has the same powers as other standing or select committees of the general assembly. Six members constitute a quorum, and the concurrence of six members is required for the recommendation of a concurrent resolution invalidating a proposed or effective rule, amendment, rescission, or part thereof, or for the suspension of a rule, amendment, rescission, or part thereof, under division (I) of section 119.03 or section 119.031 of the Revised Code.

The committee may meet during periods in which the general assembly has adjourned. At meetings of the committee, the committee may request a rule-making agency, as defined in section 119.01 of the Revised Code, to provide information relative to the agency's implementation of its statutory authority.

HISTORY: 1984 H 244, eff. 7-4-84
  1979 S 8; 1977 S 115, H 257

CROSS REFERENCES

OJur 3d: 2, Administrative Law § 63.5

---

51 Ohio Bar 318 (1978). The General Assembly's New Role in Agency Rule-Making, Frederick A. Vierow.

Chapter 111

Secretary of State

111.15 Rules filed; duties of legislative service commission; standards and procedures

(A) As used in this section:

(1) "Rule" includes any rule, regulation, bylaw, or standard having a general and uniform operation adopted by an agency under the authority of the laws governing the agency; any appendix to a rule; and any internal management rule. "Rule" does not include any order respecting the duties of employees, any finding, any determination of a question of law or fact in a matter presented to an agency, or any rule promulgated pursuant to Chapter 119., section 4141.14, division (C)(1) or (2) of section 5117.02, or section 5703.14 of the Revised Code. "Rule" includes any amendment or rescission of a rule.

(2) "Agency" means any governmental entity of the state and includes, but is not limited to, any board, department, division, commission, bureau, society, council, institution, state college or university, community college district, technical college district, or state community college. "Agency" does not include the general assembly or any court.

(3) "Internal management rule" means any rule, regulation, bylaw, or standard governing the day-to-day staff procedures and operations within an agency.

(4) "Substantive revision" has the same meaning as in division (J) of section 119.01 of the Revised Code.

(B)(1) Any rule, other than a rule of an emergency nature, adopted by any agency pursuant to this section shall be effective on the tenth day after the day on which the rule in final form and in compliance with division (B)(3) of this section is filed as follows:

(a) Two certified copies of the rule shall be filed with both the secretary of state and the director of the legislative service commission;

(b) Two certified copies of the rule shall be filed with the joint committee on agency rule review. Division (B)(1)(b) of this section does not apply to any rule to which division (D) of this section does not apply.

If all copies are not filed on the same day, the rule shall be effective on the tenth day after the day on which the latest filing is made. If an agency in adopting a rule designates an effective date that is later than the effective date provided for by division (B)(1) of this section, the rule if filed as required by such division shall become effective on the later date designated by the agency.

Any rule that is required to be filed under division (B)(1) of this section is also subject to division (D) of this section if not exempted by division (D)(1), (2), (3), (4), (5), or (6) of this section.

(2) A rule of an emergency nature necessary for the immediate preservation of the public peace, health, or safety shall state the reasons for the necessity. Copies of the emergency rule, in final form and in compliance with

division (B)(3) of this section, shall be filed as follows: two certified copies of the emergency rule shall be filed with both the secretary of state and the director of the legislative service commission, and one certified copy of the emergency rule shall be filed with the joint committee on agency rule review. The emergency rule is effective immediately upon the latest filing, except that if the agency in adopting the emergency rule designates an effective date, or date and time of day, that is later than the effective date and time provided for by division (B)(2) of this section, the emergency rule if filed as required by such division shall become effective at the later date, or later date and time of day, designated by the agency.

An emergency rule becomes invalid at the end of the ninetieth day it is in effect. Prior to that date, the agency may file the emergency rule as a nonemergency rule in compliance with division (B)(1) of this section. The agency may not refile the emergency rule in compliance with division (B)(2) of this section so that, upon the emergency rule becoming invalid under such division, the emergency rule will continue in effect without interruption for another ninety-day period.

(3) An agency shall file a rule under division (B)(1) or (2) of this section in compliance with the following standards and procedures:

(a) The rule shall be numbered in accordance with the numbering system devised by the director for the Ohio administrative code.

(b) The rule shall be prepared and submitted in compliance with the rules of the legislative service commission.

(c) The rule shall clearly state the date on which it is to be effective and the date on which it will expire, if known.

(d) Each rule that amends or rescinds another rule shall clearly refer to the rule that is amended or rescinded. Each amendment shall fully restate the rule as amended.

If the director of the legislative service commission or his designee gives an agency written notice pursuant to section 103.05 of the Revised Code that a rule filed by the agency is not in compliance with the rules of the legislative service commission, the agency shall within thirty days after receipt of the notice conform the rule to the rules of the commission as directed in the notice.

(C) All rules filed pursuant to divisions (B)(1)(a) and (2) of this section shall be recorded by the secretary of state and the director under the title of the agency adopting the rule and shall be numbered according to the numbering system devised by the director. The secretary of state and the director shall preserve the rules in an accessible manner. Each such rule shall be a public record open to public inspection and may be lent to any law publishing company that wishes to reproduce it.

(D) At least sixty days before a board, commission, department, division, or bureau of the government of the state files a rule under division (B)(1) of this section, it shall file two copies of the full text of the proposed rule with the joint committee on agency rule review, and the proposed rule shall be subject to legislative review and invalidation under division (I) of section 119.03 of the Revised Code. If a state board, commission, department, division, or bureau makes a substantive revision in a proposed rule after it is filed with the joint committee, the state board, commission, department, division, or bureau shall promptly file two copies of the full text of the proposed rule in its revised form with the joint committee. The latest version of a proposed rule as filed with the joint committee supersedes each earlier version of the text of the same proposed rule. Except as provided in division (F) of this section, a state board, commission, department, division, or bureau shall attach one copy of the rule summary and fiscal analysis prepared under section 121.24 or 127.18 of the Revised Code, or both, to each copy of a proposed rule, and to each copy of a proposed rule in revised form, that is filed under this division.

This division does not apply to any of the following:

(1) A proposed rule of an emergency nature;

(2) A rule proposed under section 1125.23, 1155.18, 1733.341, 4123.29, 4123.34, 4123.341, 4123.342, 4123.40, 4123.411, 4123.44, 4123.441, or 4123.442 of the Revised Code;

(3) A rule proposed by an agency other than a board, commission, department, division, or bureau of the government of the state;

(4) A proposed internal management rule of a board, commission, department, division, or bureau of the government of the state;

(5) A rule proposed by the Ohio student loan commission, that complies with a federal law or rule, so long as the proposed rule contains both of the following:

(a) A statement that it is proposed for the purpose of complying with a federal law or rule;

(b) A citation to the federal law or rule that requires compliance.

(6) Any proposed rule that must be adopted verbatim by an agency pursuant to federal law or rule, to become effective within sixty days of adoption, in order to continue the operation of a federally reimbursed program in this state, so long as the proposed rule contains both of the following:

(a) A statement that it is proposed for the purpose of complying with a federal law or rule;

(b) A citation to the federal law or rule that requires verbatim compliance.

(E) Whenever a state board, commission, department, division, or bureau files a proposed rule or a proposed rule in revised form under division (D) of this section, it shall also file one copy of the full text of the same proposed rule or proposed rule in revised form with the secretary of state and two copies thereof with the director of the legislative service commission. Except as provided in division (F) of this section, a state board, commission, department, division, or bureau shall attach a copy of the rule summary and fiscal analysis prepared under section 121.24 or 127.18 of the Revised Code, or both, to each copy of a proposed rule or proposed rule in revised form that is filed with the secretary of state or the director of the legislative service commission.

(F) Except as otherwise provided in this division, the auditor of state or his designee is not required to attach a rule summary and fiscal analysis to any copy of a proposed rule, or proposed rule in revised form, that he proposes under section 117.11, 117.12, or 117.43 of the Revised Code and files under division (D) or (E) of this section. If, however, the auditor of state or his designee prepares a rule summary and fiscal analysis of the original version of such a proposed rule for purposes of complying with section 121.24 of the Revised Code, he shall attach a copy of the rule summary and fiscal analysis to each copy of the original version of the proposed rule that he files under division (D) or (E) of this section.

HISTORY: 1985 H 201, eff. 7-1-85
1984 S 239, H 244; 1981 H 694, H 1; 1980 H 440; 1979 H 204, H 657, S 8; 1978 S 321; 1977 H 25, H 257; 1976 H 317; 1953 H 1; GC 161-1

Note: 1981 H 638, § 8, eff. 7-2-81, reads:
Notwithstanding sections 5111.23 to 5111.25 of the Revised Code, the Department of Public Welfare may compute the rate for public ICF-MRs operated by the Department of Mental Retardation and Developmental Disabilities according to reasonable cost principles of Title XVIII of the Social Security Act.

Section 115.15[1] and Chapter 119. of the Revised Code do not apply to rules adopted for the purpose of implementing the Title XVIII system for reimbursing state-operated ICF-MRs. The effective date of such rules shall be as early as permissable [sic] under federal regulations.

The amount of federal earnings realized as a result of using Title XVIII principles for calculating reimbursement for state-operated ICF-MRs shall first be utilized by the Department of Public Welfare in authorizing payments to nonstate-operated Medicaid providers in the event changes in federal law or regulation reduce the total estimated amount of federal financial participation available for the Title XIX program.

[1] So in original; 115.15 repealed by 1979 H 204, eff. 7-30-79; should this read "111.15"?

CROSS REFERENCES

See Baldwin's Ohio Legal Forms, Text 2919(6) note
See Baldwin's Ohio Bank Law and Regulation Manual, Text 1.07; Division of Banks Cover Letter of April 27, 1981

Definitions as used in the rules of the legislative service commission, OAC 103-1-01
Legislative service commission filing requirements, OAC Ch 103-3
Legislative service commission, format and style requirements, OAC Ch 103-5
Procedure for giving public notice of the adoption, amendment, or rescission of regulations, OAC 126-1-01
State records commission, rules and regulations, OAC 149:1-1-01
Joint mental health and mental retardation advisory and review commission, OAC 5119:80-1-04
Mental health and mental retardation citizen's advisory boards, rules, OAC 5119:81-7-04, 5119:81-17-04, 5119:81-39-04, 5119:81-43-04, 5119:81-47-04

Auditor of state, procedure for adoption of rules, 117.20
Procedure for adoption, amendment, or rescission of agency rules, 119.03
Administrative procedure, joint committee agency rule review, comparison of final form with proposed rule, finding of substantive change, 119.031
Procedures for adopting rules likely to affect individuals, small businesses or small organizations, 121.24
Rule-making agency, fiscal analysis of proposed rule, 127.18
Public utilities commission, rules for energy emergency conditions, 4935.03
Public utilities commission, rules for energy long-term forecast reports, 4935.04
Department of mental health; behavior modification committee, adoption of standards and guidelines, 5119.01

Department of rehabilitation and correction, minimum standards for jails, 5120.10

Department of mental retardation and developmental disabilities; adoption of rules relating to contracts for residential services, 5123.18

OJur 2d: 26, Health § 21; 28, Industrial Commission § 2, 3; 42, Pensions and Retirement Systems § 42; 43A, Prisons and Prisoners § 4.5; 49, State of Ohio § 17

OJur 3d: 2, Administrative Law § 59, 63, 63.5, 67, 70; 9, Banks and Financial Institutions § 109

Am Jur 2d: 2, Administrative Law § 287

---

51 Ohio Bar 318 (1978). The General Assembly's New Role in Agency Rule-Making, Frederick A. Vierow.

9 U Dayton L Rev 557 (Summer 1984). Legislative Veto in Ohio: The "Twilight Zone of Distinction," Note.

62 OS(2d) 434, 406 NE(2d) 528 (1980), Parfitt v Columbus Correctional Facility. In the absence of prejudice, a public employee in challenging his removal from employment may not assert the employer-agency's procedural rules, unless that employee is a member of the class which the rule was intended to benefit, and a rule which does not clearly grant public employees procedural rights will not be presumed to be a mandatory prerequisite to removal actions against those employees if promulgated under 111.15.

49 OS(2d) 284, 361 NE(2d) 240 (1977), Inland Steel Development Corp v PUCO. Where it is necessary to protect the public health, safety and welfare, the public utilities commission has the authority to promulgate an emergency interim order to restrict service claimed by a prospective customer pursuant to a contract with a public utility, and such order need not comply with the provisions of RC 111.15.

45 OS(2d) 86, 341 NE(2d) 585 (1976), Ohio Manufacturers Assn v PUCO. Public utilities commission had authority to adopt system of priorities for gas use, other than that provided in its rules, by emergency interim orders without following procedure for amendment of orders.

174 OS 55, 186 NE(2d) 862 (1962), State ex rel Board of Education v Holt. No rule or regulation of the school employees retirement system shall be effective unless promulgated and filed in accordance with RC 111.15.

3 App(3d) 302, 3 OBR 349, 444 NE(2d) 1353 (1982), Ohio Civil Service Employees Assn v University of Cincinnati. A public employer's interest in maintaining stable labor relations is a legitimate basis for the practice of according dues checkoff deductions only to members of recognized bargaining units.

OAG 79-088. Although RC 3745.03 exempts the rulemaking procedures of the environmental board of review from the provisions of RC Ch 119, 111.15 nevertheless requires the proposed rules of the board to be filed with the clerk of the senate for legislative review pursuant to RC 119.03(I) unless the proposed rules come within the exceptions set forth in RC 111.15(D)(1) to (7).

OAG 76-079. RC 111.15, as amended by 1976 H 317, is not applicable to the public colleges and universities, including community colleges and technical colleges, in the state of Ohio.

1941 OAG 4043. Only the filing by the public utilities commission of its rules and regulations which have a general and uniform operation is required and not the filing by it of such other orders, findings and determinations as have no such operation.

Chapter 119

Administrative Procedure

DEFINITIONS

119.01	Definitions

RULES

119.02	Compliance; validity of rules
119.03	Procedure for adoption, amendment, or rescission of rules; fiscal analyses
119.031	Comparison of final form with proposed rule; procedures in case of finding of substantive change
119.04	Effective dates of rules; compliance with standards for adoption; public records; codification
119.05	Rules compiled for distribution—Repealed

AGENCY POWERS; HEARINGS

119.06	Adjudication order of agency valid and effective; hearings; periodic registration of licenses
119.061	Power of certain agencies to suspend licenses
119.062	Registrar of motor vehicles may suspend or revoke licenses without hearing
119.07	Notice of hearing; contents; notice of order of suspension of license; publication of notice; effect of failure to give notice
119.08	Date, time, and place of adjudication hearing
119.09	Adjudication hearing
119.091	Failure to hold hearing prior to license expiration
119.092	Recovery of attorney's fees by certain prevailing parties
119.093	Attorney general to define "net worth"
119.10	Counsel to represent agency

APPEAL

119.11	Appeal from orders affecting rules; procedure; transcript; hearing; order—Repealed
119.12	Appeal by party adversely affected
119.121	Expiration of license involved in an appeal; procedure
119.13	Representation of parties and witnesses

Note: 1981 H 638, § 8, eff. 7-2-81, reads:

Notwithstanding sections 5111.23 to 5111.25 of the Revised Code, the Department of Public Welfare may compute the rate for public ICF-MRs operated by the Department of Mental Retardation and Developmental Disabilities according to reasonable cost principles of Title XVIII of the Social Security Act.

Section 115.15[1] and Chapter 119. of the Revised Code do not apply to rules adopted for the purpose of implementing the Title XVIII system for reimbursing state-operated ICF-MRs. The effective date of such rules shall be as early as permissable [sic] under federal regulations.

The amount of federal earnings realized as a result of using Title XVIII principles for calculating reimbursement for state-operated ICF-MRs shall first be utilized by the Department of Public Welfare in authorizing payments to nonstate-operated Medicaid providers in the event changes in federal law or regulation reduce the total estimated amount of federal financial participation available for the Title XIX program.

[1]So in original; 115.15 repealed by 1979 H 204, eff. 7-30-79; should this read "111.15"?

CROSS REFERENCES

See Whiteside, Ohio Appellate Practice, Text 1.18, 23.01, 23.02, 27.05
See Baldwin's Ohio School Law, Text 5.03, 13.07, 39.13
See Baldwin's Ohio Legal Forms, Form 801.77
See Gotherman & Babbit, Ohio Municipal Law, Text 44.03
See Baldwin's Ohio Bank Law and Regulation Manual, Text 5.18; Division of Banks Cover Letter of September 24, 1982

Definitions as used in the rules of the legislative service commission, OAC 103-1-01
Legislative service commission, format and style requirements, OAC 103-5-01 et seq.
Department of administrative services, procedure for adoption, amendment or rescission of rules, OAC 123:1-1-01
Department of administrative services, classification plan, OAC 123:1-7-03
Procedures for licensing solid waste disposal facilities, OAC 3745-37-07
EPA procedural rules, OAC 3745-47-01
EPA, hazardous waste, waivers, OAC 3745-50-31
EPA, registration of hazardous waste transporters, OAC 3745-53-11
Environmental board of review, internal regulations, OAC 3746-3-01
Bureau of workers' compensation rules, OAC 4123-1-01
Division of social services, issuance of renewal licensure, OAC 5101:2-12-16 et seq.
Division of social services, procedures for amending comprehensive annual services plan, OAC 5101:2-25-14
Welfare, appeals process for providers from proposed departmental actions, OAC 5101:3-1-57
Licensing of private psychiatric hospitals, OAC 5122:3-3-05, 5122:3-3-09
Department of mental health, revocation or termination of license of residential care facility, OAC 5122:3-5-04
Non-methadone drug program, hearing procedure, OAC 5122:3-9-20
Residential care facilities for the mentally retarded and developmentally disabled, definitions and license procedures, OAC 5123:2-3-01, 5123:2-3-07
Mental retardation and developmental disabilities, administrative services, placement in a licensed residential care facility of an individual residing in a developmental center, OAC 5123:2-13-01

Codifier of rules of state administrative agencies, publication of Ohio Administrative Code, 103.05
Rules filed, duties of legislative service commission, standards and procedures, fiscal analyses, 111.15
Division of oil and gas administration, rules and regulations, enforcement, 1509.03
Oil and gas, contamination of waters prohibited, liability, 1509.22
Wells for minerals other than oil or gas, chief to adopt rules, permit, 1509.221
Oil and gas board of review, 1509.35
Division of reclamation, duties of chief, 1513.02
Division of reclamation, conflict of interest prohibited, regulations, 1513.04

Reclamation of strip-mined land, performance standards, chief shall make inspection, 1513.16

Duty requirements for operator of underground coal mine, 1513.35

Division of reclamation, chief to make rules, 1514.08

Soil and water conservation commission, membership, terms, powers and duties, staff, 1515.02

Division of natural areas and preserves, duties of chief, 1517.02

Take-over bids, definitions, division of securities may prescribe rules, 1707.041

Division of securities, refusal, suspension, and revocation of license, forms, appeal, 1707.19 et seq.

Powers of director of environmental protection; variances; hazardous waste; temporary emergency permit, 3734.02

License for solid waste facility; permit for hazardous waste facility; hazardous waste facility board; hearing and appeal; renewal, modification and revision, 3734.05

Hazardous waste, rules, standards, 3734.12

Registration of transporters of hazardous waste, 3734.15

Fees for disposal and treatment of hazardous waste, 3734.18

Environmental protection agency, board to adopt regulations, 3745.03

State employment relations board subject to Ch 119, 4117.02

Bureau of workers' compensation and industrial commission, adoption of rules, 4121.30

Workers' compensation, regional boards of review, 4123.14

Foster care maintenance payments, county funds, 5101.141

Office of child support and fraud, alimony enforcement program, 5101.31

Collection of past-due child support from federal tax refunds, 5101.32

Public welfare, state funds limited to households in workfare program, rules to define what constitutes work, 5101.81

Public welfare, workfare program established, operation, 5101.83

Adult foster care facilities, regulations, 5103.31

Application and issuance of license for child care agency, 5104.03

Participation in medical assistance program, eligibility, 5111.02

Medical assistance programs, definitions, 5111.041

Medical assistance programs, contents of provider agreement, election not to continue agreement, 5111.22

Department of public welfare, poor relief, amount to be given, 5113.03

Department of mental health, persons convicted of certain offenses not to be employed, enforcement, 5119.072

Division of mental health facilities and services to adopt rules for health, safety, adequacy of treatment in residential care facilities, 5119.22

Director of mental health, duties in regulating state reimbursement, 5119.61

Department of rehabilitation and correction, duties to community and district community based correctional facilities and programs, 5120.111

Department of mental health, costs of proceedings, 5122.43

Methadone treatment to be licensed, 5122.50

Methadone treatment program, authorization, registration, prohibitions, 5122.51

Department of mental retardation and developmental disabilities, persons convicted of certain offenses not to be employed, enforcement, 5123.081

Department of mental retardation and developmental disabilities, respite care services, 5123.171

Department of mental retardation and developmental disabilities, contracts for residential services, 5123.18
Department of mental retardation and developmental disabilities, costs of proceedings, 5123.96
Rules governing county boards of mental retardation and developmental disabilities, 5126.05
County board of mental retardation and developmental disabilities, reimbursement for services promoting self sufficiency, 5126.11
Standards for funding established by department of mental retardation and developmental disabilities, 5126.13
Rules governing prisoners, employment, 5145.03
Director of environmental protection, rules for public water system, 6109.04
Water pollution control, general permit for discharge of mining wastes or installation of disposal systems, 6111.035
Water quality and effluent standards, hearings, regulations, 6111.041, 6111.042
Water pollution control, injection of wastes into wells, 6111.043
Water pollution control, notice and hearing, emergency procedures, 6111.06
Water planning powers and duties of environmental protection agency, 6111.42

OJur 2d: 41, Nurses § 5; 41, Parks, Squares and Playgrounds § 10; 42, Pensions and Retirement Systems § 33; 42, Physicians and Surgeons § 17, 23.4, 61, 62, 93, 188, 194, 205, 208; 43A, Poor Relief and Public Welfare § 73, 75.1; 48, Sales, Use, and Storage Taxes § 40; 48, Schools § 10, 225; 48, Security Regulation § 16; 53, Universities and Colleges § 5, 6; 58, Workmen's Compensation § 134, 136, 136.5

OJur 3d: 2, Administrative Law § 58, 72, 157, 163; 3, Agriculture and Crops § 17, 28.5; 6, Auctions and Auctioneers § 16; 9, Banks and Financial Institutions § 109, 525; 9, Boats, Ships, and Shipping § 18; 9, Building, Zoning, and Land Control § 11; 11, Businesses and Occupations § 148, 239.1; 15, Civil Servants and Other Public Officers and Employees § 330; 17, Consumer and Borrower Protection § 4; 28, Criminal Law § 1642; 37, Elections § 234, 243; 39, Employment Relations § 109; 40, Energy § 27; 41, Environmental Protection § 11, 81, 110, 162; 50, Fish and Game § 16, 17; 53, Harbors, Marines, and Wharves § 19 to 22; 55, Hospitals and Related Facilities; Health Care Providers § 2 to 4, 6, 127 to 131, 148; 58, Insurance § 668, 670 to 672, 941

1. In general
2. Agencies affected
3. Exceptions
4. Functions affected

1. In general

46 Ohio St L J 355 (1985). Administrative Adjudications: An Overview of the Existing Models and Their Failure to Achieve Uniformity and a Proposal for a Uniform Adjudicatory Framework, Comment.

36 Ohio St L J 662 (1975). The Ohio Division of Securities: Rulemaking, the Administrative Procedure Act and the Ohio Securities Bulletin, A. Theodore Gardiner.

35 Ohio St L J 41 (1974). Administrative Review and the Ohio Modern Courts Amendment, Ivan Cate Rutledge.

34 Ohio St L J 853 (1974). Judicial Review of Administrative Decisions in Ohio, Charles I. Kampinski.

30 Ohio St L J 1 (1969). Ombudsman in Ohio, David C. Cummins.

22 Ohio St L J 734 (1961). A Proposed "Administrative Court" for Ohio, Carl H. Fulda.

32 Cin Law Rev 33 (1963). Legislative Control Over Administrative Rule Making, Charles H. Melville.

22 Clev St L Rev 320 (1973). A Survey of the Ohio Administrative Procedures Act, Glenn R. Jones.

2 Ohio North L Rev 462 (1975). Remarks on the Attorney General's Proposed New Administrative Procedure Act for Ohio, David R. Warner, Jr.

68 OS(2d) 149, 429 NE(2d) 428 (1981), Bd of Trustees of Ohio State University v Dept of Administrative Services. A state university promulgating rules governing its classified civil service employees exercises a derivative power under RC 124.14(G), and is bound to follow the procedures in RC Ch 119.

2 App(3d) 454, 2 OBR 550, 442 NE(2d) 799 (1981), State ex rel Barron v Ohio Motor Vehicle Dealers Board. Even though the Ohio motor vehicle dealers board may delegate to the bureau of motor vehicles the investigation of the verified complaint, the board itself must conduct a probable cause hearing to assure that the investigation conducted by the bureau of motor vehicles was complete and that an impartial authority has reviewed the results of the investigation and made a decision as to whether to continue with proceedings against the licensee.

2. Agencies affected

1 App(3d) 22, 1 OBR 23, 437 NE(2d) 1215 (1981), Lewis v Parkinson. There is no right of appeal from an order of a municipal civil service commission under RC 119.12.

2 App(2d) 237, 207 NE(2d) 672 (1965), In re Petition of Martins Ferry Metropolitan Housing Authority. There are three ways in which a state board may be subjected to the Administrative Procedure Act: (1) certain boards are specifically named, (2) the legislation concerning a board specifically subjects such board to this act, and (3) a board which has authority to issue, suspend, remove or cancel licenses.

117 App 108, 191 NE(2d) 188 (1962), Graul v State Personnel Bd of Review. Proceedings before the state personnel board of review, and on appeal from such board, are governed by the Administrative Procedure Act.

114 App 111, 180 NE(2d) 861 (1961), Golubski v Board of Embalmers & Funeral Directors; overruled by 14 App(2d) 47, 236 NE(2d) 561 (1967), Jamison Plumbing & Heating Co v Rose. The board of embalmers and funeral directors is subject to the Administrative Procedure Act.

OAG 85-046. In its development of amendments to the state health plan, the statewide health coordinating council must, pursuant to RC 3702.56(C), follow the procedures set forth in RC 119.03(A), (B), (C), and (H), with the exception of requirements imposed pursuant to RC 121.24 or RC 127.18, but need not comply with RC 119.03(D), (E), (F), (G), and (I). In particular, the council must follow the public notice and hearing procedures of RC 119.03(A) and (C) and must file proposals with the secretary of state, the director of the legislative service commission, and the joint committee on agency rule review under RC 119.03(B) and (H), but proposed amendments to the state health plan are not subject to invalidation by the general assembly pursuant to RC 119.03(I).

1950 OAG 2340. The Ohio state board of optometry, by virtue of its possession of licensing powers, is subject to the rules and provisions of the Administrative Procedure Act.

1943 OAG 6458. Certificate issued by industrial commission pursuant to GC 1465-69 (RC 4123.35) is such license as will bring industrial commission in its issuance or revocation within Administrative Procedure Act.

EBR 81-16 (1983), Jones & Laughlin Steel Corp v Nichols. In promulgating hazardous waste rules, the director of the Ohio EPA is required to comply with the procedural requirements of RC Ch 119 and 3734; RC 119.03 requires an agency response to significant comments as part of the duty to give public notice of its intention to adopt rules and to receive comments on its proposed rules; RC 3745.04 grants the board exclusive original jurisdiction to review actions of the Ohio EPA and the power to compel the Ohio EPA to provide a response to significant comments or an otherwise sufficient explanation of its reasons for its actions or refusals to act.

3. Exceptions

174 OS 467, 190 NE(2d) 256 (1963), Karrick v Findlay Bd of Ed. A municipal civil service commission is not subject to the provisions of the Administrative Procedure Act in promulgating rules.

165 OS 316, 135 NE(2d) 400 (1956), Akron and Barberton Belt Railroad Co v PUCO. The public utilities commission has no authority to promulgate a rule under the Administrative Procedure Act.

162 OS 9, 120 NE(2d) 436 (1954), Craun Transportation, Inc v PUCO. In the adoption of rules the public utilities commission is not subject to the procedural requirements of GC 614-46a (RC 4903.09), and the validity of such rule can be challenged only when it is in issue in connection with a justiciable matter.

2 App(2d) 237, 207 NE(2d) 672 (1965), In re Petition of Martins Ferry Metropolitan Housing Authority. The state board of housing, in a proceeding for enlarging a metropolitan housing authority, is not subject to the Administrative Procedure Act.

110 App 527, 166 NE(2d) 253 (1959), State ex rel Columbus Bd of Ed v State Board of Education. State board of education, in making the determination required by RC 3311.06, is not subject to the provisions of the Administrative Procedure Act, its action in such matter is final, and a school district board of education may not appeal therefrom.

80 Abs 65, 154 NE(2d) 777 (CP, Cuyahoga 1958), Lakewood v Thormyer; affirmed by 111 App 403, 157 NE(2d) 431 (1959). An appeal from the decision of the director of highways declaring the necessity of a federal aid highway improvement is not governed by the Administrative Procedure Act. (111 App 403 affirmed by Lakewood v Thormeyer, 171 OS 135, 168 NE(2d) 289 (1960).)

OAG 85-046. In its development of amendments to the state health plan, the statewide health coordinating council must, pursuant to RC 3702.56(C), follow the procedures set forth in RC 119.03(A), (B), (C), and (H), with the exception of requirements imposed pursuant to RC 121.24 or RC 127.18, but need not comply with RC 119.03(D), (E), (F), (G), and (I). In particular, the council must follow the public notice and hearing procedures of RC 119.03(A) and (C) and must file proposals with the secretary of state, the director of the legislative service commission, and the joint committee on agency rule review under RC 119.03(B) and (H), but proposed amendments to the state health plan are not subject to invalidation by the general assembly pursuant to RC 119.03(I).

1954 OAG 3437. The division of shore erosion is not subject to the Administrative Procedure Act.

4. Functions affected

41 OS(2d) 115, 322 NE(2d) 878 (1975), Home Savings & Loan Assn v Boesch. The approval of an application by a building and loan association to operate a branch office pursuant to RC 1151.05 is not a licensing function within the provisions of the Administrative Procedure Act.

DEFINITIONS

119.01 Definitions

As used in sections 119.01 to 119.13 of the Revised Code:

(A) "Agency" means, except as limited by this division, any official, board, or commission having authority to promulgate rules or make adjudications in the bureau of employment services, the civil service commission, the department of industrial relations, the department of liquor control, the department of taxation, the industrial commission, the bureau of workers' compensation, the functions of any administrative or executive officer, department, division, bureau, board, or commission of the government of the state specifically made subject to sections 119.01 to 119.13 of the Revised Code, and the licensing functions of any administrative or executive officer, department, division, bureau, board, or commission of the government of the state having the authority or responsibility of issuing, suspending, revoking, or canceling licenses. Sections 119.01 to 119.13 of the Revised Code do not apply to the public utilities commission, nor do they apply to actions of the superintendent of banks, the superintendent of building and loan associations, the superintendent of credit unions, and the superintendent of insurance in the taking possession of, and rehabilitation or liquidation of, the business and property of banks, building and loan associations, insurance companies, associations, reciprocal fraternal benefit societies, and bond investment companies, nor to any action that may be taken by the superintendent of banks under sections 1113.02, 1113.05, 1125.10, and 1125.23 of the Revised Code, by the superintendent of building and loan associations under section 1155.18 of the Revised Code, or by the superintendent of credit unions under sections 1733.341, 1733.35, 1733.36, 1733.37, and 1761.03 of the Revised Code. Sections 119.01 to 119.13 of the Revised Code do not apply to actions of the industrial commission or the bureau of workers' compensation under sections 4123.01 to 4123.94 of the Revised Code with respect to all matters of adjudication, and to the actions of the industrial commission and bureau of workers' compensation under sections 4123.29, 4123.34, 4123.341, 4123.342, 4123.40, 4123.411, 4123.44, 4123.441, 4123.442, and divisions (B), (C), and (E) of section 4131.14 of the Revised Code. Sections 119.01 to 119.13 of the Revised Code do not apply to actions of the bureau of employment services except those relating to the adoption, amendment, or rescission of rules, and those relating to the issuance, suspension, revocation, or cancellation of licenses.

(B) "License" means any license, permit, certificate, commission, or charter issued by any agency. "License" does not include any arrangement whereby a person, institution, or entity furnishes medicaid services under a provider agreement with the department of human services pursuant to Title XIX of the "Social Security Act," 49 Stat. 620 (1935), 42 U.S.C. 301, as amended.

(C) "Rule" means any rule, regulation, or standard, having a general and uniform operation, adopted, promulgated, and enforced by any agency under the authority of the laws governing such agency, and includes any appendix to a rule. "Rule" does not include any internal management rule of an agency unless the internal management rule affects private rights.

(D) "Adjudication" means the determination by the highest or ultimate authority of an agency of the rights, duties, privileges, benefits, or legal relationships of a specified person, but does not include the issuance of a license in response to an application with respect to which no question is raised, nor other acts of a ministerial nature.

(E) "Hearing" means a public hearing by any agency in compliance with procedural safeguards afforded by sections 119.01 to 119.13 of the Revised Code.

(F) "Person" means a person, firm, corporation, association, or partnership.

(G) "Party" means the person whose interests are the subject of an adjudication by an agency.

(H) "Appeal" means the procedure by which a person aggrieved by a finding, decision, order, or adjudication of any agency, invokes the jurisdiction of a court.

(I) "Rule-making agency" means any board, commission, department, division, or bureau of the government of the state that is required to file proposed rules, amendments, or rescissions under division (D) of section 111.15 of the Revised Code and any agency that is required to file proposed rules, amendments, or rescissions under divisions (B) and (H) of section 119.03 of the Revised Code. "Rule-making agency" does not include any state-supported college or university.

(J) "Substantive revision" means any addition to, elimination from, or other change in a rule, an amendment of a rule, or a rescission of a rule, whether of a substantive or procedural nature, that changes any of the following:

(1) That which the rule, amendment, or rescission permits, authorizes, regulates, requires, prohibits, penalizes, rewards, or otherwise affects;

(2) The scope or application of the rule, amendment, or rescission.

(K) "Internal management rule" means any rule, regulation, or standard governing the day-to-day staff procedures and operations within an agency.

HISTORY: 1985 H 201, eff. 7-1-85
1984 H 244; 1983 H 260; 1980 H 403; 1979 H 204; 1977 H 257; 1976 S 545, H 920; 1975 H 1; 1973 H 366; 1969 H 1; 132 v S 97; 1953 H 1; GC 154-62

CROSS REFERENCES

See Merrick-Rippner, Ohio Probate Law (3rd Ed.), Text 281.18
See Whiteside, Ohio Appellate Practice, Text 23.01 to 23.03, 23.08, 33.04
See Baldwin's Ohio School Law, Text 39.13, 49.07
See Baldwin's Ohio Bank Law and Regulation Manual, Text 1.07
See Carroll, Ohio Administrative Law, Text 1.02, 1.04, 9.01

Department of mental health, public notice of rules, OAC 5122-1-02

General assembly, joint committee, agency rule review, 101.35
Secretary of state, legislative service commission, filing of temporary rules, substantive revision defined, 111.15
Procedures for rules likely to affect individuals, small businesses or small organizations, 121.24
Rule-making agency, fiscal analysis of proposed rule, 127.18

Administrator of bureau of employment services; unemployment compensation board of review to approve rules, regulations, and amendments, substantive revision defined, 4141.14

OJur 2d: 26, Health § 29.6; 27, Highways and Streets § 273.5; 28, Hospitals and Asylums § 57, 58, 62; 29, Inns and Restaurants § 10; 30, Insurance § 21, 21.5; 31, Intoxicating Liquors § 23, 156, 157, 160; 33, Labor § 10; 35, Mandamus § 93, 95, 96; 41, Parks, Squares, and Playgrounds § 10; 42, Physicians and Surgeons § 63, 202; 45, Public Utilities § 21; 48, Schools § 10; 52, Trailer Parks and Tourist Camps § 3; 52, Trademarks, Tradenames and Unfair Competition § 42, 46; 54, Unemployment Compensation § 8; 55, Wharfs § 14.1; 58, Workmen's Compensation § 133, 134

OJur 3d: 1, Abandoned, Lost, and Escheated Property § 69; 2, Administrative Law § 1, 3, 10, 26, 57 to 59, 98, 108, 157, 165, 210; 2, Advertising § 4, 14; 3, Animals § 21; 6, Atomic Energy and Ionizing Radiation § 31; 6, Auctioneers § 8; 7, Automobiles and Other Vehicles § 90; 9, Banks and Financial Institutions § 424, 507; 10, Building, Zoning, and Land Controls § 307; 10, Businesses and Occupations § 32, 45; 11, Businesses and Occupations § 156, 242; 15, Civil Servants and Other Public Officers and Employees § 182, 356; 17, Consumer and Borrower Protection § 22, 23; 35, Declaratory Judgments and Related Proceedings § 18; 39, Employment Relations § 87; 41, Environmental Protection § 56, 83

Am Jur 2d: 2, Administrative Law § 201

---

41 Cin Law Rev 589 (1972). Citizen Enforcement of Ohio's Air Quality Standards, Charles R. Johnson.

18 OS(3d) 198, 18 OBR 263, 480 NE(2d) 471 (1985), State ex rel Harris v Williams. A letter notifying a contractor of a determination by the director of industrial relations of a violation of the prevailing wage law, RC 4115.03 et seq., sent on the same date as letters notifying employees of their right to sue, is not an adjudication as defined in RC 119.01(D), and is not appealable.

12 OS(3d) 90, 12 OBR 79, 465 NE(2d) 450 (1984), Condee v Lindley. Informal instructions from the tax commissioner to public utility companies on the apportionment of situsable and non-situsable property, issued under purported authority of RC 5727.15, constitute a rule as defined by RC 119.01(C), and are therefore invalid, pursuant to RC 119.02, for noncompliance with the rulemaking procedures of RC Ch 119.

10 OS(3d) 5, 10 OBR 5, 460 NE(2d) 255 (1984), Yale, dba Yale Photography v Lindley. Because RC 5717.02 provides for an appeal to the board of tax appeals of an order of the tax commissioner, the notice and hearing requirements of RC 119.01 through 119.13 have no application to an order of the tax commissioner changing the frequency of filing sales and use tax returns, regardless of whether such order is an adjudication order under RC 119.01(D).

4 OS(3d) 201, 4 OBR 519, 448 NE(2d) 141 (1983), Ohio Academy of Trial Lawyers v Dept of Insurance. A letter from an attorney-examiner indicating that the need for a hearing requested pursuant to RC 3901.22(A) "is deemed moot" does not constitute a final order of an agency issued pursuant to an adjudication as required by RC 119.12 and as defined in RC 119.01.

68 OS(2d) 149, 429 NE(2d) 428 (1981), Bd of Trustees of Ohio State University v Dept of Administrative Services. Ohio state university is not an agency within the meaning of RC Ch 119.

53 OS(2d) 173, 373 NE(2d) 1238 (1978), State ex rel Bratenahl Local School District Bd of Ed v State Board of Education. The refusal

of the state board of education to grant a local school district an additional exception to the requirements of RC 3311.29 does not constitute an "adjudication" within the meaning of RC 119.01(D).

53 OS(2d) 173, 373 NE(2d) 1238 (1978), State ex rel Bratenahl Local School District Bd of Ed v State Board of Education. In the absence of an "adjudication" as defined in RC 119.01(D), the right to notice and hearing does not obtain and, consequently, in such a case the court of common pleas of Franklin county lacks jurisdiction under RC 119.12 to review actions taken by a state administrative agency.

17 App(3d) 86, 17 OBR 147, 477 NE(2d) 681 (Cuyahoga 1984), Garfield Heights City School Dist Bd of Ed v Gillihan. Reassignment of a part-time school bus driver to substitute driving duties because of declining enrollment is not a "disciplinary" reduction under RC 124.34; hence, a finding of jurisdiction by a municipal civil service commission cannot be appealed by the school board to common pleas court under RC 124.34; nor may appeal be taken under RC Ch 119 inasmuch as a municipal civil service commission is not an "agency" within the definition at RC 119.01(A).

8 App(3d) 188, 8 OBR 248, 456 NE(2d) 842 (Franklin 1983), Stieben v Dollison. The determination of a petitioner's right to an operator's license, or reinstatement thereof, constitutes an "adjudication" as defined by RC 119.01(D), and petitioner has available the administrative and appeal remedies provided by RC Ch 119.

8 App(3d) 188, 8 OBR 248, 456 NE(2d) 842 (Franklin 1983), Stieben v Dollison. The duties of the registrar of motor vehicles under RC Ch 4507, including RC 4507.08(A), with respect to operator's licenses as defined by RC 4507.01, constitute the exercise of licensing functions within the contemplation of RC 119.01(A).

3 App(3d) 398, 3 OBR 464, 445 NE(2d) 706 (1981), Augustine v Ohio Dept of Rehabilitation and Correction. The Ohio department of rehabilitation and correction is not an agency whose decisions are subject to judicial review by appeal pursuant to RC 119.12.

27 App(2d) 91, 273 NE(2d) 783 (1970), Clermont National Bank v Edwards. Bank which receives notice pursuant to RC 1111.02 of a hearing conducted in accordance with RC 1111.03 on an application for establishment of a new branch by applicant bank is a "party adversely affected" under RC 119.12, and has standing, under this section, to appeal an order by superintendent of banks granting application, and the granting or withholding of consent by superintendent of banks to the establishment of branch bank is an act of "adjudication" under RC 119.12.

23 App(2d) 102, 261 NE(2d) 280 (1970), Lehew v Rhodes. Section 461.2 of Ohio public assistance manual, which makes available special dietary allowance to persons receiving aid for the aged but specifically denies such allowance to persons receiving aid to disabled persons, is not a "rule" within purview of 119.01, and department of public welfare is not an "agency" thereunder or subject to act.

No. 84AP-1050 (10th Dist Ct App, Franklin, 6-27-85), Stanfield v Administrative Services Dept. The final order of the administrative services department denying disability leave benefits is appealable to the common pleas court despite the fact that the benefits were not available at the time RC 124.02 was enacted.

No. 82AP-505 (10th Dist Ct App, Franklin, 6-23-83), White Consolidated Industries v Nichols. The Ohio environmental protection agency is not a party to an adjudication hearing.

1956 OAG 6810. The state board of education should determine whether a school district has "conformed with the law" in accordance with the administrative procedure act, but may distribute funds, in conjunction with the state controlling board, to non-conforming districts. "Law" includes the Fourteenth Amendment which prohibits segregation.

1954 OAG 3437. The permits granted by the division of shore erosion are not licenses as that term is used in the Administrative Procedure Act and revocation thereof is governed by the terms of the permit.

1953 OAG 2422. The board of liquor control may determine the date, time and place of each adjudication hearing required under the provisions of either the Administrative Procedure Act or the Liquor Control Act.

RULES

119.02 Compliance; validity of rules

Every agency authorized by law to adopt, amend, or rescind rules shall comply with the procedure prescribed in sections 119.01 to 119.13, inclusive, of the Revised Code, for the adoption, amendment, or rescission of rules. Unless otherwise specifically provided by law, the failure of any agency to comply with such procedure shall invalidate any rule or amendment adopted, or the rescission of any rule.

HISTORY: 1953 H 1, eff. 10-1-53
GC 154-63

CROSS REFERENCES

OJur 2d: 26, Health § 29.6; 27, Highways and Streets § 273.5; 28, Hospitals and Asylums § 57, 58, 62; 30, Insurance § 21, 21.5; 31, Intoxicating Liquors § 23; 41, Parks, Squares, and Playgrounds § 10; 48, Schools § 10; 55, Wharfs § 14.1; 58, Workmen's Compensation § 134

OJur 3d: 1, Abandoned, Lost, and Escheated Property § 69; 2, Administrative Law § 26, 57 to 59, 62, 63, 72, 77, 98, 108, 157, 171; 2, Advertising § 4, 14; 3, Animals § 21; 4, Appellate Review § 30; 6, Atomic Energy and Ionizing Radiation § 31; 9, Banks and Financial Institutions § 424, 507; 10, Building, Zoning, and Land Controls § 156, 242; 10, Businesses and Occupations § 32, 156, 242; 17, Consumer and Borrower Protection § 22, 23; 38, Eminent Domain § 215; 39, Employment Relations § 87; 41, Environmental Protection § 56, 83

Am Jur 2d: 2, Administrative Law § 278, 300

CONSTITUTIONALITY:

30 OS(2d) 30, 282 NE(2d) 50 (1972), State v Schreckengost. RC 1541.09, authorizing division of parks and recreation to make rules and regulations necessary to proper management of parks and bodies of water under supervision and control of that division, is not an unconstitutional delegation of legislative authority.

---

36 Ohio St L J 662 (1975). The Ohio Division of Securities: Rulemaking, the Administrative Procedure Act and the Ohio Securities Bulletin, A. Theodore Gardiner.

12 OS(3d) 90, 12 OBR 79, 465 NE(2d) 450 (1984), Condee v Lindley. Informal instructions from the tax commissioner to public utility companies on the apportionment of situsable and non-situsable property, issued under purported authority of RC 5727.15, constitute a rule as defined by RC 119.01(C), and are therefore invalid, pursuant to RC 119.02, for noncompliance with the rulemaking procedures of RC Ch 119.

51 App(2d) 7, 364 NE(2d) 1386 (1977), Hansen v State Personnel Bd of Review. Pursuant to RC 119.02, the failure of any agency to comply with the required procedures shall invalidate any rule adopted.

51 App(2d) 7, 364 NE(2d) 1386 (1977), Hansen v State Personnel Bd of Review. RC 124.03(F) authorizes the state personnel board of review "to adopt and promulgate rules . . . relating to the procedure of the board in administering the laws which it has authority or duty to administer" and expressly requires that the adoption and promulgation of such rules be "in accordance with Chapter 119."

3 App(2d) 345, 210 NE(2d) 737 (1964), In re Cline. The Ohio state racing commission may appeal a judgment of a common pleas court reversing a license-revocation order of the commission, where a construction and interpretation of a commission rule is required; and, in such appeal, the correctness of the judgment that the order of the commission is not supported by any reliable, probative and substantial evidence may also be reviewed and determined.

118 App 407, 195 NE(2d) 112 (1963), In re Appeal from Rules and Regulations of the Division of Social Administration. A failure by an agency to adopt a rule as to giving notice before it initiates or takes steps to adopt a regulatory rule invalidates such regulatory rule.

99 App 49, 130 NE(2d) 837 (1954), Howell v Bryant. A directive of the department of liquor control instructing personnel to order contraceptive devices out of permit premises and directing citation of noncomplying permittees is a valid order, for such board is not required to anticipate and list by way of rules, regulations and orders the manifold reasons for the issuance of citations against liquor permit holders to show cause why permits should not be suspended or revoked.

68 Abs 19, 121 NE(2d) 463 (CP, Franklin 1954), Standard "Tote," Inc v Ohio State Racing Comm. When a party is actually present at a hearing, participates therein by offering evidence and arguments, and has ample opportunity to be heard on amendments to a rule or rules, such party cannot justly complain that the public notice of the hearing did not strictly comply with the statute. (See also Standard "Tote," Inc v Ohio State Racing Comm, 98 App 494, 130 NE(2d) 455 (1954).)

OAG 73-085. The bureau of workmen's compensation and the industrial commission have discretion to approve or disapprove the cost of chiropractic services, but may not approve the cost of any such services rendered illegally in violation of the state medical board's rules, and they are bound only by the duly adopted rules of the medical board.

1964 OAG 1122. "Modifying or rescinding orders" enacted pursuant to RC 1531.08 does not require a public hearing.

1964 OAG 1122. "Temporary written orders" may be adopted by the chief of the division of wildlife pursuant to RC 1531.08 without a public hearing and without compliance with RC 119.03.

1962 OAG 3065. Existing Rule II-2, of the director of state personnel, and proposed Rule II-2, of the director of state personnel are in conflict with RC 143.08 and are invalid.

1956 OAG 6810. The state board of education should determine whether a school district has "conformed with the law" in accordance with the Administrative Procedure Act, but may distribute funds, in conjunction with the state controlling board, to nonconforming districts. "Law" includes the Fourteenth Amendment which prohibits segregation.

1956 OAG 6199. Rule-making procedure and the effective date of amendment or annulment of rules or regulations of the Ohio board of building standards discussed.

1952 OAG 1539. The division of aid for the aged is not subject to the provisions of the Administrative Procedure Act in adopting rules governing the granting of burial awards.

119.03 Procedure for adoption, amendment, or rescission of rules; fiscal analyses

In the adoption, amendment, or rescission of any rule, an agency shall comply with the following procedure:

(A) Reasonable public notice shall be given at least thirty days prior to the date set for a hearing, in the manner and form and for the length of time as the agency determines and shall include:

(1) A statement of the agency's intention to consider adopting, amending, or rescinding a rule;

(2) A synopsis of the proposed rule, amendment, or rule to be rescinded or a general statement of the subject matter to which the proposed rule, amendment, or rescission relates;

(3) A statement of the reason or purpose for adopting, amending, or rescinding the rule;

(4) The date, time, and place of a hearing on the proposed action, which shall be not earlier than thirty nor later than fifty days after the proposed rule, amendment, or rescission is filed under division (B) of this section. In addition to public notice, the agency may give whatever other notice it considers necessary. Each agency shall adopt a rule setting forth in detail the method that the agency shall follow in giving public notice as to the adoption, amendment, or rescission of rules. The rule shall require the agency to provide the public notice required under division (A) of this section to any person who requests it and pays a reasonable fee, not to exceed the cost of copying and mailing. The methods used for notification may include, but are not limited to, mailing notices to all subscribers on a mailing list or mailing notices in addressed, stamped envelopes provided by the person requesting the notice.

(B) One copy of the full text of the proposed rule, amendment, or rule to be rescinded, accompanied by one copy of the public notice required under division (A) of this section, shall be filed with the secretary of state. Two copies of the full text of the proposed rule, amendment, or rule to be rescinded, accompanied by two copies of the public notice required under division (A) of this section, shall be filed with the director of the legislative service commission. (If in compliance with this division an agency files more than one proposed rule, amendment, or rescission at the same time, and has given a public notice under division (A) of this section that applies to more than one of the proposed rules, amendments, or rescissions, the agency shall file only one copy of the notice with the secretary of state and only two copies of the notice with the director for all of the proposed rules, amendments, or rescissions to which the notice applies.) The proposed rule, amendment, or rescission and public notice shall be filed as required by this division at least sixty days prior to the date on which the agency, in accordance with division (D) of this section, issues an order adopting the proposed rule, amendment, or rescission. The proposed rule, amendment, or rescission shall be available for at least thirty days prior to the date of the hearing at the office of the agency in printed or other legible form without charge to any person affected by the proposal. Failure to furnish such text to any person requesting it shall not invalidate any action of the agency in connection therewith. If the agency files a substantive revision in the text of the proposed rule, amendment, or rescission under division (H) of this section, it shall also promptly file one copy of the full text of the proposed rule, amendment, or rescission in its revised form with the secretary of state and two copies thereof with the director of the legislative service commission. The agency shall attach a copy of the rule summary and fiscal analysis prepared under section 121.24 or 127.18 of the Revised Code, or both, to each copy of a proposed rule or proposed rule in revised form that is filed with the secretary of state or the director of the legislative service commission.

(C) On the date and at the time and place designated in the notice, the agency shall conduct a public hearing at which any person affected by the proposed action of the agency may appear and be heard in person, by his attorney, or both, may present his position, arguments, or contentions, orally or in writing, offer and examine witnesses, and present evidence tending to show that the proposed rule, amendment, or rescission, if adopted or effectuated, will be unreasonable or unlawful.

At the hearing, the testimony, rulings on the admissibility of evidence, and proffers of evidence shall be recorded by stenographic means. Such record shall be made at the expense of the agency.

In any hearing under this section the agency may administer oaths or affirmations.

The agency shall pass upon the admissibility of evidence, but the person affected may at the time make objection to the ruling of the agency, and if the agency refuses to admit evidence the person offering the evidence shall make a proffer of the evidence, and the proffer shall be made a part of the record of such hearing.

(D) After complying with divisions (A), (B), (C), and (H) of this section, and when the time for legislative review and invalidation under division (I) of this section has expired, the agency may issue an order adopting the proposed rule or the proposed amendment or rescission of the rule, consistent with the synopsis or general statement included in the public notice. At that time the agency shall designate the effective date of the rule, amendment, or rescission, which shall not be earlier than the tenth day after the rule, amendment, or rescission has been filed in its final form as provided in section 119.04 of the Revised Code.

(E) Prior to the effective date of a rule, amendment, or rescission, the agency shall make a reasonable effort to inform those affected by the rule, amendment, or rescission and to have available for distribution to those requesting it the full text of the rule as adopted or as amended.

(F) If the governor, upon the request of an agency, determines that an emergency requires the immediate adoption, amendment, or rescission of a rule, he shall issue a written order, a copy of which shall be filed with the secretary of state, the director of the legislative service commission, and the joint committee on agency rule review, that the procedure prescribed by this section with respect to the adoption, amendment, or rescission of a specified rule is suspended. The agency may then adopt immediately the emergency rule, amendment, or rescission and it becomes effective on the date copies of the rule, amendment, or rescission, in final form and in compliance with division (A)(2) of section 119.04 of the Revised Code, are filed as follows: two certified copies of the emergency rule, amendment, or rescission shall be filed[1] with both the secretary of state and the director of the legislative service commission, and one certified copy of the emergency rule, amendment, or rescission shall be filed with the joint committee on agency rule review. If all copies are not filed on the same day, the emergency rule, amendment, or rescission shall be effective on the day on which the latest filing is made. The emergency rule, amendment, or rescission shall become invalid at the end of the ninetieth day it is in effect. Prior to that date the agency may adopt the emergency rule, amendment, or rescission as a nonemergency rule, amendment, or rescission by complying with the procedure prescribed by this section for the adoption, amendment, and rescission of nonemergency rules. The agency may not use the procedure of this division to readopt the emergency rule, amendment, or rescission so that, upon the emergency rule, amendment, or rescission becoming invalid under this division, the emergency rule, amendment, or rescission will continue in effect without interruption for another ninety-day period. This division does not apply to the adoption of any emergency rule, amendment, or rescission by the tax commissioner under division (C)(2) of section 5117.02 of the Revised Code.

(G) Rules adopted by an authority within the department of taxation or the bureau of employment services shall be effective without a hearing as provided by this section if the statutes pertaining to such agency specifically give a right of appeal to the board of tax appeals or to a higher authority within the agency or to a court, and also give the appellant a right to a hearing on such appeal. This division does not apply to the adoption of any rule, amendment, or rescission by the tax commissioner under division (C)(1) or (2) of section 5117.02 of the Revised Code, or deny the right to file an action for declaratory judgment as provided in Chapter 2721. of the Revised Code from the decision of the board of tax appeals or of the higher authority within such agency.

(H) When any agency files a proposed rule, amendment, or rescission under division (B) of this section, it shall also file with the joint committee on agency rule review two copies of the full text of the proposed rule, amendment, or rule to be rescinded in the same form and two copies of the public notice required under division (A) of this section. (If in compliance with this division an agency files more than one proposed rule, amendment, or rescission at the same time, and has given a public notice under division (A) of this section that applies to more than one of the proposed rules, amendments, or rescissions, the agency shall file only two copies of the notice with the joint committee for all of the proposed rules, amendments, or rescissions to which the notice applies.) If the agency makes a substantive revision in a proposed rule, amendment, or rescission after it is filed with the joint committee, the agency shall promptly file two copies of the full text of the proposed rule, amendment, or rescission in its revised form with the joint committee. The latest version of a proposed rule, amendment, or rescission as filed with the joint committee supersedes each earlier version of the text of the same proposed rule, amendment, or rescission. An agency shall attach one copy of the rule summary and fiscal analysis prepared under section 121.24 or 127.18 of the Revised Code, or both, to each copy of a proposed rule, amendment, or rescission, and to each copy of a proposed rule, amendment, or rescission in revised form, that is filed under this division.

This division does not apply to:

(1) An emergency rule, amendment, or rescission;

(2) Any proposed rule, amendment, or rescission that must be adopted verbatim by an agency pursuant to federal law or rule, to become effective within sixty days of adoption, in order to continue the operation of a federally reimbursed program in this state, so long as the proposed rule contains both of the following:

(a) A statement that it is proposed for the purpose of complying with a federal law or rule;

(b) A citation to the federal law or rule that requires verbatim compliance.

(I)(1) The joint committee on agency rule review may recommend the adoption of a concurrent resolution invalidating a proposed rule, amendment, rescission, or part thereof if it finds any of the following:

(a) That the rule-making agency has exceeded the scope of its statutory authority in proposing the rule, amendment, or rescission;

(b) That the proposed rule, amendment, or rescission conflicts with another rule, amendment, or rescission adopted by the same or a different rule-making agency;

(c) That the proposed rule, amendment, or rescission conflicts with the legislative intent in enacting the statute under which the rule-making agency proposed the rule, amendment, or rescission;

(d) That the rule-making agency has failed to prepare a complete and accurate rule summary and fiscal analysis of the proposed rule, amendment, or recission as required by section 121.24 or 127.18 of the Revised Code, or both.

The house of representatives and senate may adopt a concurrent resolution invalidating a proposed rule, amendment, rescission, or part thereof. The concurrent resolution shall state which of the specific rules, amendments, rescissions, or parts thereof are invalidated. A concurrent resolution invalidating a proposed rule, amendment, or rescission shall be adopted prior to the sixtieth day after the original version of the text of the proposed rule, amendment, or rescission is filed with the joint committee, except that if more than thirty days after the original version is filed the rule-making agency files a revised version of the text of the proposed rule, amendment, or rescission, a concurrent resolution invalidating the proposed rule, amendment, or rescission shall be adopted prior to the thirtieth day after the revised version is filed. If, after the joint committee on agency rule review recommends the adoption of a concurrent resolution invalidating a proposed rule, amendment, rescission, or part thereof, the house of representatives or senate does not, within the time remaining for adoption of the concurrent resolution, hold five floor sessions at which its journal records a roll call vote disclosing a sufficient number of members in attendance to pass a bill, the time within which that house may adopt the concurrent resolution is extended until it has held five such floor sessions.

Within five days after the adoption of a concurrent resolution invalidating a proposed rule, amendment, rescission, or part thereof, the clerk of the senate shall send the rule-making agency, the secretary of state, and the director of the legislative service commission a certified copy of the resolution together with a certification stating the date on which the resolution takes effect. The secretary of state and the director of the legislative service commission shall each note the invalidity of the proposed rule, amendment, rescission, or part thereof on his copy, and shall each remove the invalid proposed rule, amendment, rescission, or part thereof from the file of proposed rules. The rule-making agency shall not proceed to adopt in accordance with division (D) of this section, or to file in accordance with division (B)(1) of section 111.15 of the Revised Code, any version of a proposed rule, amendment, rescission, or part thereof that has been invalidated by concurrent resolution.

Unless the house of representatives and senate adopt a concurrent resolution invalidating a proposed rule, amendment, rescission, or part thereof within the time specified by this division, the rule-making agency may proceed to adopt in accordance with division (D) of this section, or to file in accordance with division (B)(1) of section 111.15 of the Revised Code, the latest version of the proposed rule, amendment, or rescission as filed with the joint committee. If by concurrent resolution certain of the rules, amendments, rescissions, or parts thereof are specifically invalidated, the rule-making agency may proceed to adopt, in accordance with division (D) of this section, or to file in accordance with division (B)(1) of section 111.15 of the Revised Code, the latest version of the proposed rules, amendments, rescissions, or parts thereof as filed with the joint committee that are not specifically invalidated. The rule-making agency may not revise or amend any proposed rule, amendment, rescission, or part thereof that has not been invalidated except as provided in this chapter or in section 111.15 of the Revised Code.

(2)(a) A proposed rule, amendment, or rescission that is filed with the joint committee under division (H) of this section or division (D) of section 111.15 of the Revised Code shall be carried over for legislative review to the next succeeding regular session of the general assembly if the original or any revised version of the proposed rule, amendment, or rescission is filed with the joint committee on or after the first day of December of any year.

(b) The latest version of any proposed rule, amendment, or rescission that is subject to division (I)(2)(a) of this section, as filed with the joint committee, is subject to legislative review and invalidation in the next succeeding regular session of the general assembly in the same manner as if it were the original version of a proposed rule, amendment, or rescission that had been filed with the joint committee for the first time on the first day of the session. A rule-making agency shall not adopt in accordance with division (D) of this section, or file in accordance with division (B)(1) of section 111.15 of the Revised Code, any version of a proposed rule, amendment, or rescission that is subject to division (I)(2)(a) of this section until the time for legislative review and invalidation, as contemplated by division (I)(2)(b) of this section, has expired.

(3) Invalidation of any version of a proposed rule, amendment, rescission, or part thereof by concurrent resolution shall prevent the rule-making agency from instituting or continuing proceedings to adopt any version of the same proposed rule, amendment, rescission, or part thereof for the duration of the general assembly that invalidated the proposed rule, amendment, rescission, or part thereof unless the same general assembly adopts a concurrent resolution permitting the rule-making agency to institute or continue such proceedings.

The failure of the general assembly to invalidate a proposed rule, amendment, rescission, or part thereof under this section shall not be construed as a ratification of the lawfulness or reasonableness of the proposed rule, amendment, rescission, or any part thereof or of the validity of the procedure by which the proposed rule, amendment, rescission, or any part thereof was proposed or adopted.

HISTORY: 1984 S 239, eff. 1-1-85
1984 H 244; 1983 H 291; 1981 H 694, H 1; 1979 H 657, H 204, S 8; 1978 S 321; 1977 H 25, H 257, S 43; 1976 H 317; 1969 H 1; 1953 H 1; GC 154-64

[1]Prior and current versions differ although no amendment to this language was indicated in 1984 S 239 or 1984 H 244; "two certified copies of the emergency rule, amendment, or rescission shall be filed" did not appear in 1953 H 1 or any subsequent versions.

CROSS REFERENCES

See Baldwin's Ohio Bank Law and Regulation Manual, Division of Banks Cover Letter of April 27, 1981
See Carroll, Ohio Administrative Law, Text 1.05(C) to (E), 1.05(G), 1.06(C)

Department of administrative services, division of personnel, procedure for rule changes, OAC 123:1-1-01
Department of commerce, public notice of rules, OAC 1301-1-01
Division of securities, public notice of rules, OAC 1301:6-1-03
Reclamation board of review, adoption of rules, OAC 1513-3-02
Environmental protection agency, public notice of proposed and final rules, OAC 3745-49-01
Liquor control commission, advertising of proposed regulations, OAC 4301:1-1-66
Department of public welfare, public notice of rules changes, OAC 5101-1-01
Department of rehabilitation and correction, public notice of rules changes, OAC 5120:2-1-01
Department of mental health, procedures for rules changes, OAC 5122-1-02, 5122:2-1-21, 5122:3-5-12, 5122:3-7-04

General assembly, joint committee on agency rule review, 101.35
Procedures for adopting rules likely to affect individuals, small businesses or small organizations, 121.24
Rule-making agency, fiscal analysis of proposed rule, 127.18
State employment relations board subject to Ch 119., 4117.02
Administrator of bureau of employment services; unemployment compensation board of review to approve rules, regulations, and amendments, 4141.14

OJur 2d: 26, Health § 19, 29.6; 27, Highways and Streets § 273.5; 28, Hospitals and Asylums § 57, 58, 62; 30, Insurance § 21, 21.5; 31, Intoxicating Liquors, § 24, 25, 157, 159; 41, Parks, Squares and Playgrounds § 10; 48, Schools § 10; 54, Universities and Colleges § 13.5; 55, Wharfs § 14.1; 58, Workers' Compensation § 134
OJur 3d: 1, Abandoned, Lost, and Escheated Property § 69; 2, Administrative Law § 1, 3, 10, 26, 57 to 59, 62 to 68, 70, 98, 108, 171; 2, Advertising § 4, 14; 3, Animals § 21; 6, Atomic Energy and Ionizing Radiation § 31; 6, Auctioneers § 8; 9, Banks and Financial Institutions § 424, 507; 10, Building, Zoning and Land Controls § 156, 242; 10, Businesses and Occupations § 32; 11, Businesses and Occupations § 156, 242; 15, Civil Servants and Other Public Officers and Employees § 182, 356; 17, Consumer and Borrower Protection § 22, 23; 38, Eminent Domain § 215; 39, Employment Relations § 87; 41, Environmental Protection § 14, 56, 83
Am Jur 2d: 2, Administrative Law § 278 to 287

1. In general
2. Notice of hearing
3. Filing
4. Hearing
5. Adoption
6. Effective date
7. Appeal

1. In general

51 Ohio Bar 318 (1978). The General Assembly's New Role in Agency Rule-Making, Frederick A. Vierow.

70 OS(2d) 106, 435 NE(2d) 414 (BTA 1982), McLean Trucking Co v Lindley. Tax commissioner, in apportioning taxpayer's revenues through the system-wide mileage ratio of special instruction 21, did not properly proceed under, or in compliance with, RC 5733.05(B)(2)(d); special instruction 21 is an administrative rule which was not promulgated in accordance with RC 119.03 and 5703.14 and is, therefore, invalid.

63 OS(2d) 16, 406 NE(2d) 1363 (1980), Sterling Drug, Inc v Wickham. In a declaratory judgment action seeking to invalidate a rule adopted by the state board of pharmacy, pursuant to authority granted in RC 3719.44(A)(1) to amend the controlled substances schedules in RC 3719.41 by adding a previously unscheduled drug to Schedule II, upon the ground that it is unlawful for the reason the exercise of such amending authority is legislatively restricted to drugs possessing dependency criteria enumerated in RC 3719.44(D) and that pentazocine added by the rule to Schedule II does not possess such dependency criteria, the factual conclusions of the agency as to the existence of such jurisdictional facts must be presumed to have been made upon sufficient evidence, and the burden of proof is upon the one asserting the nonexistence of such facts to prove such nonexistence by a preponderance of substantial, reliable and probative evidence upon the whole of the record sufficient to overcome such presumption and to establish the facts as otherwise than determined by the board.

51 App(2d) 7, 364 NE(2d) 1386 (1977), Hansen v State Personnel Bd of Review. Pursuant to RC 119.02, the failure of any agency to comply with the required procedures shall invalidate any rule adopted.

51 App(2d) 7, 364 NE(2d) 1386 (1977), Hansen v State Personnel Bd of Review. Included in the requirements for the adoption of an agency rule pursuant to the provisions of RC Ch 119 are: reasonable public notice by the agency including a synopsis of the proposed rule and the date, time, and place of a public hearing on the proposed action; a public hearing at which any person affected by the proposed action may present his position and present evidence tending to show that said proposed rule will be unreasonable or unlawful; and a reasonable effort by the agency prior to the effective date of the rule to inform those affected by the rule and to have available for distribution to those requesting it the full text of the rule.

14 App(2d) 47, 236 NE(2d) 561 (1967), Jamison Plumbing & Heating Co v Rose. Where an agency has followed and completed the necessary statutory procedure in adopting an amended rule, upon the arrival of the effective date of such amended rule its predecessor is, by operation of law, automatically repealed.

119 App 467, 200 NE(2d) 705 (1964), Lloyd v Industrial Comm of Ohio. The provisions of RC 119.03, having to do with the enactment of rules by an administrative agency, do not apply to a so-called "directive and order" of an administrative agency addressed "to all personnel" of such agency, and which is for the guidance of departmental procedures

to regulate the work of such agency and involves only internal procedures.

115 App 131, 184 NE(2d) 248 (1961), Maggiore v Bd of Liquor Control. The board of liquor control in the adoption of regulations is required to comply with the mandatory procedure prescribed by RC 119.03.

92 Abs 147, 189 NE(2d) 915 (CP, Franklin 1963), Acme Laundry & Dry Cleaning Co v Mahoney. The director of industrial relations has authority to make such changes in the report of a wage board as are found appropriate to safeguard the basic minimum rates established.

OAG 85-046. In its development of amendments to the state health plan, the statewide health coordinating council must, pursuant to RC 3702.56(C), follow the procedures set forth in RC 119.03(A), (B), (C), and (H), with the exception of requirements imposed pursuant to RC 121.24 or RC 127.18, but need not comply with RC 119.03(D), (E), (F), (G), and (I). In particular, the council must follow the public notice and hearing procedures of RC 119.03(A) and (C) and must file proposals with the secretary of state, the director of the legislative service commission, and the joint committee on agency rule review under RC 119.03(B) and (H), but proposed amendments to the state health plan are not subject to invalidation by the general assembly pursuant to RC 119.03(I).

OAG 73-120. While the governor may by executive order reduce the prima facie speed limits found in RC 4511.21 for specific intersections and places along highways where the proposed speed limits would be reasonable for safety purposes, there is no authority for him or any other state officer to reduce speed limits for purposes of energy conservation.

OAG 73-085. The bureau of workmen's compensation and the industrial commission have discretion to approve or disapprove the cost of chiropractic services, but may not approve the cost of any such services rendered illegally in violation of the state medical board's rules, and they are bound only by the duly adopted rules of the medical board.

1964 OAG 1122. "Temporary written orders" may be adopted by the chief of the division of wildlife pursuant to RC 1531.08 without a public hearing and without compliance with RC 119.03.

EBR 81-16 (1983), Jones & Laughlin Steel Corp v Nichols. In promulgating hazardous waste rules, the director of the Ohio EPA is required to comply with the procedural requirements of RC Ch 119 and 3734; RC 119.03 requires an agency response to significant comments as part of the duty to give public notice of its intention to adopt rules and to receive comments on its proposed rules; RC 3745.04 grants the board exclusive original jurisdiction to review actions of the Ohio EPA and the power to compel the Ohio EPA to provide a response to significant comments or an otherwise sufficient explanation of its reasons for its actions or refusals to act.

EBR 81-16 (1983), Jones & Laughlin Steel Corp v Nichols. RC 3734.12 required the director of the Ohio EPA to adopt a program of hazardous waste management which is consistent with and substantially equivalent to the federal program; substantial equivalence would require both programs to have the same effect on the regulated community; the Ohio program is not substantially equivalent in that it does not include a rule providing interested parties a right to petition the Ohio EPA for changes to the Ohio program; such failure to include a petition rule was unlawful and unreasonable; the director of the Ohio EPA is hereby ordered to adopt a petition rule for the Ohio hazardous waste program similar to the federal regulation at 40 CFR § 260.20, in accordance with RC 119.03.

EBR 78-30-49 and 75-12-16 (1982), Middletown v Nichols. Where the environmental protection agency failed to provide a synopsis for proposed water quality standards, unsuccessfully attempted only minimal compliance with the requirements of RC 119.03(A)(2), by publishing a statement which was cursory, vague and uninformative, and thereafter, adopted final regulations which substantially departed from the substance of its proposed rules, the agency violated the consistency requirements of RC 119.03(D), which is designed to ensure that agencies do not exclude meaningful public participation in rulemaking, by proposing one set of rules and then adopting sharply different ones.

EBR 78-30-49 and 75-12-16 (1982), Middletown v Nichols. Where the environmental protection agency did not release its scientific and technical rationale for proposed water quality standards in time to permit the public to comment before the end of the comment period, the agency deprived the public its right to comment guaranteed by RC 119.03.

EBR 78-30-49 and 75-12-16 (1982), Middletown v Nichols. The impropriety of private or ex parte contacts during rulemaking or adjudication can be remedied by including a memorandum or some other summary of the contact in a public record and allowing persons with opposing viewpoints to present contrary data and counter arguments to the same decisionmaker.

EBR 75-12-15-16 (1976), Akron v Williams. The environmental board of review cannot vacate, modify, or affirm the action of the director of environmental protection as the result of de novo proceedings before the board, but must enter the proper order based on the entire record.

EBR 75-12-15-16 (1976), Akron v Williams. In a quasi-legislative hearing before the environmental board of review, cross-examination of witnesses and involuntary responses by representatives of the environmental protection agency to questions and statements by appellants will not be allowed.

EBR 75-12-15-16 (1976), Akron v Williams. In quasi-legislative de novo hearings before the environmental board of review, alleged procedural errors in the rulemaking proceeding before the director of environmental protection will be heard as in an adversary proceeding.

EBR 75-7 (1976), Northern Ohio Lung Assn v Williams; reversed on remand by EBR 75-7 (1978). The environmental protection agency must apply all rules adopted by the director of environmental protection unless the rules are in clear conflict with enabling statutes, or have not been properly adopted, or are unreasonable on their faces. (See also Northern Ohio Lung Assn v Williams, Nos. 76AP-929 and 76AP-938 (App, Franklin 1977); Ohio Edison Co v Williams, EBR 75-5 (1975).)

EBR 75-7 (1976), Northern Ohio Lung Assn v Williams; reversed on remand by EBR 75-7 (1978). There is no basis in Ohio law for rulemaking by adjudication since adjudications are the result of the application of laws and rules, which are considered rigid and unchanging, to a particular fact situation by a tribunal or an administrator. (See also Northern Ohio Lung Assn v Williams, Case nos. 76AP-929 and 76AP-938 (App, Franklin 1977); Ohio Edison Co v Williams, EBR 75-5 (1975).)

EBR 73-29 (1974), Monroe Country Estates v Whitman. Regulation of water pollution by the director of environmental protection may not be effected by the issuance of internal policy statements, but only through the rulemaking procedures of RC Ch 119.

2. Notice of hearing

14 App(2d) 47, 236 NE(2d) 561 (1967), Jamison Plumbing & Heating Co v Rose. Amendments to rules which are finally adopted pursuant to RC 119.03 (D) may differ from the synopsis of proposed amendments published under paragraph (A) of such section and the full text of the proposed amendments filed under paragraph (B) of such section, provided the amendments finally adopted are sufficiently consistent with the public notice to insure that all persons affected have been afforded a reasonable opportunity to present their views on the substance and effect of the amendments at the public hearing conducted therefor.

118 App 407, 195 NE(2d) 112 (1963), In re Appeal from Rules and Regulations of the Division of Social Administration. A failure by an agency to adopt a rule as to giving notice before it initiates or takes steps to adopt a regulatory rule invalidates such regulatory rule.

113 App 113, 172 NE(2d) 726 (1961), Ohio State Federation of Licensed Nursing Homes v Public Health Council; affirmed by 172 OS 227, 174 NE(2d) 251 (1961). The public health council may revise a rule after the original proposal is presented at the public hearing required by law; and such rule, as adopted, may contain amendments, substitutions and additions to that originally proposed by the agency and considered by it at such public hearing; but such power of revision is limited by the requirement that the rule adopted be "consistent with the public notice."

68 Abs 19, 121 NE(2d) 463 (CP, Franklin 1954), Standard "Tote," Inc v Ohio State Racing Comm. A statement that an administrative agency will consider adopting, amending, or rescinding certain of its specified rules meets the requirements of the administrative procedure act. (See also Standard "Tote," Inc v Ohio State Racing Comm, 98 App 494, 130 NE(2d) 455 (1954).)

68 Abs 19, 121 NE(2d) 463 (CP, Franklin 1954), Standard "Tote", Inc v Ohio State Racing Comm. When a party is actually present at a hearing, participates therein by offering evidence and arguments, and has ample opportunity to be heard on amendments to a rule or rules, such party cannot justly complain that the public notice of the hearing did not strictly comply with the statute.

OAG 85-046. In its development of amendments to the state health plan, the statewide health coordinating council must, pursuant to RC 3702.56(C), follow the procedures set forth in RC 119.03(A), (B), (C), and (H), with the exception of requirements imposed pursuant to RC 121.24 or RC 127.18, but need not comply with RC 119.03(D), (E), (F), (G), and (I). In particular, the council must follow the public notice and hearing procedures of RC 119.03(A) and (C) and must file proposals with the secretary of state, the director of the legislative service commission, and the joint committee on agency rule review under RC 119.03(B) and (H), but proposed amendments to the state health plan are not subject to invalidation by the general assembly pursuant to RC 119.03(I).

EBR 81-16 (1983), Jones & Laughlin Steel Corp v Nichols. In promulgating hazardous waste rules, the director of the Ohio EPA is required to comply with the procedural requirements of RC Ch 119 and 3734; RC 119.03 requires an agency response to significant comments as part of the duty to give public notice of its intention to adopt rules and to receive comments on its proposed rules; RC 3745.04 grants the board exclusive original jurisdiction to review actions of the Ohio EPA and the power to compel the Ohio EPA to provide a response to significant comments or an otherwise sufficient explanation of its reasons for its actions or refusals to act.

EBR 78-30-49 and 75-12-16 (1982), Middletown v Nichols. Because the water quality standards are based on complex scientific and technical considerations, the public's right to meaningful comment requires that the Ohio environmental protection agency disclose its scientific and technical rationale at a time when this information may be used by the public to prepare comments.

EBR 78-30-49 and 75-12-16 (1982), Middletown v Nichols. The de novo hearing provision of RC 3745.05 does not curtail the public's right to meaningful comment, as provided by RC 119.03.

EBR 78-30-49 and 75-12-16 (1982), Middletown v Nichols. A procedure which allows one party to comment on proposed rules when all others are precluded from doing so, violates the provisions of RC 119.03, that all parties be allowed to participate in a single public rulemaking procedure.

3. Filing

14 App(2d) 47, 236 NE(2d) 561 (1967), Jamison Plumbing & Heating Co v Rose. Amendments to rules which are finally adopted pursuant to RC 119.03 (D) may differ from the synopsis of proposed amendments published under paragraph (a) of such section and the full text of the proposed amendments filed under paragraph (B) of such section, provided the amendments finally adopted are sufficiently consistent with the public notice to insure that all persons affected have been afforded a reasonable opportunity to present their views on the substance and effect of the amendments at the public hearing conducted therefor.

OAG 85-046. In its development of amendments to the state health plan, the statewide health coordinating council must, pursuant to RC 3702.56(C), follow the procedures set forth in RC 119.03(A), (B), (C), and (H), with the exception of requirements imposed pursuant to RC 121.24 or RC 127.18, but need not comply with RC 119.03(D), (E), (F), (G), and (I). In particular, the council must follow the public notice and hearing procedures of RC 119.03(A) and (C) and must file proposals with the secretary of state, the director of the legislative service commission, and the joint committee on agency rule review under RC 119.03(B) and (H), but proposed amendments to the state health plan are not subject to invalidation by the general assembly pursuant to RC 119.03(I).

OAG 79-088. Although RC 3745.03 exempts the rulemaking procedures of the environmental board of review from the provisions of RC Ch 119, 111.15 nevertheless requires the proposed rules of the board to be filed with the clerk of the senate for legislative review pursuant to RC 119.03(I) unless the proposed rules come within the exceptions set forth in RC 111.15(D)(1) to (7).

OAG 79-070. A "substantive revision" to a proposed rule within the meaning of RC 119.03(H) is any change which alters the meaning of the rule by changing that which is prohibited, controlled, regulated, or required by the rule; by changing the scope of the rule; or by changing any aspect of the rule which would alter the impact or application of the rule. The "final" text of a proposed rule must be filed prior to the adoption of the rule when the final text is substantively different from the "proposed" text, even if such substantive differences are consistent with the public notice and are based on the record of a public hearing.

4. Hearing

14 App(2d) 47, 236 NE(2d) 561 (1967), Jamison Plumbing & Heating Co v Rose. Amendments to rules which are finally adopted pursuant to RC 119.03(D) may differ from the synopsis of proposed amendments published under paragraph (A) of such section and the full text of the proposed amendments filed under paragraph (B) of such section, pro-

vided the amendments finally adopted are sufficiently consistent with the public notice to insure that all persons affected have been afforded a reasonable opportunity to present their views on the substance and effect of the amendments at the public hearing conducted therefor.

114 App 111, 180 NE(2d) 861 (1961), Golubski v Bd of Embalmers & Funeral Directors; overruled by 14 App(2d) 47, 236 NE(2d) 561 (1967), Jamison Plumbing & Heating Co v Rose. A hearing conducted by the board of embalmers and funeral directors prior to the adoption of various changes in the rules and regulations governing funeral directors and the conducting of funerals does not comply with the procedural requirements of the administrative procedure act, where rulings and remarks by the chairman of such board unreasonably restrict interested persons in the exercise of their rights under such act, and the hearing is adjourned after only two hours during which lengthy remarks are made by the chairman.

113 App 113, 172 NE(2d) 726 (1961), Ohio State Federation of Licensed Nursing Homes v Public Health Council; affirmed by 172 OS 227, 174 NE(2d) 251 (1961). In its consideration of proposed rules, the public health council may hold operational meetings with its staff subsequent to the public hearings required by law, in order to implement its rule-making function and arrive at a test of such rules in "final form" for adoption; and such agency may consult its departmental staff after such public hearing as to the advisability of adopting the original proposal or with respect to amendments to or substitutes for provisions of such original proposal.

Nos. 83AP-1014 to 83AP-1049 (10th Dist Ct App, Franklin, 6-7-84), Youngstown Sheet and Tube Co v Maynard. The right to be heard at a public hearing does not imply a right to receive a response setting forth the reason for the agency's agreement or disagreement with such comment.

OAG 85-046. In its development of amendments to the state health plan, the statewide health coordinating council must, pursuant to RC 3702.56(C), follow the procedures set forth in RC 119.03(A), (B), (C), and (H), with the exception of requirements imposed pursuant to RC 121.24 or RC 127.18, but need not comply with RC 119.03(D), (E), (F), (G), and (I). In particular, the council must follow the public notice and hearing procedures of RC 119.03(A) and (C) and must file proposals with the secretary of state, the director of the legislative service commission, and the joint committee on agency rule review under RC 119.03(B) and (H), but proposed amendments to the state health plan are not subject to invalidation by the general assembly pursuant to RC 119.03(I).

OAG 73-125. No person in attendance at a public rule hearing, conducted by the public health council pursuant to RC 119.03, has the right to cross-examine any witness, but the public health council may, in its sound discretion, adopt procedures permitting cross-examination during such hearings.

1964 OAG 1122. "Modifying or rescinding orders" enacted pursuant to RC 1531.08 does not require a public hearing.

EBR 571050 (12-13-84), Dayton Power & Light Co v Maynard. Where a permit to operate a power station issued by the director contains conditions on the quality of coal to be burned more stringent than the conditions applied for, and where the conditions reflect results of a "stack test" conducted with coal from the operator's usual supply, the director's exercise of discretion in determining the conditions is ministerial in nature within the purview of RC 119.01(D), and therefore, need not be preceded by an opportunity for hearing.

5. Adoption

9 App(3d) 135, 9 OBR 199, 458 NE(2d) 886 (Franklin 1983), Middletown v Nichols. RC 119.03 requires neither public disclosure of scientific and support data regarding administrative rules proposed by the director of environmental protection, nor disclosure of ex parte comments made by agencies such as the United States environmental protection agency before the close of the public comment period in order that more meaningful public comment might be made on the proposed rules; further, a new comment period need not be provided where the final rules as adopted differ substantially from the rules as proposed.

4 App(2d) 255, 211 NE(2d) 916 (1965), Maggiore v Dept of Liquor Control. An alleged noncompliance with the provisions of RC 119.03(E) by an administrative agency is not an issue which may be presented in an appeal under 119.11.

114 App 111, 180 NE(2d) 861 (1961), Golubski v Board of Embalmers & Funeral Directors; overruled by 14 App(2d) 47, 236 NE(2d) 561 (1967), Jamison Plumbing & Heating Co v Rose. The provision of RC 119.03(D) that "no rule (of an administrative board subject to such act) shall be amended except by a new rule which shall contain the entire rule as amended, and shall repeal the rule amended" is mandatory.

113 App 113, 172 NE(2d) 726 (1961), Ohio State Federation of Licensed Nursing Homes v Public Health Council; affirmed by 172 OS 227, 174 NE(2d) 251 (1961). The public health council may revise a rule after the original proposal is presented at the public hearing required by law; and such rule, as adopted, may contain amendments, substitutions and additions to that originally proposed by the agency and considered by it at such public hearing; but such power of revision is limited by the requirement that the rule adopted be "consistent with the public notice."

80 App 505, 73 NE(2d) 817 (1947), Motors Insurance Corp v Dressel. By virtue of provisions of this section, that no administrative rule shall be amended except by a new rule containing the entire rule as amended and repealing the rule amended, the new rule may be challenged and tested in its entirety.

OAG 85-046. In its development of amendments to the state health plan, the statewide health coordinating council must, pursuant to RC 3702.56(C), follow the procedures set forth in RC 119.03(A), (B), (C), and (H), with the exception of requirements imposed pursuant to RC 121.24 or RC 127.18, but need not comply with RC 119.03(D), (E), (F), (G), and (I). In particular, the council must follow the public notice and hearing procedures of RC 119.03(A) and (C) and must file proposals with the secretary of state, the director of the legislative service commission, and the joint committee on agency rule review under RC 119.03(B) and (H), but proposed amendments to the state health plan are not subject to invalidation by the general assembly pursuant to RC 119.03(I).

6. Effective date

14 App(2d) 47, 236 NE(2d) 561 (1967), Jamison Plumbing & Heating Co v Rose. RC 119.03(D) requires that the effective date of amendments to existing rules be specifically designated at the time the order adopting such amendments is issued; a declaration that the amendments will be effective ten days following their filing with the secretary of state is insufficient.

14 App(2d) 47, 236 NE(2d) 561 (1967), Jamison Plumbing & Heating Co v Rose. Where an agency has followed and completed the necessary statutory procedure in adopting an amended rule, upon the arrival

of the effective date of such amended rule its predecessor is, by operation of law, automatically repealed.

114 App 111, 180 NE(2d) 861 (1961), Golubski v Board of Embalmers & Funeral Directors; overruled by 14 App(2d) 47, 236 NE(2d) 561 (1967), Jamison Plumbing & Heating Co v Rose. The provision of RC 119.03 (D) that, in promulgating rules or changes in rules, an administrative agency "shall designate the effective date thereof" is mandatory.

OAG 85-046. In its development of amendments to the state health plan, the statewide health coordinating council must, pursuant to RC 3702.56(C), follow the procedures set forth in RC 119.03(A), (B), (C), and (H), with the exception of requirements imposed pursuant to RC 121.24 or RC 127.18, but need not comply with RC 119.03(D), (E), (F), (G), and (I). In particular, the council must follow the public notice and hearing procedures of RC 119.03(A) and (C) and must file proposals with the secretary of state, the director of the legislative service commission, and the joint committee on agency rule review under RC 119.03(B) and (H), but proposed amendments to the state health plan are not subject to invalidation by the general assembly pursuant to RC 119.03(I).

1956 OAG 6199. Rule-making procedure and the effective date of amendment or annulment of rules or regulations of the Ohio board of building standards discussed.

7. Appeal

34 Ohio St L J 853 (1974). Judicial Review of Administrative Decisions in Ohio, Charles I. Kampinski.

118 App 369, 195 NE(2d) 128 (1963), Long v Division of Watercraft. In an appeal to the common pleas court under RC 119.11 from an order of an administrative agency adopting a rule there is no burden on the agency to prove that the rule as adopted was supported by the evidence before it or that such rule is not unreasonable or unlawful.

115 App 243, 184 NE(2d) 767 (1961), In re Bd of Liquor Control's Amendments. In an appeal under RC 119.11 from an order adopting an amendment to certain of its rules by the board of liquor control, altering only the percentage mark up in the minimum price formula established for the sale of wine under authority of RC 4301.13, the attack made must be limited to the operation of such rule as amended, and the court is not required to affirmatively find that the action of the board is supported by reliable, probative and substantial evidence but only whether the adopting procedure was proper and the amendment adopted reasonable and lawful.

115 App 131, 184 NE(2d) 248 (1961), Maggiore v Bd of Liquor Control. On appeal to the common pleas court from an order of the board of liquor control adopting a regulation fixing the minimum markup for carry-out retail sales of beer and malt beverages, in the absence of a transcript of the proceedings before the board showing compliance with the procedure prescribed by RC 119.03, a finding of the common pleas court that the procedural requirements in adopting the regulation were complied with, and its judgment affirming the action of the board in adopting the regulation, are not supported by the record.

114 App 111, 180 NE(2d) 861 (1961), Golubski v Bd of Embalmers & Funeral Directors; overruled by 14 App(2d) 47, 236 NE(2d) 561 (1967), Jamison Plumbing & Heating Co v Rose. Where, on an appeal to the common pleas court from an order of the board of embalmers and funeral directors making certain changes in or additions to its rules, such board fails to file a transcript of its record of proceedings but files only an unverified stenographic transcript which includes only part of the exhibits offered, such "transcript" as filed is not sufficient to support a judgment of the common pleas court that such "board complied with

procedural requirements as provided by law in the adoption of such rule."

114 App 111, 180 NE(2d) 861 (1961), Golubski v Bd of Embalmers & Funeral Directors; overruled by 14 App(2d) 47, 236 NE(2d) 561 (1967), Jamison Plumbing & Heating Co v Rose. Where there is no specific reference in a notice of appeal from an administrative agency to the common pleas court to any alleged failure on the part of the agency to follow the provisions of the administrative procedure act in adopting a regulatory rule, the appellant is not barred from alleging such claimed procedural error for the first time in the court of appeals, and such alleged error may be considered by such court, where the common pleas court, by journal entry, holds that "said board complied with procedural requirements as provided by law in the adoption of such rule."

88 Abs 107, 184 NE(2d) 257 (CP, Franklin 1961), Columbus Green Cabs, Inc v Unemployment Compensation Bd of Review. Parties amenable to the unemployment compensation laws and represented at a hearing before the board of review for considering the adoption of amended rules who objected to certain of the amended rules as unlawful or unreasonable are parties adversely affected as contemplated by RC 119.03.

EBR 75-12-15-16 (1976), Akron v Williams. The proper proceeding before the environmental board of review on appeal of a rulemaking proceeding by the director of environmental protection is a de novo quasi-legislative appellate hearing.

119.031 Comparison of final form with proposed rule; procedures in case of finding of substantive change

(A) The chairman of the joint committee on agency rule review shall compare each rule, amendment, or rescission as filed in final form with the latest version of the same rule, amendment, or rescission as filed in proposed form.

(B) If, upon making the comparison required by division (A) of this section, the chairman of the joint committee on agency rule review finds that the rule-making agency has made a substantive revision in the rule, amendment, or rescission between the time it filed the latest version of the rule, amendment, or rescission in proposed form and the time it filed the rule, amendment, or rescission in final form, he shall promptly notify the rule-making agency, the secretary of state, and the director of the legislative service commission in writing of his finding.

(C) The joint committee on agency rule review shall review any rule, amendment, or rescission as filed in final form if, under division (B) of this section, it is found to contain a substantive revision. The joint committee may do either or both of the following:

(1) If the joint committee makes any of the findings stated in division (I)(1)(a), (b), or (c) of section 119.03 of the Revised Code, it may suspend the rule, amendment, rescission, or any part thereof. The suspension shall remain in effect until the time for legislative review and invalidation has expired under division (D) of this section, or until the general assembly adopts a concurrent resolution invalidating the rule, amendment, rescission, or any part thereof, whichever occurs first. The chairman of the joint committee shall promptly notify the rule-making agency, the secretary of state, and the director of the legislative service commission in writing of the suspension.

(2) The joint committee may recommend the adoption of a concurrent resolution invalidating the rule, amendment, rescission, or any part thereof if it makes any of the findings stated in division (I)(1)(a), (b), or (c) of section 119.03 of the Revised Code.

(D) A rule, amendment, or rescission that, under division (B) of this section, is found to contain a substantive revision shall nevertheless become effective pursuant to division (B)(1) of section 111.15, division (A)(1) of section 119.04, division (B)(1) of section 4141.14, or division (A) of section 5703.14 of the Revised Code and remain in effect as filed in final form unless:

(1) Under division (C)(1) of this section, the joint committee suspends the rule, amendment, rescission, or any part thereof; or

(2) Prior to the sixtieth day after the rule, amendment, or rescission was filed in final form, the house of representatives and senate adopt a concurrent resolution invalidating the rule, amendment, rescission, or any part thereof. If, after the joint committee on agency rule review recommends the adoption of a concurrent resolution invalidating the rule, amendment, rescission, or part thereof, the house of representatives or senate does not, within the time remaining for adoption of the concurrent resolution, hold five floor sessions at which its journal records a roll call vote disclosing a sufficient number of members in attendance to pass a bill, the time within which that house may adopt the concurrent resolution is extended until it has held five such floor sessions.

Upon the adoption of such a concurrent resolution, the clerk of the senate shall, within five days thereafter, send the rule-making agency, the secretary of state, and the director of the legislative service commission a certified copy of the resolution together with a certification stating the date on which the resolution takes effect. The secretary of state and the director shall each note the invalidity of the rule, amendment, rescission, or part thereof on his copy, and shall remove the invalid rule, amendment, rescission, or part thereof from the file of current rules. The director shall also indicate in the Ohio administrative code that the rule, amendment, rescission, or part thereof is invalid and the date of invalidation. The rule-making agency shall make appropriate adjustments to reflect the invalidity of the rule, amendment, rescission, or part thereof.

(E) Invalidation of a rule, amendment, rescission, or part thereof under this section shall prevent the rule-making agency from instituting proceedings to readopt any version of the same rule, amendment, rescission, or part thereof for the duration of the general assembly that invalidated the rule, amendment, rescission, or part thereof unless the same general assembly adopts a concurrent resolution permitting the rule-making agency to institute such proceedings.

(F) The failure of the general assembly to invalidate a rule, amendment, rescission, or part thereof under this section shall not be construed as a ratification of the lawfulness or reasonableness of the rule, amendment, rescission, or any part thereof or of the validity of the procedure by which the rule, amendment, rescission, or any part thereof was adopted.

(G) As used in this section, a rule, amendment, or rescission is filed:

(1) "In proposed form" when it is filed in such form with the joint committee under division (D) of section 111.15 or division (H) of section 119.03 of the Revised Code;

(2) "In final form" when it is filed in such form with the joint committee under division (B)(1)(b) of section 111.15, division (A)(1)(b) of section 119.04, division (B)(1)(b) of section 4141.14, or division (A)(2) of section 5703.14 of the Revised Code.

HISTORY: 1984 H 244, eff. 7-4-84

CROSS REFERENCES

General assembly, duties of joint committee on agency rule review, 101.35

119.04 Effective dates of rules; compliance with standards for adoption; public records; codification

(A)(1) Any rule adopted by any agency shall be effective on the tenth day after the day on which the rule in final form and in compliance with division (A)(2) of this section is filed as follows:

(a) Two certified copies of the rule shall be filed with both the secretary of state and the director of the legislative service commission;

(b) Two certified copies of the rule shall be filed with the joint committee on agency rule review. Division (A)(1)(b) of this section does not apply to any rule to which division (H) of section 119.03 of the Revised Code does not apply.

If all copies are not filed on the same day, the rule shall be effective on the tenth day after the day on which the latest filing is made. If an agency in adopting a rule designates an effective date that is later than the effective date provided for by this division, the rule if filed as required by this division shall become effective on the later date designated by the agency.

(2) The agency shall file the rule in compliance with the following standards and procedures:

(a) The rule shall be numbered in accordance with the numbering system devised by the director for the Ohio administrative code.

(b) The rule shall be prepared and submitted in compliance with the rules of the legislative service commission.

(c) The rule shall clearly state the date on which it is to be effective and the date on which it will expire, if known.

(d) Each rule that amends or rescinds another rule shall clearly refer to the rule that is amended or rescinded. Each amendment shall fully restate the rule as amended.

If the director of the legislative service commission or his designee gives an agency written notice pursuant to section 103.05 of the Revised Code that a rule filed by the agency is not in compliance with the rules of the commission, the agency shall within thirty days after receipt of the notice conform the rule to the rules of the commission as directed in the notice.

(3) As used in this section, "rule" includes an amendment or rescission of a rule.

(B) The secretary of state and the director shall preserve the rules filed under division (A)(1)(a) of this section in an accessible manner. Each such rule shall be a public record open to public inspection and may be lent to any law publishing company that wishes to reproduce it.

Any rule that has been adopted in compliance with section 119.03 of the Revised Code and that is in effect before January 1, 1977, may be divided into sections, numbered, provided with a subject heading, and filed with the secretary of state and the director to comply with the provisions of this section without carrying out the adoption procedure required by section 119.03 of the Revised Code. The codification of existing rules to comply with this section shall not constitute adoption, amendment, or rescission.

HISTORY: 1984 H 244, eff. 7-4-84
1981 H 694; 1977 H 25; 1976 H 317; 131 v H 628; 1953 H 1; GC 154-65

CROSS REFERENCES

Procedures for adopting rules likely to affect individuals, small businesses or small organizations, 121.24

OJur 2d: 26, Health § 29.6; 27, Highways and Streets § 273.5; 28, Hospitals and Asylums § 57, 58, 62; 30, Insurance § 21, 21.5; 41, Parks, Squares and Playgrounds § 10; 48, Schools § 10; 55, Wharfs § 14.1; 58, Workers' Compensation § 134

OJur 3d: 1, Abandoned, Lost, and Escheated Property § 69; 2, Administrative Law § 26, 57 to 59, 63.5, 66, 67, 68, 70, 98, 108, 171; 2, Advertising § 4, 14; 3, Animals § 21; 6, Atomic Energy and Ionizing Radiation § 31; 6, Auctioneers § 8; 7, Automobiles and Other Vehicles § 90; 9, Banks and Financial Institutions § 424, 507; 10, Building, Zoning and Land Controls § 156, 242, 307; 10, Businesses and Occupations § 32; 17, Consumer and Borrower Protection § 22, 23; 38, Eminent Domain § 215; 39, Employment Relations § 87; 41, Environmental Protection § 56, 83

Am Jur 2d: 2, Administrative Law § 278

119.05 Rules compiled for distribution—Repealed

HISTORY: 1976 H 317, eff. 9-30-76
1953 H 1; GC 154-66

AGENCY POWERS; HEARINGS

119.06 Adjudication order of agency valid and effective; hearings; periodic registration of licenses

No adjudication order of an agency shall be valid unless the agency is specifically authorized by law to make such order.

No adjudication order shall be valid unless an opportunity for a hearing is afforded in accordance with sections 119.01 to 119.13 of the Revised Code. Such opportunity for a hearing shall be given before making the adjudication order except in those situations where this section provides otherwise.

The following adjudication orders shall be effective without a hearing:

(A) Orders revoking a license in cases where an agency is required by statute to revoke a license pursuant to the judgment of a court;

(B) Orders suspending a license where a statute specifically permits the suspension of a license without a hearing;

(C) Orders or decisions of an authority within an agency if the rules of the agency or the statutes pertaining to such agency specifically give a right of appeal to a higher authority within such agency, to another agency, or to the board of tax appeals, and also give the appellant a right to a hearing on such appeal.

When a statute permits the suspension of a license without a prior hearing, any agency issuing an order pursuant to such statute shall afford the person to whom the order is issued a hearing upon request.

Whenever an agency claims that a person is required by statute to obtain a license, it shall afford a hearing upon the request of a person who claims that the law does not impose such a requirement.

Every agency shall afford a hearing upon the request of any person who has been refused admission to an examination where such examination is a prerequisite to the issuance of a license unless a hearing was held prior to such refusal.

Every agency shall afford a hearing upon the request of a person whose application for a license has been rejected and to whom the agency has refused to issue a license, whether it is a renewal or a new license, unless a hearing was held prior to the refusal to issue such license.

When periodic registration of licenses is required by law the agency shall afford a hearing upon the request of any licensee whose registration has been denied, unless a hearing was held prior to such denial.

When periodic registration of licenses or renewal of licenses is required by law, a licensee who has filed his application for registration or renewal within the time and in the manner provided by statute or rule of the agency, shall not be required to discontinue a licensed business or profession merely because of the failure of the agency to act on his application. Action of an agency rejecting any such application shall not be effective prior to fifteen days after notice of the rejection is mailed to the licensee.

HISTORY: 1984 H 379, eff. 7-2-84
1979 H 102; 1953 H 1; GC 154-67

CROSS REFERENCES

See Whiteside, Ohio Appellate Practice, Text 23.01, 23.03, 27.02
See Carroll, Ohio Administrative Law, Text 3.02, 13.02

Community mental health centers, certification and licensing, hearings for funds, OAC 5122:3-1-16, 5122:3-7-03
Facilities for the mentally retarded, hearings for funds, OAC 5123:1-1-16

Liquor permits, renewal, 4303.271

OJur 2d: 26, Health § 29.6; 28, Hospitals and Asylums § 57, 58, 62; 30, Insurance § 21, 21.5; 41, Parks, Squares and Playgrounds § 10; 48, Schools § 10; 55, Wharfs § 14.1; 58, Workers' Compensation § 134

OJur 3d: 1, Abandoned, Lost, and Escheated Property § 69; 2, Administrative Law § 26, 57 to 59, 81, 98, 99, 108, 113, 127, 171; 2, Advertising § 14; 3, Animals § 21; 6, Atomic Energy and Ionizing Radiation § 31; 6, Auctioneers § 8; 7, Automobiles and Other Vehicles § 85, 90, 121; 9, Banks and Financial Institutions § 424, 507; 10, Building, Zoning and Land Controls § 307; 10, Businesses and Occupations § 32; 11, Businesses and Occupations § 69, 71, 156, 242; 17, Consumer and Borrower Protection § 22, 23; 38, Eminent Domain § 215; 39, Employment Relations § 87; 40, Energy § 41; 41, Environmental Protection § 7, 56, 83

Am Jur 2d: 1, Administrative Law § 138 to 140; 2, Administrative Law § 279 to 281, 363

Revocation or suspension of license or permit to practice pharmacy or operate drugstore because of improper sale or distribution of narcotic or stimulant drugs. 17 ALR3d 1408

69 OS(2d) 1, 429 NE(2d) 1171 (1981), Ohio Boys Town, Inc v Brown. The attorney general is under a statutory duty to provide bingo licensees a hearing prior to rejection of an application for license renewal.

63 OS(2d) 232, 407 NE(2d) 527 (1980), General Motors Corp v McAvoy. Unless a contradictory statutory provision is involved, the director of the environmental protection agency must issue his actions in conformance with the requirements of RC 119.06 wherever possible and practical.

63 OS(2d) 232, 407 NE(2d) 527 (1980), General Motors Corp v McAvoy. Neither RC 3745.05 nor 3745.07 abrogates the opportunity for a prior hearing guaranteed by RC 119.06.

62 OS(2d) 297, 405 NE(2d) 714 (1980), Williams v Dollison. Appellant convicted of violating hit and run statute whose license was suspended as a result of failure to provide proof of financial responsibility was not entitled to post-suspension or revocation hearing before registrar of motor vehicles.

54 OS(2d) 159, 375 NE(2d) 417 (1978), Union Camp Corp v Whitman. The denial of a motion for a hearing de nova, by the environmental board of review, issued upon appeal of the adoption of regulations, without an adjudicatory hearing by the director of environmental protection, is an order affecting a substantial right in a special proceeding and a final order, appealable to the court of appeals of Franklin county.

18 OS(2d) 94, 247 NE(2d) 740 (1969), Toledo v Bernoir. RC 119.06 and 4509.04 authorize an owner of a motor vehicle to request and be granted a hearing pursuant to RC 119.01 et seq. to determine the validity of the registrar's order suspending his driver's license and motor vehicle registration.

8 App(3d) 347, 8 OBR 458, 457 NE(2d) 858 (Cuyahoga 1982), Solon v Solon Baptist Temple, Inc. Injunction proceedings are properly initiated under RC 3781.15 where building plans have been disapproved by a municipal building commission, since such disapproval is an appealable adjudication order effective without a hearing.

8 App(3d) 188, 8 OBR 248, 456 NE(2d) 842 (Franklin 1983), Stieben v Dollison. The determination of a petitioner's right to an operator's license, or reinstatement thereof, constitutes an "adjudication" as defined by RC 119.01(D), and petitioner has available the administrative and appeal remedies provided by RC Ch 119.

59 App(2d) 133, 392 NE(2d) 1276 (1978), Ohio State Medical Bd v Zwick. When the Ohio state medical board conducts an adjudicatory hearing pursuant to RC 4731.23, the affected party enjoys the procedural safeguards contained in RC 119.06 to 119.10 during the hearing, but does not have the right to notice of the findings or order of the hearing officer, pursuant to RC 119.09, or the opportunity to file written objections thereto.

46 App(2d) 197, 347 NE(2d) 541 (1975), Ohio Liquid Disposal, Inc v Dawe. Where an agency does not follow the statutory requirements of notice and of holding a hearing prior to issuing an adjudication order, an adverse party is not required to bring an action in mandamus to compel the agency to do that which it was aware it should do but elected not to do; the agency is estopped to assert error based on its own violations and a court of common pleas has subject matter jurisdiction over an appeal from an order made pursuant to RC 1509.081.

46 App(2d) 86, 345 NE(2d) 619 (1975), Davison v Bureau of Motor Vehicles. A notice that an examination would be held to determine the competency of the holder of a driver's license, pursuant to RC 4507.20, absent an order of revocation or suspension, is not an adjudication or appealable order.

No. H-84-9 (6th Dist Ct App, Huron, 8-17-84), Camardese v De Bord. An employer is deprived of a fair hearing and due process of law when a referee, during board review of the grant of an unemployment claim, interrupts the proceedings more than forty times, excludes the employer's affidavit concerning his reason for firing the claimant, permits the claimant to refute the banned affidavit, and then finds for the claimant on the ground that the claim is uncontroverted; exclusion of the affidavit is error, inasmuch as RC 4141.28 exempts board proceedings from rules of evidence and the most common sense of fairness is strained by the referee's rulings and decision.

No. 82AP-505 (10th Dist Ct App, Franklin, 6-23-83), White Consolidated Industries v Nichols. OAC 3745-47-03 and all other references to "draft actions" do not deny hearing rights guaranteed by RC 119.06.

61 Misc 29, 401 NE(2d) 486 (Muni, Girard 1979), Wilson v Dollison. A person who fails to claim a letter sent by certified mail at his last known address may not later complain that he did not receive notice of the suspension of his operator's license prior to the lapse of his appeal time.

76 Abs 146, 122 NE(2d) 503 (CP, Franklin 1954), Goodyear Synthetic Rubber Corp v Dept of Industrial Relations. The state fire marshal, rather than the director of industrial relations, has power over processes involving liquified petroleum gas (butadiene).

72 Abs 134, 134 NE(2d) 390 (App, Franklin 1953), Skall v Dept of Liquor Control. An applicant for a renewal of a liquor license is not entitled to a hearing before the department of liquor control at the time it considers the application for renewal unless it is requested.

717 F(2d) 308 (6th Cir 1983), Bier v Fleming. In an action by holder of harness race driver trainer license for violations of his rights by revocation of his license, state racing officials have defense of qualified good faith immunity.

538 FSupp 437 (ND Ohio 1981), Bier v Fleming; reversed by 717 F(2d) 308 (6th Cir 1983). Licensee has a property interest in a harness race driver trainer license sufficient to invoke the protection of the due process clause.

538 FSupp 437 (ND Ohio 1981), Bier v Fleming; reversed by 717 F(2d) 308 (6th Cir 1983). Due process was violated where holder of harness race driver trainer license was advised of revocation of license and then offered hearing before same tribunal that revoked license.

1959 OAG 231. The superintendent of building and loan associations does not have the power to revoke approval of a branch office of a building and loan association, previously given pursuant to RC 1151.05.

1959 OAG 231. The superintendent of building and loan associations does not have the power to revoke a certification to the secretary of state of the articles of incorporation of a proposed building and loan association, previously certified pursuant to RC 1151.03.

EBR 221086 (11-20-84), Sandusky v Maynard. The requirement in RC 119.06 of an opportunity for hearing prior to issuance of an adjudication order does not apply to findings and orders issued by the Ohio environmental protection agency in the performance of its enforcement duties, as opposed to its licensing function.

EBR 81-110 (1982), White Consolidated Industries v Nichols. RC 119.06 requires the Ohio environmental protection agency to provide the opportunity for an adjudication hearing before it issues an adjudication order. There is no provision of federal law which allows the agency to ignore its obligations under RC 119.06 to provide the opportunity for a hearing. Therefore, draft actions are unreasonable and unlawful because they may be used by the agency to deny hearing rights.

EBR 73-5 (1973), Mahoning Landfill, Inc v Bd of Health. A hearing by a local board of health for action under RC 3734.04, 3734.05, and 3734.09 is invalid if it fails to provide notice conforming to RC 119.06 and 119.07, and fails to conform procedurally with RC 119.10, which provisions are similar to those of RC 2506.03, governing administrative proceedings of units of local government.

119.061 Power of certain agencies to suspend licenses

Every agency authorized by law to adopt, amend, or rescind rules may suspend the license of any person, over whom such agency has jurisdiction within the purview of sections 119.01 to 119.13 of the Revised Code, for engaging in deceptive trade practice as defined in section 4165.02 of the Revised Code. Except as otherwise expressly provided by law existing as of November 2, 1959, no agency may make rules which would limit or restrict the right of any person to advertise in compliance with law.

HISTORY: 1972 H 511, eff. 1-1-74
130 v H 1; 128 v 318

CROSS REFERENCES

Hospitals and community health facilities, certification revocation or termination, OAC 5122:3-7-03

Fines by director of agriculture for operators' violations, hearings and other procedures, 1711.56

OJur 2d: 26, Health § 29.6; 28, Hospitals and Asylums § 57, 58, 62; 30, Insurance § 21, 21.5; 31, Intoxicating Liquors § 190; 41, Parks, Squares and Playgrounds § 10; 48, Schools § 10; 55, Wharfs § 14.1; 58, Workers' Compensation § 134

OJur 3d: 1, Abandoned, Lost, and Escheated Property § 69; 2, Administrative Law § 26, 28, 30, 57 to 59, 98, 108, 171; 2, Advertising § 4, 14; 3, Animals § 21; 6, Atomic Energy and Ionizing Radiation § 31; 6, Auctioneers § 8; 7, Automobiles and Other Vehicles § 90; 9, Banks and Financial Institutions § 424, 507; 10, Building, Zoning and Land Controls § 156, 242, 307; 10, Businesses and Occupations § 32, 45; 11, Businesses and Occupations § 68, 156, 242; 17, Consumer and Borrower Protection § 22, 23; 38, Eminent Domain § 215; 39, Employment Relations § 87; 41, Environmental Protection § 56, 83

Am Jur 2d: 1, Administrative Law § 180

---

118 App 202, 193 NE(2d) 734 (1963), International Breweries, Inc v Crouch. RC 4301.03 is a specific statute and does not come within the operation of RC 119.061.

119.062 Registrar of motor vehicles may suspend or revoke licenses without hearing

Notwithstanding section 119.06 of the Revised Code, the registrar of motor vehicles is not required to hold any hearing in connection with an order revoking or suspending a motor vehicle operator's license pursuant to section 4507.161, 4509.24, 4509.291, 4509.31, 4509.33, 4509.37, 4509.39, 4509.42, or 4509.66 of the Revised Code.

HISTORY: 1984 H 37, eff. 6-22-84
1973 S 385; 1969 H 597

CROSS REFERENCES

OJur 2d: 26, Health § 29.6; 28, Hospitals and Asylums § 57, 58, 62; 30, Insurance § 21, 21.5; 41, Parks, Squares and Playgrounds § 10; 48, Schools § 10; 55, Wharfs § 14.1; 58, Workers' Compensation § 134

OJur 3d: 1, Abandoned, Lost, and Escheated Property § 69; 2, Administrative Law § 26, 57 to 59, 98, 108, 171; 2, Advertising § 4, 14; 3, Animals § 21; 6, Atomic Energy and Ionizing Radiation § 31; 6, Auctioneers § 8; 7, Automobiles and Other Vehicles § 85, 90, 121; 9, Banks and Financial Institutions § 424, 507; 10, Building, Zoning and Land Controls § 156, 242, 307; 10, Businesses and Occupations § 32; 11, Businesses and Occupations § 156, 242; 17, Consumer and Borrower Protection § 22, 23; 38, Eminent Domain § 215; 39, Employment Relations § 87; 41, Environmental Protection § 56, 83

---

62 OS(2d) 297, 405 NE(2d) 714 (1980), Williams v Dollison. Appellant convicted of violating hit and run statute whose license was suspended as a result of failure to provide proof of financial responsibility was not entitled to post-suspension or revocation hearing before registrar of motor vehicles.

43 Misc 42, 334 NE(2d) 552 (CP, Cuyahoga 1974), Sommerville v Bureau of Motor Vehicles. The requirement in RC 119.12 for an exhaustion of administrative remedies applies to an appeal from a bureau of motor vehicles order suspending a driver's license, plates, and registration certificate.

43 Misc 29, 334 NE(2d) 8 (CP, Franklin 1975), McLaughlin v Bureau of Motor Vehicles. The rule set forth in Bell v Burson, 402 US 535 (1971), applies only to situations involving disputed civil liability, not to situations of an emergency nature where one accused of criminal offenses avoids judgment by forfeiting bond.

119.07 Notice of hearing; contents; notice of order of suspension of license; publication of notice; effect of failure to give notice

Except when a statute prescribes a notice and the persons to whom it shall be given, in all cases in which section 119.06 of the Revised Code requires an agency to afford an opportunity for a hearing prior to the issuance of an order, the agency shall give notice to the party informing him of his right to a hearing. Such notice shall be given by registered mail, return receipt requested, and shall include the charges or other reasons for such proposed action, the law or rule directly involved, and a statement informing the party that he is entitled to a hearing if he requests it within thirty days of the time of mailing the notice. The notice shall also inform the party that at the hearing he may appear in person, by his attorney, or by such other representative as is permitted to practice before the agency, or may present his position, arguments, or contentions in writing and that at the hearing he may present evidence and examine witnesses appearing for and against him. A copy of such notice shall be mailed to attorneys or other representatives of record representing the party. This paragraph does not apply to situations in which such section provides for a hearing only when it is requested by the party.

When a statute specifically permits the suspension of a license without a prior hearing, notice of the agency's order shall be sent to the party by registered mail, return receipt requested, not later than the business day next succeeding such order. Such notice shall state the reasons for the agency's action, cite the law or rule directly involved, and state that the party will be afforded a hearing if he requests it within thirty days of the time of mailing the notice. A copy of such notice shall be mailed to attorneys or other representatives of record representing the party.

Whenever a party requests a hearing in accordance with this section and section 119.06 of the Revised Code, the agency shall immediately set the date, time, and place for such hearing and forthwith notify the party thereof. The date set for such hearing shall be within fifteen days, but not earlier than seven days, after the party has requested a hearing, unless otherwise agreed to by both the agency and the party.

When any notice required by sections 119.01 to 119.13, inclusive, of the Revised Code, to be sent by registered mail, is returned because of inability to deliver, the notice required shall be published once a week for three consecutive weeks in a newspaper of general circulation in the county where the last known place of residence or business of the party is located. A copy of the newspaper, with the first publication of said notice marked, shall be mailed to the party at such address and the notice shall be deemed received as of the date of the last publication.

The failure of an agency to give the notices for any hearing required by sections 119.01 to 119.13, inclusive, of the Revised Code, in the manner provided in this section shall invalidate any order entered pursuant to such hearing.

HISTORY: 1953 H 1, eff. 10-1-53
GC 154-68

CROSS REFERENCES

See Whiteside, Ohio Appellate Practice, Text 23.01, 23.03
See Carroll, Ohio Administrative Law, Text 3.02, 15.05

Environmental protection agency, proposed actions of director, hearings and objections, mailing list, notices, appeals, 3745.07

OJur 2d: 26, Health § 29.6; 28, Hospitals and Asylums § 57, 58, 62; 30, Insurance § 21, 21.5; 31, Intoxicating Liquors § 141; 41, Parks, Squares and Playgrounds § 10; 48, Schools § 10, 195, 203; 55, Wharfs § 14.1; 58, Workers' Compensation § 134

OJur 3d: 1, Abandoned, Lost, and Escheated Property § 69; 2, Administrative Law § 26, 57 to 59, 88 to 91, 97, 98, 99, 101, 108, 125, 171; 2, Advertising § 4, 14; 3, Animals § 21; 6, Atomic Energy and Ionizing Radiation § 31; 6, Auctioneers § 8; 7, Automobiles and Other Vehicles § 90; 9, Banks and Financial Institutions § 424, 507; 10, Building, Zoning and Land Controls § 156, 242, 307; 10, Businesses and Occupations § 32, 45; 11, Businesses and Occupations § 67, 156, 242; 17, Consumer and Borrower Protection § 22, 23; 38, Eminent Domain § 215; 39, Employment Relations § 87; 41, Environmental Protection § 56, 83

Am Jur 2d: 1, Administrative Law § 353, 398 to 406

62 OS(2d) 297, 405 NE(2d) 714 (1980), Williams v Dollison. Appellant convicted of violating hit and run statute whose license was suspended as a result of failure to provide proof of financial responsibility was not entitled to post-suspension or revocation hearing before registrar of motor vehicles.

8 App(3d) 188, 8 OBR 248, 456 NE(2d) 842 (Franklin 1983), Stieben v Dollison. The determination of a petitioner's right to an operator's license, or reinstatement thereof, constitutes an "adjudication" as defined by RC 119.01(D), and petitioner has available the administrative and appeal remedies provided by RC Ch 119.

59 App(2d) 133, 392 NE(2d) 1276 (1978), Ohio State Medical Board v Zwick. When the Ohio state medical board conducts an adjudicatory hearing pursuant to RC 4731.23, the affected party enjoys the procedural safeguards contained in RC 119.06 to 119.10 during the hearing, but does not have the right to notice of the findings or order of the hearing officer, pursuant to RC 119.09, or the opportunity to file written objections thereto.

46 App(2d) 86, 345 NE(2d) 619 (1975), Davison v Bureau of Motor Vehicles. A notice that an examination would be held to determine the competency of the holder of a driver's license, pursuant to RC 4507.20, absent an order of revocation or suspension, is not an adjudication or appealable order.

39 App(2d) 47, 316 NE(2d) 481 (1973), Shady Acres Nursing Home, Inc v Canary. Where a limited term agreement between the Ohio department of public welfare and a skilled nursing home provides that a due process hearing would be afforded before rights under the agreement would be terminated due to deficiencies, no hearing is required with regard to a termination of rights ordered after the agreement has expired.

21 App(2d) 110, 255 NE(2d) 294 (1970), Tripodi, dba Naples Lounge v Liquor Control Comm. Due process of law requires that a permit holder have a right to be heard at a hearing before the liquor control commission on an alleged violation of liquor control regulations, wherein his right to continued operation under his liquor permit is in jeopardy; adequate notice of such hearing is a necessary part of this right.

21 App(2d) 110, 255 NE(2d) 294 (1970), Tripodi, dba Naples Lounge v Liquor Control Comm. The provision of RC 119.07 for giving notice to a party by registered mail, return receipt requested, informing him of his right to a hearing, prescribes adequate notice and is in compliance with due process of law, and the mailing of such notice to a permit holder at the place of business for which the permit is issued by the liquor control commission is in compliance with RC 119.07 and with due process of law.

3 App(2d) 423, 210 NE(2d) 730 (1965), Fogt v Ohio State Racing Comm. A horse trainer cited to appear before the Ohio state racing commission, who appears in person before such agency, expressly indicates he wants to proceed without counsel, specifically waives any defects in the notice of the alleged violation of a rule of such agency and consents to an amendment of the original citation to include an alleged violation of another rule of such agency, is estopped from thereafter denying the validity of such agency's order on the ground that the notice issued to him was defective in that it did not meet the requirements of RC 119.07.

109 App 477, 161 NE(2d) 543 (1959), Joseph, dba Club House Cafe v Bd of Liquor Control. In issuing a citation to show cause why a liquor permit should not be suspended or revoked it is necessary that the citation set forth with some particularity a statutory ground for suspension or revocation, but this provision has no application to a notice of the

rejection of an application for renewal of a permit; it is sufficient that the notice rejecting an application for a renewal of permit be in accord with the requirements of Regulation 65 of the department of liquor control.

103 App 347, 142 NE(2d) 268 (1957), Ohio Motor Vehicle Dealers' & Salesmen's Licensing Bd v Memphis Auto Sales. Where an automobile dealer is charged with a violation of one section of the certificate of motor vehicle title law of which he is found not guilty, a finding of the motor vehicle dealers' licensing board suspending such dealer for alleged violation of another section of such law upon which he was not charged is invalid.

91 App 277, 97 NE(2d) 688 (1950), Shearer v State Medical Bd. An order of the state medical board suspending a certificate to practice is not invalidated by reason of the board's failure to send a certified copy of such suspension order to the practitioner where the latter had full and complete notice of the board's action.

54 Misc 31, 376 NE(2d) 987 (Muni, Dayton 1978), State v Foreman. Notice under RC 4509.13 of a required security deposit and of license suspension for failure to deposit must comply with the Ohio Administrative Procedure Act, RC 119.07, both as to content and as to manner of service.

14 Misc 181, 237 NE(2d) 923 (CP, Lake 1968), Blanchard v Bureau of Unemployment Compensation. Where the administrator of the bureau of unemployment compensation rejects a claim, it is desirable, but not mandatory, that a copy of this order be mailed to claimant's counsel, if known.

69 Abs 407, 119 NE(2d) 156 (CP, Franklin 1954), Meyer v Bd of Liquor Control. Notice of hearing before board of liquor control held adequate where permit holder was notified and attorney for receiver appeared at hearing and entered a plea of guilty.

OAG 80-092. RC Ch 4735 specifically governing the division of real estate proceedings prevails over any conflicting general hearing requirements of RC Ch 119. However, RC Ch 4735 does not cover certain matters. For example, RC Ch 119 provides for due process protections regarding the contents of the letter furnishing notice of a right to a hearing.

OAG 73-125. No person in attendance at a public rule hearing, conducted by the public health council pursuant to RC 119.03, has the right to cross-examine any witness, but the public health council may, in its sound discretion, adopt procedures permitting cross-examination during such hearings.

1960 OAG 1573. Where a party to an adjudication hearing under RC Ch 119 presents his position in writing and does not testify in his own behalf, the administrative agency conducting the hearing has the right to call such party to testify under oath as upon cross-examination.

EBR 73-5 (1973), Mahoning Landfill, Inc v Bd of Health. A hearing by a local board of health for action under RC 3734.04, 3734.05, and 3734.09 is invalid if it fails to provide notice conforming to RC 119.06 and 119.07, and fails to conform procedurally with RC 119.10, which provisions are similar to those of RC 2506.03, governing administrative proceedings of units of local government.

119.08 Date, time, and place of adjudication hearing

The date, time, and place of each adjudication hearing required by sections 119.01 to 119.13, inclusive, of the Revised Code, shall be determined by the agency. If requested by the party in writing, the agency may designate as the place of hearing the county seat of the county wherein such person resides or a place within fifty miles of such person's residence.

HISTORY: 1953 H 1, eff. 10-1-53
GC 154-69

CROSS REFERENCES

See Whiteside, Ohio Appellate Practice, Text 23.01, 23.03

OJur 2d: 26, Health § 29.6; 28, Hospitals and Asylums § 57, 58, 62; 30, Insurance § 21, 21.5; 41, Parks, Squares and Playgrounds § 10; 48, Schools § 10; 55, Wharfs § 14.1; 58, Workers' Compensation § 134

OJur 3d: 1, Abandoned, Lost, and Escheated Property § 69; 2, Administrative Law § 26, 57 to 59, 98, 107, 108, 171; 2, Advertising § 4, 14; 3, Animals § 21; 6, Atomic Energy and Ionizing Radiation § 31; 6, Auctioneers § 8; 7, Automobiles and Other Vehicles § 90; 9, Banks and Financial Institutions § 424, 507; 10, Building, Zoning and Land Controls § 156, 242, 307; 10, Businesses and Occupations § 32; 11, Businesses and Occupations § 156, 242; 17, Consumer and Borrower Protection § 22, 23; 38, Eminent Domain § 215; 39, Employment Relations § 87; 41 Environmental Protection § 56, 83

Am Jur 2d: 2, Administrative Law § 353, 398 to 406

1953 OAG 2422. The board of liquor control may determine the date, time and place of each adjudication hearing required under the provisions of either the Administrative Procedure Act or the Liquor Control Act.

119.09 Adjudication hearing

As used in this section "stenographic record" means in the case of a hearing before the state personnel board of review, a record provided by stenographic means or by the use of audio electronic recording devices, as the board determines.

For the purpose of conducting any adjudication hearing required by sections 119.01 to 119.13 of the Revised Code, the agency may require the attendance of such witnesses and the production of such books, records, and papers as it desires, and it may take the depositions of witnesses residing within or without the state in the same manner as is prescribed by law for the taking of depositions in civil actions in the court of common pleas, and for that purpose the agency may, and upon the request of any party receiving notice of said hearing as required by section 119.07 of the Revised Code, shall, issue a subpoena for any witness or a subpoena duces tecum to compel the production of any books, records, or papers, directed to the sheriff of the county where such witness resides or is found, which shall be served and returned in the same manner as a subpoena in a criminal case is served and returned. The fees and mileage of the sheriff and witnesses shall be the same as that allowed in the court of common pleas in criminal cases. Fees and mileage shall be paid from the fund in the state treasury for the use of the agency in the same manner as other expenses of the agency are paid.

An agency may postpone or continue any adjudication hearing upon the application of any party or upon its own motion.

In any case of disobedience or neglect of any subpoena served on any person or the refusal of any witness to testify to any matter regarding which he may lawfully be interrogated, the court of common pleas of any county where such disobedience, neglect, or refusal occurs or any judge thereof, on application by the agency shall compel obedience by attachment proceedings for contempt, as in the case of disobedience of the requirements of a subpoena issued from such court, or a refusal to testify therein. At any adjudication hearing required by sections 119.01 to 119.13 of the Revised Code, the record of which may be the basis of an appeal to court, a stenographic record of the testimony and other evidence submitted shall be taken at the expense of the agency. Such record shall include all of the testimony and other evidence, and rulings on the admissibility thereof presented at the hearing. This paragraph does not require a stenographic record at every adjudication hearing. In any situation where an adjudication hearing is required by sections 119.01 to 119.13 of the Revised Code, if an adjudication order is made without a stenographic record of the hearing, the agency shall, on request of the party, afford a hearing or rehearing for the purpose of making such a record which may be the basis of an appeal to court. The rules of an agency may specify the situations in which a stenographic record will be made only on request of the party, otherwise such a record shall be made at every adjudication hearing from which an appeal to court might be taken.

The agency shall pass upon the admissibility of evidence, but a party may at the time make objection to the rulings of the agency thereon, and if the agency refuses to admit evidence, the party offering the same shall make a proffer thereof, and such proffer shall be made a part of the record of such hearing.

In any adjudication hearing required by sections 119.01 to 119.13 of the Revised Code, the agency may call any party to testify under oath as upon cross-examination.

The agency, or any one delegated by it to conduct an adjudication hearing, may administer oaths or affirmations.

In any adjudication hearing required by sections 119.01 to 119.13 of the Revised Code, the agency may appoint a referee or examiner to conduct said hearing. He shall have the same powers and authority in conducting said hearing as granted to the agency. Such referee or examiner shall have been admitted to the practice of law in the state and be possessed of such additional qualifications as the agency requires. The referee or examiner shall submit to the agency a written report setting forth his findings of fact and conclusions of law and a recommendation of the action to be taken by the agency. A copy of such written report and recommendation of the referee or examiner shall within five days of the date of filing thereof, be served upon the party or his attorney or other representative of record, by certified mail. The party may, within ten days of receipt of such copy of such written report and recommendation, file with the agency written objections to the report and recommendation, which objections shall be considered by the agency before approving, modifying, or disapproving the recommendation. The agency may grant extensions of time to the party within which to file such objections. No recommendation of the referee or examiner shall be approved, modified, or disapproved by the agency until after ten days after service of such report and recommendation as provided in this section. The agency may order additional testimony to be taken or permit the introduction of further documentary evidence. The recommendation of the referee or examiner may be approved, modified, or disapproved by the agency, and the order of the agency based on such report, recommendation, transcript of testimony and evidence, or objections of the parties, and additional testimony and evidence shall have the same effect as if such hearing had been conducted by the agency. No such recommendation shall be final until confirmed and approved by the agency as indicated by the order entered on its record of proceedings, and if the agency modifies or disapproves the recommendations of the referee or examiner it shall include in the record of its proceedings the reasons for such modification or disapproval.

After such order is entered on its journal, the agency shall serve by certified mail, return receipt requested, upon the party affected thereby, a certified copy of the order and a statement of the time and method by which an appeal may be perfected. A copy of such order shall be mailed to the attorneys or other representatives of record representing the party.

HISTORY: 1979 H 102, eff. 5-29-79
1953 H 1; GC 154-70

CROSS REFERENCES

See Whiteside, Ohio Appellate Practice, Text 23.01, 23.03, 23.04, 27.02
See Giannelli, Ohio Evidence Manual, Author's Comment § 101.03
See Carroll, Ohio Administrative Law, Text 3.05 to 3.08, 13.02

State personnel board of review, reports and recommendations regarding appeals, OAC 124-15-01 et seq.
Hazardous waste appeal board, record of adjudication hearings, OAC 3734-1-15
Requisites of appeals from hearings de novo and adjudication hearings, OAC 3746-7-01, 3746-9-01

Environmental protection agency, environmental board of review to conduct de novo hearings, 3745.05
Environmental protection agency, proposed actions of director; actions, hearings and objections, mailing list, notices, appeals, 3745.07
Workers' compensation, administrative procedure, 4123.08 et seq.
Unemployment compensation hearings, 4141.17

OJur 2d: 26, Health § 29.6; 28, Hospitals and Asylums § 57, 58, 62; 30, Insurance § 21, 21.5; 31, Intoxicating Liquors § 138; 41, Parks, Squares and Playgrounds § 10; 48, Schools § 10; 55, Wharfs § 14.1; 58, Workers' Compensation § 134
OJur 3d: 1, Abandoned, Lost, and Escheated Property § 69; 2, Administrative Law § 93, 102, 106, 108, 109, 111 to 115, 117, 119, 125; 6, Atomic Energy and Ionizing Radiation § 31; 9, Banks and Financial Institutions § 424, 507; 10, Building, Zoning, and Land Controls § 156, 242; 17, Consumer and Borrower Protection § 22, 23; 17, Contempt § 34; 36, Discovery and Depositions § 20, 21, 60, 67, 202; 41, Environmental Protection § 7; 44, Evidence and Witnesses § 736
Am Jur 2d: 2, Administrative Law § 397 to 426
Comment note on hearsay evidence in proceedings before state administrative agencies. 36 ALR3d 121

1. Procedure, generally
2. Hearing
3. Evidence
4. Administrative appeal

1. Procedure, generally

2 App(3d) 204, 2 OBR 223, 441 NE(2d) 584 (1981), Lies v Ohio Veterinary Medical Bd. It was not error for a court of common pleas, sitting as an appellate court to review administrative adjudications, to

allow the administrative board to amend its minutes as originally certified, under the circumstances of this case.

63 App(2d) 157, 410 NE(2d) 773 (1978), In re Appeal of Lauderbach. Where a court of common pleas alludes to but does not interpret RC 119.09, and predicates its reversal of an order of the state personnel board of review on a lack of reliable, probative and substantial evidence, the employing state agency has no right of appeal.

110 App 527, 166 NE(2d) 253 (1959), State ex rel Columbus Bd of Ed v State Board of Education and Whitehall Bd of Ed. The state board of education in making the determination as required by RC 3311.06 is not subject to the provisions of RC Ch 119, but where the board does not make an equitable division of funds and indebtedness, an original action in mandamus is possible.

106 App 74, 153 NE(2d) 404 (1957), State ex rel General Contractors Assn v Wait; affirmed by 168 OS 5, 150 NE(2d) 851 (1958). An organization of employers engaged in the construction industry, which has not and does not intend to enter into a contract with any public authority for the construction of any public improvement, is not the real party in interest in and does not have the capacity to bring an action in mandamus to compel the director of the department of industrial relations and the director of the department of highways to hold a hearing or rehearing in order to make a record, upon which an appeal to a court may be taken with respect to the determination of prevailing rates of wages for mechanics and laborers in certain counties and to enjoin such official from certifying and furnishing to any public authority such rates of wages.

101 App 550, 140 NE(2d) 626 (1955), Brenner v Bd of Liquor Control. Where there is a finding against a permit holder that he tampered with or intimidated a witness subpoenaed by the department of liquor control to testify before it, and the evidence fails to disclose a violation of law or the regulations of the board, the charge should be dismissed and the cause remanded to such board for further proceedings incident to other charges made in the proceeding.

No. 10-079 (11th Dist Ct App, Lake, 6-29-84), Dietz v State Personnel Bd of Review. When a hearing is held before an administrative law judge, the agency remains the ultimate finder of fact; the agency may reject the judge's report, even though it is explicitly based on the credibility of witnesses.

No. 81AP-958 (10th Dist Ct App, Franklin, 4-1-82), Mid-Ohio Health Planning Federation v Certificate of Need Review Bd. Where the decision to grant a certificate of need to a hospital seeking to relocate is appealed, the burden of proof is upon the appellant pursuant to RC 119.09 while the burden of demonstrating need remains with the hospital pursuant to RC 3702.54.

1961 OAG 2462. The 1961 amendments to RC 4112.05 make RC Ch 119 applicable to procedure of the civil rights commission only as they relate to the manner in which final orders of the commission are issued and served on respondents and to modification or reconsideration of final orders of the commission.

2. Hearing

8 OS(3d) 26, 8 OBR 337, 457 NE(2d) 309 (1983), Ohio Motor Vehicle Dealers Bd v Remlinger. The court of common pleas must fulfill the mandatory duty imposed upon it by RC 119.09 to compel obedience by attachment proceedings when a witness refuses to testify to matters relevant in an RC 119.09 administrative hearing, limited only by the right of the witness to refuse to testify at such hearing based upon his Fifth Amendment privilege against criminal self-incrimination, or any other applicable privilege the witness may assert.

42 OS(2d) 441, 329 NE(2d) 690 (1975), Union Camp Corp, Harchem Division v Whitman. RC 3745.05 requires the environmental board of review to conduct a hearing de novo in an appeal from an order of the director of environmental protection, except where such order results from an adjudication hearing conducted by the director in accordance with RC 119.09 and 119.10. (See also Union Camp Corp v Whitman, 54 OS(2d) 159, 375 NE(2d) 417 (1978).)

5 App(3d) 102, 5 OBR 216, 449 NE(2d) 486 (Erie 1982), Erie Care Center, Inc v Ackerman. When conducting an adjudication hearing required by RC 119.01 to 119.13, an agency is not required to make its own findings of fact, but may approve, modify, or disapprove the recommendations of the referee or examiner.

2 App(3d) 204, 2 OBR 223, 441 NE(2d) 584 (1981), Lies v Ohio Veterinary Medical Bd. The institutional decision made by an administrative board may properly be based on written findings of fact prepared by a hearing examiner appointed under RC 119.09, so long as the findings of fact constitute a basis for making informed, deliberate, and independent conclusions about the issues, and the board members need not read the entire transcript of testimony, in the absence of any affirmative demonstration that the findings of fact are in any way defective.

59 App(2d) 133, 392 NE(2d) 1276 (1978), Ohio State Medical Bd v Zwick. When the Ohio state medical board conducts an adjudicatory hearing pursuant to RC 4731.23, the affected party enjoys the procedural safeguards contained in RC 119.06 to 119.10 during the hearing, but does not have the right to notice of the findings or order of the hearing officer, pursuant to RC 119.09, or the opportunity to file written objections thereto.

54 App(2d) 160, 376 NE(2d) 596 (1977), State v Carroll. Where a license revocation hearing is held by the state medical board, pursuant to RC 4731.23, before one member of the board, the requirements of a fair hearing and due process are not met when the record affirmatively shows that the assistant attorney general who prosecuted the case was present during the subsequent deliberations of the entire board and the transcript of the evidence of the hearing was not read or considered by all the members of the board.

No. H-84-9 (6th Dist Ct App, Huron, 8-17-84), Camardese v De Bord. An employer is deprived of a fair hearing and due process of law when a referee, during board review of the grant of an unemployment claim, interrupts the proceedings more than forty times, excludes the employer's affidavit concerning his reason for firing the claimant, permits the claimant to refute the banned affidavit, and then finds for the claimant on the ground that the claim is uncontroverted; exclusion of the affidavit is error, inasmuch as RC 4141.28 exempts board proceedings from rules of evidence and the most common sense of fairness is strained by the referee's rulings and decision.

No. CA83-09-019 (12th Dist Ct App, Preble, 7-23-84), Beare v City of Eaton. Where no objection is made to unsworn testimony before a municipal civil service commission, the error is waived.

1960 OAG 1625. Where a stenographic record is made of a hearing conducted by a township board of zoning appeals under RC 519.15 the costs of such record should be borne by the party which requested or ordered that the record be made.

1958 OAG 2609. RC 119.09 does not authorize the board of liquor control to appoint one of its members who is an attorney as its referee or examiner to conduct a hearing and report to the board his findings of fact, conclusions of law, and recommendation of board action, but such board is authorized to designate any member of such board to conduct a hearing and to make up a record of the evidence, therein adduced, for review by the board as a whole.

EBR 571050 (12-13-84), Dayton Power & Light Co v Maynard. The director of environmental protection cannot issue an adjudication order, as defined in RC 119.01(D), without first providing the affected party an opportunity to request a hearing.

3. Evidence

7 App(3d) 1, 7 OBR 1, 453 NE(2d) 1262 (Clark 1982), Haley v Ohio State Dental Bd. The hearsay rule is relaxed in administrative proceedings, but the discretion to consider hearsay evidence cannot be exercised in an arbitrary manner.

120 App 163, 201 NE(2d) 605 (1963), Lakis, dba Mickey's Lounge Bar v Bd of Liquor Control. The provisions of RC 119.09 govern the board of liquor control in the matter of admitting evidence in a hearing before it, and it is not error for the board to deny a permittee the right to examine a witness of the board under RC 2317.52, which section is not controlling in such hearing.

Nos. 46202 and 46209 (8th Dist Ct App, Cuyahoga, 6-18-84), Riggar v Ohio Bureau of Employment Services. The polygraph is not an acceptable tool in the search for truth; thus, where a denial of unemployment benefits is based upon an administrative referee's conclusion that a claimant's credibility was "damaged" by his refusal to undergo a company test, the denial of benefits must be reversed and the cause remanded to the administrative body.

71 Abs 97, 130 NE(2d) 351 (App, Franklin 1955), Matteo, dba Al's Cafe v Dept of Liquor Control. Hearsay evidence may be sufficient to support revocation of a liquor permit where no objection is made thereto.

1960 OAG 1573. Where a party to an adjudication hearing under RC Ch 119 presents his position in writing and does not testify in his own behalf, the administrative agency conducting the hearing has the right to call such party to testify under oath as upon cross-examination.

4. Administrative appeal

42 OS(2d) 441, 329 NE(2d) 690 (1975), Union Camp Corp, Harchem Division v Whitman. RC 3745.05 requires the environmental board of review to conduct a hearing de novo in an appeal from an order of the director of environmental protection, except where such order results from an adjudication hearing conducted by the director in accordance with RC 119.09 and 119.10. (See also Union Camp Corp v Whitman, 54 OS(2d) 159, 375 NE(2d) 417 (1978).)

61 App(2d) 155, 400 NE(2d) 1358 (1978), United States Steel Corp v Williams. In an appeal of an action taken by the director of environmental protection in a non-adjudicatory hearing, it is prejudicial error for the board of environmental review to refuse to conduct a de novo proceeding in which all of the rights inherent to an adjudicatory hearing are allowed.

46 App(2d) 34, 345 NE(2d) 625 (1975), Babcock v Bureau of Motor Vehicles. The exceptions granted by RC 4509.19 to the security and suspension requirements of RC 4509.12 do not exempt a motorist claiming such from utilizing the administrative procedures of RC Ch 119 before an appeal is taken to a court of common pleas.

109 App 477, 161 NE(2d) 543 (1959), Joseph, dba Club House Cafe v Bd of Liquor Control. There is no statutory authority permitting the board of liquor control to order the department of liquor control to make definite and certain an order rejecting the renewal of a liquor permit; and the order of such board, on appeal, dismissing a motion to require the department of liquor control to make definite and certain such rejection order, on the ground that it was "without jurisdiction in the premises," is a proper order.

Nos. 83AP-1103 and 83AP-1140 (10th Dist Ct App, Franklin, 9-20-84), Pushay v Walter. The state board of education is not required to make its own findings of fact when rejecting the recommendation of its own referee.

Nos. 83AP-1103 and 83AP-1140 (10th Dist Ct App, Franklin, 9-20-84), Pushay v Walter. A statement by the state board of education that it has considered a referee's report and objections thereto, and that the local board of education's objections to providing transportation to students of non-public school are well-founded is sufficient to satisfy the requirement of including reasons for disapproving the recommendations of a referee in the record of its proceedings.

No. C-800857 (1st Dist Ct App, Hamilton, 2-17-82), State ex rel Wheeler v King. Where a municipality creates an inner appellate system that not only hears appeals from orders enforcing the city's regulations, but also appeals from orders enforcing the Ohio basic building code, the city ordinance is in conflict with statutory law, as the board of building appeals is the agency empowered to conduct adjudication hearings in respect to building code violations.

1960 OAG 1625. Neither a board of township trustees nor a township board of zoning appeals is authorized to require that the appellant in an appeal to such board of zoning appeals under RC 519.15 must pay the reasonable and necessary costs of postage and advertising relative to such appeal nor to require a deposit as security for the payment of such costs by the party filing the appeal.

EBR 76-37 (1977), Windlawn Township Trustees v Williams. A permit issued by the director of environmental protection is an affirmative state action, and in an adjudication hearing held in response to an objection to an issued permit, the burden of proof lies with the director.

EBR 76-20, 21, 22 (1977), Burlington Preservation Organization v Williams. In an adjudication hearing held to determine whether or not to grant a permit, the director of environmental protection and the applicant share the burden of proof, while the objectors carry the burden of proceeding.

EBR 75-12-15-16 (1976), Akron v Williams. All parties to a rulemaking proceeding before the director of environmental protection are proper parties to an appeal arising from that proceeding to the environmental board of review.

119.091 Failure to hold hearing prior to license expiration

The failure of any agency to hold an adjudication hearing before the expiration of a license shall not terminate the request for a hearing and shall not invalidate any order entered by the agency after holding the hearing. If during or after such hearing but before the issuance of an order the existing license shall expire the adjudicatory agency shall in its order in favor of the affected party provide that the licensing authority shall renew the license upon payment of the fee prescribed by law for the renewal of the license.

HISTORY: 125 v 241, eff. 10-2-53

CROSS REFERENCES

OJur 2d: 26, Health § 29.6; 28, Hospitals and Asylums § 57, 58, 62; 30, Insurance § 21, 21.5; 41, Parks, Squares and Playgrounds § 10; 48, Schools § 10; 55, Wharfs § 14.1; 58, Workers' Compensation § 134

OJur 3d: 1, Abandoned, Lost, and Escheated Property § 69; 2, Administrative Law § 26, 57 to 59, 98, 100, 108, 123, 171; 2, Advertising § 4, 14; 3, Animals § 21; 6, Atomic Energy and Ionizing Radiation §

31; 6, Auctioneers § 8; 7, Automobiles and Other Vehicles § 90; 9, Banks and Financial Institutions § 424, 507; 10, Building, Zoning and Land Controls § 156, 242, 307; 10, Businesses and Occupations § 32; 11, Businesses and Occupations § 67, 156, 242; 17, Consumer and Borrower Protection § 22, 23; 38, Eminent Domain § 215; 39, Employment Relations § 87; 41, Environmental Protection § 56, 83

119.092 Recovery of attorney's fees by certain prevailing parties

(A) As used in this section:

(1) "Eligible party" means a party to an adjudication hearing other than the following:

(a) The agency;

(b) An individual whose net worth exceeded one million dollars at the time he received notification of the hearing;

(c) A sole owner of an unincorporated business that had, or a partnership, corporation, association, or organization that had, a net worth exceeding five million dollars at the time the party received notification of the hearing, except that an organization that is described in subsection 501(c)(3) and is tax exempt under subsection 501(a) of the Internal Revenue Code, shall not be excluded as an eligible party under this division because of its net worth;

(d) A sole owner of an unincorporated business that employed, or a partnership, corporation, association, or organization that employed, more than five hundred persons at the time the party received notification of the hearing.

(2) "Fees" means reasonable attorney's fees, in an amount not to exceed seventy-five dollars per hour or a higher hourly fee that the agency establishes by rule and that is applicable under the circumstances.

(3) "Internal Revenue Code" means the "Internal Revenue Code of 1954," 68A Stat. 3, 26 U.S.C. 1, as amended.

(4) "Prevailing eligible party" means an eligible party that prevails after an adjudication hearing, as reflected in an order entered in the journal of the agency.

(B)(1) Except as provided in divisions (B)(2) and (F) of this section, if an agency conducts an adjudication hearing under this chapter, the prevailing eligible party is entitled, upon filing a motion in accordance with this division, to compensation for fees incurred by that party in connection with the hearing. A prevailing eligible party that desires an award of compensation for fees shall file a motion requesting the award with the agency within thirty days after the date that the order of the agency is entered in its journal. The motion shall do all of the following:

(a) Identify the party;

(b) Indicate that the party is the prevailing eligible party and is entitled to receive an award of compensation for fees;

(c) Include a statement that the agency's position in initiating the matter in controversy was not substantially justified;

(d) Indicate the amount sought as an award;

(e) Itemize all fees sought in the requested award. This itemization shall include a statement from any attorney who represented the prevailing eligible party, that indicates the fees charged, the actual time expended, and the rate at which the fees were calculated.

(2) Upon the filing of a motion under this section, the request for the award shall be reviewed by the referee or examiner who conducted the adjudication hearing or, if none, by the agency involved. In the review, the referee, examiner, or agency shall determine whether the fees incurred by the prevailing eligible party exceeded one hundred dollars, whether the position of the agency in initiating the matter in controversy was substantially justified, whether special circumstances make an award unjust, and whether the prevailing eligible party engaged in conduct during the course of the hearing that unduly and unreasonably protracted the final resolution of the matter in controversy. The referee, examiner, or agency shall issue a determination, in writing, on the motion of the prevailing eligible party, which determination shall include a statement indicating whether an award has been granted, the findings and conclusions underlying it, the reasons or bases for the findings and conclusions, and, if an award has been granted, its amount. The determination shall be entered in the record of the prevailing eligible party's case, and a copy of it mailed to the prevailing eligible party.

With respect to a motion under this section, the agency involved, through any representative it designates, has the burden of proving that its position in initiating the matter in controversy was substantially justified, that special circumstances make an award unjust, or that the prevailing eligible party engaged in conduct during the course of the hearing that unduly and unreasonably protracted the final resolution of the matter in controversy. A referee, examiner, or agency considering a motion under this section may deny an award entirely, or reduce the amount of an award that otherwise would be payable, to a prevailing eligible party only as follows:

(a) If the determination is that the agency has sustained its burden of proof that its position in initiating the matter in controversy was substantially justified or that special circumstances make an award unjust, the motion shall be denied;

(b) If the determination is that the agency has sustained its burden of proof that the prevailing eligible party engaged in conduct during the course of the hearing that unduly and unreasonably protracted the final resolution of the matter in controversy, the referee, examiner, or agency may reduce the amount of an award, or deny an award, to that party to the extent of that conduct;

(c) If the determination is that the fees of the prevailing eligible party were not in excess of one hundred dollars, the referee, agency, or examiner shall deny the motion.

(3) For purposes of this section, decisions by referees or examiners upon motions are final and are not subject to review and approval by an agency. These decisions constitute final determinations of the agency for purposes of appeals under division (C) of this section.

(C) A prevailing eligible party that files a motion for an award of compensation for fees under this section and that is denied an award or receives a reduced award may appeal the determination of the referee, examiner, or agency to the same court, as determined under section 119.12 of the Revised Code, as the party could have appealed the adjudication order of the agency had the party been adversely affected by it. Notices of appeal shall be filed in the manner and within the period specified in section 119.12 of the Revised Code.

Upon the filing of an appeal under this division, the agency shall prepare and certify to the court involved a complete record of the case, and the court shall conduct a hearing on the appeal. The agency and the court shall do so in accordance with the procedures established in section 119.12 of the Revised Code for appeals pursuant to that section, unless otherwise provided in this division.

The court hearing an appeal under this division may modify the determination of the referee, examiner, or agency with respect to the motion for compensation for fees only if the court finds that the failure to grant an award, or the calculation of the amount of an award, involved an abuse of discretion. The judgment of the court is final and not appealable, and a copy of it shall be certified to the agency involved and the prevailing eligible party.

(D) Compensation for fees awarded to a prevailing eligible party under this section may be paid by an agency from any funds available to it for payment of such compensation. If an agency does not pay compensation from such funds or no such funds are available, upon the filing of a referee's, examiner's, agency's, or court's determination or judgment in favor of the prevailing eligible party with the clerk of the court of claims, the determination or judgment awarding compensation for fees shall be treated as if it were a judgment under Chapter 2743. of the Revised Code and be payable in accordance with the procedures specified in section 2743.19 of the Revised Code, except that interest shall not be paid in relation to the award.

(E) Each agency that is required to pay compensation for fees to a prevailing eligible party pursuant to this section during any fiscal year shall prepare a report for that year. The report shall be completed no later than the first day of October of the fiscal year following the fiscal year covered by the report, and copies of it shall be filed with the general assembly. It shall contain the following information for the covered fiscal year:

(1) The total amount and total number of the awards of compensation for fees required to be paid by the agency;

(2) The amount and nature of each individual award that the agency was required to pay;

(3) Any other relevant information that may aid the general assembly in evaluating the scope and impact of awards of compensation for fees.

(F) The provisions of this section do not apply when any of the following circumstances are involved:

(1) An adjudication hearing was conducted for the purpose of establishing or fixing a rate;

(2) An adjudication hearing was conducted for the purpose of determining the eligibility or entitlement of any individual to benefits;

(3) A prevailing eligible party was represented in an adjudication hearing by an attorney who was paid pursuant to an appropriation by the federal or state government or a local government;

(4) An adjudication hearing was conducted by the state personnel board of review pursuant to authority conferrred [sic] by section 124.03 of the Revised Code, or by the state employment relations board pursuant to authority conferred by Chapter 4117. of the Revised Code.

HISTORY: 1984 S 102, eff. 4-11-85

Note: See note under 119.12 from 1984 S 102, § 3.

119.093 Attorney general to define "net worth"

The attorney general shall adopt a rule pursuant to this chapter that defines the term "net worth" for purposes of sections 119.092 and 2335.39 of the Revised Code. The definition shall be designed to permit agencies and courts to apply identical principles in determining whether a party to an adjudication hearing, civil action or appeal of a civil action, or appeal of an adjudication order pursuant to section 119.12 of the Revised Code is an eligible party for purposes of the provisions of sections 119.092 and 2335.39 of the Revised Code.

HISTORY: 1984 S 102, eff. 4-11-85

Note: See note under 119.12 from 1984 S 102, § 3.

119.10 Counsel to represent agency

At any adjudication hearing required by sections 119.01 to 119.13, inclusive, of the Revised Code, the record of which may be the basis of an appeal to court, and in all proceedings in the courts of this state or of the United States, the attorney general or any of his assistants or special counsel who have been designated by him shall represent the agency.

HISTORY: 1953 H 1, eff. 10-1-53
GC 154-71

CROSS REFERENCES

See Whiteside, Ohio Appellate Practice, Text 23.01, 27.02

Environmental protection agency, environmental board of review to conduct de novo hearings, 3745.05
Environmental protection agency, proposed actions of director; actions, hearings and objections, mailing list, notices, appeals, 3745.07

OJur 2d: 26, Health § 29.6; 28, Hospitals and Asylums § 57, 58, 62; 30, Insurance § 21, 21.5; 41, Parks, Squares and Playgrounds § 10; 48, Schools § 10; 55, Wharfs § 14.1; 58, Workers' Compensation § 134
OJur 3d: 1, Abandoned, Lost, and Escheated Property § 69; 2, Administrative Law § 26, 57 to 59, 61, 98, 108, 171; 2, Advertising § 4, 14; 3, Animals § 21; 6, Atomic Energy and Ionizing Radiation § 31; 6, Auctioneers § 8; 7, Automobiles and Other Vehicles § 90; 9, Banks and Financial Institutions § 424, 507; 10, Building, Zoning and Land Controls § 156, 242, 307; 10, Businesses and Occupations § 32; 11, Businesses and Occupations § 156, 242; 17, Consumer and Borrower Protection § 22, 23; 38, Eminent Domain § 215; 39, Employment Relations § 87; 41, Environmental Protection § 7, 56, 83

42 OS(2d) 441, 329 NE(2d) 690 (1975), Union Camp Corp, Harchem Division v Whitman. RC 3745.05 requires the environmental board of review to conduct a hearing de novo in an appeal from an order of the director of environmental protection, except where such order results from an adjudication hearing conducted by the director in accordance with RC 119.09 and 119.10. (See also Union Camp Corp v Whitman, 54 OS(2d) 159, 375 NE(2d) 417 (1978).)

OAG 74-089. A representative of the attorney general's office is the proper person to present complaints before hearings of the ethics commission, under present circumstances.

EBR 73-5 (1973), Mahoning Landfill, Inc v Bd of Health. A hearing by a local board of health for action under RC 3734.04, 3734.05, and 3734.09 is invalid if it fails to provide notice conforming to RC 119.06 and 119.07, and fails to conform procedurally with RC 119.10, which provisions are similar to those of RC 2506.03, governing administrative proceedings of units of local government.

APPEAL

119.11 Appeal from orders affecting rules; procedure; transcript; hearing; order—Repealed

HISTORY: 1976 H 317, eff. 9-30-76
126 v 108; 1953 H 1; GC 154-72

CROSS REFERENCES

See Carroll, Ohio Administrative Law, Text 1.06(A), 9.04

CONSTITUTIONALITY:

42 OS(2d) 436, 329 NE(2d) 686 (1975), Rankin-Thoman, Inc v Caldwell. RC 119.11, which provides for an appeal to the court of common pleas from the quasi-legislative proceedings of administrative officers and agencies, is unconstitutional, in violation of O Const Art IV, § 4(B).

---

54 OS(2d) 136, 374 NE(2d) 1378 (1978), Williams v Akron. The review of final orders or actions of administrative officers or agencies authorized by O Const Art IV, § 3(B)(2), enables the general assembly to confer upon the courts of appeals appellate jurisdiction to review the final orders of administrative officers or agencies, irrelative of the fact that it is an appeal from an administrative rule-making action.

42 OS(2d) 436, 329 NE(2d) 686 (1975), Rankin-Thoman, Inc v Caldwell. The review of proceedings of administrative officers and agencies, authorized by O Const Art IV, § 4(B), contemplates quasi-judicial proceedings only.

34 OS(2d) 93, 296 NE(2d) 261 (1973), Burger Brewing Co v Dept of Liquor Control. An action for a declaratory judgment to determine the validity of an administrative agency regulation may be entertained by a court, in the exercise of its sound discretion, where the action is within the spirit of the declaratory judgment act, a justiciable controversy exists between adverse parties, and speedy relief is necessary to the preservation of rights which may otherwise be impaired or lost, and where the prerequisites for entertaining such an action are met, an action for a declaratory judgment upon the validity of an administrative agency regulation does not constitute a judicial review of quasi-legislative proceedings of such agency. (See also Burger Brewing Co v Thomas, 42 OS(2d) 377, 329 NE(2d) 693 (1975).)

22 OS(2d) 13, 257 NE(2d) 371 (1970), Fortner v Thomas. Review of proceedings of administrative officers and agencies authorized by O Const Art IV § 4(B), contemplates quasi-judicial proceedings only, and so courts will not aid in making or revising rules of administrative officers, boards or commissions, being confined to deciding whether such rules are reasonable and lawful as applied to facts of a particular justiciable case.

22 OS(2d) 13, 257 NE(2d) 371 (1970), Fortner v Thomas. RC 119.11 may not be employed to obtain judicial review of quasi-legislative proceedings of administrative officers and agencies.

172 OS 227, 174 NE(2d) 251 (1961), Ohio State Federation of Licensed Nursing Homes v Public Health Council. Prohibition will not lie to challenge the validity of the adoption of regulations by the public health council.

119.12 Appeal by party adversely affected

Any party adversely affected by any order of an agency issued pursuant to an adjudication denying an applicant admission to an examination, or denying the issuance or renewal of a license or registration of a licensee, or revoking or suspending a license, or allowing the payment of a forfeiture under section 4301.252 of the Revised Code, may appeal from the order of the agency to the court of common pleas of the county in which the place of business of the licensee is located or the county in which the licensee is a resident, provided that appeals from decisions of the liquor control commission may be to the court of common pleas of Franklin county. If any such party is not a resident of and has no place of business in Ohio, he may appeal to the court of common pleas of Franklin county.

Any party adversely affected by any order of an agency issued pursuant to any other adjudication may appeal to the court of common pleas of Franklin county, except that appeals from orders of the fire marshal, issued under Chapter 3737. of the Revised Code, may be to the court of common pleas of the county in which the building of the aggrieved person is located.

This section does not apply to appeals from the department of taxation.

Any party desiring to appeal shall file a notice of appeal with the agency setting forth the order appealed from and the grounds of his appeal. A copy of such notice of appeal shall also be filed by appellant with the court. Unless otherwise provided by law relating to a particular agency, such notices of appeal shall be filed within fifteen days after the mailing of the notice of the agency's order as provided in this section. For purposes of this paragraph, an order includes a determination appealed pursuant to division (C) of section 119.092 of the Revised Code.

The filing of a notice of appeal shall not automatically operate as a suspension of the order of an agency. If it appears to the court that an unusual hardship to the appellant will result from the execution of the agency's order pending determination of the appeal, the court may grant a suspension and fix its terms. In the event an appeal is taken from the judgment of the court and the court has previously granted a suspension of the agency's order as provided in this section, such suspension of the agency's order shall not be vacated and shall be given full force and effect until the matter is finally adjudicated. No renewal of a license or permit shall be denied by reason of such suspended order during the period of the appeal from the decision of the court of common pleas. In the case of an appeal from the state medical board, the court may grant a suspension and fix its terms if it appears to the court that an unusual hardship to the appellant will result from the execution of the agency's order pending determination of the appeal and the health, safety, and welfare of the public will not be threatened by suspension of the order. This provision shall not be construed to limit the factors the court may consider in determining whether to suspend an order of any other agency pending determination of an appeal.

The final order of adjudication may apply to any renewal of a license or permit which has been granted during the period of the appeal.

Notwithstanding any other provision of this section, any order issued by a court of common pleas suspending the effect of an order of the liquor control commission that suspends or revokes a permit issued under Chapter 4303. of the Revised Code, or that allows the payment of a forfeiture under section 4301.352[1] of the Revised Code, shall terminate not more than fifteen months after the date of the filing of notice of appeal in the court of common pleas, even if the matter has not been finally adjudicated within that time.

Notwithstanding any other provision of this section, any order issued by a court of common pleas suspending the effect of an order of the state medical board that limits, revokes, suspends, places on probation, or refuses to register or reinstate a certificate issued by the board or reprimands the holder of such a certificate shall terminate not more than fifteen months after the date of the filing of notice of appeal in the court of common pleas, even if the matter has not been finally adjudicated within that time.

Within thirty days after receipt of notice of appeal from an order in any case wherein a hearing is required by sections 119.01 to 119.13 of the Revised Code, the agency shall prepare and certify to the court a complete record of the proceedings in the case. Failure of the agency to comply within the time allowed shall, upon motion, cause the court to enter a finding in favor of the party adversely affected. Additional time, however, may be granted by the court, not to exceed thirty days, when it is shown that the agency has made substantial effort to comply. Such record shall be prepared and transcribed and the expense thereof shall be taxed as a part of the costs on the appeal. The appellant must provide security for costs satisfactory to the court of common pleas. Upon demand by any interested party, the agency shall furnish at the cost of the party requesting it a copy of the stenographic report of testimony offered and evidence submitted at any hearing and a copy of the complete record.

Unless otherwise provided by law, in the hearing of the appeal, the court is confined to the record as certified to it by the agency. Unless otherwise provided by law, the court may grant a request for the admission of additional evidence when satisfied that such additional evidence is newly discovered and could not with reasonable diligence have been ascertained prior to the hearing before the agency.

The court shall conduct a hearing on such appeal and shall give preference to all proceedings under sections 119.01 to 119.13 of the Revised Code, over all other civil cases, irrespective of the position of the proceedings on the calendar of the court. The hearing in the court of common pleas shall proceed as in the trial of a civil action, and the court shall determine the rights of the parties in accordance with the laws applicable to such action. At such hearing, counsel may be heard on oral argument, briefs may be submitted, and evidence introduced if the court has granted a request for the presentation of additional evidence.

The court may affirm the order of the agency complained of in the appeal if it finds, upon consideration of the entire record and such additional evidence as the court has admitted, that the order is supported by reliable, probative, and substantial evidence and is in accordance with law. In the absence of such a finding, it may reverse, vacate, or modify the order or make such other ruling as is supported by reliable, probative, and substantial evidence and is in accordance with law. The court shall award compensation for fees in accordance with section 2335.39 of the Revised Code to a prevailing party, other than an agency, in an appeal filed pursuant to this section.

The judgment of the court shall be final and conclusive unless reversed, vacated, or modified on appeal. Such appeals may be taken either by the party or the agency and shall proceed as in the case of appeals in civil actions as provided in sections 2505.01 to 2505.45 of the Revised Code. Such appeal by the agency shall be taken on questions of law relating to the constitutionality, construction, or interpretation of statutes and rules of the agency, and in such appeal the court may also review and determine the correctness of the judgment of the court of common pleas that the order of the agency is not supported by any reliable, probative, and substantial evidence in the entire record. Such appeals may be taken regardless of the fact that a proceeding was pending prior to the amendment of this section expressly authorizing such appeals, provided such appeals are perfected by the filing of notice of appeal within the time prescribed by section 2505.07 of the Revised Code.

The court shall certify its judgment to such agency or take such other action necessary to give its judgment effect.

HISTORY: 1984 S 102, eff. 4-11-85
1984 H 37; 1983 H 67, H 260; 1982 H 317; 1979 H 102; 1978 H 590; 1977 H 634; 1972 S 89; 130 v H 539; 128 v 1116; 125 v 488; 1953 H 1; GC 154-73

[1]Prior and current versions differ although no amendment to this language was indicated in 1984 S 102; "4301.352" appeared as "4301.252" in 1984 H 37 and 1983 H 67.

Note: 1984 S 102, § 3, eff. 4-11-85, reads:

The provisions of sections 119.092, 119.093, 119.12, 2335.39, and 2743.19 of the Revised Code that deal with awards of compensation for fees, as enacted by this act, shall apply only as follows:

(A) To adjudication hearings that are both commenced and conducted on or after July 1, 1985;

(B) To civil actions that are both commenced and conducted on or after July 1, 1985;

(C) To appeals of civil actions, provided that both the civil action and the appeal of the civil action are commenced and conducted on or after July 1, 1985;

(D) To appeals of adjudication orders of agencies pursuant to section 119.12 of the Revised Code, provided that both the adjudication hearing related to the adjudication order and the appeal of the adjudication order are commenced on or after July 1, 1985.

CROSS REFERENCES

See Baldwin's Ohio Township Law, Text 89.09
See Whiteside, Ohio Appellate Practice, Text 3.13, 23.01, 23.05, 23.07 to 23.13, 27.06, 33.04, 33.06, 33.07, 33.10, 33.11, 35.07, 35.08, 35.10; Forms 33.10, 33.13, 33.20

See Baldwin's Ohio School Law, Text 49.07, 49.09, 49.10

See Gotherman & Babbit, Ohio Municipal Law, Forms 27.01(Rule IX)(4), 33.04, 33.05, 33.09, 33.10

See Baldwin's Ohio Bank Law and Regulation Manual, Text 1.07

See Carroll, Ohio Administrative law, Text 1.06(A), 3.08(B), 3.11(A), 3.11(B)(2), 3.11(E), 9.08

Environmental board of review, bonds, OAC 3746-5-14

Department of rehabilitation and correction, employee discipline, OAC 5120-7-05

Adult parole authority, licensing requirements for a halfway house or community residential center as a licensed facility for the care and treatment of parolees, probationers, and furloughees, OAC 5120:1-3-02

Licensure of residential care facilities for the mentally ill, waivers and variances, OAC 5122:3-5-05

Funds for community facilities for the mentally retarded, appeals, OAC 5123:1-1-16

Procedure for withdrawal of bid, hearing, 9.31

Department of development, procedures for designation or rescission, appeals, 122.701

When liquor permit holder may be permitted to elect a forfeiture in lieu of suspension, 4301.252

Cancellation or suspension of permit, appeal to liquor control commission, 4301.28

Adult foster care facility, appeal of license revocation, 5103.34

Medicaid providers, orders against, 5111.06

Department of rehabilitation and correction, minimum standards for jails, appeals, 5120.10

Scope of rules, applicability, construction, exceptions, Civ R 1(C)

OJur 2d: 26, Health § 29.6; 28, Hospitals and Asylums § 57, 58, 62; 30, Insurance § 21, 21.5, 94.12; 31, Intoxicating Liquors § 144, 146, 148, 156 to 166; 35, Mandamus § 93, 95, 96; 40, New Trial § 49; 41, Parks, Squares and Playgrounds § 10; 42, Physicians and Surgeons § 63; 43A, Prisons § 4.5; 45, Veterans § 11; 48, Schools § 10; 49, State Fire Marshal § 11; 55, Wharfs § 14.1; 58, Workers' Compensation § 134

OJur 3d: 1, Abandoned, Lost, and Escheated Property § 69; 2, Administrative Law § 26, 57, 58, 59, 97, 98, 102, 108, 128, 155, 156, 157, 165, 170, 171, 177, 180 to 185, 193 to 196, 198, 199, 202 to 205, 207 to 210, 212 to 215; 2, Advertising § 4, 14; 3, Animals § 21; 4, Appellate Review § 689; 6, Atomic Energy and Ionizing Radiation § 31; 6, Auctioneers § 8; 7, Automobiles and Other Vehicles § 90, 142; 8, Banks and Financial Institutions § 52; 9, Banks and Financial Institutions § 424, 507; 10, Brokers § 20; 10, Building, Zoning and Land Controls § 156, 242, 307; 10, Businesses and Occupations § 32, 73; 11, Businesses and Occupations § 156, 212, 242; 15, Civil Servants and Other Public Officers and Employees § 174, 182, 185; 17, Consumer and Borrower Protection § 22, 23; 22, Courts and Judges § 333, 352; 38, Eminent Domain § 215; 39, Employment Relations § 87; 41, Environmental Protection § 56, 83

Am Jur 2d: 2, Administrative Law § 553 to 775

Applicability of stare decisis doctrine to decisions of administrative agencies. 79 ALR2d 1126

1. In general
2. Effect on other remedies
3. Party adversely affected
4. Matters appealable
5. Matters not appealable
6. Venue
7. Appeals in Franklin County
8. Notice of appeal
9. Time for filing
10. Suspension of order
11. Record of proceedings
12. Additional evidence
13. Procedure
14. Reliable, probative and substantial evidence
15. In accordance with law
16. Appeal by agency available
17. Appeal by agency denied
18. Scope of review
19. Disposition of appeal

1. In general

28 Ohio St L J 75 (1967). Ohio Sovereign Immunity: Long Lives the King, Ronald E. Schultz.

45 Cin Law Rev 108 (1976). The Applicability of the Sixth or Seventh Amendment Right to a Jury Trial in OSHA Penalty Proceedings, Gina A. West.

9 Akron L Rev 713 (1976). The Availability of Mandamus as a Vehicle for Administrative Review, Jane E. Bond.

12 U Tol L Rev 37 (1980). Patterns of Judicial Review of Administrative Decisions, F. Patrick Hubbard.

17 OS(3d) 226, 17 OBR 466, 479 NE(2d) 254 (1985), Miller v Industrial Relations Dept. An agency may appeal a decision of a common pleas court to a court of appeals only on questions of law, although once an appeal is perfected on such grounds the appellate court has jurisdiction to determine also whether the lower court's judgment is supported by the evidence.

14 OS(3d) 64, 14 OBR 456, 471 NE(2d) 488 (1984), Ohio Motor Vehicle Dealers Bd v Central Cadillac Co. The hearing required by RC 119.12 may be limited to a review of the record, or, at the judge's discretion, may involve briefs, oral argument, or newly discovered evidence.

9 App(3d) 198, 9 OBR 309, 459 NE(2d) 247 (Franklin 1983), Poole v Maloney. The appointing authority of a municipal department has no express statutory right to appeal the decision of a municipal civil service commission which reinstated a classified employee who was terminated for "lack of funds."

9 App(3d) 142, 9 OBR 207, 458 NE(2d) 895 (Preble 1983), Beare v Eaton. A municipal civil service employee who was removed from employment for disciplinary reasons may appeal the adverse decision of the civil service commission to the court of common pleas either under RC 119.12 or 2506.01.

8 App(3d) 105, 8 OBR 139, 456 NE(2d) 577 (Cuyahoga 1983), State Medical Bd v Mt. Sinai Hospital. RC 4731.341 is an independent special statute which expressly provides for an injunction action to abate a public nuisance, the unlawful practice of medicine; it does not provide for an administrative hearing as a condition precedent to the injunction action.

70 App(2d) 219, 436 NE(2d) 543 (1980), Painesville Raceway, Inc v Dept of Liquor Control. RC 119.12 confers upon the court of appeals appellate jurisdiction over administrative appeals taken by a state agency from decisions of the court of common pleas on questions of law relating to the constitutionality, construction, or interpretation of state statutes and rules of the agency.

51 App(2d) 92, 367 NE(2d) 63 (1976), Bolin v White. The court of claims has no jurisdiction to review decisions of the department of public welfare.

46 App(2d) 197, 347 NE(2d) 541 (1975), Ohio Liquid Disposal, Inc v Dawe. Where an agency does not follow the statutory requirements of notice and of holding a hearing prior to issuing an adjudication order, an adverse party is not required to bring an action in mandamus to compel the agency to do that which it was aware it should do but elected not to do; the agency is estopped to assert error based on its own violations and a court of common pleas has subject matter jurisdiction over an appeal from an order made pursuant to RC 1509.081.

40 App(2d) 285, 319 NE(2d) 212 (1973), Blue Cross of Northwest Ohio v Superintendent of Insurance. Rule-making by an administrative agency must be accomplished by the adoption of rules and regulations pursuant to statutory procedure and cannot be accomplished indirectly by adjudicatory determination.

39 App(2d) 47, 316 NE(2d) 481 (1973), Shady Acres Nursing Home, Inc v Canary. Subchapter XIX of the Social Security Act (42 USC 9985) does not authorize the summary decertification of a nursing home indirectly receiving benefits under its provisions, and where payments are discontinued without a hearing through the action of a state agency during the term of an existing agreement between the state and the home, establishing the conditions pursuant to which the payments are made, such action is invalid.

98 App 494, 130 NE(2d) 455 (1954), Standard "Tote," Inc v Ohio State Racing Comm. The Administrative Procedure Act authorizes an appeal to the court of appeals from an adverse decision rendered by the common pleas court upon a duly perfected appeal questioning the validity of rules adopted by the Ohio state racing commission, and such review is judicial rather than administrative.

No. 84AP-1085 (10th Dist Ct App, Franklin, 7-2-85), In re Application of Stover. An appeal of an adverse administrative decision to the common pleas court is a statutory proceeding under RC 119.12 and the rules of civil procedure are inapplicable pursuant to Civ R 1(C); therefore vacation of the judgment of the court under Civ R 60 is not available.

No. 411 (4th Dist Ct App, Vinton, 8-31-84), Dodrill dba Jim Dodrill Auto Sales v Motor Vehicle Dealers Board. The Motor Vehicle Dealers Board is not an "agency of a political subdivision," and appeals from the board are pursuant to RC Ch 119, not RC Ch 2506.

No. 44659 (8th Dist Ct App, Cuyahoga, 12-16-82), Minello v Orange City School District Bd of Ed. Trial court commits error in dismissing an appeal of a judgment rendered by the state personnel board of review for want of prosecution without a hearing or notice of hearing as required by state statute.

73 Abs 260, 137 NE(2d) 885 (App, Franklin 1953), In re Appeal of Socotch. It is not a ground for dismissal of an appeal from an order of the board of liquor control refusing to renew a permit that there is pending before the court an appeal from an order in a contempt proceeding requiring the permit to be granted.

2. Effect on other remedies

53 OS(2d) 18, 371 NE(2d) 841 (1978), State ex rel Bargar v Ross. A discharged state employee who has been denied relief in an appeal from a decision of the state personnel board of review cannot thereafter seek relief in mandamus.

172 OS 109, 173 NE(2d) 347 (1961), State ex rel Toledo-Maumee Raceways, Inc v Ohio State Racing Comm. A writ of mandamus may not be employed as a substitute for appeal and will not issue to control the discretion of the state racing commission or to direct in what particular way it shall proceed or decide a particular matter.

168 OS 445, 155 NE(2d) 897 (1959), State ex rel Oliver v State Civil Service Comm. Mandamus is not available to challenge the discharge of an employee by the bureau of unemployment compensation, inasmuch as the relator has a remedy by way of appeal.

147 OS 359, 71 NE(2d) 483 (1947), State ex rel Stein v Sohngen. Insofar as GC 6064-27 (RC 4301.28) provides that any person deeming himself aggrieved thereby may appeal to board of liquor control from action of department of liquor control refusing to issue permit, and this section provides further appeal to court of common pleas of Franklin county, writ of mandamus will not be issued to require department to issue liquor permit after refusal by department, as adequate remedy is provided by law and as writ will not issue as substitute for appeal.

1 App(3d) 141, 1 OBR 449, 439 NE(2d) 958 (1981), Ninth Street Church of Christ, Inc v Reich. Although a church, which wants to protest the issuance of a liquor permit, may be entitled to a hearing pursuant to RC 4303.26, neither RC Ch 4303 nor Ch 119 authorize the church to appeal the subsequent decision of the director of liquor control concerning the liquor permit application to the court of common pleas.

14 Misc 9, 233 NE(2d) 147 (CP, Montgomery 1967), Handler v Dept of Commerce. A proceeding by an administrative agency to revoke a license, commenced while an appeal to common pleas court is pending from an earlier order revoking such license on the same alleged grounds, when the agency has since terminated the earlier proceeding by reinstating the license on its own motion, cannot give rise to a valid order of revocation in the later proceeding, since the agency's jurisdiction is barred by the pendency of the earlier appeal at the time of commencing the second action to revoke.

70 Abs 485, 128 NE(2d) 762 (App, Franklin 1954), Green v Ohio State Racing Comm. A writ of prohibition will not issue to prohibit the state racing commission from considering charges which would lead to an individual's being ruled off the race-tracks of the state, since an adequate remedy at law is available through the Administrative Procedure Act.

66 Abs 232, 116 NE(2d) 455 (CP, Franklin 1953), In re Appeal of Socotch; reversed by 73 Abs 260, 137 NE(2d) 855 (App, Franklin 1953). Where the board of liquor control rejects an application for a permit, and a previous order of a common pleas court finding the board in contempt for failure to issue such permit is before an appellate court, common pleas court will not take jurisdiction of the second appeal since it is between the same parties and involves the same subject matter.

3. Party adversely affected

67 OS(2d) 106, 423 NE(2d) 161 (1981), Genoa Banking Co v Mills. Any bank receiving notice of a branch bank application pursuant to RC Ch 1111 is a proper party to bring an appeal of the approval of the application by the superintendent of banks pursuant to RC Ch 119.

34 OS(2d) 93, 296 NE(2d) 261 (1973), Burger Brewing Co v Liquor Control Comm. An action for a declaratory judgment to determine the

validity of an administrative agency regulation may be entertained by a court, in the exercise of its sound discretion, where the action is within the spirit of the Declaratory Judgments Act, a justiciable controversy exists between adverse parties, and speedy relief is necessary to the preservation of rights which may otherwise be impaired or lost, and where the prerequisites for entertaining such an action are met, an action for a declaratory judgment upon the validity of an administrative agency regulation does not constitute a judicial review of quasi-legislative proceedings of such agency.

29 OS(2d) 139, 280 NE(2d) 371 (1972), A. B. Jac, Inc v Liquor Control Comm. Ohio liquor control commission has a right of appeal from judgment of court of common pleas where all essential elements of violation in question were stipulated at the hearing before the commission and where court of common pleas reverses order of liquor control commission upon the basis of a question of law interpreting application of a regulation of the commission.

172 OS 394, 176 NE(2d) 214 (1961), In re Removal of Taylor. Where the mayor of a city is a party in an appeal to the common pleas court from an order of the municipal civil service commission affirming an order of the mayor removing the chief of police from office, and the judgment of the court reinstates the chief of police, the mayor is a proper party and has a right to appeal to the court of appeals.

27 App(2d) 237, 273 NE(2d) 903 (1971), In re Highland Holiday Subdivision. Board of county commissioners has no standing to appeal an order of court of common pleas ordering them to approve a plat submitted to them pursuant to RC Ch 711.

27 App(2d) 91, 273 NE(2d) 783 (1970), Clermont National Bank v Edwards. Bank which receives notice pursuant to RC 1111.02 of a hearing conducted in accordance with RC 1111.03 on an application for establishment of a new branch by applicant bank is a "party adversely affected" under RC 119.12, and has standing, under this section, to appeal an order by superintendent of banks granting application, and the granting or withholding of consent by superintendent of banks to the establishment of branch bank is an act of "adjudication" under RC 119.12.

No. 82AP-75 (10th Dist Ct App, Franklin, 11-18-82), Assignment of New Riegel Local School District to Vanguard Joint Vocational School District v Walter. Where the state board of education assigns a school district to membership in a joint vocational school district pursuant to RC 3313.90, the school district has the right of appeal to the court of common pleas.

4. Matters appealable

67 OS(2d) 378, 423 NE(2d) 1105 (1981), Pitts v Dept of Transportation. An order of the state personnel board of review issued on appeal from a final decision of an appointing authority relative to job abolishments is appealable, pursuant to the provisions of RC 119.12.

14 App(3d) 101, 14 OBR 115, 470 NE(2d) 200 (Franklin 1983), Wahle v Industrial Relations Dept. The provisions of RC Ch 2506 are inapplicable to an appeal from an order of the board of building standards; rather, such an appeal is governed by RC Ch 119 and 3781.

8 App(3d) 306, 8 OBR 414, 456 NE(2d) 1245 (Franklin 1982), In re Assignment of New Riegel Local School District to the Vanguard Joint Vocational School District. A resolution by the state board of education, assigning a school district to membership in a joint vocational school district pursuant to RC 3313.90 and 3313.911, is of a quasi-judicial nature and, therefore, subject to review as an adjudication under RC 119.12.

8 App(3d) 188, 8 OBR 248, 456 NE(2d) 842 (Franklin 1983), Stieben v Dollison. The determination of a petitioner's right to an operator's license, or reinstatement thereof, constitutes an "adjudication" as defined by RC 119.01(D), and petitioner has available the administrative and appeal remedies provided by RC Ch 119.

3 App(3d) 398, 3 OBR 464, 445 NE(2d) 706 (1981), Augustine v Ohio Dept of Rehabilitation and Correction. The Ohio department of rehabilitation and correction is not an agency whose decisions are subject to judicial review by appeal pursuant to RC 119.12.

27 App(2d) 91, 273 NE(2d) 783 (1970), Clermont National Bank v Edwards. Bank which receives notice pursuant to RC 1111.02 of a hearing conducted in accordance with RC 1111.03 on an application for establishment of a new branch by applicant bank is a "party adversely affected" under RC 119.12, and has standing, under this section, to appeal an order by superintendent of banks granting application, and the granting or withholding of consent by superintendent of banks to the establishment of branch bank is an act of "adjudication" under RC 119.12.

120 App 168, 201 NE(2d) 707 (1963), State ex rel Kendrick v Masheter; affirmed by 176 OS 232, 199 NE(2d) 13 (1964). A decision of the state personnel board of review affirming an order of an appointing authority "laying off" an employee in the classified service of the state is a final appealable order, and such employee may appeal therefrom to the court of common pleas of Franklin county.

117 App 108, 191 NE(2d) 188 (1962), Graul v State Personnel Bd of Review. An order of the state personnel board of review classifying employees in the attorney general's office is appealable, pursuant to the provisions of RC Ch 119 and 143.011.

110 App 286, 163 NE(2d) 391 (1959), State ex rel Buchard v State Bd of Examiners of Architects. RC 4743.03 is permissive, and the review provided for therein is not a prerequisite to an appeal to the courts under RC 119.12.

No. CA83-05-045 (12th Dist Ct App, Clermont, 3-19-84), Turner-Brannock v Bureau of Employment Services. Where an intermittent claims examiner with the bureau of employment services was dismissed because a certified civil servant had been selected from an eligibility list to fill the former's position, such claims examiner was not dismissed for disciplinary reasons, and therefore appeal of her dismissal could only properly be made under RC 119.12, rather than RC 124.34.

No. 11170 (9th Dist Ct App, Summit, 2-16-84), In re Removal of Roach v Fairlawn. An appeal of a discharge from a municipal police force must be brought under RC Ch 2506, and may not be brought pursuant to RC 119.12, which is relevant only to appeals from decisions of state agencies.

5. Matters not appealable

17 OS(3d) 105, 17 OBR 224, 477 NE(2d) 1134 (1985), State ex rel Carter v Cleveland City School Dist Bd of Ed. Where a civil service appeal is settled before a civil service commission hearing is held, there is no decision from which a party to the proceeding may appeal when the other party violates the terms of the settlement.

66 OS(2d) 152, 420 NE(2d) 990 (1981), Bd of Ed of Marion City School District v Bd of Ed of Elgin Local School District. The act of the Ohio state board of education disapproving a transfer of territory pursuant to RC 3311.06 is a legislative act, and, as such, is not appealable pursuant to RC 119.12.

53 OS(2d) 173, 373 NE(2d) 1238 (1978), State ex rel Bratenahl Local School District Bd of Ed v State Board of Education. In the

absence of an "adjudication" as defined in RC 119.01(D), the right to notice and hearing does not obtain and, consequently, in such a case the court of common pleas of Franklin county lacks jurisdiction under RC 119.12 to review actions taken by a state administrative agency.

42 OS(2d) 436, 329 NE(2d) 686 (1975), Rankin-Thoman, Inc v Caldwell. RC 119.11, which provides for an appeal to the court of common pleas from the quasi-legislative proceedings of administrative officers and agencies, is unconstitutional, in violation of O Const Art IV, § 4(B).

41 OS(2d) 115, 322 NE(2d) 878 (1975), Home Savings & Loan Assn v Boesch. The approval of an application by a building and loan association to operate a branch office pursuant to RC 1151.05 is not a licensing function within the provisions of the Administrative Procedure Act.

172 OS 394, 176 NE(2d) 214 (1961), In re Removal of Taylor. A person who becomes chief of police of a city without taking the civil service examination required by law is not in the classified service, is not entitled to the benefits of the civil service law, and has no right of appeal to the municipal civil service commission from an order of removal by the mayor of the city or to the common pleas court from a decision of the municipal civil service commission affirming the mayor's removal order.

11 App(3d) 277, 11 OBR 457, 464 NE(2d) 610 (Cuyahoga 1983), Walt's Friendly Tavern v Dept of Liquor Control. RC 119.12 provides only for the appeal of an adjudication by an administrative agency, and the results of a local-option election are not appealable under that statute.

4 App(3d) 78, 4 OBR 130, 446 NE(2d) 493 (Franklin 1982), In re Transfer of Territory from Cleveland City School District. The act of the Ohio state board of education disapproving a transfer of territory pursuant to RC 3311.24 is similar to disapproval of a transfer pursuant to RC 3311.06 and, as such, is a legislative act, which is not appealable pursuant to RC 119.12.

1 App(3d) 22, 1 OBR 23, 437 NE(2d) 1215 (1981), Lewis v Parkinson. There is no right of appeal from an order of a municipal civil service commission under RC 119.12.

49 App(2d) 303, 361 NE(2d) 1072 (1976), Diebler v Denton. Appeals from state personnel board of review to the common pleas court of the county of residence (other than Franklin county) of those matters coming within the operation of RC 124.34 must be grounded under the appeal provisions of that section.

46 App(2d) 86, 345 NE(2d) 619 (1975), Davison v Bureau of Motor Vehicles. A notice that an examination would be held to determine the competency of the holder of a driver's license, pursuant to RC 4507.20, absent an order of revocation or suspension, is not an adjudication or appealable order.

46 App(2d) 34, 345 NE(2d) 625 (1975), Babcock v Bureau of Motor Vehicles. The exceptions granted by RC 4509.19 to the security and suspension requirements of RC 4509.12 do not exempt a motorist claiming such from utilizing the administrative procedures of Ch 119 before an appeal is taken to a court of common pleas.

44 App(2d) 115, 355 NE(2d) 868 (1975), Fair v School Employees Retirement System. Neither RC 119.12 nor 2506.01 confer a remedy of appeal from a decision of the school employees retirement board denying an application for disability retirement.

1 App(2d) 480, 205 NE(2d) 118 (1963), Roxy Musical Bar, Inc v Bd of Liquor Control. The overruling by the board of liquor control of a motion to make a departmental order definite and certain is not a final order within the provisions of RC 119.12 and is not appealable.

120 App 163, 201 NE(2d) 605 (1963), Lakis, dba Mickey's Lounge Bar v Bd of Liquor Control. Where the board of liquor control, following a hearing at which permittee's preliminary motions are overruled, finds "the permittee in violation of charges set forth" and by subsequent order suspends permittee's license and recites the number of days for which such license is suspended, such finding of a "violation of charges" lacks finality and is not subject to appeal, and the board retains jurisdiction to continue hearings, and such subsequent order only provides the necessary basis for an appeal.

43 Misc 42, 334 NE(2d) 552 (CP, Cuyahoga 1974), Sommerville v Bureau of Motor Vehicles. The requirement in RC 119.12 for an exhaustion of administrative remedies applies to an appeal from a bureau of motor vehicles order suspending a driver's license, plates, and registration certificate.

OAG 75-027. A determination made by the commissioners of the sinking fund pursuant to O Const Art VIII, § 2j, concerning an applicant's eligibility for compensation from the Vietnam conflict compensation fund is not appealable pursuant to RC 119.12.

6. Venue

69 OS(2d) 577, 433 NE(2d) 223 (1982), Harris v Lewis. Involuntary reductions in pay must comply with RC 124.34 and may be appealed only to the court of common pleas in the county of the employee's residence.

64 OS(2d) 102, 413 NE(2d) 816 (1980), Davis v State Personnel Bd of Review. A member of the classified civil service, aggrieved by a decision of the state personnel board of review affirming his removal or reduction in pay for disciplinary reasons, must bring his appeal, if at all, in the court of common pleas of the county of his residence.

58 OS(2d) 67, 388 NE(2d) 1226 (1979), Scott v Reinier. Where the state personnel board of review modifies an appointing authority's removal order to a suspension order, the case remains a "case of removal" within the meaning of RC 124.34, and an appeal lies to the court of common pleas.

40 OS(2d) 107, 321 NE(2d) 603 (1974), In re Termination of Employment of Pratt. A party adversely affected by an order of the state personnel board of review may appeal the order of the board to the court of common pleas of the county in which the affected employee resides, and may, in that court, raise the issue of the board's jurisdiction to issue the order.

29 OS(2d) 188, 281 NE(2d) 9 (1972), State ex rel Ohio Assn of Insurance Agents, Inc v Dept of Insurance. Mandamus will not lie to compel department of insurance to revoke license of agency on ground it is not owned by residents of Ohio where they have not sought adjudication under Administrative Procedure Act.

168 OS 520, 156 NE(2d) 740 (1959), Welsh v Ohio State Medical Bd. An appeal from the action of the state medical board in denying an application for restoration of a revoked hydrotherapy license may be taken to the court of common pleas in the county in which the applicant is a resident or has his place of business.

38 Misc 31, 311 NE(2d) 880 (CP, Pickaway 1974), Tootle v Wood; affirmed by 40 App(2d) 576, 321 NE(2d) 623 (1974). Where a plaintiff's driving license and registration were suspended, the decision of the bureau is sustained on an appeal to the common pleas court and there is no further appeal, plaintiff could not thereafter bring a declaratory judgment action seeking to restrain the bureau from suspending her driving rights.

7. Appeals in Franklin County

34 Ohio St L J 853 (1974). Judicial Review of Administrative Decisions in Ohio, Charles I. Kampinski.

22 Clev St L Rev 229 (1973). Ohio Revised Code Chapter 2506—Judicial Review of Administrative Rulings, Marshall J. Wolf and Donald M. Robiner.

67 OS(2d) 106, 423 NE(2d) 161 (1981), Genoa Banking Co v Mills. The action of the superintendent of banks approving or disapproving a branch application constitutes an exercise by an agency of a licensing function and is appealable to the court of common pleas pursuant to RC 119.12. Any bank receiving notice of a branch bank application pursuant to RC Ch 1111 is a proper party to bring said appeal.

54 OS(2d) 159, 375 NE(2d) 417 (1978), Union Camp Corp v Whitman. The denial of a motion for a hearing de nova, by the environmental board of review, issued upon appeal of the adoption of regulations, without an adjudicatory hearing by the director of environmental protection, is an order affecting a substantial right in a special proceeding and a final order, appealable to the court of appeals of Franklin county.

176 OS 232, 199 NE(2d) 13 (1964), State ex rel Kendrick v Masheter. An order of the state personnel board of review issued on appeal from a final decision of an appointing authority relative to layoff is appealable to the court of common pleas of Franklin county.

164 OS 275, 131 NE(2d) 390 (1955), Andrews v Bd of Liquor Control. Where the court of common pleas reverses an order of the board of liquor control, such board may appeal to the court of appeals for Franklin county, which court may affirm or reverse the judgment of the court of common pleas in accordance with the nature and scope of the appellate jurisdiction of the court of common pleas.

16 App(3d) 124, 16 OBR 131, 474 NE(2d) 691 (Franklin 1984), Gil Lieber Buick Oldsmobile, Inc v Motor Vehicle Dealers Bd. The requirement of RC 119.12 that the court "shall conduct a hearing on such appeal" means that the court must set a date for a hearing and that briefs are timely if filed by that date; it is error to dismiss an appeal for failure to file briefs by an earlier date pursuant to a local rule applicable where no date is set by statute.

10 App(3d) 229, 10 OBR 324, 461 NE(2d) 919 (Lake 1983), Ludwig v Willoughby-Eastlake City School District Bd of Ed. Classified employees in the "state service" who have been laid off must appeal orders of the state personnel board of review to the Franklin county court of common pleas; classified employees of a municipal civil service commission who have been laid off must appeal to the common pleas court in the county where they reside.

49 App(2d) 303, 361 NE(2d) 1072 (1976), Diebler v Denton. Where an order of removal of the appointing authority has been modified on appeal by the state personnel board of review to constitute an order of suspension there exists no right of appeal from the modified order to the court of common pleas of any county of residence other than Franklin county, and such courts of common pleas are without jurisdiction to entertain same. (Disagreed with by Scott v Reinier, 60 App(2d) 289, 396 NE(2d) 1041 (1978) and In re Stanley, 56 App(2d) 1, 381 NE(2d) 212 (1978); 60 App(2d) 289 affirmed by 58 OS(2d) 67, 388 NE(2d) 1226 (1979).)

49 App(2d) 303, 361 NE(2d) 1072 (1976), Diebler v Denton. There is no constitutional provision conferring upon a classified civil service employee a right of appeal from the state personnel board of review to a court of common pleas of the county of residence and no statutory provision conferring such right upon an employee in cases of suspension from employment for disciplinary reasons, with the exception of an

appeal to the court of common pleas of Franklin county. (Disagreed with by Scott v Reinier, 60 App(2d) 289, 396 NE(2d) 1041 (1978) and In re Stanley, 56 App(2d) 1, 381 NE(2d) 212 (1978); 60 App(2d) 289 affirmed by 58 OS(2d) 67, 388 NE(2d) 1226 (1979).)

1 App(2d) 336, 204 NE(2d) 692 (1965), In re Removal of Zeigler; affirmed by 4 OS(2d) 46, 212 NE(2d) 419 (1965). An order of the state personnel board of review issued on appeal from a final decision of an appointing authority relative to layoff is not appealable to the court of common pleas of the county in which the employee resides, but is appealable exclusively to the court of common pleas of Franklin county.

No. 7555 (2d Dist Ct App, Montgomery, 4-8-82), Hoffman v Montgomery County Commrs. Where the state personnel board of review decision upheld appellant's discharge due to abolition of the position, said discharge does not constitute "removal or reduction in pay for disciplinary reasons" within the meaning of RC 124.34 and an appeal from said determination must be filed in the common pleas court of Franklin County pursuant to RC 119.12; an appeal to any other common pleas court will not lie because of lack of subject matter jurisdiction. A court that lacks subject matter jurisdiction, has no power to transfer venue pursuant to Civ R 3(C)(1) because said action has not been properly commenced; said action must be dismissed pursuant to Civ R 12(H)(2).

8. Notice of appeal

CONSTITUTIONALITY:

49 App(2d) 402, 361 NE(2d) 271 (1976), Townsend v Bd of Building Appeals. The requirement of RC 119.12 that a notice of appeal be filed within fifteen days after the mailing of the notice of the agency's order is constitutional.

---

156 OS 255, 102 NE(2d) 8 (1951), Moore v Foreacher. Where an appeal is taken to the common pleas court from a decision of the bureau of unemployment compensation board of review, that portion of GC 1346-4 (RC 4141.28) which reads, "such notice of appeal shall set forth the decision appealed from," does not require that the decision appealed from be incorporated in the notice of appeal by being copied into it or attached thereto and made part thereof by reference.

91 App 28, 105 NE(2d) 80 (1951), Moore v Foreacher; affirmed by 156 OS 255, 102 NE(2d) 8 (1951). In perfecting an appeal from a decision of the unemployment compensation board of review to the common pleas court it is not required that the notice of appeal set forth verbatim the entire contents of the decision appealed from and the statutory requirement for notice is sufficiently met by designating the decision appealed from by its proper board of review docket number and narrating the substance of the other relevant portions thereof.

94 Abs 392, 201 NE(2d) 305 (CP, Franklin 1964), Columbus v Upper Arlington. Any method of service of a notice of appeal productive of certainty of accomplishment is countenanced.

9. Time for filing

14 App(3d) 463, 14 OBR 583, 472 NE(2d) 69 (Summit 1984), Troutman v Mitchum. The time for appeal of an administrative decision is not extended by a motion for reconsideration made within the appeal period which is denied after the appeal period has run.

49 App(2d) 402, 361 NE(2d) 271 (1976), Townsend v Bd of Building Appeals. The depositing of a notice of appeal in the US mail is not the equivalent of filing a notice of appeal with the agency whose order is being appealed, pursuant to RC 119.12.

96 App 128, 121 NE(2d) 257 (1953), Hart v Bd of Liquor Control. In perfecting an appeal from a decision of the board of liquor control to the common pleas court it is mandatory that the notice of appeal be filed within fifteen days from the mailing of the board's decision, and the provision of § 9 of Reg. 65 of the board for application for rehearing within thirty days after the board's decision does not extend the fifteen-day period.

41 Misc 139, 324 NE(2d) 802 (CP, Wayne 1974), Bolt v Bureau of Motor Vehicles. RC 119.12 requires that the notice of appeal must be filed with the agency whose order is appealed from within the fifteen-day period and that it must actually be received by said bureau not later than the fifteenth day, and in this case the filing of the notice with the court does not comply with RC 119.12 for the purpose of establishing jurisdiction to hear the appeal on the merits.

39 Misc 103, 315 NE(2d) 842 (CP, Montgomery 1973), Boomershine v Bureau of Motor Vehicles. The term "file" as used in RC 119.12 means actual receipt by the agency of the notice of appeal.

72 Abs 189, 134 NE(2d) 82 (App, Franklin 1955), Arndt v Scott. The fifteen day requirement of RC 119.12 is mandatory, even though a constitutional question is involved.

10. Suspension of order

92 App 78, 109 NE(2d) 545 (1951), Lewis v Anspon. Where, after revocation of a real estate broker's license, the broker appeals to the common pleas court and the court enters an order suspending such revocation, such suspension order supersedes the order of revocation as of the date of the latter's issuance, and such broker is not, by force of such revocation order, deprived of his right to do business under his license.

Nos. 84AP-225 and 84AP-362 (10th Dist Ct App, Franklin, 9-27-84), Plotnick v State Medical Bd. The fifteen-month limitation upon suspension of execution of orders of the medical board at RC 119.12 is not unconstitutional on its face and does not on its face deny equal protection of the law.

11. Record of proceedings

67 OS(2d) 363, 423 NE(2d) 1099 (1981), State ex rel Crockett v Robinson. Relator reinstated to position with city government on the ground that the civil service commission failed to timely file its record with the court of common pleas as mandated by RC 119.12 is entitled to mandamus ordering payment of back pay, including across-the-board salary increases and interest, but not attorneys' fees nor credit for vacation, holiday, or sick leave.

60 OS(2d) 13, 396 NE(2d) 743 (1979), Smith v Bd of Trustees of Chester Twp. Under RC 2506.02, the administrative body from which an appeal is taken has the duty, upon the filing of a praecipe, to prepare and file a complete transcript as defined therein, including the duty to initially pay the cost of preparing the same.

48 OS(2d) 153, 357 NE(2d) 1067 (1976), Lorms v Dept of Commerce, Division of Real Estate. An agency's omission of items from the certified record of an appealed administrative proceeding does not require a finding for the appellant, pursuant to RC 119.12, when the omissions in no way prejudice him in the presentation of his appeal.

5 OS(2d) 229, 215 NE(2d) 397 (1966), McKenzie v Ohio State Racing Comm. There is a sufficient certification by "the agency" under RC 119.12 where a member or employee of the agency certifies that what purports to be a record of such proceedings "is a complete record" thereof, that "any copies of material herein ... are certified to be true

copies of the original matter," and that such certificate is made "by order of the" agency "and acting in its behalf," unless it is made to appear affirmatively that the one so certifying did not have authority to do so or that the record so certified is not a complete record of the proceedings.

177 OS 55, 202 NE(2d) 305 (1964), Matash v Dept of Insurance. Where an appeal from an order of an administrative agency has been duly made to the common pleas court and the agency has not prepared and certified to the court a complete record of the proceedings within twenty days after receipt of the notice of appeal and the court has granted the agency no additional time to do so, the court must, upon motion of the appellant, enter a finding in favor of the appellant and render a judgment for the appellant.

14 App(3d) 267, 14 OBR 296, 470 NE(2d) 919 (Franklin 1984), Luther v Employment Services Bureau. Where an agency's complete failure to certify a record results in entry of judgment against the agency pursuant to Matash v Dept of Insurance, 177 OS 55, 202 NE(2d) 305 (1964), such failure cannot be excusable neglect for purposes of vacating the judgment pursuant to Civ R 60(B)(1).

9 App(3d) 237, 9 OBR 410, 459 NE(2d) 584 (Franklin 1983), Genoa Banking Co v Mills. Where the superintendent of banks failed to certify the record of administrative proceedings to the court of common pleas within thirty days after receipt of a notice of appeal, the court need not enter judgment for the adversely affected party unless the party demonstrates either that the presentation of his case was prejudiced by such failure or that the trial court made a prejudicial error resulting directly from the late certification.

7 App(3d) 189, 7 OBR 236, 454 NE(2d) 982 (Hamilton 1982), Sayler v State Racing Comm. When the court of common pleas vacates a suspension order of the Ohio state racing commission because of the commission's failure to certify a complete record to the court, if the commission issues a second suspension order, the doctrine of res judicata is inapplicable to proceedings on the second order because the judgment vacating the first order was based on technical or procedural grounds and was not a review on the merits of the appeal.

2 App(3d) 430, 2 OBR 524, 442 NE(2d) 771 (1981), Alban v Ohio Real Estate Comm. The mere omission of an item from the certified record of the proceedings of an administrative agency upon the appeal of one of its decisions does not require a reversal of the order pursuant to RC 119.12, where that which has been omitted in no way prejudices the appellant in the presentation of his appeal.

2 App(3d) 204, 2 OBR 223, 441 NE(2d) 584 (1981), Lies v Ohio Veterinary Medical Bd. The court of common pleas, in conducting its review of the administrative record under RC 119.12, has a mandatory duty to examine and consider the record in its entirety including the transcript of the proceedings before the hearing examiner.

64 App(2d) 243, 412 NE(2d) 418 (1979), Richmond v Bd of Review, Bureau of Employment Services. Although the requirement in RC 4141.26 that the board of review shall file with the clerk a certified transcript of the record of the proceedings before the board within thirty days after the filing of a written demand by the appellant is mandatory, when the board files the transcript beyond the thirty-day time limit, the issue is the sanction, if any, to be imposed, not whether the requirement is mandatory, and where the transcript is not timely filed, the trial court may, within the exercise of its discretion, order such transcript stricken from the record, or allow the late filing where excusable neglect is demonstrated pursuant to Civ R 6(B).

41 App(2d) 37, 322 NE(2d) 139 (1974), Checker Realty Co v Ohio Real Estate Comm. A "complete record of proceedings" in a case is a precise history of the proceedings from their termination.

41 App(2d) 37, 322 NE(2d) 139 (1974), Checker Realty Co v Ohio Real Estate Comm. The mere omission of an item from the certified record of the proceedings of an administrative agency, upon the appeal of one of its decisions, does not require a reversal of the order issued pursuant to RC 119.12, where that which has been omitted in no way prejudices the appellant in the presentation of his appeal.

9 App(2d) 25, 222 NE(2d) 789 (1967), Young v Board of Review. When the only copy of the adjudication order contained in the record of proceedings of an administrative board certified to a common pleas court in connection with an appeal to that court by a party adversely affected by such order is itself contained in an unsigned copy of a letter addressed to such person, certified in that copy to be such, the requirements of RC 119.12 that the board prepare and certify a complete record of the proceedings in the case have not been complied with, and, upon motion, the common pleas court is required to enter a finding in favor of the party adversely affected by the adjudication order. (Disapproved by Lorms v Dept of Commerce, Division of Real Estate, 48 OS(2d) 153, 357 NE(2d) 1067 (1976).)

5 App(2d) 161, 214 NE(2d) 265 (1966), Brockmeyer v Ohio Real Estate Comm; overruled by 41 App(2d) 37, 322 NE(2d) 139 (1974), Checker Realty Co v Ohio Real Estate Comm. The provisions of RC 119.12 requiring an administrative agency to certify a complete record and requiring the court to enter a finding in favor of the appellant where the agency fails to so certify are mandatory.

5 App(2d) 161, 214 NE(2d) 265 (1966), Brockmeyer v Ohio Real Estate Comm; overruled by 41 App(2d) 37, 322 NE(2d) 139 (1974), Checker Realty Co v Ohio Real Estate Comm. A record certified by an agency, which does not contain the agency's order, is not a "complete record of the proceedings" as required by RC 119.12.

4 App(2d) 413, 213 NE(2d) 188 (1964), Bd of Real Estate Examiners v Peth. In an appeal from a decision of the Ohio real estate commission to the common pleas court the transmittal of a record filed in the common pleas court and consisting of a group of detached exhibits, none of which bears the filing stamp of the commission, and papers, some of which are merely unsigned carbon copies of letters, accompanied by a letter of transmittal bearing only the rubber stamp facsimile of the signature of the secretary of the commission, is not a certification of a complete record of the proceedings in the case, as required by RC 119.12.

1 App(2d) 283, 204 NE(2d) 569 (1965), McKenzie v Ohio State Racing Comm; reversed by 5 OS(2d) 229, 215 NE(2d) 397 (1966). The additional ten-day period provided in RC 119.12 for an administrative agency to certify the record to the common pleas court must be computed with reference to the date of the notice of appeal, and the failure of the agency to fully comply within a total of thirty days requires a reversal of the agency's order and a judgment for the party adversely affected by its order.

1 App(2d) 126, 204 NE(2d) 82 (1964), Tisone v Bd of Liquor Control. In an appeal from a decision of the board of liquor control to the common pleas court, the requirement of RC 119.12 that "the agency shall prepare and certify to the court a complete record of the proceedings in the case," is satisfied by a certification of a complete record of the proceedings by the clerk of the board of liquor control.

119 App 1, 196 NE(2d) 338 (1962), Ohio Real Estate Comm v Evans. The Ohio real estate commission on an appeal from an order adversely affecting a license to the common pleas court is required to

prepare and certify to such court a complete record of the proceedings in the case by affixing the signatures thereto of the three commissioners of the Ohio real estate commission, and the signature of the secretary is insufficient. (Disapproved by McKenzie v Ohio State Racing Comm, 5 OS(2d) 229, 215 NE(2d) 397 (1966).)

113 App 538, 173 NE(2d) 389 (1960), Stephan v State Veterinary Medical Board. The word, "shall," as used in that provision of RC 119.12 requiring that, in an appeal to the common pleas court from certain orders of an administrative agency, "within ten days ... after receipt of notice of appeal ... the agency shall prepare and certify to the court a complete record of the proceedings in the case," is mandatory requirement, and in an appeal to the common pleas court from an order of the veterinary medical board suspending a license to practice veterinary medicine, where the board fails to prepare and certify to the court a complete record of the proceedings in the case within ten days, the sustaining of the appellant's motion for judgment in his favor is not erroneous.

No. 8674 (2d Dist Ct App, Montgomery, 5-21-84), McCullion v Edmundson. RC 119.12 clearly implies that an administrative agency shall be accorded an opportunity to respond to a motion filed by an appellant who seeks to penalize an agency for failing to properly certify an administrative record.

13 Misc 39, 230 NE(2d) 691 (CP, Hamilton 1967), Fahrenbruck v State Bd of Landscape Architect Examiners. Where an administrative agency fails to prepare and certify the record of a proceeding within twenty days after receipt of a notice of appeal, its order will be reversed.

12. Additional evidence

1 App(3d) 10, 1 OBR 51, 437 NE(2d) 319 (1981), Zieverink v Ackerman. In an appeal to the court of common pleas from the decision of a state agency, if the appellant presented evidence before the state agency in the administrative hearing, concerning the constitutionality of the statute at issue, as applied to the appellant, he is then entitled to have the court of common pleas determine the constitutionality of the statute, as applied to him, but where the appellant has not presented such evidence before the agency, he is precluded from raising the constitutional issue by introducing new evidence before the court of common pleas unless such evidence was "newly discovered and could not with reasonable diligence have been ascertained prior to the hearing before the agency."

5 App(2d) 161, 214 NE(2d) 265 (1966), Brockmeyer v Ohio Real Estate Comm; overruled by 41 App(2d) 37, 322 NE(2d) 139 (1974), Checker Realty Co v Ohio Real Estate Comm. There is no provision in RC 119.12 which authorizes either the common pleas court or the court of appeals to order a diminution of the record by an administrative agency to correct an omission or other deficiency in the record as certified, where the time within which to certify has expired.

109 App 289, 165 NE(2d) 19 (1959), In re Owner-Trainer Topper. A court of common pleas may grant a request for the admission of additional evidence when satisfied that such additional evidence is newly discovered and could not with reasonable diligence have been ascertained prior to the hearing before the agency from which an appeal to such court is taken.

106 App 494, 153 NE(2d) 153 (1958), City Products Corp v Bd of Liquor Control. In an appeal from the order of an administrative agency to the common pleas court, the hearing contemplated by RC 119.12 consists of a consideration of the record as certified to it by the agency, the briefs and oral arguments of counsel, and, if the court has granted a request for it, newly discovered evidence, so that in an appeal from the

board of liquor control to the common pleas court, in the absence of a request by the appellant to present new evidence, a hearing upon the transcript of the proceedings and testimony before the board, the original papers and the briefs and arguments of counsel, is a full and complete hearing. (See also City Products Corp, dba Pilsner Brewing Co v Bd of Liquor Control, 79 Abs 481, 156 NE(2d) 347 (App, Franklin 1958)).

106 App 494, 153 NE(2d) 153 (1958), City Products Corp v Bd of Liquor Control. Where, in an appeal from an order of the board of liquor control suspending a permit there is no showing that the appellant either offered any new evidence or requested permission to offer any new evidence in the common pleas court; but, on the other hand, rested its case in the common pleas court upon the evidence offered before the board of liquor control, the appellant has received the hearing prescribed by RC 119.12. (See also City Products Corp, dba Pilsner Brewing Co v Bd of Liquor Control, 79 Abs 481, 156 NE(2d) 347 (App, Franklin 1958)).

68 Abs 318, 122 NE(2d) 121 (CP, Franklin 1953), Vito v Bd of Liquor Control. On an appeal from the board of liquor control the court of common pleas will not order a more complete record, especially where there is no showing the record omits any matters.

13. Procedure

66 OS(2d) 192, 421 NE(2d) 128 (1981), Plumbers & Steamfitters Joint Apprenticeship Committee v Ohio Civil Rights Comm. The Ohio civil rights commission is not subject to the thirty-day (formerly twenty-day) record certification requirement of RC 119.12.

62 OS(2d) 297, 405 NE(2d) 714 (1980), Williams v Dollison. Appellant convicted of violating hit and run statute whose license was suspended as a result of failure to provide proof of financial responsibility was not entitled to post-suspension or revocation hearing before registrar of motor vehicles.

162 OS 37, 120 NE(2d) 730 (1954), Mantho v Bd of Liquor Control. Although neither the director of liquor control nor the board of liquor control nor the department of liquor control had authority to prosecute an appeal from a judgment of the common pleas court with respect to the issuance or renewal of liquor permits, at the time such an appeal was taken, nevertheless, where such appeal was prosecuted by the board of liquor control and no objection was raised to the prosecution of such appeal in the court of appeals, and the appeal was heard and judgment was rendered by the court of appeals, such judgment was valid and cannot thereafter be set aside or vacated on the ground of lack of jurisdiction of the court of appeals.

151 OS 222, 85 NE(2d) 113 (1949), Farrand v State Medical Bd. The word "appeal," as used in this section, means the proceedings whereby a court reviews the action or decision of an administrative agency and affirms, reverses, vacates or modifies an order of the agency complained of in the appeal and does not authorize a trial de novo.

16 App(3d) 124, 16 OBR 131, 474 NE(2d) 691 (Franklin 1984), Gil Lieber Buick Oldsmobile, Inc v Motor Vehicle Dealers Bd. The requirement of RC 119.12 that the court "shall conduct a hearing on such appeal" means that the court must set a date for a hearing and that briefs are timely if filed by that date; it is error to dismiss an appeal for failure to file briefs by an earlier date pursuant to a local rule applicable where no date is set by statute.

3 App(3d) 351, 3 OBR 408, 445 NE(2d) 722 (1982), In re Appeal of Bidlack. The jurisdiction of an administrative agency is terminated at the end of the appeal period, or, when an appeal is filed, and "reconsideration" of an agency's decision within that period means the actual rendi-

tion of a new or reconsidered decision before the expiration of the appeal period.

59 App(2d) 133, 392 NE(2d) 1276 (1978), Ohio State Medical Bd v Zwick. When the Ohio state medical board conducts an adjudicatory hearing pursuant to RC 4731.23, the affected party enjoys the procedural safeguards contained in RC 119.06 to 119.10 during the hearing, but does not have the right to notice of the findings or order of the hearing officer, pursuant to RC 119.09, or the opportunity to file written objections thereto.

4 App(2d) 147, 211 NE(2d) 885 (1963), Fugate v Columbus. An appeal to the common pleas court by a member of the police department of a city from an order of the municipal civil service commission is an appeal on questions of law and fact, and where the appellant proceeds in the common pleas court on the record made before the commission he is presumed to have waived his right to a trial de novo; the judgment rendered therein by the common pleas court must be supported by a preponderance of the evidence, and it is error for the court to base an affirmance of the order of the commission on a finding that the order appealed from is supported by reliable probative and substantial evidence.

2 App(2d) 112, 206 NE(2d) 587 (1964), Grecian Gardens, Inc v Bd of Liquor Control. A rule of the common pleas court authorizing the dismissal of an appeal for want of prosecution upon failure of the appellant to file his brief or his demand for a transcript of the record, is invalid insofar as it applies to an appeal from an order of an agency under RC 119.12.

1 App(2d) 283, 204 NE(2d) 569 (1965), McKenzie v Ohio State Racing Comm; reversed by 5 OS(2d) 229, 215 NE(2d) 397 (1966). A motion, objecting to a record certified by an administrative agency under RC 119.12, is timely if filed any time prior to the final judgment.

118 App 170, 193 NE(2d) 542 (1963), Stark v Dept of Health. An order of a common pleas court dismissing an appeal from an order of the Ohio department of health cannot be appealed on questions of law and fact to the court of appeals.

111 App 279, 170 NE(2d) 747 (1960), Swallow Bar, Inc v Bd of Liquor Control. Where, on appeal by the board of liquor control from a decision of the court of common pleas reversing a ruling of the board suspending a liquor permit, it appears that the trial court found insufficient evidence of an element necessary to be proved, and only a question of fact is presented on such appeal, a motion to dismiss such appeal will be sustained.

111 App 79, 165 NE(2d) 658 (1960), In re Application of Welsh. There is no provision whereby the state medical board is empowered to reconsider an application seeking the reinstatement of a license after an order revoking a license has become final either on appeal or by reason of the failure of the licensee to appeal as provided by RC 119.12.

111 App 79, 165 NE(2d) 658 (1960), In re Application of Welsh. There is no provision whereby the board is empowered to reconsider an application seeking the reinstatement of a license after an order revoking a license has become final either on appeal or by reason of the failure of the licensee to appeal.

109 App 289, 165 NE(2d) 19 (1959), In re Owner-Trainer Topper. Where an appeal on questions of law relating to the construction of interpretation of RC 119.12 is perfected to the court of appeals from the common pleas court, the court of appeals is permitted to review and determine the correctness of the judgment of the common pleas court; and, in such review and determination, the court of appeals must follow

the same procedure enjoined by RC 119.12 on the common pleas court in arriving at its determination.

108 App 413, 154 NE(2d) 646 (1958), Buckeye Lake Hotel Co v Bd of Liquor Control. A motion to dismiss an appeal by the board of liquor control is filed prematurely where it is filed only twenty-seven days after the notice of appeal and before the board had filed any assignment of errors.

108 App 413, 154 NE(2d) 646 (1958), Buckeye Lake Hotel Co v Bd of Liquor Control. Where, in an appeal from an order of the board of liquor control revoking the retail liquor permits of a permit holder, the common pleas court reduces the penalty to a suspension, and the board files a notice of appeal to the court of appeals, appellee's motion to dismiss the appeal on jurisdictional grounds, filed before appellant has filed its assignment of errors and when appellant still has time to file it, is prematurely filed and such motion will be overruled.

104 App 316, 137 NE(2d) 777 (1956), Quinn v State Bd of Real Estate Examiners. On an appeal from the court of common pleas sustaining a decision of the board of real estate examiners revoking a broker's license, the court of appeals does not hear the matter de novo.

No. CA-6448 (5th Dist Ct App, Stark, 11-26-84), Adams v Canton Civil Service Comm. The failure to request a hearing on an administrative appeal acts as a submission of the case upon the briefs under local rules of procedure and the dismissal of the case for failure to prosecute is erroneous.

10 Misc 225, 225 NE(2d) 859 (CP, Tuscarawas 1963), Liquor Control Comm v Bartolas. A court may entertain a motion for new trial in a proceeding in common pleas court on an appeal from an order of an administrative agency.

80 Abs 253, 158 NE(2d) 899 (App, Franklin 1958), DiNardo, dba Coliseum Palace v Bd of Liquor Control. A court of appeals will not overrule an order of the court of common pleas denying rehearing of an order by such court affirming an order of the board of liquor control revoking appellant's permits where the alleged ground is new evidence and where such evidence was in the hands of appellant's counsel prior to the hearing in the common pleas court.

74 Abs 540, 141 NE(2d) 671 (App, Franklin 1956), Burger v Bd of Liquor Control. In an appeal from an order of the department of liquor control a decision will be reversed where the trial court judge considered it as an appeal on questions of law and not de novo.

69 Abs 407, 119 NE(2d) 156 (CP, Franklin 1954), Meyer v Bd of Liquor Control. Notice of hearing before board of liquor control held adequate where permit holder was notified and attorney for receiver appeared at hearing and entered a plea of guilty.

14. Reliable, probative and substantial evidence

44 OS(2d) 78, 337 NE(2d) 783 (1975), Blue Cross Hospital Plan, Inc v Jump. Superintendent of insurance was not justified in denying rate increase to Blue Cross on ground it had not represented the interests of its subscribers by attempting to control rising hospital costs.

17 OS(2d) 69, 246 NE(2d) 549 (1969), Dept of Liquor Control v Santucci. Where the holder of permits to sell alcoholic beverages is charged with the violation of law and regulations of the liquor control commission on the permit premises, his plea of guilty to such charges, knowingly and voluntarily made at the hearing thereon before the commission, is equivalent to testimony on his part that the facts set forth in such charges are true, and a suspension of his permits for a prescribed length of time by the commission, acting within its powers, is authorized,

so that on the permit holder's appeal to the court of common pleas that court may properly determine that the orders against him by the commission were supported by "reliable, probative and substantial evidence."

12 OS(2d) 76, 232 NE(2d) 407 (1967), Doelker v Accountancy Bd of Ohio. On an appeal from an order of an agency revoking a license, the common pleas court may affirm that order only "if it finds upon consideration of the entire record and such additional evidence as the court has admitted, that the order is supported by reliable, probative, and substantial evidence and is in accordance with law," and this means that such evidence must not only exist but must be in the record in order to support an affirmance.

70 App(2d) 219, 436 NE(2d) 543 (1980), Painesville Raceway, Inc v Dept of Liquor Control. In an appeal taken from the decision of an administrative agency to the court of common pleas pursuant to RC 119.12, the court of common pleas is not required to determine whether the order of the agency is supported by reliable, probative and substantial evidence where that court determines that the decision of the administrative agency is grounded upon a misinterpretation of the applicable law and is contrary to law.

69 App(2d) 108, 430 NE(2d) 967 (1980), Western Reserve Psychiatric Hospital v Knight. In the event an appeal is taken from an order of the state personnel board of review to the court of common pleas pursuant to RC 119.12, the order of the board must be affirmed if it is supported by reliable, probative and substantial evidence and is in accordance with law; if the evidence supports the order, a court may not substitute its judgment for the board's.

2 App(2d) 112, 206 NE(2d) 587 (1964), Grecian Gardens, Inc v Bd of Liquor Control. An appeal from an order of the board of liquor control to the common pleas court may not be dismissed without examination of the record to find whether the order appealed from is or is not supported by "reliable, probative and substantial evidence."

114 App 200, 181 NE(2d) 275 (1961), Blankenship v State ex rel Braden. On an appeal to the common pleas court from an order of the motor vehicle dealers and salesmen licensing board, sustaining an order of the registrar of motor vehicles rejecting the application of a licensed motor vehicle salesman to transfer his license from a former employer to a new employer, where the record before the court is not a complete record of the proceedings in the case, a judgment of affirmance, based upon a finding that the order is supported by reliable, probative and substantial evidence, is against the manifest weight of the evidence.

104 App 316, 137 NE(2d) 777 (1956), Quinn v State Bd of Real Estate Examiners. A court of appeals, in an appeal on questions of law from a decision of the court of common pleas affirming a decision of the state board of real estate examiners revoking a real estate broker's license, is confined in its jurisdiction on review to a consideration of the record made before such board and in the common pleas court and whether the common pleas court erred in sustaining the order of the board as being supported by reliable, probative and substantial evidence and as being in accordance with law.

94 App 92, 114 NE(2d) 736 (1953), In re Touchman. In an appeal to the court of common pleas from an order of the home inspection section of the division of aid for the aged, department of public welfare, denying an application for renewal of a license to operate a rest home, a general finding on the issues joined complied with the statutory requirement, and error was not committed in such appeal where the record disclosed that the court of common pleas found that "violations were found to exist and that they did exist is shown by the preponderance of the evidence," and based its judgment of affirmance on such finding.

53 Misc 13, 372 NE(2d) 1345 (CP, Montgomery 1977), In re Removal of Bronkar. As a "temporary" court of appeals under RC 119.12, the court of common pleas must view the evidence on appeal from the state personnel board of review from an appellate perspective, and the findings of the board must be affirmed if supported by reliable, probative, and substantial evidence, and if in accordance with law.

1 Misc 109, 205 NE(2d) 613 (CP, Franklin 1964), Lakis v Dept of Liquor Control. If there were some reliable, probative and substantial evidence adduced (even though it was disputed) to support a finding of the liquor control commission, a court should affirm its finding.

90 Abs 137, 187 NE(2d) 641 (CP, Muskingum 1962), Ohio Real Estate Comm v Cohen. "Reliable," "probative," and "substantial" defined.

82 Abs 191, 156 NE(2d) 175 (CP, Franklin 1955), Salvatore v Bd of Liquor Control. Where the evidence showed that a party had nothing in his hands when he went into the appellant's place of business, that he engaged the appellant in conversation at which time the appellant nodded towards an investigator for the department of liquor control, that later such party came out of the place of business to look around, went back into the place of business and came out with a bottle of wine in a brown sack, the board was justified in finding that the wine was purchased in appellant's premises.

78 Abs 468, 153 NE(2d) 334 (App, Franklin 1957), Khoury v Bd of Liquor Control. Where the board of liquor control affirmed an order of the department of liquor control refusing to renew a permit on grounds different from those relied on by the department, and the court of common pleas found that not only was the record before the court devoid of reliable, substantial and probative evidence to support the order of the board, but that such order was unsupported by any evidence shown to be relevant to the issue before the board, the court of common pleas did not err in remanding the case to the board to accord the appellant the right to a hearing on his appeal from the order of the department.

75 Abs 304, 144 NE(2d) 912 (CP, Franklin 1956), Collinwood Slovenian Home Co v Bd of Liquor Control. An affidavit that certain bottles contained six per cent beer cannot be accepted as reliable or trustworthy where the person making the affidavit is identified only as "chief chemist" and his qualifications are not established by the evidence, and a suspension of a permit by the board of liquor control based upon such affidavit and without any testimony tracing the bottles to such person is not supported by sufficient evidence.

74 Abs 141, 139 NE(2d) 493 (CP, Franklin 1956), Kostecki, dba Bill's Bar v Bd of Liquor Control. A hearing before the board of liquor control on a complaint charging a violation of the liquor laws is not a proceeding in which an affidavit may be used.

74 Abs 141, 139 NE(2d) 493 (CP, Franklin 1956), Kostecki, dba Bill's Bar v Bd of Liquor Control. Extra judicial confessions are not competent to prove the body of the offense.

74 Abs 69, 139 NE(2d) 55 (App, Franklin 1953), Bd of Liquor Control v Walnut Cafe, Inc. A cigarette vendor whose employer paid the owner of a liquor permit for the cigarette and hat concession on the premises was an agent of the permit holder rather than an independent contractor, but evidence that she had solicited a patron to buy her a "drink" and that such "drink" was furnished, without more information is insufficient to prove that such drink was intoxicating liquor.

73 Abs 577, 139 NE(2d) 870 (App, Franklin 1954), Mullins, dba Luke's Restaurant v Bd of Liquor Control. The department of liquor control is justified in denying a D-2 permit upon a finding that the

premises are fifty feet from a library and that a large number of children using the library would be required to pass the premises.

71 Abs 166, 130 NE(2d) 717 (App, Franklin 1954), Fernberg, dba Hinky Dinks v Bd of Liquor Control. A court of appeals may reverse the judgment of a common pleas court if it finds that the action of the board of liquor control in refusing to renew the permit of a licensee is founded upon evidence having a probative and substantial relation to the establishment and maintenance of sobriety and good order upon the permit premises and its environs, and is conducive to the establishment and maintenance of public decency, sobriety and good order generally.

15. In accordance with law

4 OS(3d) 201, 4 OBR 519, 448 NE(2d) 141 (1983), Ohio Academy of Trial Lawyers v Dept of Insurance. A letter from an attorney-examiner indicating that the need for a hearing requested pursuant to RC 3901.22(A) "is deemed moot" does not constitute a final order of an agency issued pursuant to an adjudication as required by RC 119.12 and as defined in RC 119.01.

170 OS 233, 163 NE(2d) 678 (1959), Henry's Cafe, Inc v Bd of Liquor Control. On appeal from an order of an agency to the court of common pleas, the power of the court to modify such order is limited to the ground of an absence of a finding that the order is supported by reliable, probative, and substantial evidence, and such court has no authority to modify a penalty that the agency was authorized to and did impose, on the ground that the agency abused its discretion.

12 App(2d) 52, 230 NE(2d) 662 (1967), Battles v Ohio State Racing Comm. If the unreasonableness or illegality of an administrative rule in its application to a particular set of facts or circumstances is determined, then such rule has no force or validity, as so applied, by virtue of the last paragraph of RC 119.11 and, upon such determination, no issue of its constitutionality may be determined in an appeal under 119.12.

3 App(2d) 345, 210 NE(2d) 737 (1964), In re Cline. The Ohio state racing commission may appeal a judgment of a common pleas court reversing a license-revocation order of the commission, where a construction and interpretation of a commission rule is required; and, in such appeal, the correctness of the judgment that the order of the commission is not supported by any reliable, probative and substantial evidence may also be reviewed and determined.

104 App 208, 148 NE(2d) 81 (1957), Arvay, dba Arvay's Recreation v Bd of Liquor Control. An appeal to the court of appeals from a judgment of the common pleas court in a cause appealed thereto from an order of the board of liquor control is appealable on questions of law only.

No. 8745 (2d Dist Ct App, Montgomery, 7-6-84), In re Moreo v City of Vandalia. A common pleas court, on remand from a reversal of its decision in a civil service appeal, need not return the cause to the civil service commission for trial de novo or reconsideration, but may itself determine the civil servant's rights and issue a final order.

14 Misc 9, 233 NE(2d) 147 (CP, Montgomery 1967), Handler v Dept of Commerce. RC 4727.16, when properly construed in relation to RC 119.12 and 4727.03, does not require a revocation of a pawnbroker's license automatically upon the mere assertion of two convictions for violations of any of the sections of the pawnbroker's law.

82 Abs 25, 163 NE(2d) 72 (App, Franklin 1959), Mogavero, dba Lombardo's Restaurant v Bd of Liquor Control. A mere allegation by the board of liquor control that the court erred in its interpretation and application of a regulation of the board is not sufficient to sustain the board's right to appeal unless its allegation is supported by the record.

80 Abs 138, 158 NE(2d) 543 (App, Franklin 1959), Henry's Cafe, Inc v Bd of Liquor Control; affirmed by 170 OS 233, 163 NE(2d) 678 (1959). Where the court of common pleas found that an order of the board of liquor control revoking a permit was supported by reliable, probative, and substantial evidence, its further finding that the penalty pronounced was contrary to law was inconsistent and unauthorized.

78 Abs 386, 153 NE(2d) 163 (App, Montgomery 1956), Bretscher v Robinson. An order by the superintendent of insurance revoking an insurance agent's license must recite a finding of fact upon which such order is based.

77 Abs 425, 150 NE(2d) 475 (App, Franklin 1957), Currier, dba Marie's Tavern v Bd of Liquor Control. If in a proceeding for the issuance of a liquor permit there is evidence that the permit premises are within 500 feet of a named institution and that an authorized representative of such institution objected to issuance of a permit, there is sufficient proof upon which the department or board may exercise its discretion to refuse the permit.

16. Appeal by agency available

60 OS(2d) 85, 397 NE(2d) 764 (1979), In re Dismissal of Mitchell. Where on an appeal from the state personnel board of review the trial court premises its conclusion upon an interpretation of the statutes and the regulations which provide the procedural mechanism by which the employer could have exempted the employee from classified status, the employer has a right of appeal even though the employee did not raise a question of law relating to the constitutionality, construction, or interpretation of the statutes or rules of the agency.

46 OS(2d) 436, 349 NE(2d) 304 (1976), Rrawu, Inc v Liquor Control Comm. The liquor control commission is entitled to appeal the judgment of a trial court to the court of appeals where stipulation made at the hearing before the commission admitted violation of the regulation of the commission, and the trial court's judgment entry reversing the order of the commission is based only upon a finding that the "order of the liquor control commission is not supported by reliable, probative and substantial evidence . . .."

166 OS 229, 141 NE(2d) 294 (1957), Katz v Dept of Liquor Control. An administrative agency may appeal from a judgment of the court of common pleas, rendered on appeal from a decision of such agency, only upon questions of law relating to the constitutionality, construction or interpretation of statutes and rules and regulations of the agency, but when such appeal is perfected the reviewing court has jurisdiction to review and determine the correctness of the judgment of the court of common pleas that the order of the agency is not supported by any reliable, probative and substantial evidence in the entire record.

3 App(2d) 345, 210 NE(2d) 737 (1964), In re Cline. The Ohio state racing commission may appeal a judgment of a common pleas court reversing a license-revocation order of the commission, where a construction and interpretation of a commission rule is required; and, in such appeal, the correctness of the judgment that the order of the commission is not supported by any reliable, probative and substantial evidence may also be reviewed and determined.

118 App 255, 190 NE(2d) 34 (1962), Trianon Bowling Lanes, Inc v Dept of Liquor Control. The department of liquor control may appeal, from a common pleas court judgment reversing the board of liquor control, only on questions of law relating to the constitutionality, construction or interpretation of statutes and the regulations of such agency, and a reviewing court may consider the sufficiency of the evidence involved only where such question of constitutionality, construction or interpretation is involved.

117 App 173, 191 NE(2d) 736 (1963), Zarachowicz v Bd of Liquor Control. The board of liquor control may appeal from a decision of a court of common pleas which interprets a regulation of such board and finds such regulation and the enactment thereof to be an abuse of discretion and invalid.

79 Abs 266, 155 NE(2d) 466 (App, Franklin 1958), Schott, dba Duke's Restaurant v Bd of Liquor Control. Where the issue involved in the denial of a liquor permit was whether the applicant was the owner or operator of the business, the board of liquor control was entitled to appeal from an order of the court reversing the board.

73 Abs 397, 137 NE(2d) 788 (App, Franklin 1953), Tuma v Bd of Liquor Control. The department of liquor control may appeal from the decision of a court of common pleas.

17. Appeal by agency denied

46 OS(2d) 41, 346 NE(2d) 141 (1976), State ex rel Osborn v Jackson. The director of a state department does not have a right of appeal to the court of common pleas of Franklin county from an order of the state personnel board of review disaffirming the director's layoff order of an employee for alleged lack of work, and the court of common pleas has no jurisdiction to hear such an attempted appeal.

162 OS 37, 120 NE(2d) 730 (1954), Mantho v Bd of Liquor Control. Although neither the director of liquor control nor the board of liquor control nor the department of liquor control had authority to prosecute an appeal from a judgment of the common pleas court with respect to the issuance or renewal of liquor permits, at the time such an appeal was taken, nevertheless, where such appeal was prosecuted by the board of liquor control and no objection was raised to the prosecution of such appeal in the court of appeals, and the appeal was heard and judgment was rendered by the court of appeals, such judgment was valid and cannot thereafter be set aside or vacated on the ground of lack of jurisdiction of the court of appeals.

160 OS 234, 115 NE(2d) 840 (1953), In re Millcreek Local District High School. Neither the director of education nor the high school board have the right to appeal from a judgment of the court of common pleas rendered on appeal from an order of the department of education.

160 OS 9, 113 NE(2d) 360 (1953), Corn v Bd of Liquor Control. There is no constitutional or legislative authority for an appeal by the board of liquor control, the department of liquor control, or the director of liquor control from a judgment of the court of common pleas rendered on appeal from a decision of the board of liquor control.

158 OS 302, 109 NE(2d) 8 (1952), A. DiCillo & Sons v Chester Zoning Bd of Appeals. Neither a township board of zoning appeals nor any of its members as such have a right to appeal from the judgment of a court, rendered on appeal from a decision of such board and reversing and vacating that decision.

63 App(2d) 157, 410 NE(2d) 773 (1978), In re Appeal of Lauderbach. Where a court of common pleas alludes to but does not interpret RC 119.09, and predicates its reversal of an order of the state personnel board of review on a lack of reliable, probative and substantial evidence, the employing state agency has no right of appeal.

60 App(2d) 245, 396 NE(2d) 792 (1978), In re Application of Blue Cross. The superintendent of insurance of Ohio has no right to appeal a judgment rendered by a court of common pleas which reverses a decision of the superintendent.

1 App(2d) 219, 204 NE(2d) 404 (1964), Mentor Marinas, Inc v Bd of Liquor Control. Where in an appeal by an administrative agency from an adverse judgment in the common pleas court the trial court has made

no specific determination as to the meaning or application of a particular statute, rule or regulation, the court of appeals is without jurisdiction to review the judgment.

120 App 385, 202 NE(2d) 634 (1963), In re Job Abolishment of Jenkins. An "appointing authority" has no right of appeal to the common pleas court from a decision of the state personnel board of review disaffirming a job abolishment by such "appointing authority."

119 App 133, 197 NE(2d) 370 (1963), Zarachowicz v Bd of Liquor Control. The board of liquor control cannot appeal from a judgment of a common pleas court reversing a decision of such board, where no question of law was before such common pleas court which merely held in its journal entry that "the decision of the board of liquor control is not sustained by substantial, probative and reliable evidence and is not in accordance with law."

115 App 463, 185 NE(2d) 576 (1961), Cranwood Steak House, Inc v Bd of Liquor Control. An order of the common pleas court reversing a decision of the board of liquor control as not supported by reliable, probative and substantial evidence may not be appealed by the board of liquor control.

106 App 59, 151 NE(2d) 686 (1958), Gay, dba Johnny's Recreation v Bd of Liquor Control. The right to appeal by the department of liquor control is not authorized in a case where the only error complained of was the finding by the court of common pleas that the defense of entrapment was well taken.

80 Abs 327, 154 NE(2d) 754 (App, Cuyahoga 1958), Metropolitan Savings Assn v Burdsall. An administrative agency may not appeal from a judgment of a common pleas court determining that an order of the superintendent of the division of building and loan associations refusing to certify articles of incorporation to the secretary of state was arbitrary, capricious and unlawful because not supported by reliable, probative and substantial evidence.

18. Scope of review

63 OS(2d) 108, 407 NE(2d) 1265 (1980), University of Cincinnati v Conrad. Court of common pleas was acting in accordance with its statutory power under RC 119.12 in electing not to give credence to testimony of employee and instead relying on testimony of police officer.

166 OS 229, 141 NE(2d) 294 (1957), Katz v Dept of Liquor Control. An administrative agency may appeal from a judgment of the court of common pleas, rendered on appeal from a decision of such agency, only upon questions of law relating to the constitutionality, construction or interpretation of statutes and rules and regulations of the agency, but when such appeal is perfected the reviewing court has jurisdiction to review and determine the correctness of the judgment of the court of common pleas that the order of the agency is not supported by any reliable, probative and substantial evidence in the entire record.

164 OS 275, 131 NE(2d) 390 (1955), Andrews v Bd of Liquor Control. Scope of review of decisions of board of liquor control by Franklin county common pleas court discussed.

151 OS 222, 85 NE(2d) 113 (1949), Farrand v State Medical Bd. The word "appeal," as used in this section, means the proceedings whereby a court reviews the action or decision of an administrative agency and affirms, reverses, vacates or modifies an order of the agency complained of in the appeal and does not authorize a trial de novo.

14 App(3d) 101, 14 OBR 115, 470 NE(2d) 200 (Franklin 1983), Wahle v Industrial Relations Dept. In an appeal of an order of the board of building standards that denies a person's application for approval as the chief building official of a municipal building department, the proper

standard for review by the common pleas court is provided by RC 119.12, rather than RC 3781.101; the standard of review found in RC 3781.101 has no application to the appeal of an adjudication order.

7 App(3d) 237, 7 OBR 300, 455 NE(2d) 9 (Hamilton 1982), Conners v Dept of Commerce, Div of Real Estate. An order of the Ohio real estate commission that is within the scope of the commission's authority and that modifies the recommendation of its hearing examiner by changing the duration of the disciplinary suspension is not subject to review by the court of common pleas, and the fact that the commission failed to state its reasons for its modification is of no legal significance on appeal.

7 App(3d) 1, 7 OBR 1, 453 NE(2d) 1262 (Clark 1982), Haley v Ohio State Dental Bd. A court reviewing a decision of an administrative agency is confronted with the issue of whether the decision is against the manifest weight of the evidence, not whether the agency abused its discretion; the existence of some reliable, probative, and substantial evidence is sufficient to support such findings.

70 App(2d) 219, 436 NE(2d) 543 (1980), Painesville Raceway, Inc v Dept of Liquor Control. Whether the provisions of RC Ch 4303 preclude the department of liquor control from issuing more than one liquor permit to separate applicants for the same location is a question of interpretation of state statutes and rules and regulations of the liquor control commission, and is within the perimeters of the appellate jurisdiction of the court of appeals pursuant to RC 119.12.

50 App(2d) 391, 364 NE(2d) 44 (1976), Shady Acres Nursing Home, Inc v Bd of Building Appeals. A court of common pleas has no power to grant a new trial from a judgment rendered in an administrative appeal under RC 119.12.

46 App(2d) 120, 346 NE(2d) 337 (1975), Farrao v Bureau of Motor Vehicles. Under RC 119.12, where a court finds that an order of the bureau of motor vehicles is supported by reliable, probative and substantial evidence, it is without authority to reverse or modify it.

12 App(2d) 52, 230 NE(2d) 662 (1967), Battles v Ohio State Racing Comm. In an appeal under RC 119.12, a common pleas court does not have jurisdiction to review the reasonableness and lawfulness, in its general application, of a rule adopted by an administrative agency but derives jurisdiction under the provisions of the last paragraph of RC 119.11 to review the reasonableness or legality of the rule in its application to the particular set of facts or circumstances involved in the adjudication pertaining to licensing resulting in the order from which the appeal under RC 119.12 has been perfected.

1 App(2d) 263, 204 NE(2d) 535 (1965), Rahal v Liquor Control Comm. The liquor control commission has no authority to pass on the constitutionality of a statute, and a party need not raise such a question before the commission in order to be entitled to present it in the common pleas court.

111 App 435, 172 NE(2d) 628 (1960), State Racing Comm v Robertson. Upon an appeal to the common pleas court from an order of an administrative agency, such court, in the absence of a finding that such order is not supported by reliable, probative and substantial evidence and is not in accordance with law, may not modify the penalty imposed by such agency; but the court of appeals, upon review of a judgment of the court of common pleas, has jurisdiction to consider and review the record of the proceedings before the agency and in the common pleas court to determine whether such court may have erred in finding that such order is supported by reliable, probative and substantial evidence and is in accordance with law.

109 App 289, 165 NE(2d) 19 (1959), In re Owner-Trainer Topper. The jurisdiction of the court of appeals, in an appeal by an administra-

tive agency from a judgment of a common pleas court on appeal from an order of such agency, is limited and controlled by RC 119.12.

97 App 8, 119 NE(2d) 309 (1953), Socotch v Krebs. In an appeal to the common pleas court from an order of the board of liquor control affirming a finding of the department of liquor control rejecting the appellant's application for the transfer of a liquor permit, the court is without jurisdiction to make an order respecting the issuance or renewal of such permit.

91 App 277, 97 NE(2d) 688 (1950), Shearer v State Medical Bd. In an appeal to the common pleas court from an order of the state medical board suspending the certificate of one licensed to practice, the test to be applied by the reviewing court is whether the decision of the state medical board is against the manifest weight of the evidence, and it is reversible error for the reviewing court to affirm the decision of such board on the ground that it "has not been guilty of an abuse of discretion or acted arbitrarily or capriciously."

No. 411 (4th Dist Ct App, Vinton, 8-31-84), Dodrill dba Jim Dodrill Auto Sales v Motor Vehicle Dealers Board. Abuse of discretion is not within the scope of review of RC 119.12, and a party on appeal may not use discovery to inquire into the rationale for an administrative adjudicative order, or to obtain information on the disposition of similar administrative cases.

53 Misc 13, 372 NE(2d) 1345 (CP, Montgomery 1977), In re Bronkar. The hearing envisioned by RC 119.12 on an appeal from the state personnel board of review requires a close consideration by the court of common pleas of the record as certified to it by the board, the written briefs, and the oral argument of counsel.

77 Abs 457, 150 NE(2d) 461 (App, Franklin 1957), Mangold, dba Clover Club v Bd of Liquor Control. The court of appeals does not have jurisdiction to hear an appeal filed by an administrative agency pursuant to RC 119.12 where the question presented is limited to a review of the correctness of the judgment of a court of common pleas holding that the order of the administrative agency is not supported by reliable, probative and substantial evidence.

74 Abs 492, 141 NE(2d) 787 (CP, Franklin 1957), Khoury v Bd of Liquor Control; affirmed by 78 Abs 468, 153 NE(2d) 334 (App, Franklin 1957). A court is not required to determine the issue as to "advisability" of issuing liquor permits; but only to find whether the order of the board, in the exercise of its discretion, upon consideration of the entire record, "is supported by reliable, probative and substantial evidence and is in accordance with law."

67 Abs 53, 118 NE(2d) 697 (CP, Franklin 1953), Fawcett v Bd of Liquor Control. In reviewing an order of the board of liquor control affirming the action of the director of liquor control in refusing to issue a permit because the permit premises were within 500 feet of a church and school, the court is not required to determine the issue as to "advisability" of issuing such permits; but only to find whether the order of the board in the exercise of its discretion upon consideration of the entire record is supported by reliable, probative and substantial evidence and is in accordance with law.

19. Disposition of appeal

170 OS 233, 163 NE(2d) 678 (1959), Henry's Cafe, Inc v Bd of Liquor Control. On appeal from an order of an agency to the court of common pleas, the power of the court to modify such order is limited to the ground of an absence of a finding that the order is supported by reliable, probative, and substantial evidence, and such court has no authority to modify a penalty that the agency was authorized to and did impose, on the ground that the agency abused its discretion.

1 App(2d) 470, 205 NE(2d) 100 (1964), Broadway Enterprise, Inc v Bd of Liquor Control. In an appeal from an order of the board of liquor control suspending a liquor permit, the common pleas court, finding that the order of the board is supported by reliable, probative and substantial evidence and is in accordance with law and affirming the order of the board, is without authority to modify the penalty.

112 App 264, 172 NE(2d) 336 (1960), Evans v Bd of Liquor Control. The court of common pleas has no authority to modify the penalty imposed by the board of liquor control revoking a liquor permit for violations of the Liquor Control Act, where, on an appeal from such order of the board, the court considers the entire record and the evidence before it and determines that the order of the board is supported by reliable, probative and substantial evidence.

112 App 264, 172 NE(2d) 336 (1960), Evans v Bd of Liquor Control. Where evidence was stipulated into the record at the hearing before the board of liquor control of a conviction of the bartender for a violation of RC 4301.22, and the board revoked plaintiff's license therefor, the court of common pleas did not have authority to reduce the penalty to a suspension.

108 App 417, 159 NE(2d) 632 (1958), Bd of Liquor Control v Buckeye Lake Hotel Co. A reviewing court which finds that the decision of the board of liquor control is supported by the evidence has no jurisdiction to modify the penalty imposed.

108 App 417, 159 NE(2d) 632 (1958), Bd of Liquor Control v Buckeye Lake Hotel Co. A reviewing court has the power to modify an order of the board of liquor control appealed from only when it does not find that such order is supported by "reliable, probative, and substantial evidence"; and where such court finds that an order of the board of liquor control is supported by "reliable, probative and substantial evidence and is in accordance with law" it has no authority to modify the penalty imposed by such board.

106 App 391, 152 NE(2d) 282 (1958), In re Revocation of License. The common pleas court, on an appeal from an order of the state board of real estate examiners revoking the license of a real estate broker for misconduct, may, where it finds that "the penalty imposed is unduly extreme and harsh," modify the order of the board and impose a lesser penalty.

106 App 211, 149 NE(2d) 150 (1958), Carpenter v Sinclair. On the record action of the common pleas court in revoking appellant's real estate brokers license was unjustified, and the court of appeals will substitute instead a thirty day revocation.

No. 84AP-1085 (10th Dist Ct App, Franklin, 7-2-85), In re Application of Stover. An appeal of an adverse administrative decision to the common pleas court is a statutory proceeding under RC 119.12 and the rules of civil procedure are inapplicable pursuant to Civ R 1(C); therefore vacation of the judgment of the court under Civ R 60 is not available.

14 Misc 9, 233 NE(2d) 147 (CP, Montgomery 1967), Handler v Dept of Commerce. When a court finds that the order of an administrative agency appealed pursuant to RC 119.01 et seq. is not supported by reliable, probative, and substantial evidence or is not in accordance with law it may reverse, vacate, or modify such order.

74 Abs 459, 141 NE(2d) 889 (App, Franklin 1956), Delmonte Cafe, Inc v Dept of Liquor Control. Where the court finds that an order of the board of liquor control is supported by reliable, probative, and substantial evidence and is in accordance with law, it has no power to modify the penalty imposed by reducing it. (See also City Products Corp, dba

Pilsner Brewing Co v Bd of Liquor Control, 79 Abs 481, 156 NE(2d) 347 (App, Franklin 1958).)

119.121 Expiration of license involved in an appeal; procedure

The expiration of the license involved in an appeal filed pursuant to section 119.12 of the Revised Code shall not affect the appeal. If during an appeal the existing license shall expire the court in its order in favor of an aggrieved person shall order the agency to renew the license upon payment of the fee prescribed by law for the license.

HISTORY: 125 v 241, eff. 10-2-53

CROSS REFERENCES

Hospitals and community mental health facilities, revocation or termination of certification, OAC 5122:3-7-03

OJur 2d: 26, Health § 29.6; 28, Hospitals and Asylums § 57, 58, 62; 30, Insurance § 21, 21.5; 31, Intoxicating Liquors § 148, 166; 41, Parks, Squares and Playgrounds § 10; 48, Schools § 10; 55, Wharfs § 14.1; 58, Workers' Compensation § 134

OJur 3d: 1, Abandoned, Lost, and Escheated Property § 69; 2, Administrative Law § 26, 57 to 59, 98, 108, 157, 171, 210; 2, Advertising § 4, 14; 3, Animals § 21; 6, Atomic Energy and Ionizing Radiation § 31; 6, Auctioneers § 8; 7, Automobiles and Other Vehicles § 90; 9, Banks and Financial Institutions § 424, 507; 10, Building, Zoning and Land Controls § 156, 242, 307; 10, Businesses and Occupations § 32; 11, Businesses and Occupations § 73, 156, 242; 17, Consumer and Borrower Protection § 22, 23; 38, Eminent Domain § 215; 39, Employment Relations § 87; 41, Environmental Protection § 56, 83

Am Jur 2d: 2, Administrative Law § 208

119.13 Representation of parties and witnesses

At any hearing conducted under sections 119.01 to 119.13 of the Revised Code, a party or an affected person may be represented by an attorney or by such other representative as is lawfully permitted to practice before the agency in question, but, except for hearings held before the state personnel board of review under section 124.03 of the Revised Code, only an attorney at law may represent a party or an affected person at a hearing at which a record is taken which may be the basis of an appeal to court.

At any hearing conducted under sections 119.01 to 119.13 of the Revised Code, a witness, if he so requests, shall be permitted to be accompanied, represented, and advised by an attorney, whose participation in the hearing shall be limited to the protection of the rights of the witness, and who may not examine or cross-examine witnesses, and the witness shall be advised of his right to counsel before he is interrogated.

HISTORY: 1977 H 260, eff. 6-16-77
129 v 1052; 1953 H 1; GC 154-74

CROSS REFERENCES

See Whiteside, Ohio Appellate Practice, Text 23.01, 23.04

Witnesses, 9.84
State employment relations board, power to establish standards of practice, 4117.02

Proceedings held by unemployment compensation board of review, lay representation, 4141.07

OJur 2d: 26, Health § 29.6; 28, Hospitals and Asylums § 57, 58, 62; 30, Insurance § 21, 21.5; 41, Parks, Squares and Playgrounds § 10; 48, Schools § 10; 55, Wharfs § 14.1; 58, Workers' Compensation § 134

OJur 3d: 1, Abandoned, Lost, and Escheated Property § 69; 2, Administrative Law § 26, 57 to 59, 61, 98, 108, 171; 2, Advertising § 4, 14; 3, Animals § 21; 6, Atomic Energy and Ionizing Radiation § 31; 6, Auctioneers § 8; 7, Automobiles and Other Vehicles § 90; 9, Banks and Financial Institutions § 424, 507; 10, Building, Zoning and Land Controls § 156, 242, 307; 10, Businesses and Occupations § 32, 45; 11, Businesses and Occupations § 156, 242; 7, Consumer and Borrower Protection § 22, 23; 38, Eminent Domain § 215; 39, Employment Relations § 87; 41, Environmental Protection § 56, 83

Am Jur 2d: 2, Administrative Law § 273

Comment note—Right to assistance by counsel in administrative proceedings. 33 ALR3d 229

---

12 Misc 227, 230 NE(2d) 693 (CP, Hamilton 1967), Kelly v Liquor Control Comm. It is not a ground for reversal in a hearing before the liquor control commission that a witness other than the permit holder was not advised of his right to counsel.

OAG 73-041. The representation of a complainant by a layman, in a proceeding before a county board of revision in which a record is made, constitutes the unauthorized practice of law under RC 4705.01.

Chapter 2506

Appeals From Orders of Administrative Officers, and Agencies

2506.01 Appeal from decisions of any agency of any political subdivision
2506.02 Filing of transcript
2506.03 Hearing of appeal
2506.04 Finding and order of court

CROSS REFERENCES

See Whiteside, Ohio Appellate Practice, Text 1.18, 21.03, 25.01 to 25.05, 25.07, 25.09, 33.07, 33.12; Forms 11.582
See Baldwin's Ohio School Law, Text 49.01, 49.07, 59.06
See Gotherman & Babbit, Ohio Municipal Law, Text 16.05, 37.58, 37.64, 37.65, 45.08, 45.28, 45.29; Forms 33.22

Suspension, revocation or denial of solid waste disposal facility or site license; hearing; appeal, 3734.09

---

34 Ohio St LJ 853 (1974). Judicial Review of Administrative Decisions in Ohio, Charles I. Kampinski.

30 Ohio St LJ 1 (1969). Ombudsman in Ohio, David C. Cummings.

53 Cin L Rev 681 (1984). Judicial Review of Administrative Regulations: An Overview, Russell L. Weaver.

22 Clev St L Rev 229 (1973). Ohio Revised Code Ch 2506—Judicial Review of Administrative Rulings, Marshall Wolf and Donald Robiner.

14 App(3d) 22, 14 OBR 26, 469 NE(2d) 989 (Summit 1984), Carlyn v Davis. Upon the entrance of an order allowing an annexation, the remedy available to township trustees is injunctive relief pursuant to RC 709.07, and the underlying trial court decision allowing annexation is not dispositive of the trustees' action for injunction, as the trustees could not be a party to such underlying action and would effectively be denied their only remedy.

7 App(3d) 304, 7 OBR 387, 455 NE(2d) 709 (Cuyahoga 1983), Woods v Civil Service Comm. Where a ruling of a municipal civil service commission is appealed to the court of appeals, and the municipal civil service commission is named appellee rather than the municipality, the appellant's motion to amend the notice of appeal in the court of common pleas should be granted when the municipality has participated in the proceedings and was served a copy of the notice of appeal.

No. 10433 (9th Dist Ct App, Summit, 5-19-82), In re Annexation of 1,544.61 Acres of Land in Northampton Twp to the City of Akron. Intervention pursuant to Civ R 24(B) is permissive and the trial court does not abuse its discretion in denying township trustees intervention in an administrative appeal filed pursuant to Ch 2506 challenging the denial of a petition for annexation.

2506.01 Appeal from decisions of any agency of any political subdivision

Every final order, adjudication, or decision of any officer, tribunal, authority, board, bureau, commission, department or other division of any political subdivision of the state may be reviewed by the common pleas court of the county in which the principal office of the political subdivision is located, as provided in sections 2505.01 to 2505.45, inclusive, of the Revised Code, and as such procedure is modified by sections 2506.01 to 2506.04, inclusive, of the Revised Code.

The appeal provided in sections 2506.01 to 2506.04, inclusive, of the Revised Code is in addition to any other remedy of appeal provided by law.

A "final order, adjudication, or decision" does not include any order from which an appeal is granted by rule, ordinance, or statute to a higher administrative authority and a right to a hearing on such appeal is provided; any order which does not constitute a determination of the rights, duties, privileges, benefits, or legal relationships of a specified person; nor any order issued preliminary to or as a result of a criminal proceeding.

HISTORY: 127 v 963, eff. 9-16-57

CROSS REFERENCES

See Baldwin's Ohio Township Law, Text 3.02, 59.04, 59.10, 59.13, 59.25
See Whiteside, Ohio Appellate Practice, Text 21.08, 25.01, 25.03 to 25.05, 33.12; Forms 11.58, 11.581
See Baldwin's Ohio School Law, Text 41.08, 49.07, 49.08
See Gotherman & Babbit, Ohio Municipal Law, Text 15.72, 15.94, 15.96, 45.28; Forms 33.21, 33.23
See Carroll, Ohio Administrative law, Text 3.11(B)(2)

OJur 2d: 58, Zoning § 176, 179

1. In general
2. Alternative remedies
3. Appeal authorized
4. Appeal precluded
5. Procedure

1. In general

35 Ohio St LJ 41 (1974). Administrative Review and the Ohio Modern Courts Amendment, Ivan Cate Rutledge.

12 WRU Law Rev 645 (1961). Some Aspects of Appellate Procedure in Ohio, Judge Lee E. Skeel.

5 OS(3d) 141, 5 OBR 273, 449 NE(2d) 771 (1983), In re Appeal of Bass Lake Community, Inc. Township trustees lack standing to contest appeal by applicants from order denying application for annexation.

42 OS(2d) 436, 329 NE(2d) 686 (1975), Rankin-Thoman v Caldwell. 119.11, which provides for an appeal to the court of common pleas from the quasi-legislative proceedings of administrative officers and agencies, is unconstitutional, in violation of O Const Art IV, § 4(B).

42 OS(2d) 436, 329 NE(2d) 686 (1975), Rankin-Thoman v Caldwell. The review of proceedings of administrative officers and agencies, authorized by O Const Art IV, § 4(B), contemplates quasi-judicial proceedings only.

42 OS(2d) 368, 328 NE(2d) 808 (1975), Cincinnati Bell, Inc v Glendale. The test which courts of common pleas apply when hearing appeals pursuant to Ch 2506 is not whether any legal justification exists for a holding of the board of zoning appeals, but rather whether the ordinance, in proscribing a landowner's proposed use of his land, bears a reasonable relationship to the public health, safety, welfare, or morals.

38 OS(2d) 298, 313 NE(2d) 400 (1974), C. Miller Chevrolet, Inc v Willoughby Hills. In an appeal under Ch 2506 from the denial of an application for a variance by a zoning board of appeals, there is a presumption that the board's determination is valid, and the burden of showing invalidity of the board's determination rests on the party contesting that determination.

38 OS(2d) 23, 309 NE(2d) 900 (1974), Mobil Oil Corp v Rocky River. In an appeal, pursuant to Ch 2506, which challenges the constitutionality of a zoning ordinance as applied, the issue for determination is whether the ordinance, in proscribing a landowner's proposed use of his land, has any reasonable relationship to the legitimate exercise of police power by the municipality.

36 OS(2d) 62, 303 NE(2d) 890 (1973), De Long v Bd of Ed of Southwest School District. The review of proceedings of administrative officers and agencies under 2506.01 contemplates quasi-judicial proceedings only.

8 App(3d) 424, 8 OBR 548, 457 NE(2d) 883 (Trumball 1982), Howland Realty Co v Wolcott. The action of referendum is not an appeal since it is not conducted by a higher administrative authority, and it is not subject to a right of hearing thereon.

8 App(3d) 176, 8 OBR 236, 456 NE(2d) 829 (Cuyahoga 1982), Wade v Cleveland. While application of the doctrine of res judicata is generally made with regard to actions which have proceeded to judicial review and determination, it is similarly applicable to actions which have been reviewed before an administrative body, in which there has been no appeal made pursuant to RC 2506.01.

63 App(2d) 34, 409 NE(2d) 258 (1979), Central Motors Corp v Pepper Pike. A declaration of unconstitutionality of a zoning ordinance and a determination of a reasonable use or uses in a declaratory judgment action have the same legal effect as a successful Ch 2506 appeal,

and where a property owner is successful in an attack on constitutionality under Ch 2506, the court has determined that the prohibition against a proposed use is unconstitutional. When, in a declaratory judgment action, a court determines unconstitutionality of a zoning ordinance as applied to a particular parcel of property and a reasonable use or uses for the property, any action taken to prevent or deny development of the property for that reasonable use will also be considered an unconstitutional act and, any prohibition against the reasonable use found by the court is unconstitutional.

49 App(2d) 77, 359 NE(2d) 459 (1976), Flair Corp v Brecksville. An appeal may be taken under Ch 2506 from the action or refusal to act of a city council when that body is acting in a quasi-judicial capacity but not when it acts or refuses to act in its legislative capacity.

49 App(2d) 77, 359 NE(2d) 459 (1976), Flair Corp v Brecksville. Where a planning commission of a municipality is only a recommending agency, its recommendation is not a final order from which an appeal may be taken under Ch 2506.

48 App(2d) 1, 355 NE(2d) 495 (1976), Standard Oil Co v Warrensville Hts. A property owner may attack the constitutionality of a zoning ordinance either in a declaratory judgment action under Ch 2721, or in an appeal to the common pleas court from an administrative agency under Ch 2506; it is not necessary to seek legislative rezoning as a condition precedent to maintaining a declaratory judgment action attacking the constitutionality of a zoning ordinance, nor is it necessary to attempt to exhaust administrative remedies and take an appeal under Ch 2506, prior to initiating declaratory judgment action if the administrative remedies are not equally as serviceable as a declaratory judgment action, are unusually expensive or onerous, seeking such remedies would constitute vain acts, or if the administrative agency does not have authority to grant the relief sought.

45 App(2d) 163, 341 NE(2d) 860 (1975), State ex rel Dean v Huddle. Where a decision by an administrative department to lay off an employee does not require notice, a hearing, and the opportunity to contest the action through the presentation of evidence, it may not be the subject of an appeal pursuant to 2506.01.

44 App(2d) 115, 335 NE(2d) 868 (1975), Fair v School Employees Retirement System. Neither 119.12 nor 2506.01 confer a remedy of appeal from a decision of the school employees retirement board denying an application for disability retirement.

4 App(2d) 171, 211 NE(2d) 880 (1965), Petitioners for Incorporation v Bd of Twinsburg Twp Trustees. The board of trustees of a township is an agency of a political subdivision of the state within the meaning of 2506.01.

No. 411 (4th Dist Ct App, Vinton, 8-31-84), Dodrill dba Jim Dodrill Auto Sales v Motor Vehicle Dealers Board. The Motor Vehicle Dealers Board is not an "agency of a political subdivision," and appeals from the board are pursuant to RC Ch 119, not RC Ch 2506.

No. 11170 (9th Dist Ct App, Summit, 2-16-84), In re Removal of Roach v Fairlawn. An appeal of a discharge from a municipal police force must be brought under RC Ch 2506, and may not be brought pursuant to RC 119.12, which is relevant only to appeals from decisions of state agencies.

706 F(2d) 985 (6th Cir 1983), Doe v Staples; cert denied 104 SCt 1301, 79 LEd(2d) 701 (1984). The county welfare department, when removing children from a natural parent, must give notice to the parents prior to or at the time of removal stating reasons for removal, and must give parents a full opportunity to present witnesses at a hearing at which they may be represented by retained counsel, and such hearing must be

held before a neutral hearing officer, who is to state in writing the decision reached and reasons therefor.

OAG 84-101. A decision by a board of county commissioners to levy an assessment pursuant to RC 1515.24 for the costs of maintenance or repair of an improvement may be appealed in accordance with the provisions of RC Ch 2505 and 2506.

2. Alternative remedies

66 OS(2d) 304, 421 NE(2d) 530 (1981), Schomaeker v First National Bank of Ottawa. A person entitled under Ch 2506 to appeal the order of a planning commission granting a variance pursuant to a village ordinance is not entitled to a declaratory judgment where failure to exhaust administrative remedies is asserted and maintained.

54 OS(2d) 354, 376 NE(2d) 1343 (1978), State ex rel Board of County Commissioners v Court of Common Pleas of Butler County. 307.56 and 2506.01 do not patently and unambiguously restrict court of common pleas from hearing appeal of clerk of courts from decision of county commissioners denying budget request of clerk.

42 OS(2d) 263, 328 NE(2d) 395 (1975), Driscoll v Austintown Associates. The availability of a Ch 2506 action to review the denial of a variance sought by the owner of a specific tract of land does not preclude a declaratory judgment action which challenges the constitutionality of the zoning restrictions on that land.

34 OS(2d) 222, 297 NE(2d) 525 (1973), State ex rel Kronenberger-Fodor Co v Parma. In a zoning case, where a constitutional process of appeal has been legislatively provided, the sole fact that pursuing such process would encompass more delay and inconvenience than seeking a writ of mandamus is insufficient to prevent the process from constituting a plain and adequate remedy in the ordinary course of the law.

34 OS(2d) 59, 295 NE(2d) 657 (1973), State ex rel Benton's Village Sanitation Service v Usher. A writ of mandamus will not issue to compel a district board of health to issue a license to operate a solid waste disposal site or facility pursuant to Ch 3734.

14 OS(2d) 226, 237 NE(2d) 392 (1968), State ex rel Marshall v Civil Service Comm. Where a municipal civil service commission formally rejects the application of a municipal civil service employee to take a promotional examination for the reason that he does not meet the minimum qualifications established by rule of the commission for taking the examination, the employee has a plain appeal under 2506.01 to the court of common pleas of the county in which the commission is located, and adequate remedy in the ordinary course of the law, and he may not properly resort to an action in mandamus against the commission under 2731.02 to enforce his claimed right to take the examination.

9 OS(2d) 95, 223 NE(2d) 824 (1967), State ex rel Federal Homes Properties, Inc v Singer. In any instance of a refusal, for whatever reason, of an administrative official to act timely upon an application for a permit, either mandamus in the common pleas court or a mandatory injunction would appear to be an appropriate remedy to compel his decision, and if the response of the official is to refuse the permit, the right to test the correctness of his decision is furnished by way of appeal to the court of common pleas, after all administrative remedies of appeal, if any, are exhausted.

1 OS(2d) 100, 205 NE(2d) 14 (1965), State ex rel Weaver v Faust. The writ of prohibition will not issue at the instance of a party who alleges irregularities in the proceedings of an administrative board and anticipates that such board will deprive him of procedural and substantive rights.

176 OS 147, 197 NE(2d) 897 (1964), State ex rel Conant v Jones. Mandamus may not be used as a substitute for appeal under Ch 2506.

175 OS 361, 194 NE(2d) 850 (1963), State ex rel Ruggiero v Common Pleas Court of Cuyahoga County. Procedendo will not lie where an adequate remedy by appeal is available.

174 OS 109, 186 NE(2d) 839 (1962), State ex rel Steyer v Szabo. Where a municipal civil service commission rejected relator's contention that he was entitled to be certified as chief of police, an appeal to the common pleas court is the correct remedy and quo warranto did not lie.

171 OS 553, 173 NE(2d) 117 (1961), State ex rel Ricketts v Balsly. Mandamus is not the proper remedy for appealing from the decision of a building inspector to compel the issuance of a building permit and zoning certificate.

171 OS 343, 170 NE(2d) 847 (1960), State ex rel Fredrix v Beachwood. Refusal of a village to grant a request for rezoning should not be tested by a mandamus action.

171 OS 318, 170 NE(2d) 487 (1960), State ex rel Gund Co v Solon. Review of final orders of a village building commissioner or board of zoning appeals should be under Ch 2506 rather than by application for a writ of mandamus directing the issuance of a building permit.

9 App(3d) 142, 9 OBR 207, 458 NE(2d) 895 (Preble 1983), Beare v Eaton. A municipal civil service employee who was removed from employment for disciplinary reasons may appeal the adverse decision of the civil service commission to the court of common pleas either under RC 119.12 or 2506.01.

64 App(2d) 90, 411 NE(2d) 504 (1979), Ruprecht v Cincinnati. Where civil service employee is given an official reprimand and the loss of five "off days" as a disciplinary action by the appointing authority and where the action of the appointing authority is upheld by the municipal civil service commission, neither 124.34 nor 2506.01 provides the employee with a right of appeal to the court of common pleas since the specific statutory provision (124.34) prevails over the general statutory provision (2506.01).

63 App(2d) 34, 409 NE(2d) 258 (1979), Central Motors Corp v Pepper Pike. The issues to be determined in a declaratory judgment action attacking the constitutionality of a zoning ordinance may include an objective determination as to whether the ordinance is unreasonable, arbitrary and confiscatory and not based on the public health, safety, morals and general welfare, and thus whether or not it is unconstitutional; the prayer for relief may include a request for a determination of a reasonable use or uses of the property if the zoning ordinance is declared unconstitutional, or in the alternative, the issue may be framed more narrowly such as in a Ch 2506 appeal, as to whether the prohibition against a specific proposed use is constitutional.

59 App(2d) 155, 392 NE(2d) 1316 (1978), Gates Mills Investment Co v Pepper Pike. When a party files an action in declaratory judgment under Ch 2721 seeking a declaration that a zoning ordinance is unconstitutional and the defendant municipality raises the affirmative defense of failure to exhaust administrative remedies and the plaintiff counters by contending that seeking such administrative relief would be an onerous or vain act, these preliminary issues must be resolved before the case is tried on its merits.

47 App(2d) 125, 352 NE(2d) 606 (1975), Gannon v Perk. A declaratory judgment action brought under Ch 2721, seeking a declaration regarding the legality of layoffs by the city of Cleveland of policemen and firemen, is a legal action and may be maintained even though the parties bringing the action have the alternative, but not exclusive, rem-

edy of appeal to the civil service commission and to the courts under Ch 2506.

40 App(2d) 166, 318 NE(2d) 433 (1973), State ex rel Dahmen v Youngstown. Mandamus is the proper remedy of one who has been illegally removed from the classified service, as where he has been removed under the guise of abolishing his position but in fact such abolishment was a mere pretext for displacing him and putting in his place another who, under a different title, is to perform substantially the same duties.

34 App(2d) 98, 296 NE(2d) 290 (1972), Brooks v Cook Chevrolet, Inc. Where an administrative agency has jurisdiction to make an order in a matter pending before it, and a right of appeal from such order to the court of common pleas is provided by law to any person adversely affected thereby, such person is not authorized to bring an independent action in equity to enjoin the carrying out of such order, where the grounds relied upon in seeking the injunction are such as could be fully litigated in the appeal authorized by law.

11 App(2d) 84, 228 NE(2d) 913 (1967), State ex rel Marshall v Columbus Civil Service Comm; reversed by 14 OS(2d) 226, 237 NE(2d) 392 (1968). A rejection by the secretary and personnel director of a civil service commission of an application of a relator to take a promotional, competitive examination for the classified civil service position of fire chief, without communicating such action to the civil service commission, is not a final order which could have been appealed by the relator to the common pleas court pursuant to Ch 2506; and, for such reason, relator does not have available an adequate and effective remedy at law.

116 App 329, 187 NE(2d) 170 (1962), State ex rel Thomas v Ludewig. A common pleas court does not abuse its discretion in allowing a writ of mandamus merely because the relator has an adequate remedy in the ordinary course of law.

112 App 87, 163 NE(2d) 778 (1960), State ex rel Trusz v Middleburg Hts. The deciding factor as to whether relief by way of mandamus is available where an appeal from a final decision of a zoning board of appeals is possible under Ch 2505 and Ch 2506 is whether such appeal provides an adequate remedy in the ordinary course of the law.

No. 11661 (9th Dist Ct App, Summit, 10-24-84), Burch v Cuyahoga Falls. An appeal from a municipal civil service commission order may be brought under either RC 124.34 or 2506.01, and the failure of a common pleas court to specify under which section it is ruling is not error.

49 Misc 36, 360 NE(2d) 761 (CP Montgomery 1976), In re Sergent. Ch 2506 governs appeals from orders of administrative officers, including appeals from orders of a board of education under 3319.081(C).

39 Misc 11, 314 NE(2d) 403 (CP Hamilton 1973), Public Employees Council No. 51 v University of Cincinnati. A labor union is not a party entitled to a quasi-judicial hearing before a municipal service commission, and is therefore not entitled to an appeal from a decision of the commission under 2506.01 et seq.

93 Abs 353, 198 NE(2d) 479 (1964), Feinstein v Whitehall. Before attacking validity of municipal licensing ordinance, petitioner should have exhausted administrative remedies under Ch 2506.

88 Abs 306, 182 NE(2d) 638 (1961), State ex rel Hershey Builders, Inc v Brewer. Mandamus will issue to compel a board of zoning appeals to deliver a certificate of compliance previously authorized and issued.

OAG 83-072. If a person fails to build a portion of a fence assigned to him under RC 971.04 and has not appealed the decision making the assignment, a board of township trustees may proceed to have such fence built in accordance with RC 971.07(A); a party who has failed to avail himself of the appeal provided under RC 2506.01 may not collaterally attack a decision of a board of township trustees made after an RC 971.04 proceeding through an action for an injunction or declaratory judgment.

3. Appeal authorized

66 OS(2d) 304, 421 NE(2d) 530 (1981), Schomaeker v First National Bank of Ottawa. A person owning property, who has previously indicated an interest in the proposed use of contiguous property by a prior court action challenging the use, and who attends a hearing on the variance together with counsel, is within that class of persons directly affected by the administrative decision and is entitled to appeal under Ch 2506.

61 OS(2d) 273, 400 NE(2d) 908 (1980), Walker v Eastlake. Where the civil service commission of a municipality removes a classified employee from his position for disciplinary reasons, that decision may be appealed to the court of common pleas pursuant to 2506.01.

34 OS(2d) 32, 295 NE(2d) 404 (1973), Haught v Dayton. Action of municipal civil service board in amending rules to provide that employees working in emergency employment act employment should be permitted to work regardless of their relative city-wide length of service could be appealed under Ch 2506 by employees wrongfully dismissed as a result thereof.

20 OS(2d) 128, 254 NE(2d) 18 (1969), State ex rel Cunagin Construction Corp v Creech. The written denial of a planning commission of the validity of an application for a building permit and its refusal to act on the same constituted a final act, the lawfulness of which is subject to review by appeal pursuant to 2506.01 et seq., and hence mandamus is not available as a remedy to compel issuance of the application.

13 OS(2d) 1, 233 NE(2d) 500 (1968), Donnelly v Fairview Park. The failure or refusal of a municipal council to approve a plan for the resubdivision of land which meets the terms of a zoning ordinance adopted and in existence in an administrative act, and an appeal from such failure or refusal to approve lies to the court of common pleas under Ch 2506.

7 OS(2d) 21, 218 NE(2d) 460 (1966), Jacobs v Maddux. Where a board of township trustees acts to deny a petition for incorporation of a village for the reason that the petition does not conform to the requirements of 707.15, the action of the board is quasi-judicial in nature and an appeal may be taken from such action under 2506.01.

174 OS 330, 189 NE(2d) 69 (1963), State ex rel Fagain v Stork. A decision of a municipal civil service commission affirming the action of the director of civil service in discharging an employee for physical unfitness is appealable under Ch 2506.

173 OS 168, 180 NE(2d) 591 (1962), Roper v Richfield Bd of Zoning Appeals. A resident, elector and property owner of a township, who appears before a township board of zoning appeals, is represented by an attorney, opposes and protests the changing of a zoned area from residential to commercial, and advises the board, on the record, that if the decision of the board is adverse to him he intends to appeal from the decision to a court, has a right of appeal to the common pleas court if the appeal is properly and timely made.

14 App(3d) 372, 14 OBR 477, 471 NE(2d) 845 (Cuyahoga 1984), FRC of Kamms Corner, Inc v Cleveland Bd of Zoning Appeals. A constitutional challenge to a zoning ordinance shall be tried originally in the common pleas court, with the court permitting the parties to offer additional evidence.

49 App(2d) 101, 359 NE(2d) 445 (1974), State ex rel Stec v Bd of Ed of Lorain City School District. An original action for a declaratory

judgment is a proper method to determine if a teacher is entitled to a continuing service contract and an action in mandamus will lie to compel a school board to tender such a contract if a clear legal duty to do so is demonstrated.

40 App(2d) 166, 318 NE(2d) 433 (1973), State ex rel Dahmen v Youngstown. A decision of a municipal civil service commission can be appealed pursuant to 2506.01.

33 App(2d) 177, 294 NE(2d) 230 (1972), In re Locke. The law and fact appeal provided the chiefs and members of city fire and police departments is not exclusive, and an appeal may also be taken pursuant to the provisions of Ch 2506.

28 App(2d) 175, 275 NE(2d) 637 (1971), Fox v Johnson. Resident, property owner and elector of township who appears before township board of zoning appeals and is represented by attorney and who opposed granting of variance permitting commercial use in residential area has right to appeal to common pleas court pursuant to 2506.01.

27 App(2d) 204, 273 NE(2d) 800 (1971), Shelby Realty, Inc v Springdale. If board of zoning appeals upholds refusal of building department to grant building permit, applicant for permit has the right to judicial review in court of common pleas.

21 App(2d) 49, 254 NE(2d) 711 (1969), Bell v Lawrence County General Hospital Bd of Trustees. Public employees whose employment has been terminated pursuant to the provisions of Ch 4117 have the right of appeal to the court of common pleas, pursuant to Ch 2506.

12 App(2d) 87, 231 NE(2d) 81 (1967), State ex rel Smith v Johnson. An elector who files a protest with a board of elections pursuant to 3513.262, which protest is overruled by such board of elections, can appeal to the common pleas court pursuant to Ch 2506; if such an appeal is filed, a candidate whose petitions are being challenged is a necessary party to such an appeal and must be joined as a party defendant.

3 App(2d) 32, 209 NE(2d) 218 (1965), Bieger v Moreland Hills. Where, by the zoning ordinance of a village, a board of zoning appeals is created to hear appeals from the action of the inspector of buildings, acting under the authority of the zoning ordinance, and by the provision of such ordinance the village council is made an appellate body to review the orders of the board of zoning appeals, the council, in reviewing an order appealed to it from an order of the board of zoning appeals, acts in an administrative and quasi-judicial capacity and its order in such case is appealable to the court of common pleas under the provisions of Ch 2506.

2 App(2d) 201, 207 NE(2d) 573 (1965), In re Appeal of Clements. Under a city ordinance which provides that the city planning and zoning commission, subject to confirmation and approval of city council, may, after public notice and hearing and subject to such conditions and safeguards as the city planning and zoning commission may establish, grant a variance in certain use districts, where the city council, after public hearing, accepts a recommendation of the planning and zoning commission and determines that a variance be granted to a certain individual property owner on a particular parcel of real property, the city council is fulfilling a purely administrative function and thereby acting in an administrative or quasi-judicial capacity, and an appeal may be taken from such action of the council to the court of common pleas under Ch 2506.

119 App 15, 196 NE(2d) 333 (1963), In re Appeal of McDonald. A decision of a board of zoning appeals as to whether to grant a zoning variance is made in a judicial capacity and may be appealed on the grounds of reasonableness alone.

118 App 125, 193 NE(2d) 437 (1962), State ex rel Fagain v Stork; affirmed by 174 OS 330, 180 NE(2d) 69 (1963). A final order of a municipal civil service commission, entered on July 28, 1961, and concerning other than police and fire personnel, is appealable pursuant to Ch 2506.

115 App 472, 180 NE(2d) 27 (1962), Shaker Coventry Corp v Shaker Heights Bd of Zoning Appeals. The proper method to test the validity of a zoning ordinance and for a judicial review of the final orders of administrative boards of municipalities is by way of appeal under the procedure set forth in Ch 2506, and the refusal of a zoning board of appeals to accept jurisdiction, where a building commissioner could not issue a building permit because of conflict with an ordinance, does not result in a deprivation of such right to appeal.

No. 10763 (9th Dist Ct App, Summit, 2-2-83), In re Annexation of 201.2 Acres of Land in Bath Twp to the City of Akron. Since RC 2506.04 provides that the judgment of a court may be appealed by any party, it is presumed that a nonaggrieved board of township trustees is a proper party to a RC 2506.01 appeal.

No. 43544 (8th Dist Ct App, Cuyahoga, 1-14-82), Treska v Trumble. Trial court has jurisdiction to review a decision of a municipal civil service commission pursuant to 2506.01.

9 Misc 11, 314 NE(2d) 403 (CP Hamilton 1973), Public Employees Council No. 51 v University of Cincinnati. A municipal civil service commission performs a quasi-judicial function in interpreting its own rules and the civil service laws as bearing upon the matters before it, so that a final order issued pursuant to such interpretation is subject to judicial review under 2506.01 et seq.

23 Misc 311, 261 NE(2d) 918 (1970), Medley v Portsmouth Civil Service Comm. An order refusing to grant approval for sick leave and disallowing compensation therefor upon request of member of city fire department constitutes suspension of pay and is appealable to civil service commission pursuant to 143.27.

14 Misc 144, 237 NE(2d) 641 (1965), Beerman v Kettering. An appeal provided by city charter of an order of a board of zoning appeals to be reviewed by council results in a proceeding which is quasi-judicial rather than legislative and therefore one which is subject to further appeal under Ch 2506 by the common pleas court. (See also Beerman v Kettering, 120 App 309, 201 NE(2d) 887 (1963).)

470 F(2d) 163 (6th Cir 1972), Burks v Perk. Judicial review is available of a final decision of a mayor removing municipal civil service commission members.

OAG 84-101. A decision by a board of county commissioners to levy an assessment pursuant to RC 1515.24 for the costs of maintenance or repair of an improvement may be appealed in accordance with the provisions of RC Ch 2505 and 2506.

OAG 83-072. In hearing and deciding a partition fence complaint under RC 971.04, a board of township trustees must allow each landowner who wishes to do so to present evidence that the cost of the erection of the fence will exceed any increase in the value of his land; a decision of a board of township trustees making an assignment of partition fences in accordance with RC 971.04, is appealable to the court of common pleas under RC 2506.01; such an appeal subsequent to an RC 971.04 proceeding, must, in accordance with RC 2505.07, be perfected within ten days of service of the board's written order.

4. Appeal precluded

67 OS(2d) 139, 423 NE(2d) 184 (1981), Moraine v Bd of County Commrs of Montgomery County. An appeal pursuant to 2506.01 from

the denial of an amendment to a comprehensive zoning plan is improper, since such action is a legislative function.

59 OS(2d) 48, 391 NE(2d) 736 (1979), State ex rel Rieke v Hausrod. No administrative appeal is available under 2506.01 from a decision of a mayor terminating a policeman's employment and from the city civil service commission's order denying him a hearing on the basis he was a probationary employee.

36 OS(2d) 62, 303 NE(2d) 890 (1973), De Long v Bd of Ed of Southwest School District. The action of a board of education in deciding not to reemploy a school teacher whose limited employment contract is due to expire is not a quasi-judicial proceeding subject to judicial review under 2506.01.

32 OS(2d) 150, 290 NE(2d) 562 (1972), M. J. Kelley Co v Cleveland. The review of proceedings of administrative officers and agencies, authorized by O Const Art IV, § 4(B), contemplates quasi-judicial proceedings only, and administrative actions of administrative officers and agencies not resulting from quasi-judicial proceedings are not appealable to the court of common pleas under 2506.01.

6 OS(2d) 155, 216 NE(2d) 877 (1966), Tuber v Perkins. The action of a board of township trustees in adopting or amending a zoning regulation is a legislative action and does not fall under 2506.01 providing for appeals to the court of common pleas from final orders of administrative bodies.

176 OS 146, 198 NE(2d) 48 (1964), Berg v Struthers. An appeal will not lie under Ch 2506 from the refusal of a city council to grant a requested zoning change, since such refusal was a legislative action.

175 OS 197, 191 NE(2d) 837 (1963), Remy v Kimes. Ch 2506 is not applicable to the legislative action of a city commission in passing an annexation ordinance.

14 App(3d) 101, 14 OBR 115, 470 NE(2d) 200 (Franklin 1983), Wahle v Industrial Relations Dept. The provisions of RC Ch 2506 are inapplicable to an appeal from an order of the board of building standards; rather, such an appeal is governed by RC Ch 119 and 3781.

13 App(3d) 64, 13 OBR 69, 467 NE(2d) 1390 (Franklin 1983), Welch v Cason. While the appointing authority of a municipal corporation has no right of appeal under RC 2506.01 in his official capacity, he does have a right under RC 124.34 to appeal a final order of a municipal civil service commission that orders the reinstatement of a municipal employee who was removed because such employee was absent without leave.

69 App(2d) 115, 432 NE(2d) 210 (1980), State ex rel Moss v Franklin County Bd of Elections. The determination of a board of elections with respect to a protest against a nominating petition is not appealable.

40 App(2d) 166, 318 NE(2d) 433 (1973), State ex rel Dahmen v Youngstown. The action of a municipal board of health abolishing a position under the classified municipal service is not quasi-judicial and, therefore, not appealable to the court of common pleas under 2506.01.

36 App(2d) 111, 303 NE(2d) 101 (1973), State ex rel Wedgewood 129 Corp v Olenick. The action by the county auditor of refusing to submit the complaint of a taxpayer as to the assessment of real property to the county board of revision is a ministerial act that is not quasi-judicial and is not appealable under 2506.01.

18 App(2d) 34, 246 NE(2d) 592 (1969), Stocker v Wood. In refusing to amend comprehensive zoning legislation, a board of county commissioners acts in a legislative capacity and is not amenable to the provisions of the administrative appeals act.

18 App(2d) 11, 246 NE(2d) 368 (1969), Szymanski v Toledo. Action of a committee of the whole of a city council to report a proposed

ordinance to council as disapproved is not reviewable under the provisions of Ch 2506.

11 App(2d) 84, 228 NE(2d) 913 (1967), State ex rel Marshall v Columbus Civil Service Comm; reversed by 14 OS(2d) 226, 237 NE(2d) 392 (1968). A rejection by the secretary and personnel director of a civil service commission of an application of a relator to take a promotional, competitive examination for the classified civil service position of fire chief, without communicating such action to the civil service commission, is not a final order which could have been appealed by the relator to the common pleas court pursuant to Ch 2506; and, for such reason, relator does not have available an adequate and effective remedy at law.

5 App(2d) 187, 214 NE(2d) 681 (1965), In re Application of Latham. Ch 2506 does not confer jurisdiction upon a court of common pleas to hear an appeal from the action of a board of county commissioners denying an application for rezoning.

2 App(2d) 201, 207 NE(2d) 573 (1965), In re Appeal of Clements. An appeal will not lie under Ch 2506 from the passage by a city council of a zoning ordinance changing a parcel of real property from a U2 use district to a U4 use district, because such a zoning ordinance is a purely legislative act.

2 App(2d) 197, 207 NE(2d) 385 (1963), Bailes v Martino. Property owners who appear individually at a hearing before a zoning board of appeals having to do with an application for a zoning-variance certificate and participate only in an extremely limited way, and who are not parties to and do not participate in an appeal from the decision of such board to the common pleas court, are not entitled to appeal the judgment of the common pleas court to the court of appeals.

118 App 457, 195 NE(2d) 380 (1963), In re Passage of Ordinance No. 105-62. The provisions of Ch 2506 do not apply to the adoption of an ordinance by a municipal council, and confer no right of appeal from such council action on a resident of such municipality.

No. CA-8998 (2d Dist Ct App, Montgomery, 4-18-85), In re Anderson. RC 505.62, which permits township trustees to appear in an appeal under RC Ch 2506 if the board of trustees was represented at the annexation hearing, gives the board of county commissioners no right to be a party to such an appeal; indeed, it confirms the fact that the board has no standing and cannot be a party to an annexation appeal for any purpose; misjoinder of the board is not a "technicality" and denial of a motion to dismiss the board is prejudical error; *amicus curiae* briefs from the commissioners must not be encouraged.

No. 84-CA-3026 (5th Dist Ct App, Licking, 6-5-84), Chilcote v Newark. The general right to appeal conferred by RC 2506.01 is limited by RC 124.34 to civil service removals or reductions in pay for disciplinary reasons.

No. 11540 (9th Dist Ct App, Summit, 5-9-84), Rivers v Quirk. RC 124.34 provides the exclusive right of appeal for civil service employees.

No. CA 2951 (5th Dist Ct App, Licking, 7-7-83), Cashdollar v Bd of Ed Northridge High School. A one-day suspension of a student is not appealable if the board of education has not entered an appropriate resolution on its minutes.

No. 1-81-64 (3d Dist Ct App, Allen, 7-16-82), Finfrock v Spencerville Local School District Bd of Ed. Where a school bus driver, who was suspended for cause after an informal hearing of the school board, has appealed the findings to common pleas court, the school employee's failure to object to the lack of due process protection at the school board hearing during the proceedings in the trial court, constituted a waiver of such rights.

25 Misc 175, 266 NE(2d) 864 (1970), In re Annexation in Mad River Twp. Municipal corporation to which annexation of territory is proposed by petition of landowners is neither party to annexation proceedings nor "person aggrieved" within meaning of Ch 2506 and so may not effect appeal from decision of board of county commissioners.

5. Procedure

64 OS(2d) 102, 413 NE(2d) 816 (1980), Davis v State Personnel Bd of Review. A member of the classified civil service, aggrieved by a decision of the state personnel board of review affirming his removal or reduction in pay for disciplinary reasons, must bring his appeal, if at all, in the court of common pleas of the county of his residence.

60 OS(2d) 13, 396 NE(2d) 743 (1979), Smith v Bd of Trustees of Chester Twp. Under 2506.02, the administrative body from which an appeal is taken has the duty, upon the filing of a praecipe, to prepare and file a complete transcript as defined therein, including the duty to initially pay the cost of preparing the same.

46 OS(2d) 99, 346 NE(2d) 157 (1976), Dvorak v Athens Municipal Civil Service Comm. Where an appeal is taken to the court of common pleas under Ch 2506, the hearing is confined to the transcript of the administrative body, unless one of the conditions specified in 2506.03 appears on the face of the transcript or by affidavit.

44 OS(2d) 73, 337 NE(2d) 777 (1975), Gates Mills Investment Co v Pepper Pike. The availability of a Ch 2506 action to review the denial of a variance sought by the owner of a specific tract of land does not preclude a declaratory judgment action to decide questions regarding the applicability of a zoning ordinance to a particular parcel of land even though the appellant has not applied for a building permit or a variance.

26 OS(2d) 37, 268 NE(2d) 280 (1971), Gold Coast Realty v Cleveland Bd of Zoning Appeals. Where appeal is filed from decision of municipal commissioner of building to municipality's board of zoning appeals, either municipality or its commissioner of building is party adverse to appellant and necessary to appeal, and where such adverse and necessary party appears and participates in such appeal such party remains adverse and necessary in further appeal to court of common pleas under Ch 2506, even though not named as such in appellant's notice of appeal filed therein.

18 OS(2d) 23, 247 NE(2d) 471 (1969), State ex rel Broadway Petroleum Corp v Elyria. Where legislation has specifically provided for review by a city board of zoning appeals of the determination of its building inspector in refusing a building permit, neither the building inspector, the city nor its mayor may attack or avoid a decision of that board in judicial proceedings, except as authorized by legislation to do so.

15 OS(2d) 177, 239 NE(2d) 26 (1968), Thomas v Webber. Except to the extent they may conflict with Ch 2506, 2505.04 and 2505.05 apply to the perfection of an appeal and the form of a notice of appeal, pursuant to Ch 2506, from the decision of an agency of a political subdivision.

7 OS(2d) 85, 218 NE(2d) 428 (1966), State ex rel Sibarco Corp v Berea. Where a zoning ordinance is unconstitutional to the extent that it is applied to prohibit a proposed use of certain property, and where a building commissioner denies an application for a building permit because that proposed use of that property is prohibited by that zoning ordinance, and the owner of the property duly exhausts his administrative remedies by an unsuccessful appeal to the board of zoning appeals, an appeal to the common pleas court pursuant to Ch 2506 from the final order of the board of zoning appeals will provide the owner of the property with a plain and adequate remedy to prevent the unconstitu-

tional application of the zoning ordinance as a basis for refusing the building permit.

14 App(3d) 124, 14 OBR 139, 470 NE(2d) 224 (Summit 1984), Roseman v Reminderville. Once jurisdiction has been questioned for failure to properly perfect an appeal under RC Ch 2506, the trial court must examine the record and other necessary evidence to determine whether the action was commenced properly; in such a case, the moving party must meet the burden of proving the deficiency which would divest the court of jurisdiction over the appeal.

14 App(3d) 124, 14 OBR 139, 470 NE(2d) 224 (Summit 1984), Roseman v Reminderville. The provision by Civ R 52 for the making of separate findings of fact and conclusions of law is inapplicable to an appeal brought under RC Ch 2506; in the case of such an appeal, the trial court is only authorized to determine whether the order appealed from is unconstitutional, illegal, arbitrary, capricious, unreasonable, or unsupported by the preponderance of substantial, reliable, and probative evidence on the whole record.

4 App(3d) 213, 4 OBR 318, 447 NE(2d) 765 (Franklin 1982), Franklin Township v Marble Cliff. In an appeal pursuant to RC Ch 2506, where a transcript of administrative hearings is filed which contains gaps and omissions, the judgment of the court of common pleas predicated thereon will not be disturbed unless the complaining parties can demonstrate that there is a reasonable likelihood that the outcome would have been different had they been permitted to introduce additional evidence.

53 App(2d) 183, 372 NE(2d) 1360 (1976), Tolson v Oregon. A municipal ordinance approving the recommendation of the assessment equalization board as to the amount to be assessed against a landowner is a final appealable order although the municipal council has not yet adopted an ordinance determining that it shall proceed with the project and although the total cost of the improvement is subject to revision.

44 App(2d) 325, 338 NE(2d) 547 (1975), SMC, Inc v Laudi. While a municipal board of zoning appeals is without jurisdiction to hear or decide the constitutionality of zoning ordinances, a court of common pleas does sustain such jurisdiction in an appeal from a board of zoning appeals, and upon such appeal the issue of the constitutionality of zoning restrictions must be tried de novo by the court, so that either party may request, or the court on its own motion may require, the presentation of evidence in addition to that presented to the board of zoning appeals.

44 App(2d) 113, 335 NE(2d) 872 (1975), Sofer v Cincinnati Metropolitan Housing Authority. Where a trial court orders a dismissal in an appeal from a decision of an administrative agency without having before it a transcript of proceedings, which the agency has been directed by the court to submit, its action fails to comply with the requirements of 2506.02.

40 App(2d) 166, 318 NE(2d) 433 (1973), State ex rel Dahmen v Youngstown. The time for perfecting an appeal pursuant to Ch 2506 is determined by 2505.07 and is ten days after entry of the decision of the board or officer from which the appeal is taken.

33 App(2d) 177, 294 NE(2d) 230 (1972), In re Locke. The time for perfecting an appeal pursuant to Ch 2506 is controlled by 2505.07 and is ten days after entry of the decision of the commission.

33 App(2d) 177, 294 NE(2d) 230 (1972), In re Locke. The review granted pursuant to Ch 2506 is not the equivalent of a de novo review granted under the law and fact appeal set forth in 143.27.

25 App(2d) 125, 267 NE(2d) 595 (1971), Lakewood Homes, Inc v Lima Bd of Adjustment. In administrative appeal under 2506.01 et seq.,

time for perfecting appeal is determined by 2505.07 and is ten days from entry of decision of board or officer from which appeal is taken.

19 App(2d) 63, 249 NE(2d) 921 (1969), Chester Township Bd of Trustees v Kline. Where the records of a township board of zoning appeals do not clearly indicate what constitutes the "matter for review" and when it was "entered" in its records, a reviewing court has jurisdiction to entertain the matter for review, if the notice of appeal is filed within ten days after the applicant receives the decision of the board.

119 App 249, 188 NE(2d) 185 (1963), Floyd Stamps Rambler, Inc v Euclid Planning and Zoning Comm. Where a municipal ordinance provides that the action of such municipality's planning and zoning commission in granting or refusing permits as a variance from the zoning ordinance is always "subject to confirmation or approval" of such municipality's council, the municipal council acts, in such instances, as a quasi-judicial body performing an administrative function, and an appeal to the courts in a zoning matter in such case may be taken only from a decision of such council.

118 App 71, 193 NE(2d) 396 (1962), Minarik v Board of Review. An appeal from the state personnel board of review will be dismissed where, in the papers forwarded by such board, there is no copy of any notice of appeal, no certificate or statement that all the original papers were forwarded, and no certificate authenticating the transcript or record of testimony.

115 App 472, 180 NE(2d) 27 (1962), Shaker Coventry Corp v Shaker Heights Bd of Zoning Appeals. The proper method to test the validity of a zoning ordinance and for a judicial review of the final orders of administrative boards of municipalities is by way of appeal under the procedure set forth in Ch 2506, and the refusal of a zoning board of appeals to accept jurisdiction, where a building commissioner could not issue a building permit because of conflict with an ordinance, does not result in a deprivation of such right to appeal.

115 App 96, 184 NE(2d) 538 (1961), Maughan v Davis Investment Co. It is not error for a common pleas court to dismiss an attempted appeal from a decision of a municipal board of zoning adjustment where no notice of appeal was filed with such board or its duly appointed clerk.

111 App 449, 173 NE(2d) 168 (1960), Fleischmann v Medina Supply Co. Where, in an appeal to the court of common pleas from an administrative agency of a local political subdivision the transcript of the proceeding furnished the court by the agency does not contain all the evidence submitted to it on the trial of the issues before the agency, and when such transcript does not contain the conclusions of fact supporting the decision appeal to the court, the court is required to hear such additional evidence as may be introduced by either party in the proceeding on appeal; which is one on questions of law, and upon the conclusion of the hearing on appeal, the court must enter its judgment on the record as thus created.

No. 8609 (2d Dist Ct App, Montgomery, 7-26-84), Blake v Council of Kettering. A city council resolution granting a variance and conditional use permit on appeal from a board of zoning appeals decision need not set forth formal findings of fact; it is sufficient that the decision be made upon the basis of compliance with statutory criteria, and this may be shown by the nature of the evidence received by the council.

24 Misc 10, 263 NE(2d) 325 (1970), Rosenberg v Cleveland Bd of Building Standards. Law of Ohio makes no provision whereby common pleas court can remand appeal to administrative office or body appealed from for further proceedings, other than to enter an order consistent with the finding and opinion of court.

23 Misc 211, 258 NE(2d) 470 (1970), Lakewood Homes, Inc v Lima Bd of Adjustment; modified by 25 App(2d) 125, 267 NE(2d) 595 (1971). Time for perfecting an appeal from an administrative agency of a political subdivision, as prescribed by 2505.07, does not commence until record of action to be appealed is entered in writing in office of such agency.

22 Misc 54, 256 NE(2d) 631 (1970), Levitt v Cleveland. When an appeal has been filed from an order of an officer to an administrative agency, and from that agency to the court of common pleas and it is clear that the purported appeals are each a sham, filed solely for the purpose of delaying the execution of the administrative order, the court should dismiss the appeal and properly order the costs of the transcripts taxed as costs.

22 Misc 54, 256 NE(2d) 631 (1970), Levitt v Cleveland. An administrative appeal under an ordinance which requires that it be made by a "person aggrieved" is not properly filed where signed only by the owner's attorney and not accompanied by a letter of authorization from the owner.

22 Misc 54, 256 NE(2d) 631 (1970), Levitt v Cleveland. An ordinance requiring that an administrative appeal be filed with a statement of the grounds thereof is reasonable, and the failure of the notice of appeal to state the facts upon which it is contended that the officer's ruling should be reversed is sufficient basis to refuse to take testimony relating to such an appeal.

22 Misc 54, 256 NE(2d) 631 (1970), Levitt v Cleveland. Refusal of an administrative agency to grant a continuance of a hearing on the grounds of alleged conflict with an appearance of an attorney in a court is not an abuse of discretion where it is not shown that there was a direct conflict in the time of the appearances.

17 Misc 193, 243 NE(2d) 777 (1969), Grimes v Cleveland. Ch 2506 is supplemental to the requirements of Ch 2505 for appeal to the common pleas court from final orders of administrative agencies.

419 US 565, 95 SCt 729, 42 LE(2d) 725 (1975), Goss v Lopez. Student is entitled to due process in connection with a suspension of up to ten days to the extent of being entitled to oral or written notice of the charges against him and if he denies the charges an explanation of the evidence the authorities have and an opportunity to present his version, and such notice should precede student's removal from school except where his presence endangers persons or property or threatens disruption of the academic process.

339 FSupp 1194 (1972), Burks v Perk; reversed by 470 F(2d) 163 (1972). In action by members of city civil service commission against the mayor challenging the validity of proceedings for their removal, the federal courts will apply the doctrine of abstention to allow the Ohio courts to determine the validity of the city charter provisions providing therefor, but the state removal proceedings will be stayed until such determination is made by the state court.

1964 OAG 810. A board of township trustees has no authority to employ special counsel to appeal a decision of a township board of zoning appeals unless the township is a party to the proceeding before the township board of zoning appeals.

1963 OAG 102. During the pendency of appeals prosecuted under 2506.01 to 2506.04 and 2505.01 to 2505.45, county officials are bound by the doctrine of "lis pendens" to maintain the status quo.

2506.02 Filing of transcript

Within thirty days after filing the notice of appeal, the officer or body from which the appeal is taken shall, upon the filing of a precipe, prepare and file in the court to which the appeal is taken, a complete transcript of all the original papers, testimony and evidence offered, heard and taken into consideration in issuing the order appealed from. The costs of such transcript shall be taxed as a part of the costs of the appeal.

HISTORY: 127 v 963, eff. 9-16-57

CROSS REFERENCES

See Whiteside, Ohio Appellate Practice, Text 25.05 to 25.07; Forms 11.04, 11.583
See Baldwin's Ohio School Law, Text 49.07, 59.06
See Gotherman & Babbit, Ohio Municipal Law, Text 45.28; Forms 33.24 to 33.26

OJur 2d: 58, Zoning § 180

---

67 OS(2d) 363, 423 NE(2d) 1099 (1981), State ex rel Crockett v Robinson. Relator reinstated to position with city government on the ground that the civil service commission failed to timely file its record with the court of common pleas as mandated by 119.12 is entitled to mandamus ordering payment of back pay, including across-the-board salary increases, and interest, but not attorneys' fees nor credit for vacation, holiday, or sick leave.

60 OS(2d) 13, 396 NE(2d) 743 (1979), Smith v Bd of Trustees of Chester Twp. Under 2506.02, the administrative body from which an appeal is taken has the duty, upon the filing of a praecipe, to prepare and file a complete transcript as defined therein, including the duty to initially pay the cost of preparing the same.

4 App(3d) 213, 4 OBR 318, 447 NE(2d) 765 (Franklin 1982), Franklin Township v Marble Cliff. In an appeal pursuant to RC Ch 2506, where a transcript of administrative hearings is filed which contains gaps and omissions, the judgment of the court of common pleas predicated thereon will not be disturbed unless the complaining parties can demonstrate that there is a reasonable likelihood that the outcome would have been different had they been permitted to introduce additional evidence.

61 App(2d) 14, 399 NE(2d) 92 (1978), Zurow v Cleveland. When an administrative agency, such as a board of zoning appeals, acts in a quasi-judicial capacity in hearing an appeal from a denial of a building permit by a building commissioner it must administer oaths to witnesses. The failure to administer oaths is error; if timely objection is not made this error is waived throughout the entire proceedings, including the appellate level.

44 App(2d) 113, 335 NE(2d) 872 (1975), Sofer v Cincinnati Metropolitan Housing Authority. Where a trial court orders a dismissal in an appeal from a decision of an administrative agency without having before it a transcript of proceedings, which the agency has been directed by the court to submit, its action fails to comply with the requirements of 2506.02.

1 App(2d) 84, 203 NE(2d) 859 (1963), Grant v Washington Twp. Where no transcript has been filed as provided in Ch 2506, the common pleas court has no basis or authority upon which to permit the introduction of evidence and no authority to proceed with the appeal.

111 App 449, 173 NE(2d) 168 (1960), Fleischmann v Medina Supply Co. Where, in an appeal to the court of common pleas from an administrative agency of a local political subdivision the transcript of the proceeding furnished the court by the agency does not contain all the evidence submitted to it on the trial of the issues before the agency, and when such transcript does not contain the conclusions of fact supporting the decision appealed to the court, the court is required to hear such additional evidence as may be introduced by either party in the proceeding on appeal; which is one on questions of law, and upon the conclusion of the hearing on appeal, the court must enter its judgment on the record as thus created.

No. CA-2991 (5th Dist Ct App, Licking, 2-13-84), Thomas v Lima Twp Bd of Zoning Appeals. Where a board of zoning appeals failed to file findings of fact and conclusions of law in upholding a denial of a zoning certificate, any procedural defect was cured when the common pleas court conducted an evidentiary hearing.

No. 82-C-44 (7th Dist Ct App, Columbiana, 4-26-83), Van Fossen v Beaver Local School District Bd of Ed. Trial court erred in considering a notice of appeal filed by a suspended employee of a board of education, where the transcript filed with the trial court by the employee consisted of miscellaneous papers which were neither certified nor verified.

No. 82 CA 35 (7th Dist Ct App, Mahoning, 3-23-83), Kenney v South Range Local School District Bd of Ed. Where a suspended school bus driver appeals the decision of a hearing by the school board, an affidavit filed by the board treasurer does not constitute a transcript of the hearing, where such affidavit consists simply of a narrative of the proceedings at the hearing and it cannot be ascertained whether testimony given at the hearing was given by sworn witnesses.

49 Misc 36, 360 NE(2d) 761 (CP Montgomery 1976), In re Sergent. When a board of education fails to conduct a full hearing complete with transcript in terminating a nonteaching employee's contract, it is the same as if that board did nothing, and its judgment is void ab initio.

24 Misc 10, 263 NE(2d) 325 (1970), Rosenberg v Cleveland Bd of Building Standards. Since, in matters of appeal from orders of administrative officers and agencies of any political subdivision of the state, 2506.03 confines court to the transcript as filed pursuant to 2506.02, motion for judgment on the transcript made by appellant to trial court on appeal from a final order of board of building standards and building appeals of city of Cleveland is unnecessary and redundant.

22 Misc 54, 256 NE(2d) 631 (1970), Levitt v Cleveland. When an appeal has been filed from an order of an officer to an administrative agency, and from that agency to the court of common pleas and it is clear that the purported appeals are each a sham, filed solely for the purpose of delaying the execution of the administrative order, the court should dismiss the appeal and properly order the costs of the transcripts taxed as costs.

2506.03 Hearing of appeal

The hearing of such appeal shall proceed as in the trial of a civil action but the court shall be confined to the transcript as filed pursuant to section 2506.02 of the Revised Code unless it appears on the face of said transcript or by affidavit filed by the appellant that:

(A) The transcript does not contain a report of all evidence admitted or proffered by the appellant.

(B) The appellant was not permitted to appear and be heard in person or by his attorney in opposition to the order appealed from:

(1) To present his position, arguments and contentions;

(2) To offer and examine witnesses and present evidence in support thereof;

(3) To cross-examine witnesses purporting to refute his position, arguments and contentions;

(4) To offer evidence to refute evidence and testimony offered in opposition to his position, arguments and contentions;

(5) To proffer any such evidence into the record, if the admission thereof is denied by the officer or body appealed from.

(C) The testimony adduced was not given under oath.

(D) The appellant was unable to present evidence by reason of a lack of the power of subpoena by the officer or body appealed from or the refusal, after request, of such officer or body to afford the appellant opportunity to use the power of subpoena when possessed by the officer or body.

(E) The officer or body failed to file with the transcript, conclusions of fact supporting the order, adjudication or decision appealed from; in which case, the court shall hear the appeal upon the transcript and such additional evidence as may be introduced by any party. At the hearing, any party may call as if on cross-examination, any witness who previously gave testimony in opposition to such party.

HISTORY: 127 v 963, eff. 9-16-57

CROSS REFERENCES

See Baldwin's Ohio Township Law, Text 59.27

See Whiteside, Ohio Appellate Practice, Text 25.06, 25.07; Forms 11.011

See Baldwin's Ohio School Law, Text 59.06

See Gotherman & Babbit, Ohio Municipal Law, Text 45.28; Forms 33.26 to 33.28

OJur 2d: 58, Zoning § 180

---

63 OS(2d) 26, 406 NE(2d) 1095 (1980), Noernberg v Brook Park. A court of common pleas has no jurisdiction over the indefinite suspension of a city civil service employee when the employee fails to file an available administrative appeal, even though the legal basis for the suspension is subsequently nullified.

58 OS(2d) 202, 389 NE(2d) 1113 (1979), Dudukovich v Lorain Metropolitan Housing Authority. In an appeal under Ch 2506 the court of common pleas must weigh the evidence in the record, and whatever additional evidence may be admitted pursuant to 2506.03, to determine whether there exists a preponderance of reliable, probative and substantial evidence to support the agency decision.

46 OS(2d) 99, 346 NE(2d) 157 (1976), Dvorak v Athens Municipal Civil Service Comm. Where an appeal is taken to the court of common pleas under Ch 2506, the hearing is confined to the transcript of the administrative body, unless one of the conditions specified in 2506.03 appears on the face of the transcript or by affidavit.

46 OS(2d) 99, 346 NE(2d) 157 (1976), Dvorak v Athens Municipal Civil Service Comm. Where an affidavit is filed pursuant to 2506.03, in a Ch 2506 appeal, the reviewing court must consider its content in its disposition of the case.

38 OS(2d) 298, 313 NE(2d) 400 (1974), C. Miller Chevrolet, Inc v Willoughby Hills. In an appeal under Ch 2506 from the denial of an application for a variance by a zoning board of appeals, there is a

presumption that the board's determination is valid, and the burden of showing invalidity of the board's determination rests on the party contesting that determination.

27 OS(2d) 1, 271 NE(2d) 831 (1971), Capello v Mayfield Heights. In an appeal from a ruling of an administrative board, a court of common pleas may not base its affirmance solely upon the transcript of the proceedings before the board, where that transcript does not contain reliable and probative evidence to support the board's ruling.

15 OS(2d) 177, 239 NE(2d) 26 (1968), Thomas v Webber. A person who is an elector and freeholder of an area of a township sought to be incorporated and who is designated to act as agent for those who sign a petition for incorporation of that area, has general authority to act on behalf of all who sign such petition to accomplish the purpose sought by their petition, including authority to act for them on appeal from any decision of the township trustees approving their petition or any court decision reversing such decision of the township trustees.

1 OS(2d) 100, 205 NE(2d) 14 (1965), State ex rel Weaver v Faust. The writ of prohibition will not issue at the instance of a party who alleges irregularities in the proceedings of an administrative board and anticipates that such a board will deprive him of procedural and substantive rights.

168 OS 113, 151 NE(2d) 533 (1958), Mentor Lagoons, Inc v Mentor Twp Zoning Bd. In order to reverse a decision of a township board of zoning appeals in refusing to authorize a variance from the terms of a zoning resolution, it is not necessary for the common pleas court to find that the board abused its discretion but it is sufficient if that court finds that the decision of the board in refusing to authorize the requested variance represents an unreasonable exercise of that discretion.

9 App(3d) 224, 9 OBR 395, 459 NE(2d) 566 (Cuyahoga 1983), Resek v Seven Hills. Members of a police or fire department and police and fire chiefs may use either of two different routes of appeal to the court of common pleas from a municipal civil service commission decision ordering demotion, suspension, or removal from office: (1) an appeal on questions of law and fact brought under RC 124.34 and governed by RC Ch 2505 allows the court to hear additional evidence, and to replace the judgment of the commission with its own; (2) an appeal brought pursuant to RC Ch 2506 allows additional evidence only in statutorily enumerated circumstances, and due deference must be given to the administrative determination of evidentiary questions.

4 App(3d) 213, 4 OBR 318, 447 NE(2d) 765 (Franklin 1982), Franklin Township v Marble Cliff. In an appeal pursuant to RC Ch 2506, where a transcript of administrative hearings is filed which contains gaps and omissions, the judgment of the court of common pleas predicated thereon will not be disturbed unless the complaining parties can demonstrate that there is a reasonable likelihood that the outcome would have been different had they been permitted to introduce additional evidence.

61 App(2d) 14, 399 NE(2d) 92 (1978), Zurow v Cleveland. When an administrative agency, such as a board of zoning appeals, acts in a quasi-judicial capacity in hearing an appeal from a denial of a building permit by a building commissioner it must administer oaths to witnesses. The failure to administer oaths is error; if timely objection is not made this error is waived throughout the entire proceedings, including the appellate level.

44 App(2d) 325, 338 NE(2d) 547 (1975), SMC, Inc v Laudi. While a municipal board of zoning appeals is without jurisdiction to hear or decide the constitutionality of zoning ordinances, a court of common pleas does sustain such jurisdiction in an appeal from a board of zoning appeals, and upon such appeal the issue of the constitutionality of zoning

restrictions must be tried de novo by the court, so that either party may request, or the court on its own motion may require, the presentation of evidence in addition to that presented to the board of zoning appeals.

34 App(2d) 168, 296 NE(2d) 842 (1973), Schoell v Sheboy. In an appeal under Ch 2506 to the common pleas court, the court can consider only the evidence presented in the transcript of the administrative hearing, unless it is manifest on the face of the transcript, or by affidavit filed with the court alleging that the transcript is deficient in one or more of the respects enumerated in 2506.03(A) to (E).

33 App(2d) 94, 292 NE(2d) 642 (1972), Libis v Akron Bd of Zoning Appeals. No provision is made in 2506.03 for interrogation, as witnesses, of the members of the administrative body that made the ruling being appealed.

33 App(2d) 94, 292 NE(2d) 642 (1972), Libis v Akron Bd of Zoning Appeals. There is no statutory or procedural rule which prevents a member of the administrative body from stating for the record, at the end of that hearing on which he is sitting, the reasons by which he arrived at his conclusions.

31 App(2d) 199, 287 NE(2d) 814 (1972), 12701 Shaker Blvd Co v Cleveland. Mere filing of an affidavit does not automatically quicken the statutory right to offer additional testimony in defense of one's property on appeal from a ruling of the board of zoning appeals to the court of common pleas, nor does it compel that court to take additional evidence, unless the record supports some one of the deficiencies enumerated in 2506.03.

18 App(2d) 188, 247 NE(2d) 789 (1969), Williamson v Trustees of Chester Twp. 2506.03 does not provide for a trial de novo in the common pleas court in an appeal thereto from a township board of zoning appeals.

1 App(2d) 84, 203 NE(2d) 859 (1963), Grant v Washington Twp. In an appeal to the common pleas court under Ch 2506, the hearing is confined to the transcript of the administrative body, unless the transcript shows one of the specified deficiencies listed in 2506.03.

1 App(2d) 84, 203 NE(2d) 859 (1963), Grant v Washington Twp. Where no transcript has been filed as provided in Ch 2506, the common pleas court has no basis or authority upon which to permit the introduction of evidence and no authority to proceed with the appeal.

117 App 55, 189 NE(2d) 651 (1962), In re Appeal of Manning. In an appeal from a decision of a board of zoning appeals to the court of common pleas, the court of common pleas has no power to determine the case de novo, but is authorized only to determine the legal justification of the board's decision—not only by what evidence was before the board, but also by supplemental evidence before the court if the latter is permitted by 2506.03; and the court may then, "consistent with its findings, ... affirm, reverse, vacate, or modify the order, adjudication or decision" from which the appeal was taken.

No. 48396 (8th Dist Ct App, Cuyahoga, 12-27-84), McCreery v Brecksville Bd of Zoning Appeals. Where an appeal from a denial of a variance by a board of zoning appeals raises constitutional issues, a trial court errs in not granting a hearing at which evidence may be presented on those issues.

No. CA-2991 (5th Dist Ct App, Licking, 2-13-84), Thomas v Lima Twp Bd of Zoning Appeals. Where a board of zoning appeals failed to file findings of fact and conclusions of law in upholding a denial of a zoning certificate, any procedural defect was cured when the common pleas court conducted an evidentiary hearing.

No. 82-C-44 (7th Dist Ct App, Columbiana, 4-26-83), Van Fossen v Beaver Local School District Bd of Ed. Trial court erred in considering a notice of appeal filed by a suspended employee of a board of education, where the transcript filed with the trial court by the employee consisted of miscellaneous papers which were neither certified nor verified.

No. 10285 (9th Dist Ct App, Summit, 1-27-82), Concerned Taxpayers of Stow v Stow. Failure to timely object to testimony not given under oath at planning committee and city council meetings waives such error and is not grounds under 2506.03 for the presentation of extrinsic evidence in a zoning dispute.

49 Misc 36, 360 NE(2d) 761 (CP Montgomery 1976), In re Sergent. When a board of education fails to conduct a full hearing complete with transcript in terminating a nonteaching employee's contract, it is the same as if that board did nothing, and its judgment is void ab initio.

25 Misc 156, 262 NE(2d) 586 (1970), Cortner v National Cash Register Co. In appeal from administrative agency to common pleas court, court may not consider matters outside transcript of hearing below, in absence of statutory authority.

24 Misc 10, 263 NE(2d) 325 (1970), Rosenberg v Cleveland Bd of Building Standards. Since, in matters of appeal from orders of administrative officers and agencies of any political subdivision of the state, 2506.03 confines court to the transcript as filed pursuant to 2506.02, motion for judgment on the transcript made by appellant to trial court on appeal from a final order of board of building standards and building appeals of city of Cleveland is unnecessary and redundant.

22 Misc 54, 256 NE(2d) 631 (1970), Levitt v Cleveland. Right of a party to administrative proceeding to have testimony of witnesses to be taken under oath is waived by going forward without objection.

15 Misc 17, 238 NE(2d) 578 (1968), Box v Cleveland. An appeal from the action of a municipal board must be decided upon the basis of evidence in the record certified to the common pleas court, which must be shown to have been by sworn testimony.

95 Abs 86, 200 NE(2d) 366 (1964), In re Appeal of Sun Oil Co. Summary judgment is not available on appeal to the common pleas court from an order of township trustees denying a rezoning application.

89 Abs 140, 185 NE(2d) 76 (1959), Broad-Miami Co v Bd of Zoning Appeals. Failure of a board of zoning adjustment to file with the transcript "conclusions of fact supporting the order," as referred to in paragraph (E) of 2506.03 affords another basis for the taking of additional testimony before the court that such conclusions of fact, if filed, might be considered by the court, and thus throw light on the question of the "unreasonableness" of the order.

EBR 73-5, Mahoning Landfill, Inc v Board of Health. A hearing by a local board of health for action under 3734.04, 3734.05, and 3734.09 is invalid if it fails to provide notice conforming to 119.06 and 119.07, and fails to conform procedurally with 119.10, which provisions are similar to those of 2506.03, governing administrative proceedings of units of local government.

2506.04 Finding and order of court

The court may find that the order, adjudication or decision is unconstitutional, illegal, arbitrary, capricious, unreasonable, or unsupported by the preponderance of substantial, reliable and probative evidence on the whole record. Consistent with its findings, the court may affirm, reverse, vacate, or modify the order, adjudication or decision, or remand the cause to the officer or body appealed from with instructions to enter an order consistent with the findings or opinion of the court. The judgment of the court may be appealed by any party on questions of law pursuant to sections 2505.01 to 2505.45, inclusive, of the Revised Code.

HISTORY: 127 v 963, eff. 9-16-57

CROSS REFERENCES

See Whiteside, Ohio Appellate Practice, Text 25.07 to 25.09; Forms 11.02, 11.03

See Gotherman & Babbit, Ohio Municipal Law, Text 37.58; Forms 33.27, 33.28

OJur 2d: 58, Zoning § 179

---

2 OS(3d) 108, 2 OBR 658, 443 NE(2d) 166 (1982), State ex rel Bd of Trustees of Springfield Twp v Davis. Absent an injunction or order staying further action, "the adoption by the city council of an ordinance accepting annexation renders moot a case seeking to enjoin annexation."

66 OS(2d) 93, 420 NE(2d) 103 (1981), Brown v Cleveland. Refusal to grant variance to permit non-conforming gasoline station to add grocery lines, a permitted use, was not unreasonable; where the reasonableness of a zoning regulation is fairly debatable, it will be upheld.

58 OS(2d) 202, 389 NE(2d) 1113 (1979), Dudukovich v Lorain Metropolitan Housing Authority. In an appeal under Ch 2506 the court of common pleas must weigh the evidence in the record, and whatever additional evidence may be admitted pursuant to 2506.03, to determine whether there exists a preponderance of reliable, probative and substantial evidence to support the agency decision.

42 OS(2d) 368, 328 NE(2d) 808 (1975), Cincinnati Bell, Inc v Glendale. The test which courts of common pleas apply when hearing appeals pursuant to Ch 2506 is not whether any legal justification exists for a holding of the board of zoning appeals, but rather whether the ordinance, in proscribing a landowner's proposed use of his land, bears a reasonable relationship to the public health, safety, welfare, or morals.

39 OS(2d) 36, 313 NE(2d) 280 (1974), Superior Uptown, Inc v Cleveland. A cause of action for money damages cannot be maintained against a municipality for losses sustained as the result of the adoption of a rezoning ordinance which is subsequently declared invalid.

38 OS(2d) 298, 313 NE(2d) 400 (1974), C. Miller Chevrolet, Inc v Willoughby Hills. In an appeal under Ch 2506 from the denial of an application for a variance by a zoning board of appeals, there is a presumption that the board's determination is valid, and the burden of showing invalidity of the board's determination rests on the party contesting that determination.

26 OS(2d) 37, 268 NE(2d) 280 (1971), Gold Coast Realty, Inc v Cleveland Bd of Zoning Appeals. Where appeal is filed from decision of municipal commissioner of building to municipality's board of zoning appeals, either municipality or its commissioner of building is party adverse to appellant and necessary to appeal, and where such adverse and necessary party appears and participates in such appeal such party remains adverse and necessary in further appeal to court of common pleas under Ch 2506, even though not named as such in appellant's notice of appeal filed therein.

15 OS(2d) 177, 239 NE(2d) 26 (1968), Thomas v Webber. A person who is a freeholder and elector of territory sought to be incorporated by a petition filed pursuant to 707.15 and who has signed such petition becomes a party to an appeal to the common pleas court pursuant to Ch 2506 from an order of the township trustees approving such petition, whether or not such person has participated in the proceedings before

the common pleas court; and, as such a party, he may appeal to the court of appeals from a judgment of the common pleas court reversing the order of the township trustees.

7 OS(2d) 32, 218 NE(2d) 179 (1966), Arcaro Brothers Builders, Inc v North College Hill Zoning Bd of Appeals. Where chairman of zoning board of appeals refused permission to have any witnesses sworn, and allowed unidentified statements to be recorded in the transcript, the record in the appeal contained no evidence and decision of board was not supported by preponderance thereof.

175 OS 361, 194 NE(2d) 850 (1963), State ex rel Ruggiero v Common Pleas Court of Cuyahoga County. Procedendo will not lie where an adequate remedy by appeal is available.

14 App(3d) 124, 14 OBR 139, 470 NE(2d) 224 (Summit 1984), Roseman v Reminderville. The provision by Civ R 52 for the making of separate findings of fact and conclusions of law is inapplicable to an appeal brought under RC Ch 2506; in the case of such an appeal, the trial court is only authorized to determine whether the order appealed from is unconstitutional, illegal, arbitrary, capricious, unreasonable, or unsupported by the preponderance of substantial, reliable, and probative evidence on the whole record.

39 App(2d) 177, 317 NE(2d) 65 (1973), Cole v Marion Township Bd of Zoning Appeals. When upon the evidence a change in the purposes set forth in an application for a variance occurs while an appeal is pending in a common pleas court from a decision of a board of township zoning appeals denying such variance and remand to the board of zoning appeals would not result in the exercise of a discretion but would merely result in denial of the application as a matter of law, and where the common pleas court would on remand be required, without exercising any discretion and as a matter of law, to affirm the decision of the board of zoning appeals denying the application, the court of appeals will not remand the cause either to the board of zoning appeals or to the common pleas court but will render the judgment the common pleas court should have rendered affirming the decision of the board denying the application.

33 App(2d) 177, 294 NE(2d) 230 (1972), In re Locke. The review granted pursuant to Ch 2506 is not the equivalent of a de novo review granted under the law and fact appeal set forth in 143.27.

27 App(2d) 204, 273 NE(2d) 800 (1971), Shelby Realty, Inc v Springdale. Court of common pleas has no authority to order that a "variance" be made to a zoning ordinance.

19 App(2d) 63, 249 NE(2d) 921 (1969), Chester Township Bd of Trustees v Kline. Where the records of a township board of zoning appeals do not clearly indicate what constitutes the "matter for review" and when it was "entered" in its records, a reviewing court has jurisdiction to entertain the matter for review, if the notice of appeal is filed within ten days after the applicant receives the decision of the board.

18 App(2d) 188, 247 NE(2d) 789 (1969), Williamson v Trustees of Chester Twp. A common pleas court does not have authority, in an appeal from a township board of zoning appeals, to remand the cause to such board with instructions that it allow a variance on certain conditions.

119 App 15, 196 NE(2d) 333 (1963), In re Appeal of McDonald. A decision of a board of zoning appeals as to whether to grant a zoning variance is made in a judicial capacity and may be appealed on the grounds of reasonableness alone.

117 App 55, 189 NE(2d) 651 (1962), In re Appeal of Manning. In an appeal from a decision of a board of zoning appeals to the court of common pleas, the court of common pleas has no power to determine the

case de novo, but is authorized only to determine the legal justification of the board's decision—not only by what evidence was before the board, but also by supplemental evidence before the court if the latter is permitted by 2506.03; and the court may then, "consistent with its findings,... affirm, reverse, vacate, or modify the order, adjudication or decision" from which the appeal was taken.

111 App 449, 173 NE(2d) 168 (1960), Fleischmann v Medina Supply Co. Where, in an appeal to the court of common pleas from an administrative agency of a local political subdivision the transcript of the proceeding furnished the court by the agency does not contain all the evidence submitted to it on the trial of the issues before the agency, and when such transcript does not contain the conclusions of fact supporting the decision appealed to the court, the court is required to hear such additional evidence as may be introduced by either party in the proceeding on appeal; which is one on questions of law, and upon the conclusion of the hearing on appeal, the court must enter its judgment on the record as thus created.

No. C-830813 (1st Dist Ct App, Hamilton, 8-15-84), Gabbard v Norwood Bd of Appeals. The trial court's failure to state in so many words that the decision of a municipal board of zoning appeals was supported by a preponderance of the evidence is insignificant when the court's decision makes clear that the standard was applied.

No. CA83-04-033 (12th Dist Ct App, Clermont, 7-30-84), Hiett v Goshen Twp Bd of Trustees. In an appeal to a common pleas court from the dismissal of a township police chief by the township board of trustees, if the court finds that only one of several charges against the chief is supported by the record, it has the authority to modify the penalty imposed by the board to a six-month suspension.

No. 10763 (9th Dist Ct App, Summit, 2-2-83), In re Annexation of 201.2 Acres of Land in Bath Twp to the City of Akron. Since RC 2506.04 provides that the judgment of a court may be appealed by any party, it is presumed that a nonaggrieved board of township trustees is a proper party to a RC 2506.01 appeal.

No. 10763 (9th Dist Ct App, Summit, 2-2-83), In re Annexation of 201.2 Acres of Land in Bath Twp to the City of Akron. RC 709.07 may not be used as a substitute for a RC 2506.04 appeal from a decision of the common pleas court.

56 Misc 27, 382 NE(2d) 1200 (CP, Mahoning 1976), Wells v Horsley. A decision of the court of claims upon the merits of an action is a final judgment and conclusively determines the rights, questions of law and the facts in issue between the parties to the dispute and is a bar to a future action between the same parties on those issues.

24 Misc 10, 263 NE(2d) 325 (1970), Rosenberg v Cleveland Bd of Building Standards. The general rule that a court will not substitute its judgment for that of an administrative agency when its finding and determination involves only questions of ministerial or administrative character is applicable to rule of the board of building standards and building appeals requiring one not the owner of record of a building in question to have a letter of authorization from owner in order to appeal to board.

23 Misc 211, 258 NE(2d) 470 (1970), Lakewood Homes, Inc v Lima Bd of Adjustment; modified by 25 App(2d) 125, 267 NE(2d) 595 (1971). On appeal from administrative agency of political subdivision, court of common pleas is not limited to mere curbing of extreme actions, positively illegal ones, or abuses of discretion, but may correct, revise, or reverse action appealed from on any reasonable ground.

14 Misc 149, 237 NE(2d) 644 (1965), Beerman v Kettering. In an appeal to common pleas court pursuant to 2506.04 the whole record,

including any supplemental evidence received by the court, must be considered in determining whether the decision of a board is unreasonable or unsupported by the preponderance of substantial, reliable and probative evidence. (See also Beerman v Kettering, 120 App 309, 201 NE(2d) 887 (1963).)

95 Abs 28, 197 NE(2d) 828 (1964), Ruggiero v Brooklyn Bd of Zoning Appeals. A common pleas court is without authority to remand a case, submitted to it on appeal from an order of an administrative agency, back to such agency for further proceedings.

89 Abs 140, 185 NE(2d) 76 (1959), Broad-Miami Co v Columbus Bd of Zoning Adjustment. The judicial test or criterion on an appeal from a decision of a municipal board of zoning adjustment is whether the order in question was unreasonable.

APPENDICES

A. Table of Cases
B. Table of Laws and Rules Construed
C. Bibliography

Appendix A
Table of Cases

This table is arranged alphabetically letter-by-letter; i.e., each group of words comprising a case name is considered as a continuous series of letters. For example, *Harrison; State v* precedes *Harris; United States v.*

For citation and subsequent case history, consult the Text Section(s) listed.

Casename	Text Section(s)
A	
A. Dicillo & Sons, Inc v Chester Zoning Bd of Appeals	3.08
Administrator, Bureau of Employment Services; Powell v	7.04
Administrator, Bureau of Unemployment Compensation; Tatman v	7.04
Akron; Williams v	1.06
Alaska v A.L.I.V.E. Voluntary	1.05
A.L.I.V.E. Voluntary; Alaska v	1.05
American Petroleum Institute v Costle	1.07
Appeal of Peabody Coal Co, In re	3.09
Armstrong v Manzo	1.03
Arvay v Bd of Liquor Control	15.05
Atkinson; State ex rel Cleveland Railway Co v	21.07
Ayres; National Tube Co v	3.09
B	
Barker, State ex rel v Manchin	1.05
Bd of Embalmers & Funeral Directors; State ex rel Homan v	1.07
Bd of Liquor Control; Arvay v	15.05
Bd of Liquor Control; Lakis v	3.11
Bd of Liquor Control; Roxy Musical Bar, Inc v	3.11
Bd of Liquor Control; Silverstein v	3.11
Bd of Liquor Control; Stouffer Corp v	1.06
Bd of Liquor Control; Wittenberg v	3.08
Bd of Review; Bohannon v	7.07
Bd of Review; Hepner v	7.04
Bd of Review; Kilgore v	7.07
Bd of Review; Leach v	7.07
Beck, State ex rel v Hummel	3.08
Belden v Union Central Life Insurance Co	1.03
Blake; State ex rel Wilms v	21.04
Bloch v Glander	3.08
Blue Cross of Northwest Ohio v Superintendent of Insurance	1.07
Board of Tax Appeals v Zangerle	3.06
Bockrath; State ex rel Wuebker v	3.09
Boesch; Home Savings & Loan Assn v	3.01
Bohannon v Board of Review	7.07
Bolin v White	13.04
Bosch, State ex rel v Industrial Comm	21.04
Bozarth; State ex rel Williams v	1.06, 11.03
Brook Park v Cuyahoga County Budget Comm	3.06
Brown; Ohio Boys Town, Inc v	3.02
Brown; State ex rel Federated Department Stores, Inc v	5.02
Brown; State ex rel Newell v	5.01, 5.04
Bryant; State ex rel Jones v	15.05

Casename	Text Section(s)
Buckeye Power, Inc v Whitman	1.06
Bucyrus v Ohio Dept of Health	3.05, 3.06
Burdette, State ex rel v Dayton Walther Corp	21.04
Burger Brewing Co v Liquor Control Comm	1.06, 3.01, 5.03, 9.04
Burt Realty Corp v Columbus	3.11

C

Casename	Text Section(s)
Caldwell; Rankin-Thoman, Inc v	1.06, 3.01, 3.11, 5.05
Campbell v Maynard	11.02
Caramico v Secretary of Housing & Urban Development	1.03
Carpenter; Meneley v	3.05, 3.08
Chemical Foundation; United States v	3.06
Chester Zoning Bd of Appeals; A. Dicillo & Sons, Inc v	3.08
Cincinnati; Cincinnati ex rel Crotty v	11.03
Cincinnati ex rel Crotty v Cincinnati	11.03
Cincinnati, Wilmington & Zanesville RR Co v Clinton County Commrs	1.03
Citizens Committee to Preserve Lake Logan v Williams	11.03
ClenDening; State ex rel Nolan v	5.04
Cleveland Bd of Zoning; Vlad v	3.11
Cleveland; Cleveland Electric Illuminating Co v	3.11
Cleveland Electric Illuminating Co v Cleveland	3.11
Cleveland Electric Illuminating Co v Williams	1.01
Cleveland; Levitt v	3.05
Cleveland v Piskura	1.03
Cleveland Police Relief Fund Bd of Trustees; State ex rel Wichman v	1.07

Casename	Text Section(s)
Cleveland Railway Co, State ex rel v Atkinson	21.07
Cleveland; Yee Bow v	1.03
Clinton County Commrs; Cincinnati, Wilmington & Zanesville RR Co v	1.03
Collopy; State ex rel Geyer v	5.04
Columbus; Burt Realty Corp v	3.11
Columbus Gas & Fuel Co, State ex rel v PUCO	3.05
Co-operative Legislative Committee of Transportation Brotherhoods v PUCO	3.11
Connor; Skiba v	21.08
Consumer Energy Council v Federal Energy Regulatory Comm	1.05
Copperweld Steel Co v Industrial Comm	5.05
Costle; American Petroleum Institute v	1.07
Cuff; Haba v	3.09
Cundiff, State ex rel v Industrial Comm	3.08
Cuyahoga County Budget Comm; Brook Park v	3.06

D

Casename	Text Section(s)
Dayton; Dayton Newspapers, Inc v	1.05
Dayton Newspapers, Inc v Dayton	1.05
Dayton Walther Corp; State ex rel Burdette v	21.04
Dell; Industrial Comm v	3.09
Dept of Commerce; Handler v	3.09
Dept of Industrial Relations; Goodyear Synthetic Rubber Corp v	3.06
Dickerson; State ex rel Moskowitz v	5.02
Dover Corp, State ex rel v Industrial Comm	21.06

Casename	Text Section(s)
Dudukovich v Lorain Metropolitan Housing Auth	3.11
Duff v PUCO	17.04

E

East Ohio Gas Co v PUCO	3.08
Eggers v Morr	3.11
EPA; Mision Industrial, Inc v	1.06, 1.07
Evatt; Zangerle v	1.06, 3.01

F

Farrand v Ohio Medical Board	3.11
FCC; Office of Communication of United Church of Christ v	3.04
Federal Energy Regulatory Comm; Consumer Energy Council v	1.05
Federal Trade Commission v Ruberoid Co	23.01
Federated Department Stores, Inc, State ex rel v Brown	5.02
Fortner v Thomas	3.01, 9.04
Franklin County Regional Planning Comm; State ex rel Ohio Power Co v	5.04
Franz; Tcherepnin v	9.06
Frick-Gallagher Mfg Co; State ex rel Hutt v	21.04

G

Gannon v Perk	5.03
Gates Mills Investment Co v Pepper Pike	3.11
General Motors Corp v McAvoy	3.01, 3.02, 3.06, 11.02
Geyer, State ex rel v Collopy	5.04
Giles; UAW v	7.02
Glander; Bloch v	3.08
Glander; Kroger Grocery & Baking Co v	1.01
Goldberg v Kelly	1.03

Casename	Text Section(s)
Goodyear Synthetic Rubber Corp v Dept of Industrial Relations	3.06
Grannis v Ordean	1.03
Green v State Civil Service Comm	5.05
Grossman v PUCO	17.04
Gullatt Cleaning & Laundry Co; State ex rel Schneider v	1.03

H

Haba v Cuff	3.09
Haines, State ex rel v Industrial Comm	21.07
Handler v Dept of Commerce	3.09
Harmon v State	1.03
Harris, State ex rel v Industrial Comm	21.07
Helle v PUCO	3.09
Hepner v Board of Review	7.04
Hipp; State v	3.01
Hocking Valley Railway Co v PUCO	3.11
Homan, State ex rel v Bd of Embalmers & Funeral Directors	1.07
Home Savings & Loan Assn v Boesch	3.01
Hummel; State ex rel Beck v	3.08
Hutt, State ex rel v Frick-Gallagher Mfg Co	21.04

I

Independent Broker-Dealers' Trade Assn v SEC	1.03
Industrial Comm; Copperweld Steel Co v	5.05
Industrial Comm v Dell	3.09
Industrial Comm; Simmons v	3.08
Industrial Comm; State ex rel Bosch v	21.04
Industrial Comm; State ex rel Cundiff v	3.08
Industrial Comm; State ex rel Dover Corp v	21.06
Industrial Comm; State ex rel Haines v	21.07

Casename	Text Section(s)
Industrial Comm; State ex rel Harris v	21.07
Industrial Comm; State ex rel Kildow v	1.06
Industrial Comm; State ex rel Nicodemus v	21.08
Industrial Comm; State ex rel Timken Roller Bearing Co v	5.04
In re Appeal of Peabody Coal Co	3.09
In re McKenzie	7.04
In re Milton Hardware Co	3.05

J

Casename	Text Section(s)
Jennings; State v	9.09
Jones, State ex rel v Bryant	15.05
Joseph v US Civil Service Comm	1.07

K

Casename	Text Section(s)
Keaton v State	3.02
Keeler, State ex rel v Levine	3.06
Kelly; Goldberg v	1.03
Kildow, State ex rel v Industrial Comm	1.06
Kilgore v Bd of Review	7.07
Kroger Grocery & Baking Co v Glander	1.01
Kyne; Leedom v	3.11

L

Casename	Text Section(s)
Lake Geauga Printing Co; Simon v	7.07
Lakis v Bd of Liquor Control	3.11
Laughlin v PUCO	3.07
Leach v Bd of Review	7.07
Leedom v Kyne	3.11
Lehew v Rhodes	13.04
Levine; State ex rel Keeler v	3.06
Levitt v Cleveland	3.05
Lieux, State ex rel v Westlake	3.11
Liquor Control Comm; Burger Brewing Co v	1.06, 3.01, 5.03, 9.04
Liquor Control Comm; Tripodi v	3.02
Lorain Metropolitan Housing Auth; Dudukovich v	3.11

M

Casename	Text Section(s)
Manchin; State ex rel Barker v	1.05
Manzo; Armstrong v	1.03
Marble Cliff Quarries Co, State ex rel v Morse	5.02
Masterson, State ex rel v Racing Comm	5.04
Maynard; Campbell v	11.02
Maynard, State ex rel v Whitfield	11.03
Maynard; Youngstown Sheet & Tube Co v	1.07
McAvoy; General Motors Corp v	3.01, 3.02, 3.06, 11.02
McAvoy; Truck world, Inc v	11.03
McKenzie, In re	7.04
Meneley v Carpenter	3.05, 3.08
Messenger; State v	1.07
Meyer v Parr	5.05
Michaels, State ex rel v Morse	5.02
Middletown v Nichols	11.02
Milton Hardware Co, In re	3.05
Mision Industrial, Inc v EPA	1.06, 1.07
Mitchell, State ex rel v Robbins & Myers, Inc	21.04
Morr; Eggers v	3.11
Morrison; State ex rel Wright v	5.02
Morse; State ex rel Marble Cliff Quarries Co v	5.02
Morse; State ex rel Michaels v	5.02
Moskowitz, State ex rel v Dickerson	5.02

N

Casename	Text Section(s)
National Tube Co v Ayres	3.09
Natural Resources Defense Counsel; Vermont Yankee Nuclear Power Corp v	1.03
New Bremen v PUCO	9.07
Newell, State ex rel v Brown	5.01, 5.04
New York Central RR Co v PUCO (1952)	3.05

Casename	Text Section(s)
New York Central RR Co v PUCO (1936)	1.03
New York State Banking Dept; Stratford Factors v	3.05
Nichols; Middletown v	11.02
Nichols; White Consolidated Industries v	11.02
Nicodemus, State ex rel v Industrial Comm	21.08
NLRB v Wyman-Gordon Co	1.07
Nolan, State ex rel v ClenDening	5.04

O

Casename	Text Section(s)
Office of Communication of United Church of Christ v FCC	3.04
Ohio Bell Telephone Co v PUCO	3.06
Ohio Boys Town, Inc v Brown	3.02
Ohio Dept of Health; Bucyrus v	3.05, 3.06
Ohio Medical Board; Farrand v	3.11
Ohio Medical Bd; Shearer v	3.06
Ohio Power Co, State ex rel v Franklin County Regional Planning Comm	5.04
Ohio; Slagle v	3.06
Ohio State Federation of Licensed Nursing Homes v Public Health Council	1.07
Opinion of the Justices to the Governor	1.05
Ordean; Grannis v	1.03

P

Casename	Text Section(s)
Parr; Meyer v	5.05
Pepper Pike; Gates Mills Investment Co v	3.11
Perk; Gannon v	5.03
Pirnie; Taub v	3.06
Piskura; Cleveland v	1.03
Powell v Administrator, Bureau of Employment Services	7.04

Casename	Text Section(s)
Powell v Young	3.11
Public Health Council; Ohio State Federation of Licensed Nursing Homes v	1.07
PUCO; Co-operative Legislative Committee of Transportation Brotherhoods v	3.11
PUCO; Duff v	17.04
PUCO; East Ohio Gas Co v	3.08
PUCO; Grossman v	17.04
PUCO; Helle v	3.09
PUCO; Hocking Valley Railway Co v	3.11
PUCO; Laughlin v	3.07
PUCO; New Bremen v	9.07
PUCO; New York Central RR Co v (1952)	3.05
PUCO; New York Central RR Co v (1936)	1.03
PUCO; Ohio Bell Telephone Co v	3.06
PUCO; State ex rel Columbus Gas & Fuel Co v	3.05
PUCO; Sylvania Home Telephone Co v	9.07

R

Casename	Text Section(s)
Raabe v State	1.03
Racing Comm; State ex rel Masterson v	5.04
Rankin-Thoman, Inc v Caldwell	1.06, 3.01, 3.11, 5.05
Reynolds; United States v	3.05
Rhodes; Lehew v	13.04
Robbins & Myers, Inc; State ex rel Mitchell v	21.04
Roxy Musical Bar, Inc v Bd of Liquor Control	3.11

S

Casename	Text Section(s)
Salfi; Weinberger v	3.11
Schneider, State ex rel v Gullatt Cleaning & Laundry Co	1.03

Casename	Text Section(s)	Casename	Text Section(s)
SEC; Independent Broker-Dealers' Trade Assn v	1.03	Timken Roller Bearing Co, State ex rel v Industrial Comm	5.04
Secretary of Housing & Urban Development; Caramico v	1.03	Tripodi v Liquor Control Comm	3.02
Shearer v Ohio Medical Bd	3.06	Truck world, Inc v McAvoy	11.03
Shively v Stewart	3.05	**U**	
Silverstein v Bd of Liquor Control	3.11	UAW v Giles	7.02
Simmons v Industrial Comm	3.08	Union Camp Corp v Whitman	1.06
Simmons, State ex rel v Wieber	3.09	Union Central Life Insurance Co; Belden v	1.03
Simon v Lake Geauga Printing Co	7.07	United States v Chemical Foundation	3.06
Skiba v Connor	21.08	United States v Reynolds	3.05
Slagle v Ohio	3.06	US Civil Service Comm; Joseph v	1.07
State Civil Service Comm; Green v	5.05		
State ex rel—see name of party		**V**	
State; Harmon v	1.03	Vermont Yankee Nuclear Power Corp v Natural Resources Defense Counsel	1.03
State v Hipp	3.01		
State v Jennings	9.09		
State; Keaton v	3.02		
State v Messenger	1.07	Vlad v Cleveland Bd of Zoning	3.11
State; Raabe v	1.03		
Sterling Drug, Inc v Wickham	1.05, 1.06	**W**	
Stewart; Shively v	3.05	Warren Molded Plastics, Inc v Williams	1.06, 11.03
Stouffer Corp v Bd of Liquor Control	1.06	Weinberger v Salfi	3.11
Stratford Factors v New York State Banking Dept	3.05	Westlake; State ex rel Lieux v	3.11
Stringer; Zavatsky v	21.04	White; Bolin v	13.04
Superintendent of Insurance; Blue Cross of Northwest Ohio v	1.07	White Consolidated Industries v Nichols	11.02
		Whitfield; State ex rel Maynard v	11.03
Sylvania Home Telephone Co v PUCO	9.07	Whitman; Buckeye Power, Inc v	1.06
		Whitman; Union Camp Corp v	1.06
T		Wichman, State ex rel v Cleveland Police Relief Fund Bd of Trustees	1.07
Tatman v Administrator, Bureau of Unemployment Compensation	7.04	Wickham; Sterling Drug, Inc v	1.05, 1.06
Taub v Pirnie	3.06	Wieber; State ex rel Simmons v	3.09
Tcherepnin v Franz	9.06		
Thomas; Fortner v	3.01, 9.04	Williams v Akron	1.06

Casename	Text Section(s)
Williams; Citizens Committee to Preserve Lake Logan v	11.03
Williams; Cleveland Electric Illuminating Co v	1.01
Williams, State ex rel v Bozarth	1.06, 11.03
Williams; Warren Molded Plastics, Inc v	1.06, 11.03
Wilms, State ex rel v Blake	21.04
Wittenberg v Bd of Liquor Control	3.08
Wright, State ex rel v Morrison	5.02

Casename	Text Section(s)
Wuebker, State ex rel v Bockrath	3.09
Wyman-Gordon Co; NLRB v	1.07
Y	
Yee Bow v Cleveland	1.03
Young; Powell v	3.11
Youngstown Sheet & Tube Co v Maynard	1.07
Z	
Zangerle; Board of Tax Appeals v	3.06
Zangerle v Evatt	1.06, 3.01
Zavatsky v Stringer	21.04

Appendix B
Table of Laws and Rules Construed

ABBREVIATIONS

App R—Rules of Appellate Procedure
OAC—Ohio Administrative Code
O Const—Constitution of the State of Ohio
RC—Revised Code

O Const	Text Section(s)
Art II, § 1	1.03
Art IV, § 2(B)(2)(c)	1.06
Art IV, § 3(B)(2)	1.06
Art IV, § 4	3.11
Art IV, § 4(B)	3.01

OAC	Text Section(s)
1509-1-03	19.03
1509-1-04	19.03
1513-3-08	19.02
3745-5-15	11.03
3745-47	11.02
3746-5	11.03
3746-7	11.03
3746-9-01	11.03
3746-13-01	11.03
4121-3-09	21.02
4121-3-15(C)	21.05
4121-3-18	21.02
4121-3-18(A)(4)	21.03
4121-3-20	21.07
4121-3-28	21.06
4146-3-01	7.02, 7.05
4146-3-02	7.02
4146-5-01	7.02
4146-5-03	7.05
4146-5-04	7.04
4146-7	7.02
4146-7-02	7.05
4146-15-01	7.05
4146-15-03	7.05
4146-21-02	7.04
4146-21-03	7.02
4146-21-04	7.04
4146-23	7.02
4146-23-01	7.03
4146-23-02	7.02
4146-23-03	7.03
4146-23-05	7.03
4146-25-01	7.02
4146-25-02(B)	7.06
4301:1-1-12	15.05
4301:1-1-16	15.04, 15.05
4301:1-1-64	15.02
4301:1-1-65(A)	15.05
4901-1	17.03

OAC	Text Section(s)
4901-9-01	17.03
5101:1-35-04 to -07	13.04
5101:3-2-0712(B)	13.03
5101:3-50-11	13.02
5101:3-50-22	13.02
5101:3-50-24(A)	13.02
5101:4-9	13.04

RC	Text Section(s)
103.05	1.01
111.15	1.04
119.01	1.02, 1.04, 9.01
119.02	1.05
119.03	1.05, 1.06
119.06	3.02
119.07	3.02, 3.08, 15.05
119.08	3.02
119.09	3.02, 3.05 to 3.08, 13.02
119.11	1.06, 9.04
119.12	1.06, 3.08, 3.11
127.18(B)	1.05
149.41	1.05
1509.33	19.03
1509.36	19.03
1509.37	19.03
1513.02	19.02
1513.13	19.02
1513.14	19.02
1707.041(B)(4)	9.01
1707.09	9.02
1707.13	9.06
1707.20(D)	9.01
1707.22	9.01
1707.23	9.07
2505.01(A)	9.09
2505.03	3.11
2505.07	3.11
2505.21	9.09
2506.01	3.11
Ch 2721	5.03
2721.02	5.03
3734.01	11.02
3734.05	11.04
3734.13(B)	11.02
3745.04 to 3745.08	11.02, 11.03
4121.13	21.01, 21.07

RC	Text Section(s)	RC	Text Section(s)
4121.131	21.01	4903.12	17.03
4121.34(B)	21.01	4903.13	17.03
4121.35	21.01	4905.02	17.02
4123.343	21.06	4905.03	17.02
4123.35	21.01	4905.26	17.04
4123.515	21.03	4905.301	17.04
4123.516	21.01 to 21.03	4905.302	17.04
4123.519	21.03, 21.04, 21.06	4909.18	17.04
4123.57	21.05	4909.19	17.04
4123.65	21.01	4909.34	17.04
4141.24(F)	15.03	4909.42	17.04
4141.28	3.10	4909.66	17.04
4141.28(J)	7.03, 7.04	4921.02	17.05
4151.14	3.10	4921.07	17.05
4301.28	15.02	4921.10	17.05
4303.27	15.03	5111.06	13.02
4303.272	15.04	5739.14	15.03
4303.29	15.02		
4303.292(A)(1)	15.03	**App R**	**Text Section(s)**
4901.02	17.01	App R 1	9.09
4901.13	17.03	App R 12(A)	9.09
4903.081	17.03		

Appendix C
Bibliography

Books, Treatises, and Serials

Administrative Law Review, Administrative Law Section, American Bar Association (1960-___).

Barry, D. and Whitcomb, H., *The Legal Foundations of Public Administration* (1981).

Cooper, F., *State Administrative Law* (1965).

Davis, K., *Administrative Law Treatise* (2d ed 1978-1982).

Edles, G. and Nelson, J., *Federal Regulatory Process: Agency Practices and Procedures* (1981-1984).

Fischer, H., et al, *Pike and Fischer Administrative Law* (2d series 1952-1985).

Gellhorn, W., *Federal Administrative Proceedings* (1941).

Journal of the National Association of Administrative Law Judges, National Association of Administrative Law Judges (1981-___).

Landis, J., *The Administrative Process* (1938).

Mashaw, J., *Due Process in the Administrative State* (1985).

Mezines, B., et al, *Administrative Law* (1977-1985).

Office of the Chairman, Administrative Conference of the United States, *Federal Administrative Procedure Sourcebook* (1985).

Ohio Legislative Service Commission, *The Ohio Administrative Procedure Act* (1975).

Regulation, American Enterprise Institute for Public Policy Research (1977-___).

Rosenberg, M. and McGovern, B., eds, *Current Issues in Regulatory Reform* (1980).

Schwartz, B., *Administrative Law* (2d ed 1983).

United States Department of Justice, *Attorney General's Manual on the Administrative Procedure Act* (1973).

Young, J., *Young's Workmen's Compensation Law of Ohio* (2d ed 1971).

Law Review and Journal Articles

Boley, *Administrative Conference of the United States: A Selected Bibliography 1968-1980*, 33 Ad L Rev 235 (1981).

Brown, *Sexual Harassment in Employment: Procedure for Filing a Complaint with the Ohio Civil Rights Commission*, 10 Capital L Rev 531 (1981).

Brown, *The Trend of Workers' Compensation in Ohio: Ohio Puts the Worker Back into Workers' Compensation*, 13 Capital L Rev 521 (1984).

Brubaker and Northrop, *Appellate Review of Administrative Rule Making in Ohio—Prospects for Revival*, 37 Ohio St L J 471 (1976).

Comment, *Blankenship v. Cincinnati Milacron Chemicals, Inc: Some Fairness for Ohio Workers and Some Uncertainty for Ohio Employers*, 15 Tol L Rev 403 (1983).

Comment, *Municipal Home Rule in Ohio: A Mechanism for Local Regulation of Hazardous Waste Facilities*, 16 Tol L Rev 553 (1985).

Comment, *The Ohio Liquor Control Commission's Right to Regulate*, 9 Akron L Rev 695 (1976).

Comment, *S.B. 269: The Impact of Federal Legislation on Ohio's Hazardous Waste Disposal Program*, 7 Dayton L Rev 567 (1982).

Comment, *Third Party's Rights Under Ohio's Workmen's Compensation System: Will Comparative Negligence Relieve the Inequities?*, 11 Capital L Rev 285 (1981).

Cryder, Faulk, and McKirahan, *Strip Mining: The Ohio Experience*, 4 Capital L Rev 169 (1975).

Emens and Fullmer, *Ohio Securities Laws Amended (Again)*, 58 Ohio Bar 654 (1985).

Emens and Lowe, *Ohio Oil and Gas Conservation Law—The First Ten Years (1965-1975)*, 37 Ohio St L J 31 (1976).

Farmer and Feldman, *Fraud in Securities Transactions: A Comparison of Civil Remedies Under the Ohio Securities Act, the Uniform Securities Act, and the Federal Securities Acts*, 49 Cin L Rev 814 (1980).

Landey, *The Federal Regulatory Process: An Overview of an Enervated System*, 36 Ad L Rev 75 (1984).

Leaffer, *Automatic Fuel Adjustment Clauses: Time for a Hearing*, 30 Case WR L Rev 228 (1980).

McAvoy, *Hazardous Waste Management in Ohio: The Problem of Siting*, 9 Capital L Rev 435 (1980).

Melle, *Ohio's Merit Principle: Its Abuse in Nondisciplinary Personnel Actions*, 8 Capital L Rev 491 (1979).

Meyers and Williams, *Petroleum Conservation in Ohio*, 26 Ohio St L J 591 (1965).

Note, *Administrative Law*, 8 Ohio North L Rev 639 (1981), 9 Ohio North L Rev 597 (1982), 10 Ohio North L Rev 689 (1983), 11 Ohio North L Rev 459 (1984).

Note, *The Ohio Division of Securities: Rulemaking, the Administrative Procedure Act and the Ohio Securities Bulletin*, 36 Ohio St L J 662 (1975).

Note, *Public Utilities*, 16 Akron L Rev 659 (1983).

Note, *Public Utilities*, 51 Cin L Rev 203 (1982).

Note, *Public Utilities Commission*, 11 Ohio North L Rev 575 (1984).

Note, *Workers' Compensation*, 8 Ohio North L Rev 866 (1981), 9 Ohio North L Rev 785 (1982), 10 Ohio North L Rev 810 (1983), 11 Ohio North L Rev 625 (1984).

Sargent, *On the Validity of State Takeover Regulation: State Responses to MITE and Kidwell*, 14 Securities L Rev 221 (1982).

Sargentich, *The Reform of the American Administrative Process: The Contemporary Debate*, 1984 Wis L Rev 385 (1984).

Smith, *Development of Environmental Law Through the Administrative Process*, 4 Capital L Rev 203 (1975).

Strauss, *Regulation of Hazardous Waste Transportation in Ohio*, 52 Transp Prac J 349 (1985).

Tseng, *Recent Developments in Ohio Administrative Law: Regulating the Regulators?*, 4 Ohio North L Rev 317 (1977).

Wiley, *Workers' Compensation in Ohio: Scope of Employment and the Intentional Tort*, 17 Akron L Rev 249 (1983).

INDEX

Ohio Revised Code sections are cited by section number.

Text sections are cited with the prefix T.

Cross references to another main heading are in CAPITAL LETTERS.

ADJUDICATION, T 3.01 to T 3.11
See also HEARINGS; ORDERS; particular agency concerned.
Appeals from—See ADMINISTRATIVE REVIEW; JUDICIAL REVIEW, generally.
Attorneys—See ATTORNEYS.
Burden of proof—See BURDEN OF PROOF.
Commencement of action, T 3.02, T 3.05(A)
  Forced by courts, T 5.01, T 5.02
Continuances—See CONTINUANCES.
Definitions—See DEFINITIONS.
Depositions—See DEPOSITIONS.
Discovery—See DISCOVERY.
Estoppel, applicability, T 3.09(B)
Examiners—See HEARING EXAMINERS.
Fact-finding hearing for administrative review, T 3.10
Findings—See FINDINGS.
Hearings—See HEARINGS.
Initiation of proceeding—See Commencement of action, this heading.
Intervention in proceedings, T 3.04
Judicial review of orders—See JUDICIAL REVIEW.
Jurisdiction—See JURISDICTION.
Legislative basis for, T 1.07(C)
Licenses—See LICENSES AND PERMITS.
Mandamus used to force commencement of, T 5.01, T 5.02
"Mental processes" rule, T 3.06(A)
Notice—See NOTICE, generally.
Orders—See ORDERS, generally.
Parties to proceedings—See PARTIES TO PROCEEDINGS.
Policy development, by, T 3.01(B)
Postponements—See CONTINUANCES.
Power to perform, T 1.07(C)
Prehearing procedure—See PREHEARING PROCEDURE.
Procedural charts—See CHARTS.
Public participation, T 3.04
Referees—See HEARING EXAMINERS.
Review—See ADMINISTRATIVE REVIEW; JUDICIAL REVIEW.
Rulemaking, distinguished from, T 3.01(B)
Rules of procedure, T 1.02, T 3.05(A)
Transcripts—See RECORDS AND REPORTS.
Witnesses and testimony—See WITNESSES AND TESTIMONY.

ADMINISTRATIVE APPELLATE PROCEDURE ACT, T 3.11(C)(1); 2506.01

ADMINISTRATIVE CODE, T 1.01
See also RULES AND RULEMAKING POWERS, generally.

ADMINISTRATIVE PROCEDURE—See ADJUDICATION.

ADMINISTRATIVE REVIEW, T 3.10
Appeals from—See JUDICIAL REVIEW.
Diagnosis related groups (DRG) prospective payments
  Reconsideration process, T 13.03
Employment services bureau rules, T 1.05(D); 119.03(G)
Environmental review board, T 11.03
  See also ENVIRONMENTAL REVIEW BOARD, generally.
Estoppel applicable to agencies, T 3.09(B)
Exhaustion of administrative remedies, T 3.11(B)(3)
  Prerequisite for judicial review, T 3.10, T 3.11(B)(1)
Fact-finding hearing, T 3.10
Industrial commission—See WORKERS' COMPENSATION, at
    Administrative appeals process.
Liquor control commission, T 15.01 to T 15.08
  See also LIQUOR CONTROL COMMISSION.
Members of review board, qualifications, T 3.10
Objections to hearing examiner's report, T 3.07(C)
Oil and gas board of review, T 19.03(A)
Reconsideration process
  Diagnosis related groups (DRG) prospective payments, T 13.03
Records must support agency findings to be upheld, T 3.08(B);
  119.12
Rehearings, T 3.09(C)
Types, T 3.10
Unemployment compensation board of review, T 7.01 to T 7.09
  See also UNEMPLOYMENT COMPENSATION BOARD OF
    REVIEW.

ADMINISTRATIVE RULES—See RULES AND RULEMAK-
    ING POWERS.

ADMISSIBILITY OF EVIDENCE—See also EVIDENCE, gener-
    ally.
Adjudication hearing, T 3.06(F); 119.09
Denial, T 3.06(E)
Proposed rule hearing, T 1.05(D)

AFFIDAVITS
Liquor permit business closing, reasons, T 15.04

AGENCIES
Environmental protection agency, T 11.01 to T 11.09
  See also ENVIRONMENTAL PROTECTION AGENCY.

APPELLATE REVIEW—See ADMINISTRATIVE REVIEW; JUDICIAL REVIEW.

ATTORNEYS
Agencies, counsel to in adjudication hearings, 119.10
Environmental review board, appeals to, T 11.03(A)(2)
Fees, 119.092
   Compensation for—See PARTIES TO PROCEEDINGS, at Compensation for attorney fees.
   Defined, 119.092(A)
   Unemployment compensation board of review hearings, limitations, T 7.01
Human services department—See HUMAN SERVICES DEPARTMENT, at Legal services office.
Industrial commission hearing officers, T 21.01(B)
Judicial review proceedings, 119.13
License suspension hearing, T 3.03
Liquor permit business, involvement in purchase of, T 15.03
Oil and gas division, areas of concern, T 19.03
Public utilities commission hearings, examiners, T 17.03(A), T 17.03(C)
Reclamation division, areas of concern, T 19.02
Securities division hearings, duties, T 9.03, T 9.08
Unemployment compensation board of review hearing examiners—See UNEMPLOYMENT COMPENSATION BOARD OF REVIEW, at Hearing examiners.

BOARDS
Environmental review board, T 11.03
  See also ENVIRONMENTAL REVIEW BOARD.
Hazardous waste facility board, T 11.04
  See also HAZARDOUS WASTE FACILITY BOARD.
Oil and gas board of review—See OIL AND GAS BOARD OF REVIEW.
Reclamation board of review—See RECLAMATION REVIEW BOARD.
Unemployment compensation board of review, T 7.01 to T 7.09
  See also UNEMPLOYMENT COMPENSATION BOARD OF REVIEW.

BRIEFS
Environmental review board proceedings, T 11.03(B)
Public utilities commission hearings, T 17.03(B)(3)

BURDEN OF PROOF, T 3.06(A)
See also EVIDENCE, generally.
Environmental review board hearing, T 11.03(B)
Judicial review of rules, T 1.06(B)
Unemployment compensation board of review hearings, T 7.05
Witnesses, effect on order of presentation, T 3.06(C)

BUREAUS
Employment services bureau—See EMPLOYMENT SERVICES BUREAU.

BUREAUS—*continued*
Workers' compensation bureau—See WORKERS' COMPENSATION BUREAU.

CEASE AND DESIST ORDERS
Securities division, T 9.07

CHARTS
Employment services bureau, procedural chart, T 7.09
Environmental protection agency
  Organizational chart, T 11.05
  Procedural chart, adjudication, T 11.08
Environmental review board, organizational chart, T 11.06
Hazardous waste facility board
  Organizational chart, T 11.07
  Procedural chart, adjudication, T 11.09
Human services department
  Chapter 119 adjudication proceedings, procedural chart, T 13.06
  Organizational chart, T 13.05
  State hearing process, procedural chart, T 13.07
Industrial commission, organizational chart, T 21.11
Liquor control department
  Organizational chart, T 15.07
  Procedural chart, adjudication, T 15.08
Natural resources department
  Organizational chart, T 19.07
  Procedural chart, T 19.08
Public utilities commission
  Complaint proceedings, procedural chart, T 17.08
  Judicial review, procedural chart, T 17.11
  Motor carrier applications proceedings, chart, T 17.10
  Organizational chart, T 17.07
  Rate change application proceedings, chart, T 17.09
Securities division
  Enforcement, adjudicative procedural chart, T 9.12
  Organizational chart, T 9.11
  Registration of securities, adjudicative procedural chart, T 9.13
Unemployment compensation board of review, organizational chart, T 7.08
Workers' compensation
  Organizational chart of industrial commission, T 21.11
  Procedural chart, adjudication, T 21.12
Workers' compensation bureau, organizational chart, T 21.10

CIVIL SERVICE
Liability insurance for employees, T 9.06
Unemployment compensation board of review hearing examiners, T 7.01

CLAIMS—See COMPLAINTS.

COAL MINING
License of operator, suspension, T 19.02(A)
Notice of violation, T 19.02(A)

COAL MINING—*continued*
Reclamation board of review decisions, T 19.02(B)
  Appeal to court of appeals, T 19.02(C)
Reclamation division—See RECLAMATION DIVISION.
Strip mining, reclamation standards, T 19.02
Technical aspects, T 19.04
Violation, notice, T 19.02(A)

COMMENCEMENT OF ACTIONS, T 3.02, T 3.05(A)
Forced by courts, T 5.01, T 5.02

COMMERCE DEPARTMENT, SECURITIES DIVISION, T 9.01 to T 9.13
See also SECURITIES DIVISION.

COMMISSIONS
Industrial commission, T 21.01 to T 21.12
  See also WORKERS' COMPENSATION.
Legislative service commission—See LEGISLATIVE SERVICE COMMISSION DIRECTOR.
Liquor control commission, T 15.01 to T 15.08
  See also LIQUOR CONTROL COMMISSION.
Power siting commission, discovery procedures, T 3.05(B)
Public utilities commission, T 17.01 to T 17.11
  See also PUBLIC UTILITIES COMMISSION.

COMMITTEES
Joint committee on agency rule review—See JOINT COMMITTEE ON AGENCY RULE REVIEW.

COMMON CARRIERS
Motor carriers—See MOTOR CARRIERS.

COMPLAINTS
Commencement of action by, T 3.05(A)
Environmental protection agency, verification, T 11.02(A)
Public utilities commission, T 17.04(A)
  Procedural charts, T 17.08
Workers' compensation claims—See WORKERS' COMPENSATION, at Claims.

CONFERENCES, PREHEARING—See PREHEARING PROCEDURE.

CONFLICT OF LAWS
Rule conflicting with statute, T 1.06(C)(3)

CONTINUANCES, T 3.02, T 3.05(C); 119.09
Environmental review board hearings, T 11.03(C)
Environmental review board, stay of proceeding, T 11.03(B)
Human services department, prehearing conference, T 13.02(C)
Notice, T 3.02
Unemployment compensation board of review hearing, T 7.05

COUNSEL IN PROCEEDINGS—See ATTORNEYS.

COURTS OF APPEALS—See also JUDICIAL REVIEW, for general provisions.
Environmental protection agency, appeals from, T 1.07(A)
Reclamation review board, appeals from, T 19.02(C)

COURTS OF COMMON PLEAS—See also JUDICIAL REVIEW, for general provisions.
Administrative Appellate Procedure Act, T 3.11(C)(1); 2506.01
Franklin county, appeals to, T 3.11(A); 119.12
Industrial commission decisions, appeals from, T 21.04(A)
Oil and gas review board decisions, appeal from, T 19.03(B)
Powers of review, T 3.11(C)(1); 2506.01
Unemployment compensation board of review, appeals from, T 7.07

DAMAGES
Action for, T 5.05

DECLARATORY JUDGMENTS, T 3.11(C)(2)
Commencement of adjudication by, T 5.01, T 5.03
Environmental protection agency rules, T 1.06(A)
Rulemaking decisions
  Burden of proof, T 1.06(B)
  Review by declaratory judgment, T 1.06
    See also JUDICIAL REVIEW, at Rules, of.

DEFINITIONS
Adjudication, T 3.01(A); 119.01(D)
  Hearing, 119.01(E)
  Parties to, T 3.03; 119.01(G), 119.092(A)
Agency, T 1.04; 111.15(A), 119.01(A)
  Rulemaking agency, 119.01(I)
Attorney fees, 119.092(A)
Environmental review board, T 11.03(A)
Hearings, 119.01(E)
Internal management rules, 119.01(K)
Internal revenue code, 119.092(A)
Judicial review, 119.01(H)
License, T 3.01(A); 119.01(B)
Net worth, attorney general to define, 119.093
Party in adjudication, T 3.03; 119.01(G), 119.092(A)
Person, 119.01(F)
Procedural rules, T 1.02
Public record, T 1.05(C)
Rulemaking agency, 119.01(I)
Rules—See RULES AND RULEMAKING POWERS.

DE NOVO HEARINGS
Courts, by, T 3.11(E)
Environmental review board, T 11.03(B)

DEPARTMENTS
Commerce department, securities division, T 9.01 to T 9.13
  See also SECURITIES DIVISION.
Human services department, T 13.01 to T 13.07
  See also HUMAN SERVICES DEPARTMENT.

DEPARTMENTS—*continued*
Liquor control department, T 15.01 to T 15.08
  See also LIQUOR CONTROL DEPARTMENT.
Natural resources department, T 19.01 to T 19.08
  See also NATURAL RESOURCES DEPARTMENT.
Taxation department, appeals from rules, T 1.05(D); 119.03(G)

DEPOSITIONS, T 3.06(B)
Authorization, T 3.05(B); 119.09
Environmental review board, T 11.03(B)

DIAGNOSIS RELATED GROUPS (DRG) PROSPECTIVE PAYMENTS
Reconsideration process, T 13.03

DISCOVERY, T 3.05(B)
Environmental protection agency procedure, T 11.02(C), T 11.02(D)(2)
Environmental review board proceedings, T 11.03(C)
Human services department prehearing conference, T 13.02(C)
Power siting commission, T 3.05(B)
Prehearing conference, T 3.05(B), T 13.02(C)
Public utilities commission hearing, T 17.03(B)(1)
Securities division hearing, T 9.03

DIVISIONS
Oil and gas division, T 19.03
  See also OIL AND GAS DIVISION.
Reclamation division—See RECLAMATION DIVISION.
Securities division, T 9.01 to T 9.13
  See also SECURITIES DIVISION.

DRIVERS' LICENSES
Suspension without hearing, 119.062

DUE PROCESS—See also HEARINGS; NOTICE, generally.
Rulemaking procedure, T 1.03(B)
Securities division, T 9.06

EMERGENCY RULES, T 1.05(G); 111.15(B), 119.03(F)
See also RULES AND RULEMAKING POWERS, generally.

EMPLOYMENT SERVICES BUREAU
Appeals from rules, T 1.05(D); 119.03(G)
Chart, procedural, T 7.09

ENVIRONMENTAL PROTECTION AGENCY, T 11.01 to T 11.09
See also ADJUDICATION, for general provisions.
Appeals to environmental review board, T 11.03
  See also ENVIRONMENTAL REVIEW BOARD, generally.
Charts
  Organizational chart, T 11.05
  Procedural chart, adjudication, T 11.08
Complaints, verified, T 11.02(A)

ENVIRONMENTAL PROTECTION AGENCY—*continued*
Director, powers and duties, T 11.02(A)
Discovery procedure, T 11.02(C), T 11.02(D)(2)
Enforcement orders, T 11.02(A)
Environmental review board, T 11.03
  See also ENVIRONMENTAL REVIEW BOARD.
Hazardous waste facility board, T 11.04
  See also HAZARDOUS WASTE FACILITY BOARD.
Hearing examiners, T 11.02(C), T 11.02(D)(2)
Hearings, T 3.02, T 11.02(C), T 11.02(D)(1)
  See also HEARINGS, for general provisions.
  Appeals from—See ENVIRONMENTAL REVIEW BOARD.
  Discovery, T 11.02(C), T 11.02(D)(2)
  Transcripts of hearings, T 11.02(D)(2)
  Witnesses, order of presentation, T 3.06(C)
Judicial review of rules, T 1.06(A)
Orders, T 11.02(A)
Organizational chart, T 11.05
Permits, issuance, T 11.02(A)
Petition for rule changes, T 1.07(B)
Pollutants, discharge, T 11.02(A)
Programs administered by, T 11.02
Proposed actions, T 11.02(C)
Proposed rules, T 1.07(A)
  See also PROPOSED RULES, for general provisions.
Records, hearings, T 11.02(D)(2)
Rules and rulemaking powers—See also RULES AND RULEMAKING POWERS, for general provisions.
  Issuance by director, T 11.02(A)
  Judicial review, T 1.06(A)
  Petitions for changes in, T 1.07(B)
  Proposed rules, T 1.07(A)
    See also PROPOSED RULES, for general provisions.
  Public hearing prior to rule adoption, T 11.02(B)
Sewage disposal permits, T 11.02(A)
Solid waste disposal facility unit, T 11.02(A)
Transcripts of hearings, T 11.02(D)(2)
Violations, determination, T 11.02(A)

ENVIRONMENTAL REVIEW BOARD, T 11.03
See also ADJUDICATION, for general provisions.
Appeals from to courts of appeals, T 1.06(A), T 1.07(A), T 11.03(B)
Appointment of members, T 11.03(A)(2)
Attorneys in proceedings, T 11.03(A)(2)
Briefs, filing, T 11.03(C)
Burden of proceeding, T 11.03(B)
Charts, organizational, T 11.06
De novo hearings, T 11.03(B)
Depositions, T 11.03(B)
Discovery, T 11.03(C)
Evidentiary rules, T 11.03(B)
Final orders, T 11.03(D)
Franklin county court of appeals, board's decisions appealed to, T 11.03(B)

ENVIRONMENTAL REVIEW BOARD—*continued*
Hearings, T 3.10
  See also HEARINGS, for general provisions.
  Administrative procedures, T 11.03(B)
  Conduct of, T 11.03(C)
  Continuances, T 11.03(C)
  Definition, T 11.03(A)
  De novo, T 11.03(B)
  Discovery, T 11.03(C)
Jurisdiction, T 11.03(A)
  Exclusivity, T 11.03(A)(2)
Members
  Appointment, T 11.03(A)(2)
  Qualifications, T 3.10
Notice of appeal, T 11.03(B)
Organizational chart, T 11.06
Parties to proceedings, T 11.03(B)
Qualifications of members, T 3.10
Records, T 11.03(B)
Right to appeal to review board, T 11.02(C)
Scope of review, T 11.03(D)
Stay of proceeding, T 11.03(B)
Subpoena powers, T 11.03(B)
Testimony, liberal policy towards admissibility, T 11.03
Third-party appeals, T 11.03(A)(1)

ESTOPPEL
Applicability to agencies, T 3.09(B)

EVIDENCE, T 3.06(F), T 3.06(G); 119.09
See also WITNESSES AND TESTIMONY.
Admissibility
  Adjudication hearing, T 3.06(F); 119.09
  Denial, T 3.06(E)
  Proposed rule hearing, T 1.05(D)
Burden of proof
  Environmental review board hearing, T 11.03(B)
  Unemployment compensation board of review hearings, T 7.05
  Witnesses, effect on order of presentation, T 3.06(C)
Depositions—See DEPOSITIONS.
Discovery—See DISCOVERY.
Environmental review board, T 11.03(B)
Hearsay rule, T 3.06(F)
Judicial review
  Additional, introduction into record, T 3.11(E); 119.12
  Agency decision, evidence to support; consideration, T 3.11(D); 119.12
  Evidence to support, T 3.08(B)
Liquor control commission hearing, T 15.05(E)
Orders, supporting, T 3.08(B)
Proposed rule hearing, T 1.05(D)
Rules of, T 3.06(F)
  Environmental review board, applied to, T 11.03(B)
  Liquor control department, applied to, T 15.02

FACT-FINDING HEARING
Administrative review, T 3.10

FEDERAL ADMINISTRATIVE PROCEDURE ACT, T 1.03(B)

FEES AND COSTS—See particular subject concerned.
Attorney fees—See ATTORNEYS.

FILING OF RULES, 111.15
Emergency rules, T 1.05(G); 119.03(F)
Final rule, T 1.05(F); 111.15(B), 119.031(G), 119.03(D), 119.04(A)
Fiscal analysis of rule—See FISCAL ANALYSIS OF RULES.
Proposed rules—See PROPOSED RULES.
Public access to agency files, T 1.05(C)

FINAL RULES—See also RULES AND RULEMAKING POWERS, generally.
Comparison with proposed rules, T 1.05(F); 119.031
Date effective, T 1.05(F); 111.15(B), 119.03(D), 119.04(A)
Filing, T 1.05(F); 111.15(B), 119.031(G), 119.03(D), 119.04(A)
Notice of adoption, T 1.05(F); 119.03(D)

FINDINGS, T 3.08
Evidence to support, T 3.08(B)
Hearing examiners—See HEARING EXAMINERS, at Reports.
Judicial review, 2506.04
Posthearing procedures, T 3.07(A)
Records, T 3.07(B), T 3.08(C)
  Written record, T 3.08(A)
Rehearings on, T 3.09(B)
Written record, T 3.08(A)

FINES AND FORFEITURES
Liquor permit violations, T 15.05(C)

FISCAL ANALYSIS OF RULES
Filing requirements, 111.15(E), 111.15(F)
  Joint committee on agency rule review, T 1.05(B); 119.03(H)
  Legislative service commission director, T 1.05(B)
  Secretary of state, T 1.05(B)

FORMS
Liquor permits definitions/privileges, T 15.06
Reclamation board of review
  Appeal, notice, T 19.05
Reclamation division
  Violation, notice, T 19.06
Workers' compensation bureau, T 21.09

FRANKLIN COUNTY
Common pleas courts, appeals to, T 3.11(A); 119.12
  Unemployment compensation board of review decisions, T 7.07

GAMBLING
Liquor permit holder, T 15.05(A)

GENERAL ASSEMBLY
Fiscal analysis of proposed ruled filed with, T 1.05(B)
Joint committee on agency rule review—See JOINT COMMITTEE ON AGENCY RULE REVIEW.
Legislative powers, delegation, T 1.03(A)
Legislative service commission director—See LEGISLATIVE SERVICE COMMISSION DIRECTOR.
Proposed rule
  Filed with, T 1.04
  Invalidation—See PROPOSED RULES.
Senate clerk
  Fiscal analysis of proposed rule filed with, T 1.05(B)
  Proposed rule filed with, T 1.04

GOVERNOR
Emergency rules, powers, T 1.05(G); 119.03(F)

HANDICAP REIMBURSEMENT HEARINGS, T 21.06
Appeal from decision of, T 21.06(F)
Application for, T 21.06(D)
Costs, reimbursable, T 21.06(B)
Docket, T 21.06(E)
Employer eligibility, T 21.06(C)
Evidence, T 21.06(E)
Purpose of, T 21.06(A)

HAZARDOUS WASTE FACILITY BOARD, T 11.04
Charts
  Organizational chart, T 11.07
  Procedural chart, adjudication, T 11.09
Hearings, T 11.04
Members, T 11.04
Organizational chart, T 11.07
Permit issuance, T 11.04
Purpose, T 11.04

HEARING EXAMINERS
Appeals from decisions, 2506.01
Appointment, T 3.06(D); 119.09
Duties, T 3.06(D); 119.09
Environmental protection agency, T 11.02(C), T 11.02(D)(2)
Hazardous waste facility board, T 11.04
Human services department—See HUMAN SERVICES DEPARTMENT.
Industrial commission—See WORKERS' COMPENSATION.
Liquor control department, objections to permit issuance, T 15.02(B)
Public utilities commission, T 17.03(A), T 17.03(C)
Recommendations
  Action on, T 3.07(C); 119.09
  Modifications, T 3.08(A); 119.09

HEARING EXAMINERS—*continued*
Reports, T 3.08
  Copies to parties, T 3.07(B); 119.09
  Filing, T 3.07(B)
  Findings of fact, T 3.07(A)
  Human services department examiner, T 13.02(E)
  Objections to, T 3.07(C); 119.09
  Public utilities commission, T 17.03(C)
  Recommendations to agency, T 3.06(D); 119.09
  Written report, T 3.08(A)
Securities division, T 9.03

HEARINGS, T 3.02, T 3.06; 119.06
Attorneys—See ATTORNEYS.
Commencement—See COMMENCEMENT OF ACTIONS.
Continuance—See CONTINUANCES.
Definition, 119.01(E)
De novo hearings
  Courts, by, T 3.11(E)
  Environmental review board, T 11.03(B)
Depositions—See DEPOSITIONS.
Discovery—See DISCOVERY.
Environmental protection agency—See ENVIRONMENTAL PROTECTION AGENCY.
Environmental review board—See ENVIRONMENTAL REVIEW BOARD.
Evidence—See EVIDENCE.
Examiners—See HEARING EXAMINERS.
Exemptions, T 3.02; 119.06
Findings—See FINDINGS.
Handicap reimbursement, T 21.06
  See also HANDICAP REIMBURSEMENT HEARINGS.
Hazardous waste facility board, T 11.04
Hearsay, T 3.06(F)
Human services department—See HUMAN SERVICES DEPARTMENT.
Industrial commission—See WORKERS' COMPENSATION.
Initiation—See INITIATION OF PROCEEDING.
Intervention in proceeding, T 3.04
License, revocation or suspension—See LICENSES AND PERMITS, at Hearings.
Liquor permit violations—See LIQUOR CONTROL COMMISSION.
Location, 119.08
  Requested by party affected, T 3.02; 119.08
Notice—See NOTICE.
Objections, T 3.06(E)
Orders issued before, T 3.05(E)
Parties—See PARTIES TO PROCEEDINGS.
Posthearing procedure—See POSTHEARING PROCEDURE.
Postponement—See CONTINUANCES.
Prefiled testimony, T 3.06(B)
Prehearing procedure—See PREHEARING PROCEDURE.
Presumptions, T 3.06(A)
Procedural rules, T 3.05(A)

HEARINGS—*continued*
Proposed rule, on—See PROPOSED RULES.
Public assistance recipients, for—See HUMAN SERVICES DEPARTMENT.
Public utilities commission—See PUBLIC UTILITIES COMMISSION.
Records—See RECORDS AND REPORTS.
Referees—See HEARING EXAMINERS.
Regularity of administrative action, T 3.06(A)
Rehearings, T 3.09(B)
  Public utilities commission, T 17.03(D)
Request for, T 3.02; 119.06
  Notice of right to request, T 3.02; 119.07
  Time limitation, T 3.02; 119.07
Scheduling, T 3.02; 119.08, 119.09
  Time limitation, 119.07
Securities division—See SECURITIES DIVISION.
Unemployment compensation board of review—See UNEMPLOYMENT COMPENSATION BOARD OF REVIEW.
Witnesses—See WITNESSES AND TESTIMONY.

HEARSAY
Adjudication proceedings, T 3.06(F)

HUMAN SERVICES DEPARTMENT, T 13.01 to T 13.07
See also ADJUDICATION, for general provisions.
Attorney general assigns lawyer to represent, T 13.02(B)
Charts
  Chapter 119 adjudication proceedings, T 13.06
  Organizational chart, T 13.05
  State hearing process, T 13.07
Continuances, prehearing conference, T 13.02(C)
Diagnosis related groups (DRG) prospective payments, reconsideration process, T 13.03
Discovery, requests for
  Prehearing conference, T 13.02(C)
Duties, T 13.01
Hearing examiners—See also HEARING EXAMINERS, for general provisions.
  Assignment, T 13.02(E)
  Objections to reports, T 13.02(E)
  Recipient hearings, T 13.04(C)
  Reconsideration process for DRG payments, T 13.03
Hearings for providers, T 13.01, T 13.02
  See also HEARINGS, for general provisions.
  Audit of providers, basis for, T 13.02(A)
  Burden of proof, T 13.02(D)
  Licenses; denial, revocation or suspension, T 13.02(A)
  Prehearing conference, T 13.02(C)
  Request for, T 13.02(B)
  Resolution prior to final hearing, T 13.02(C)
  Scheduling, T 13.02(C)
  Stenographic record, T 13.02(D)
  Witnesses and testimony, T 13.02(F)

HUMAN SERVICES DEPARTMENT—*continued*
Hearings for recipients, T 13.01, T 13.04
  See also HEARINGS, for general provisions.
  Appeals from, T 13.04(D)
  "Appeals summary", T 13.04(B)
  Decisions, T 13.04(D)
  Final action, T 13.04(E)
  Hearing examiner, T 13.04(C)
  Public assistance programs requiring special hearings, T 13.04(F)
  Reasons for initiating, T 13.04(A)
  Time limits for hearing requests, T 13.04(A)
Legal services office, T 13.01
  Hearing requests handled by, T 13.02(B)
  Objections to hearing examiner's report filed with, T 13.02(E)
  Reconsideration process for hospital prospective payments, T 13.03
Licenses for providers; revocation, denial or suspension, T 13.02(A)
Orders, T 13.02(A)
  Final order, T 13.02(F)
Organizational chart, T 13.05
Persons affected by, T 13.01
Prehearing conferences, T 13.02(C)
Procedural charts, T 13.06, T 13.07
Programs under department control, T 13.01
Prospective payments, reconsideration process, T 13.03
Provider hearings—See Hearings for providers, this heading.
Questionnaire submitted prior to prehearing conference, T 13.02(C)
Recipient hearings—See Hearings for recipients, this heading.
Reconsideration process for diagnosis related groups (DRG) prospective payments, T 13.03
Records
  Hearing examiner's report, T 13.02(E)
  Stenographic record, T 13.02(D)

INDUSTRIAL COMMISSION, T 21.01 to T 21.12
See also ADJUDICATION, for general provisions; WORKERS' COMPENSATION.

INITIATION OF PROCEEDING, T 3.02, T 3.05(A)
Forced by courts, T 5.01, T 5.02

INJUNCTIVE RELIEF, T 5.05

INSURANCE
Liability, civil service, T 9.06
Workers' compensation insurance, T 21.01(A)

INTERNAL REVENUE CODE
Definition, 119.092(A)

INTERVENTION, T 3.04

INVALIDATION OF RULES, 119.031(D), 119.031(F)
Availability of public copies, lack of as grounds, T 1.07(A)
Failure to comply with rulemaking procedure, T 1.06(C); 119.02

INVALIDATION OF RULES—*continued*
Issues, T 1.06(A)
Notice, T 1.05(E)
Proposed rule—See PROPOSED RULES.
Readoption of rule after, 119.031(E)

JOINT COMMITTEE ON AGENCY RULE REVIEW
Comparison of final form with proposed rule, T 1.05(F); 119.031
Emergency rules filed with, T 1.05(G); 119.03(F)
Established by general assembly, T 1.05(E); 101.35
Final rules
  Comparison to original, T 1.05(F); 119.031
  Copies filed with, T 1.05(F); 111.15(B), 119.04(A)
Fiscal analysis of proposed rule filed with, T 1.05(B); 119.03(H)
Proposed rules
  Filing with, T 1.05(B); 119.03(H)
  Recommendation for invalidation, T 1.05(E); 119.03(I)
  Reviewed by, T 1.04; 111.15(D), 119.03(H)

JUDGMENTS—See FINDINGS.
Declaratory—See DECLARATORY JUDGMENTS.

JUDICIAL REVIEW, T 3.11, T 5.01 to T 5.05; 119.12, 2506.01 to 2506.04
Attorneys in proceedings, 119.13
Avoiding, T 3.11(B)(3)
Collateral attack, T 5.01, T 5.05
Commencement of agency action by, T 5.01, T 5.02
Common pleas court—See COURTS OF COMMON PLEAS.
Counsel in proceedings, 119.13
Court of appeals—See COURTS OF APPEALS.
Damages, action for, T 5.05
Declaratory judgments—See DECLARATORY JUDGMENTS.
De novo hearing, T 3.11(E)
Enforcement action, defense for
  Administrative determination, attack of as defense, T 5.05
Environmental protection agency rules, T 1.06(A)
Evidence
  Additional, introduction into record, T 3.11(E); 119.12
  Agency decision, evidence to support; consideration, T 3.11(D); 119.12
  Evidence to support, T 3.08(B)
"Exhaustion of administrative remedies" doctrine, T 3.11(B)(3)
  Prerequisite, T 3.10, T 3.11(B)(1)
Filing of transcript, 2506.02
Finality of order or decision, prerequisite, T 3.11(B)(2); 2506.01
Findings, 2506.04
Forms of, T 3.11(C)
Guidelines for in statutes, T 3.11(C)(1)
Industrial commission proceedings, T 21.04
Injunctive relief, T 5.05
Issues, T 3.11(D)
Jurisdiction
  "Primary jurisdiction" doctrine, T 3.11(B)(1)

JUDICIAL REVIEW—*continued*
Licensing decisions, of, 119.12
  Expiration of license during, effect, 119.121
Limitations, T 3.11(B), T 3.11(D)
  "Primary jurisdiction" doctrine, T 3.11(B)(1)
  "Prior resort" doctrine, T 3.11(B)(1)
Liquor control commission decisions, T 3.11(A); 119.12
Location of appeal, 119.12
Mandamus—See MANDAMUS.
Notice of appeal, T 3.11(C)(1); 119.12
Oil and gas division appeals, T 19.03(B)
Parties, representation, 119.13
Powers of review, T 3.11(D)
Prerequisite, exhaustion of administrative remedies, T 3.10, T 3.11(B)(1), T 3.11(B)(3)
"Primary jurisdiction" doctrine, T 3.11(B)(1)
"Prior resort" doctrine, T 3.11(B)(1)
"Private attorney general" concept, T 3.04
Prohibition, writ of, T 3.11(C)(2), T 5.04
  Unauthorized judicial power, prevention, T 5.01
Public utilities commission appeals, T 17.03(E)
  Procedural chart, T 17.11
Reclamation division appeals, T 19.02(C)
Records
  Review of, T 3.11(E); 119.12
  Transcripts of hearings as basis for review, T 3.06(G); 119.09, 2506.03
Right to, T 3.02, T 3.11(A), T 3.11(B)(2); 119.06, 119.12
Rules, of, T 1.06
  Comments on by public, right to, T 1.06(C)(2)
  Consistency requirement, T 1.06(C)(1); 119.03(D)
  Constitutionality issues, T 1.06(A)
  Failure of agency to comply with rulemaking procedure, T 1.06(C); 119.02
  Limitations, T 1.06(A)
  Public notice of proposed rules, T 1.06(C)(1)
  Reasonableness of rule, T 1.06(C)(4)
  Rules conflicting with statute, T 1.06(C)(3)
  Standards of review, T 1.06(B)
Scope of, T 3.11(D)
Securities division, T 9.09
Standards for rulemaking, T 1.03(A)
Statutory guidelines, T 3.11(C)(1)
Supreme Court, appeals to from public utilities commission, T 17.03(E)
Timing, T 3.11(B)(2)
Transcripts of hearings as basis for, T 3.06(G); 119.09, 2506.03
Unemployment compensation board of review hearings, T 7.07

JURISDICTION
Environmental review board, T 11.03(A)
Industrial commission, T 21.01(B), T 21.01(D)
Invocation by complaint, T 3.05(A)
"Primary" jurisdiction doctrine in judicial review, T 3.11(B)(1)

JURISDICTION—*continued*
Public utilities commission, T 17.02(A)
  Motor carrier companies, T 17.05

LAWYERS—See ATTORNEYS.

LEGISLATIVE SERVICE COMMISSION DIRECTOR
Emergency rules filed with, T 1.05(G); 119.03(F)
Final rules filed with, T 1.05(F); 111.15(B), 119.04(A)
Fiscal analysis of proposed rule filed with, T 1.05(B)
Numbering of rules, 111.15(C)
Preservation of rules, 111.15(C), 119.04(B)
Proposed rules filed with, T 1.04, T 1.05(B); 111.15(E), 119.03(B)

LEGISLATURE, STATE—See GENERAL ASSEMBLY.

LIABILITY INSURANCE
Civil service, T 9.06

LICENSES AND PERMITS
Coal mine operator, suspension of license for reclamation violation, T 19.02(A)
Definition of license, T 3.01(A); 119.01(B)
Denial of, appeal—See Judicial review of decision, this heading.
Driver's license, suspension without hearing, 119.062
Environmental protection agency, T 11.02(A)
Expiration
  Hearing, during, 119.091
  Judicial review, during; effect, 119.121
Hazardous waste facilities installation, T 11.04
Hearings, T 3.02, T 3.03; 119.06
  See also HEARINGS, for general provisions.
  Counsel in, T 3.03
  Failure to hold before expiration, 119.091
  Issuance, exemption from adjudication, T 3.01(A); 119.01(D)
  Liquor permits
    Objections to issuance—See LIQUOR CONTROL COMMISSION, at Permit denial, appeals to.
    Violations—See LIQUOR CONTROL COMMISSION.
  Notice, T 3.02
  Party to, T 3.03
  Record, T 3.03
Human services providers; denial, revocation, or suspension, T 13.02(A)
Issuance, exemption from adjudication, T 3.01(A); 119.01(D)
Judicial review of decision, 119.12
  Expiration of license during, 119.121
Liquor permits—See LIQUOR PERMITS.
Medicaid provider; refusal, revocation, or suspension, T 13.02(A)
Motor vehicle driver's license, suspension without hearing, 119.062
Securities—See SECURITIES DIVISION.
Suspension
  Agency, by, 119.061
  Appeal, 119.12
  Hearing on request—See Hearings, this heading.
  Notice sent to party affected, T 3.08(C); 119.07

LIQUOR CONTROL COMMISSION, T 15.01 to T 15.08
See also ADJUDICATION, for general provisions.
Duties, T 15.01
Fines for permit violations, T 15.05(C)
Permit denial, appeals to, T 15.02(B), T 15.05(D)
  Evidence, T 15.05(E)
  Franklin county common pleas court, T 3.11(A); 119.12
Violation hearings, T 15.01, T 15.05(B)
  Evidence, T 15.05(E)
  Fines imposed, T 15.05(C)
  Notice, T 15.05(B)
  Plea bargain offers, T 15.05(B)
  Scheduling, T 15.05(B)

LIQUOR CONTROL DEPARTMENT, T 15.01 to T 15.08
See also ADJUDICATION, for general provisions.
Appeals from—See LIQUOR CONTROL COMMISSION.
Application for permits—See LIQUOR PERMITS.
Charts
  Organizational chart, T 15.07
  Procedural chart, adjudication, T 15.08
Complaints, investigation of, T 15.05(A)
Evidence rules applied, T 15.02
Hearings
  Objections to permit issuance—See LIQUOR CONTROL COMMISSION, at Permit denial, appeals to.
  Permit holder violations—See LIQUOR CONTROL COMMISSION, at Violation hearings.
Local option status, T 15.02(A)
Organizational chart, T 15.07
Permits—See LIQUOR PERMITS.
Quota register of available permits, T 15.02(A)
Safekeeping of liquor permit, T 15.04
Violations of liquor law, T 15.05
  Hearing—See LIQUOR CONTROL COMMISSION, at Violation hearings.

LIQUOR PERMITS
Application for, T 15.02(A)
  Denial—See Denial, appeal to liquor control commission, this heading.
Availability, T 15.02(A)
  Municipality, to, T 1.06(C)(4)
Business holding
  Closing without notification to department, T 15.04
  Purchase, T 15.03
Denial, appeal to liquor control commission, T 15.02(B), T 15.05(D)
  Appeal from commission decision to Franklin county common pleas court, T 3.11(A); 119.12
  Evidence, T 15.05(E)

LIQUOR PERMITS—*continued*
Fines for violations, T 15.05(C)
Form, retail permit definition/privileges, T 15.06
Franklin county common pleas court, appeals to, T 3.11(A); 119.12
Gambling by permit holder, T 15.05(A)
Hearings
  Objections to new permit issuance—See Denial, appeal to liquor control commission, this heading.
  Permit holder violations—See LIQUOR CONTROL COMMISSION, at Violation hearings.
Issuance, T 15.02(B)
Leasing of permit business, prohibited, T 15.03(A)
Municipality, number available to, T 1.06(C)(4)
Notice
  Closure of business, notice to liquor control department required, T 15.04
  Denial of permit, notice of appeal, T 15.02(B)
  Issuance of permit, T 15.02(B)
  Violation, T 15.05(A)
    Hearing, T 15.05(B)
Objections to issuance, T 15.02(B)
Prostitution, effect on, T 15.05(A)
Purchase of existing permit business, T 15.03
  Attorney's responsibilities, T 15.03
  Time involved, T 15.03(A)
Quota register of available permits, T 15.02(A)
Renewal, T 15.02(B)
Revoking for violations, T 15.05(C)
Safekeeping with liquor control department, T 15.04
Transfer of, T 15.02(A), T 15.03(C)
  Management agreement used during transition period, T 15.03(B)
  Simultaneous with closing of purchase, T 15.03(B)
  Time involved, T 15.03(A)
  Unpaid taxes impediment, T 15.03(C)
Violations, T 15.05
  Fines, T 15.05(C)
  Hearings—See LIQUOR CONTROL COMMISSION.
  Nature of offense, T 15.05(A)

MANDAMUS, T 3.11(C)(2)
Commencement of adjudication by, T 5.01, T 5.02
Industrial commission proceedings, T 21.04(B)

"MENTAL PROCESSES" RULE, T 3.06(A)

MOTOR CARRIERS, T 17.05
Common carrier applicants, T 17.05(A)
  Procedural chart, T 17.10
Private companies, applications to public utilities commission, T 17.05(B)
Qualifications, T 17.05(A)

MOTOR VEHICLES
Driver's license, suspension without hearing, 119.062

NATURAL RESOURCES DEPARTMENT, T 19.01 to T 19.08
Charts
  Organizational chart, T 19.07
  Procedural chart, T 19.08
Coal mining—See COAL MINING.
Enforcement authority, increase in power, T 19.01
Oil and gas board of review, T 19.03(A)
  Appeals from to common pleas court, T 19.03(B)
    See also JUDICIAL REVIEW, generally.
Oil and gas division—See OIL AND GAS DIVISION.
Organization
  Changes in, T 19.01
  Chart, T 19.07
Reclamation division—See RECLAMATION DIVISION.
Regulatory bodies within, T 19.01

NOTICE
Coal mining violation, T 19.02(A)
Continuance, T 3.02
Environmental review board appeals, T 11.03(B)
Final rule, adoption, T 1.05(F); 119.03(D)
Hearings, T 3.02; 119.07
  Continuance, T 3.02
Industrial commission review board hearings, T 21.02(A), T 21.03(B), T 21.08(A)
Intervention in adjudication proceedings, T 3.04
Invalidation of rules, T 1.05(E)
License suspension hearing, T 3.02
Liquor control commission hearing, T 15.05(B)
Liquor permits—See LIQUOR PERMITS.
Mailing lists of agencies, T 1.05(B)
Oil and gas review board, appeals to, T 19.03(A)
Permanent partial disability hearing, T 21.05(B)
Persons affected by rules, 119.03(E)
Prenotice rulemaking procedures, T 1.05(A)
Proposed rule—See PROPOSED RULES.
Public notice rule, T 1.05(C); 111.15(C)
  Proposed rules, T 1.05(B); 119.03(A)
Public utilities commission rehearing, T 17.03(D)
Reclamation division violation, T 19.02(A)
Unemployment compensation board of review proceedings, T 7.02, T 7.05
Workers' compensation claim hearing, T 21.02(A)

OATHS AND AFFIRMATIONS
Proposed rule hearings, T 1.05(D)

OIL AND GAS BOARD OF REVIEW, T 19.03(A)
Appeals from to common pleas court, T 19.03(B)
  See also JUDICIAL REVIEW, generally.

OIL AND GAS DIVISION, T 19.03
Attorneys, areas of concern, T 19.03
Charts, procedural, T 19.08
Drilling, technical aspects, T 19.04

OIL AND GAS DIVISION—*continued*
Reorganization, T 19.01
Review board, T 19.03(A)
  Appeals from to Franklin county common pleas court, T 19.03(B)

ORDERS, T 3.08
Appeals from—See ADMINISTRATIVE REVIEW; JUDICIAL REVIEW.
Effective date, T 3.09(A)
Environmental protection agency, T 11.02(A)
Environmental review board, T 11.03(D)
Evidence supporting, documented, T 3.08(B)
Finalization, T 3.09(A); 119.09
  Determination, T 3.11(B)(1), T 3.11(B)(2)
Hearing, issued before, T 3.05(E)
Human services department, T 13.02(A), T 13.02(E)
Issuance prior to hearing, T 3.05(E)
Journal of agency, entered in, T 3.08(C); 119.09
Judicial review—See JUDICIAL REVIEW, generally.
Modifying or vacating, estoppel to preclude, T 3.09(B)
Notice sent to parties affected, T 3.08(C); 119.09
Prehearing conference, T 3.05(E)
Prohibition writs, issuance, T 5.01, T 5.04
Records and reports, T 3.08(C), T 3.09(A); 119.09
  Evidence supporting, documented, T 3.08(B)
  Finalization, T 3.09(A); 119.09
  Journal required of agency, T 3.08(C), T 3.09(A); 119.09
Res judicata effect, T 3.09(D)
Securities division, contempt orders, T 9.10
Validity, T 3.02; 119.06

PARTIES TO PROCEEDINGS
Attorneys for—See ATTORNEYS.
Compensation for attorney fees, 119.092(B)
  Denial, 119.092(C)
  Payment, 119.092(D)
  Report by agency, 119.092(E)
Definition, T 3.03; 119.01(G), 119.092(A)
Environmental protection agency hearings
  Right to appeal, T 11.02(C)
Environmental review board, T 11.03(B)
Hearing examiner's report, copies furnished to, T 3.07(B); 119.09
Judicial review, representation in, 119.13
License suspension hearing, T 3.03
Location of hearing, requested by, T 3.02; 119.08
Public utilities commission hearings, T 17.03
Right to request hearing, T 3.02; 119.06
  Notice of right, T 3.02; 119.07
  Time limitation, T 3.02; 119.07
Unemployment compensation board of review hearing, T 7.04

PERMITS—See LICENSES AND PERMITS.

PETITIONS
Rulemaking, for, T 1.07(B)

POLICY DEVELOPMENT
Adjudication, by, T 3.01(B)
Informal, T 5.01 to T 5.05
  Judicial review of rules, T 1.06

POSTHEARING PROCEDURE, T 3.07
Briefs, T 3.07(A)
Findings of fact, T 3.07(A)
Hearing examiner's report, filing, T 3.07(B)
  See also HEARING EXAMINERS, at Reports, generally.
Review—See ADMINISTRATIVE REVIEW; JUDICIAL
    REVIEW.

POSTPONEMENTS—See CONTINUANCES.

POWER SITING COMMISSION
Discovery procedures, T 3.05(B)
  See also DISCOVERY, for general provisions.

PREHEARING PROCEDURE, T 3.05
Conferences
  Human services department, T 13.02(C)
  Public utilities comission, T 17.03(B)(2)
  Record, T 3.05(D)
  Securities division, T 9.08
  Witnesses, order of; determined during, T 3.06(C)
Discovery—See DISCOVERY.
Orders issued, T 3.05(E)
Pleadings and motions, T 3.05(A)

"PRIMARY JURISDICTION" DOCTRINE, T 3.11(B)(1)

"PRIOR RESORT" DOCTRINE, T 3.11(B)(1)

"PRIVATE ATTORNEY GENERAL" CONCEPT, T 3.04

PROCEEDINGS—See ADJUDICATION; HEARINGS.

PROHIBITION, WRITS, T 3.11(C)(2), T 5.04

PROPOSED RULES—See also RULES AND RULEMAKING
    POWERS, generally.
Amendment of proposed rule—See Revisions, this heading.
Business and industry, proposed by, T 1.05(A)
Comments on by public, right to, T 1.06(C)(2); 119.03(C)
Comparison with final rules, T 1.05(F); 119.031
Copies, availability, T 1.05(B)
Documentation, availability, T 1.05(C), T 1.06(C)(2)
Drafting, T 1.05(A)
Environmental protection agency, T 1.07(A)
Filing, T 1.04, T 1.05(B); 111.15(D), 111.15(E), 119.031(G),
    119.03(B)
  Fiscal analysis—See FISCAL ANALYSIS OF RULES.
  Joint committee on agency rule review, T 1.05(B); 119.03(H)

PROPOSED RULES—*continued*
Filing—*continued*
  Legislative service commission director, T 1.04, T 1.05(B); 111.15(E), 119.03(B)
  Secretary of state, T 1.04, T 1.05(B), T 1.07(A); 111.15(B), 111.15(E), 119.03(B)
  Senate clerk, T 1.04
  Time limitation, T 1.04, T 1.05(B); 111.15(D), 111.15(E), 119.03(B)
Final rules—See FINAL RULES.
Fiscal analysis—See FISCAL ANALYSIS OF RULES.
Hearings, T 1.05(B)
  Evidence, T 1.05(D)
  Notice—See Notice, this heading.
  Oaths, T 1.05(D)
  Records—See Stenographic records, this subheading.
  Required, T 1.05(D); 119.03(C)
  Scheduling, T 1.05(D); 119.03(A)
  Stenographic records, T 1.05(D), T 1.05(H); 119.03(C)
    Agency's expense, T 1.07(A); 119.03(C)
  Time limitations for holding, T 1.05(D); 119.03(A)
  Witnesses, T 1.05(D)
Invalidation, 119.031(D), 119.031(F)
  General assembly, by, T 1.04, T 1.05(E); 119.03(I)
  Readoption of rule after, 119.031(E)
  Reasons, 119.03(I)
  Time limitation, T 1.05(E); 119.03(I)
Joint committee on agency rule review—See JOINT COMMITTEE ON AGENCY RULE REVIEW.
Notice, T 1.06(C)(1), T 1.07(A); 119.03(A)
  Hearing, T 1.05(B), T 1.05(D), T 1.06(C)(1), T 1.07(A); 119.03(A)
  Invalidation, T 1.05(E)
  Persons affected by, 119.03(E)
Persons affected by, notice to, 119.03(E)
Promulgation as final rule—See FINAL RULES.
Public notice—See Notice, this heading.
Records
  Hearing records, T 1.05(D), T 1.05(H), T 1.07(A); 119.03(C)
  Public access to supporting documentation, T 1.05(C)
Review—See JOINT COMMITTEE ON AGENCY RULE REVIEW.
Revisions, 119.031(B)
  Filing, T 1.04; 111.15(D)
  Review for, 119.031(A)
    Joint committee on agency rule review, 119.031(C)
  Substantive revisions, definition, 119.01(J)
Statutory authority, T 1.05(A)
Substantive language, T 1.05(A)
Summary—See RULE SUMMARY.

PROSTITUTION
Liquor permit holder, T 15.05(A)

PUBLIC HEARINGS—See HEARINGS.

PUBLIC NOTICE—See NOTICE.

PUBLIC UTILITIES COMMISSION, T 17.01 to T 17.11
See also ADJUDICATION, for general provisions.
Adjudicatory authority, T 17.02(D)
Appeals from to Supreme Court, T 17.03(E)
  See also JUDICIAL REVIEW, generally.
Appointment of members, T 17.01
Charts
  Complaint proceedings, T 17.08
  Judicial review, procedural chart, T 17.11
  Motor carrier applications, procedure, T 17.10
  Organizational, T 17.07
  Rate change application proceedings, T 17.09
Complaint proceeding, T 17.04(A)
  Procedural chart, T 17.08
Departments of, T 17.02(B)
Fuel clause hearings, T 17.04(C)
  Electric fuel component rate hearings, T 17.04(C)(1)
  Gas cost recovery hearings, T 17.04(C)(2)
Hearing examiners—See also HEARING EXAMINERS, generally.
  Attorney serving as, T 17.03(A)
  Report, T 17.03(C)
Hearings, T 17.03, T 17.06
  See also HEARINGS, generally.
  Briefs, T 17.03(B)(3)
  Discovery, T 17.03(B)(1)
  Fuel clause hearing—See Fuel clause hearings, this heading.
  Initiating, reasons for, T 17.02(D)
  Memoranda, T 17.03(B)(1), T 17.03(B)(3)
  Miscellaneous hearings, T 17.06
  Nontransportation hearings—See Nontransportation hearings, this heading.
  Pleadings and motions, T 17.03(B)(1)
  Prehearing conferences, T 17.03(B)(2)
  Rehearings, T 17.03(D)
  Testimony, expert and nonexpert, T 17.03(B)(2)
Information availability, T 17.02(C)
Judicial review, T 17.03(E)
  Procedural chart, T 17.11
    See also JUDICIAL REVIEW, generally.
Jurisdiction, T 17.02(A)
  Motor carrier companies, T 17.05
Legal counsel, T 17.02(B)
Members, appointment, T 17.01
Motions served by mail, response time, T 17.03(B)(1)
Motor carrier regulation, T 17.05
  See also MOTOR CARRIERS.
Nontransportation hearings, T 17.04
  Complaint proceeding, T 17.04(A)
    Procedural chart, T 17.08
  Gas and electric fuel clause hearings, T 17.04(C)
  Rate increase application, T 17.04(B)
    Procedural chart, T 17.08

PUBLIC UTILITIES COMMISSION—*continued*
Organizational chart, T 17.07
Prehearing conference, T 17.03(B)(2)
Railroads
  Investigation, T 3.05(A)
  Jurisdiction of, T 17.02(A)
Rates, application for change in by public utility, T 17.04(B)
  Chart of proceedings, T 17.09
Reports
  Briefs, T 17.03(B)(3)
  Hearing examiners, T 17.03(C)
  Memoranda, T 17.03(B)(1), T 17.03(B)(3)
  Staff report, T 17.04(B)
Supreme Court, appeals to from commission decisions, T 17.03(E)
Tariff of utility company, T 17.02(C)

RAILROADS
Investigation by public utilities commission, T 3.05(A)
Jurisdiction of public utilities commission, T 17.02(A)

RATES
Public utilities, application for change, T 17.04(B)
  Procedural chart, T 17.09

RECLAMATION DIVISION, T 19.02
See also ADJUDICATION, for general provisions.
Appeals to court of appeals, T 19.02(C)
  See also JUDICIAL REVIEW, generally.
Attorneys, areas of concern, T 19.02
Charts, procedural, T 19.08
Coal mining permit
  Suspension for violation, T 19.02(A)
  Underground, T 19.02
Enforcement powers, T 19.02(A)
Forms
  Violation, notice, T 19.06
Notice of violation, T 19.02(A)
  Form, T 19.06
Reorganization, T 19.01
Review board, T 19.02(B)
Violations, notice, T 19.02(A)
  Form, T 19.06

RECLAMATION REVIEW BOARD
Decisions, T 19.02(B)
  Appeal to court of appeals, T 19.02(C)
Form, notice of appeal, T 19.05

RECORDS AND REPORTS
Attorney fees, compensation; agency report, 119.092(E)
Definition of public record, T 1.05(C)
Environmental review board, T 11.03(B)
Errors, correction by agency, T 3.09(C)
Files, agency; public access to, T 1.05(C)

RECORDS AND REPORTS—*continued*
Findings of fact, hearing examiner, T 3.07(B), T 3.08
  Written, T 3.08(A)
Handbooks published by agencies
  Intervention procedure, T 3.04
Hearing examiners—See HEARING EXAMINERS, at Reports.
Hearings, T 1.05(D), T 1.05(H); 119.03(C)
  See also particular agency concerned.
  Agency expense, 119.09
  Appeals, basis for, T 3.06(G); 119.09
  Errors, correction, T 3.09(C)
  Filing, T 3.07(B)
  Findings to be supported by, T 3.07(B), T 3.08(B)
  Nunc pro tunc entries, T 3.09(C)
  Proposed rule, T 1.07(A); 119.03(C)
  Reliability of evidence, T 3.08(B)
Human services department—See HUMAN SERVICES DEPARTMENT.
Intervention, handbooks published by agency, T 3.04
Journal, agency
  Adjudication order entered in, T 3.08(C), T 3.09(A); 119.09
Judicial review—See JUDICIAL REVIEW.
License suspension hearing, T 3.03
Liquor control department, permits available, T 15.02(A)
Nunc pro tunc entries, T 3.09(C)
Prehearing conference, T 3.05(D)
Proposed rules—See PROPOSED RULES.
Public utilities commission—See PUBLIC UTILITIES COMMISSION, at Reports.
Referees—See HEARING EXAMINERS, at Reports.
Rulemaking record, 119.03(A), 119.03(B), 119.03(C)
  Docket, T 1.07(A)
Securities division records, subpoena, T 9.03
Unemployment compensation board of review—See UNEMPLOYMENT COMPENSATION BOARD OF REVIEW.

REFEREES—See HEARING EXAMINERS.

REGULATIONS—See RULES AND RULEMAKING POWERS.

REHEARINGS, T 3.09(B)
Public utilities commission, T 17.03(D)

REPORTS—See RECORDS AND REPORTS.

RES JUDICATA
Applicability to agencies, T 3.09(D)

REVIEW—See ADMINISTRATIVE REVIEW; JUDICIAL REVIEW.
Rules—See JOINT COMMITTEE ON AGENCY RULE REVIEW.

RULES AND RULEMAKING POWERS, T 1.01 to T 1.07
Administering of laws, T 1.03(A)
Administrative code, establishment, T 1.01
Adoption of rules, T 1.03(A)
  See also PROPOSED RULES, for general provisions.
  Adoption under RC 111.15, T 1.04
  Adoption under RC 119.03 and RC 119.04, T 1.05
Amendments, T 1.05
  See also PROPOSED RULES, for general provisions.
Appeal from rulemaking decisions, T 1.06
  See also ADMINISTRATIVE REVIEW; JUDICIAL REVIEW,
    at Rules, of.
Case-by-case adjudication, based on, T 1.07(C)
Codification, T 1.01
Commerce department, securities division—See SECURITIES
    DIVISION.
Conflicting with statutes, T 1.06(C)(3)
Consistency requirement, T 1.06(C)(1); 119.03(D)
Constitutional issues, T 1.03
  Due process requirements, T 1.03(B)
  Judicial review of rules, T 1.06(A)
  Legislative powers, delegation, T 1.03(A)
  Separation of powers, T 1.03(A)
Declaratory relief, T 1.06
  See also JUDICIAL REVIEW, at Rules, of.
Definitions, T 1.01; 111.15(A), 119.01(C)
  Internal management rules, 119.01(K)
  Procedural rules, T 1.02
  Revision, 119.01(J)
  Rulemaking agency, 119.01(I)
  Self-executing, T 1.02
  Substantive rules, T 1.02
    Revision, 119.01(J)
Delegation of legislative powers, T 1.03(A)
Distinguished from adjudication, T 3.01(B)
Docket, T 1.07(A)
Due process, T 1.03(B)
  See also PROPOSED RULES, at Notice.
Emergency rules, T 1.05(G); 111.15(B), 119.03(F)
Enforcement, T 1.07(C)
Enumeration, 111.15(C)
Environmental protection agency—See ENVIRONMENTAL
    PROTECTION AGENCY.
Evidence rules—See EVIDENCE.
Expiration date, T 1.05(F); 119.04(A)
Failure to comply with rulemaking procedure, 119.02
Federal regulations, incorporation in rules, T 1.03(A)
Filing—See FILING OF RULES.
Final rules—See FINAL RULES.
Fiscal analysis—See FISCAL ANALYSIS OF RULES.
Governor's order for emergency rules, T 1.05(G); 119.03(F)
Grounds for invalidation—See INVALIDATION OF RULES.
Hazardous waste facility board, T 11.04
Internal management rules, T 1.02; 119.01(C)
  Definition, 119.01(K)

RULES AND RULEMAKING POWERS—*continued*
Invalidation—See INVALIDATION OF RULES.
Joint committee on agency rule review—See JOINT COMMITTEE ON AGENCY RULE REVIEW.
Judicial review of rules, T 1.06
  See also JUDICIAL REVIEW, at Rules, of.
Legislative oversight, T 1.05(E)
Legislative service commission—See LEGISLATIVE SERVICE COMMISSION DIRECTOR.
Model rules as basis, T 1.05(A)
Notice, T 1.05(C); 111.15(C)
  Proposed rules—See PROPOSED RULES.
Numbering, 111.15(C)
Petitions for, T 1.07(B)
Preservation, 111.15(C), 119.04(B)
Procedural rules, definition, T 1.02
Proposed rules—See PROPOSED RULES.
Public notice rule, T 1.05(C); 111.15(C)
  Proposed rules, T 1.05(B); 119.03(A)
Publishing, T 1.01; 111.15(C)
Reasonableness requirement, T 1.06(C)(4)
Records, 119.03(A), 119.03(B), 119.03(C)
  Docket, T 1.07(A)
Rescission, T 1.05
  See also PROPOSED RULES, for general provisions.
Review, proposed rules—See JOINT COMMITTEE ON AGENCY RULE REVIEW.
Revisions—See PROPOSED RULES, at Revisions.
Securities division—See SECURITIES DIVISION.
Self-executing rules, definition, T 1.02
Separation of agency powers, T 1.07(C)
Standards for promulgation, T 1.03(A)
Statutes
  Conflicting with, T 1.06(C)(3)
  Distinct from, T 1.03(A)
Substantive rules, T 1.02
Summaries—See RULE SUMMARY.
Types of rules, T 1.02
Unauthorized, T 1.06(C)(3)

RULE SUMMARY, 111.15(E)
Filing requirements, 111.15(F)
Joint committee on agency rule review, filed with, T 1.05(B); 119.03(H)

SECRETARY OF STATE
Emergency rules filed with, T 1.05(G); 119.03(F)
Final rules filed with, T 1.04, T 1.05(F); 111.15(B), 119.04(A)
Fiscal analysis of proposed rule filed with, T 1.05(B)
Preservation of rules, 111.15(C), 119.04(B)
Proposed rules filed with, T 1.04, T 1.05(B), T 1.07(A); 111.15(B), 111.15(E), 119.03(B)

SECURITIES ACT, T 9.02

SECURITIES DIVISION, T 9.01 to T 9.13
See also ADJUDICATION, for general provisions.
Administrative procedure act applicable to, T 9.01
Appeals from—See ADMINISTRATIVE REVIEW; JUDICIAL REVIEW, generally.
Attorneys
  Hearings, duties, T 9.03
  Preparation of case against division, T 9.08
"Cease and desist" proceeding, T 9.07
Charts
  Enforcement, adjudication process, T 9.12
  Organizational chart, T 9.11
  Securities registration, chart of adjudication procedure, T 9.13
Contempt orders, T 9.10
Dealer, licensing—See Licensing of dealers and salesmen, this heading.
Discovery, T 9.03
Due process, T 9.06
Enforcement section, T 9.08
  Procedural chart, T 9.12
Hearings, T 9.03, T 9.06, T 9.08
  See also HEARINGS, for general provisions.
  Attorneys, duties, T 9.03, T 9.08
  Discovery, T 9.03
  Due process, T 9.06
  Examiners, T 9.03
  License
    Denial, T 9.03, T 9.05
    Violations, T 9.06, T 9.07
  Prehearing conference, T 9.08
  Reasons for, T 9.02
  Registration
    Application, denial, T 9.03
    Suspension, T 9.06
  Subpoenas—See Subpoenas, this heading.
  Takeover bids, T 9.01
  Unlicensed persons, violations, T 9.07
Investigative powers, T 9.07
Issuer's selling rights, suspension, T 9.06
Judicial review, T 9.09
  See also JUDICIAL REVIEW, generally.
Licensing of dealers and salesmen, T 9.05
  Administrative procedure act, subject to, T 9.01
  Denial, hearing, T 9.05
  Suspension, T 9.06
  Violations, hearing, T 9.06, T 9.07
Organizational chart, T 9.11
Policy statements of division used in hearing, T 9.03
Prehearing conference, T 9.08
Public access to information, T 9.03, T 9.08
Records of
  Public access, T 9.03, T 9.08
  Subpoenaed for hearing, T 9.03
Registration of securities, T 9.02
  Denial, hearing, T 9.03

SECURITIES DIVISION—*continued*
Registration of securities—*continued*
  Procedural chart, adjudication, T 9.13
  Suspension, hearing, T 9.06
Rules and rulemaking powers, T 9.04
  See also RULES AND RULEMAKING POWERS, for general provisions.
  Administrative procedure act, subject to, T 9.01
Salesmen, licenses—See Licensing of dealers and salesmen, this heading.
Securities Act, T 9.02
Subpoenas
  Attorneys, by, T 9.03
  Commissioner subpoenaed, T 9.08
  Contempt of division's subpoenas, T 9.10
  Powers of, T 9.07
  Records for hearing, T 9.03
Violations, proceedings, T 9.06, T 9.07

SENATE CLERK
Fiscal analysis of proposed rule filed with, T 1.05(B)
Proposed rule filed with, T 1.04

SUBPOENAS
Environmental review board powers, T 11.03(B)
Issued by agencies, T 3.05(B); 119.09
Securities division—See SECURITIES DIVISION.

SUMMARIES OF RULES—See RULE SUMMARY.

SUPREME COURT
Public utilities commission, appeals from, T 17.03(E)

TAXATION
Liquor permit transfer, unpaid taxes impediment to, T 15.03(C)

TAXATION DEPARTMENT
Appeals from rules, T 1.05(D); 119.03(G)

TESTIMONY—See WITNESSES AND TESTIMONY.

TRANSCRIPTS—See RECORDS AND REPORTS.

UNEMPLOYMENT COMPENSATION BOARD OF REVIEW,
  T 7.01 to T 7.09
See also ADJUDICATION, for general provisions.
Appeals from referee decisions, T 7.06, T 7.07
  See also ADMINISTRATIVE REVIEW; JUDICIAL REVIEW, generally.
Attorney as hearing examiner, T 7.01
Attorneys for parties, T 7.01
Benefit charge hearings, T 7.03
Benefit hearings, T 7.02, T 7.04
  See also Hearings, this heading.
  Appeals from to common pleas courts, T 7.07
Chart, organizational, T 7.08

UNEMPLOYMENT COMPENSATION BOARD OF REVIEW—
continued
  Civil service employees, T 7.01
    Decisions, appeals from, T 7.06
    Responsibilities, T 7.01, T 7.05
    Subpoena powers, T 7.05
  Common pleas courts, appeal of board's decision to, T 7.07
    See also JUDICIAL REVIEW, generally.
  Counsel representing claimant, fees, T 7.01
  Eligibility notice hearing—See Benefit hearings, this heading.
  Employer contribution disputes—See Liability hearings, this heading.
  Employment services bureau—See EMPLOYMENT SERVICES BUREAU.
  Fraud hearings, T 7.04
  Hearing examiners—See also HEARING EXAMINERS, generally.
    Appointment, T 7.01
    Attorneys, licensed, T 7.01
    Decisions, appeals from, T 7.06, T 7.07
  Hearings, T 7.02 to T 7.05
    See also HEARINGS, for general provisions.
    Benefit charge hearings, T 7.03
    Benefit hearings, T 7.02, T 7.04
    Burden of proof, T 7.03, T 7.05
    Conduct of, T 7.05
    Continuances, T 7.05
    Cross-examination of witnesses, T 7.04, T 7.05
    Eligibility notice dispute—See Benefit hearings, this heading.
    Examiners—See Hearing examiners, this heading.
    Filing for, time limitation, T 7.02
    Fraud hearings, T 7.04
    Issues considered, T 7.05
      Liability hearings, T 7.03
    Liability hearing, T 7.02, T 7.03
    Location, T 7.04
    Notice of, T 7.02, T 7.05
    Objections during, T 7.02
    Open to public, T 7.01
    Order of testimony, T 7.05
    Participants, T 7.03, T 7.04
    Procedural rules, T 7.02
    Record of, T 7.02, T 7.03
      Review, T 7.05
    Referees—See Hearing examiners, this heading.
    Residence of appellee, effect on hearing, T 7.04
    Scheduling, T 7.05
      Benefit and eligibility notice hearing, T 7.04
    "Split hearing", T 7.04, T 7.05
    Subpoena requests, T 7.05
    Telephone conference hearing, T 7.04
    Types of disputes, T 7.02
    Witnesses and testimony—See Witnesses and testimony, this heading.
  Judicial review, T 7.06, T 7.07
    See also JUDICIAL REVIEW, generally.

UNEMPLOYMENT COMPENSATION BOARD OF REVIEW— *continued*
Liability hearings, T 7.02, T 7.03
  See also Hearings, this heading.
  Appeals from to Franklin county common pleas court, T 7.07
Members, T 7.01
Notice of hearing, T 7.02, T 7.05
Organizational chart, T 7.08
Records and reports
  Appeals to common pleas courts, T 7.07
  Hearing, T 7.02, T 7.03
    Review of record, T 7.05
  Mechanical record of testimony, T 7.02
Referees—See Hearing examiners, this heading.
"Split hearing", T 7.04
  Continuance, T 7.05
Subpoena powers, T 7.05
Telephone conference hearings, T 7.04
Witnesses and testimony
  Benefit hearing, T 7.04
  Eligibility notice hearing, T 7.04
  Fraud hearings, T 7.04
  Liability hearings, T 7.03
  Order of testimony, T 7.05
  Testimony mechanically recorded, T 7.02

WELFARE DEPARTMENT—See now HUMAN SERVICES DEPARTMENT.

WITNESSES AND TESTIMONY, T 3.06(B); 119.09
See also EVIDENCE, generally.
Credibility, investigation by courts, T 3.11(D)
Cross-examination, T 3.06(B); 119.09
  Unemployment compensation board of review hearing, T 7.04, T 7.05
Depositions—See DEPOSITIONS.
Discovery—See DISCOVERY.
Environmental review board proceedings, T 11.03
Hearsay, T 3.06(F)
Human services department provider hearing, T 13.02(F)
Order of presentation, T 3.06(C)
  Unemployment compensation board of review hearing, T 7.05
Prefiled testimony, T 3.06(B)
Proposed rule hearing, T 1.05(D)
Subpoenas—See SUBPOENAS.
Transcripts—See RECORDS AND REPORTS, at Hearings.
Unemployment compensation board of review hearing—See UNEMPLOYMENT COMPENSATION BOARD OF REVIEW.

WORKERS' COMPENSATION, T 21.01 to T 21.12
See also ADJUDICATION, for general provisions.
Adjudicatory nature of, T 21.01(A)
Administrative appeals process, T 21.03
  See also ADMINISTRATIVE REVIEW, generally.

WORKERS' COMPENSATION—*continued*
Administrative appeals process—*continued*
  Forms available at workers' compensation bureau offices, T 21.01(B)
Attorneys to be hearing examiners, T 21.01(B)
Bureau—See WORKERS' COMPENSATION BUREAU.
Charts
  Organizational, T 21.11
  Procedural chart, adjudication, T 21.12
Claims
  Final authority in settling, T 21.01(D)
  Hearings on, T 21.02(A)
  Opening of file initiated by workers' compensation bureau, T 21.01(E)
Forms, T 21.09
Handicap reimbursement—See HANDICAP REIMBURSEMENT HEARINGS.
Hearing examiners, T 21.01(B)
  See also HEARING EXAMINERS, for general provisions.
  Appeals from decision, T 21.02(B), T 21.03(A)
    Late appeals, liberal policy, T 21.08
Hearings, T 21.08
  See also HEARINGS, for general provisions.
  Applications for settlement, T 21.08(B)
  Claims hearing, T 21.02(A)
  Handicap reimbursement, T 21.06
    See also HANDICAP REIMBURSEMENT HEARINGS.
  Initiating, T 21.08(D)
  Notice, T 21.02(A), T 21.03(B), T 21.08(A)
  Permanent and total disability, T 21.08(C)
  Permanent partial disability, T 21.05
  Regional boards of review, procedure, T 21.03(B)
  Safety violation hearings, T 21.07(D)
    Appeal of hearing, T 21.07(E)
    Rehearing, T 21.07(E)
    Writ of mandamus, T 21.07(E)
Judicial review, T 21.04
  See also JUDICIAL REVIEW, generally.
  Common pleas courts, T 21.04(A)
  Mandamus, petition for, T 21.04(B)
Jurisdiction of industrial commission, T 21.01(B), T 21.01(D)
Mandamus, petition for to appeal industrial commission decision, T 21.04(B)
Members of industrial commission, appointment, T 21.01(D)
Notice of hearing, T 21.02(A), T 21.03(B), T 21.08(A)
Organizational chart, T 21.11
Permanent partial disability
  Appeal of hearing officer's decision, T 21.05(D)
  Application for determination, T 21.05(A)
    Docket assigned, T 21.05(B)
  Compensation for, T 21.05(C)
  Hearings, T 21.05
    Scheduling, notice, T 21.05(B)
  Mandamus, petition for, T 21.05(D)
  Notice of hearing, T 21.05(B)

WORKERS' COMPENSATION—*continued*
Permanent partial disability—*continued*
  Physical examination to determine, T 21.05(A)
    Report evaluated by hearing officer, T 21.05(C)
Regional review boards, T 21.01(C), T 21.03(A), T 21.03(B)
  Appeals from orders of, T 21.03(C)
Safety requirements, T 21.07
  Additional benefits due to violations, application for, T 21.07(A), T 21.07(B)
    Hearings on, T 21.07(D), T 21.07(E)
  Industry standards, T 21.07(A)
  Investigation of violations, T 21.07(C)
Scheduling of claims hearing, T 21.02(A)

WORKERS' COMPENSATION BUREAU
Administrative body, T 21.01(A)
Benefits
  Additional benefits eligibility due to safety violations, T 21.07(A)
  Stayed during appeal, T 21.03(A)
Chart, organizational, T 21.10
Claims
  Evaluation, T 21.01(A)
  File, opening, T 21.01(E)
  Notice of hearing, T 21.02(A)
Forms, T 21.09
Insurance, T 21.01(A)
Organizational chart, T 21.10

WRITS
Mandamus, T 5.01, T 5.02
Prohibition, T 5.01, T 5.04